Anthropology and the Behavioral and Health Sciences

Anthropology and the Behavioral and Health Sciences

OTTO von MERING
and
LEONARD KASDAN,
Editors

University of
Pittsburgh Press

GN
29
A 57

SBN 8229–3189–3
Library of Congress Catalog Card Number 75–93289
Copyright © 1970, University of Pittsburgh Press
Manufactured in the United States of America

Contents

List of Contributors

ROY M. ACHESON — Yale University

PAUL T. BAKER — Pennsylvania State University

CLIFFORD R. BARNETT — Stanford University

CYRIL S. BELSHAW — University of British Columbia

HENRY W. BROSIN — University of Pittsburgh

C. R. CARPENTER — Pennsylvania State University and University of Georgia

BERNARD S. COHN — University of Chicago

MALCOLM COLLIER — American Anthropological Association, Chicago

LLOYD R. COLLINS — McDonnell Aircraft, St. Louis

GEORGE DALTON — Northwestern University

ALBERT DAMON — Harvard University

L. WILLIAM EARLEY, deceased — Formerly with the University of Pittsburgh

ELIZABETH EDDY — University of Florida

ROBERT L. EMRICH — United States Department of Justice, Washington, D.C.

LLOYD FALLERS — University of Chicago

ZACHARY GUSSOW — Louisiana State University

JULES HENRY, deceased — Formerly with Washington University

DONALD L. HOCHSTRASSER — University of Kentucky

CHARLES C. HUGHES — Michigan State University

EDWARD E. HUNT, JR. — Penn State University

LEONARD KASDAN — Michigan State University

ARI KIEV — Cornell University Medical College

SOLON T. KIMBALL — University of Florida

BERTRAM S. KRAUS — University of Pittsburgh

WILTON M. KROGMAN — University of Pennsylvania

GABRIEL W. LASKER — Wayne State University

WILLIAM P. McLURE — University of Illinois

MELVIN MEDNICK — Temple University

HORACE M. MINER — University of Michigan

COENRAAD MOORREES	Forsyth Dental Center, Boston
RICHARD L. PARK	University of Michigan
STEVEN POLGAR	University of North Carolina
SUZANNE RIPLEY	University of Virginia
ARTHUR J. RUBEL	University of Notre Dame
RICHARD F. SALISBURY	McGill University
HARVEY B. SARLES	University of Minnesota
RICHARD G. SNYDER	University of Michigan and Highway Safety Research Institute
T. D. STEWART	Smithsonian Institute
ROBERT C. SUGGS	Alexandria, Virginia
JESSE W. TAPP, JR.	University of Kentucky
SYLVIA THRUPP	University of Michigan
ARTHUR J. VIDICH	New School for Social Research
OTTO von MERING	University of Pittsburgh
ANTHONY F. C. WALLACE	University of Pennsylvania
MURRAY L. WAX	University of Kansas
EDWARD WELLIN	University of Wisconsin at Milwaukee
JOHN WHITING	Harvard University

Acknowledgments

We wish to give special thanks to Harold Gould, Bertram S. Kraus, Richard L. Park, Harvey M. Sarles, and Alexander Spoehr, who encouraged and supported us in the initial planning to bring together the many contributors of this book. We are equally grateful to Morton H. Fried, Marshall Sahlins, Lyle Saunders, John J. Honigmann, Thomas Sebeok, George D. Spindler, Peter Hammond, James F. Bosma, Donald C. Marshall, William P. Lebra, and Thomas Gladwin for their able chairmanship of the twelve symposium sessions during the 1966 annual American Anthropological Association meeting, when the original papers and commentaries comprising this book were first presented. Our warm thanks go to Philip Hallen, president of the Maurice Falk Medical Fund, who was our munificent host at a special luncheon for members of this symposium.

In particular, we want to state our appreciation to every contributor for his exemplary patience and help throughout the long process of polishing and updating the final draft of the manuscript. Moreover, we wish to express our gratitude to Mrs. Ada Brandegee, Mrs. Sandra Lord, Mrs. Arlene Abady, and Miss Bonnie Harrington for their exceptional editorial counsel in readying the manuscript for publication. We also want to thank Miss Lorraine Burkhart and Mrs. Sharon Bodnar for their steady secretarial assistance during every phase of the preparation of this book. We are warmly appreciative of the bibliographic contributions of Mr. Jeremiah O'Mara.

OTTO VON MERING
LEONARD KASDAN

July 1969

Anthropology and the Behavioral and Health Sciences

Otto von Mering/Leonard Kasdan

INTRODUCTION:
The Craft and Discipline
of Anthropology

Background

All the papers and commentaries appearing in this volume were originally presented as a symposium at the annual meeting of the American Anthropological Association in Pittsburgh, Pennsylvania, November 1966. Subsequently, every participant had an opportunity to revise and update his contribution.

Several related influences prompted the editors to organize a symposium and publish the resultant papers concerning the place and relationship of anthropology within the broad spectrum of the behavioral and health sciences. Our common experience of holding joint academic appointments in anthropology as well as in other university departments was, and perhaps remains, the most immediate influence. The rapidly growing body of lore and fact about the desirability, utility, and even necessity of such working relationships within academe and other research centers reflects a need for making available an edited volume of the papers and commentaries presented in symposia such as this.

Anthropologists increasingly find themselves to be performing their activities in contexts where many of their colleagues are trained in other disciplines and, conversely, where anthropology departments are including on their staffs individuals whose training has been in fields other than anthropology. Furthermore, both private and governmental

3

granting agencies have been encouraging interdisciplinary research and collaboration at an accelerating rate. These contexts emphasize the behavioral sciences as a unified problem area, in contrast to the compartmentalized interests of the traditional disciplines.

In examining these trends, we concluded that the traditional boundaries between disciplines and subdisciplines are slowly breaking down, and that within the field of anthropology important conceptual, methodological, and curricular changes are occurring which warrant examination. Hence, we brought together a group of knowledgeable anthropologists who are engaged in such reevaluation in the context of their work with colleagues from other sciences and disciplines. Because we anticipated that they would explore and analyze the implications of this experience primarily from the anthropologist's point of view, we also invited scientists and teachers from circumjacent behavioral and health sciences who would bring diverging viewpoints to the symposium.

Taking stock of the scope and aims of anthropology as one of the "sciences of man" is, of course, not new to the anthropologist. Since World War II an impressive series of comprehensive statements have appeared concerning its many-sided contributions to the understanding of biological and social man, his limitations and potentialities. *The Science of Man in the World Crisis* (Linton, 1945) set the precedent for other studies that would present periodically a balanced inventory and appraisal of anthropology as a science and discipline. Thus, the First International Symposium on Anthropology in 1952 resulted in the twin publications, *Anthropology Today: An Encyclopedic Inventory* (Kroeber, 1953) and *An Appraisal of Anthropology Today* (Tax et al., 1953).

Largely as a result of the growing significance of anthropology as an academic discipline and field of research, subsequent appraisals also began to focus on the special academic problems and interdisciplinary requirements of teaching anthropology. As before, a series of symposia, organized for this purpose, became the vehicle for bringing out *The Teaching of Anthropology* (Mandelbaum, Lasker, and Albert, 1963). Like the aforementioned volumes, it has had a telling impact on the anthropologist as a researcher and teacher. Concurrently, the growing need to communicate to a broader audience the many uses of, and changes in, the field of anthropology led to the timely publication of *Horizons of Anthropology* (Tax, 1964).

The more we reflect on the many-faceted content of these varied appraisals of anthropology, the more apparent is the historical significance of the processes of mutual stimulation, the borrowing of concepts, and the overlap of problem areas that characterize the behavioral and health sciences. What appears compelling, even new to us, however, is the increasing complexity of these issues within the institutional growth of anthropology, particularly in the United States, and the growing pertinence of anthropology for understanding vital contemporary problems. The implications of these developments for the growth of the field, the recruitment of students and their training, and anthropology's increasing professionalization remain largely unexamined.

A surprising number of anthropologists still feel that their traditional analytical tools, developed largely in studying "exotic" societies, have quite suddenly acquired great relevance to the social policy and health sciences of today. This reaction may have resulted from the anthropologist's inclination to be more introspective than circumspective about the many changes and controversies that have overtaken his field in the last decade. In the meantime, however, the neighboring sciences and disciplines have moved rapidly to borrow and adapt many anthropological tools and techniques for their own purposes. If at times they have done so with less than deliberate speed, their reason is nonetheless unassailable: to obtain firsthand knowledge about the confluence of biosocial forces making for cultural stability and selective resistance to planned technological, economic, and political change.

Parallel to, and seemingly independent of, these developments, present-day anthropologists also have been moving away from a primary concern with simple, relatively small-scale social systems to a concern with problems of complex biosocial systems, their functions and changes with time. This gradual shift of emphasis has urged many anthropologists to reevaluate their own concepts and methodologies, and to supplement them with the theories and tools from those disciplines and sciences which developed them through research into Western industrial societies.

As so many times before in the annals of scientific endeavor, the process of reciprocal borrowing has not been systematic, but rather an artifact of the pragmatics of day-to-day research. Regardless of the immediate trials and benefits of this process, another reason for taking a closer look at anthropology is the new relevance of this field to those of our scientific neighbors and the growing convergence of ideas and methods between the two. This is compounded by the fact that these neighbors sometimes become our keenest competitors in work formerly regarded as our exclusive province.

Our planning for this volume on the relationship of anthropology to the circumjacent disciplines and sciences also was stimulated by recent symposia by British and American anthropologists. The results of one appeared in a book edited by Max Gluckman, *Closed Systems and Open Minds: The Limits of Naivety in Social Anthropology* (1964); the other, beginning in 1965 under the aegis of the Association of Social Anthropology comprises a series of volumes appearing in Britain (*ASA Monographs 1– ; 1965–   ).

Closed Systems and Open Minds addresses itself to the problem of what methods and assumptions are common to social anthropological analysis, and to the question of how they are related to the approaches of other social sciences. The contributors examined these issues by reanalyzing scientific procedures followed in their own selected empirical researches. During this reexamination, the authors also became concerned with the nature of their relationships with other social science disciplines.

The first four Association of Social Anthropology monographs deal with some of the same problems. These papers discuss general and special theoretical issues, such as the relevance of selected analytical models to social anthropology. With the exception of the ASA monograph on economics (no. 6, 1967) and, to a very limited extent, of the ASA monograph on history (no. 7, 1968), the relationship of social anthropology to other sciences and disciplines is not directly approached in any of these publications. On the whole, the various authors dealt with this problematic issue only to the extent necessary for their particular contributions.

Although the present book does cover some of the same ground as its predecessors, it differs in two ways. First, its definition of anthropology is in the American tradition of four major areas of specialization, including many subdisciplines not normally subsumed under social anthropology. Consequently, this book addresses itself to the much broader problem of the special and general relationships between the behavioral and health sciences *and* anthropology. A second distinguishing feature is the manner in which the charge to contributors was conceived.

Both the Gluckman volume and the ASA monographs focused on methodological and theoretical issues *within* the field of social anthropology. The problems of the conceptual and working relationships with other disciplines were derivative issues.

The scope and nature of these relationships is the primary focus of this book, although the approach to this issue was left entirely to each author. The content of their deliberations is, therefore, both more wide-ranging and inclusive. We feel that these qualities are an accurate reflection of the many-faceted nature of American anthropology, as well as the more varied experience of American anthropologists in establishing relationships with other disciplines and sciences.

The Charge to the Contributors

To preface this document, we have selected some of Fred Eggan's extremely pertinent observations about the state of anthropology, delivered in his Peabody Museum Centennial lecture in the spring of 1967:

The history of anthropology has been one of gradually increasing complexity as race, language, and culture were first differentiated, and, later, culture, society and personality were conceptualized. The central problems of anthropology remain, and we keep returning to them periodically with new methods and new data. The interrelations of biological, psychological, social, and cultural factors and the problems of adapting to varied geographical and social environments make anthropology a complicated science indeed. But the simpler formulations of the past have not sufficed, and we will make progress only as we develop new ideas and new ways to cooperate with disciplines.

We can begin to see a new organization for anthropology emerging, centering on man and his works and providing a spectrum of specialized fields which interlock with those of the social and behavioral sciences. Ultimately, there will be no sharp boundaries — as there are none in the biological and physical sciences today — but culture, society and personality will be major foci of attention, both individually and in their interrelationships. What the role of anthropology will be in this larger field is not yet clear, but its broad comparative treatment of social and cultural phenomena should assure it a central position (Eggan, 1968).

The desire to think through the many ramifications of the contemporary interrelatedness of anthropological endeavors with those of the neighboring fields, and the wish to share our preliminary reflections with the symposium contributors prompted us to prepare a series of formal statements on (1) the theme, (2) the task, and (3) the issues. Taken as a whole, these statements became the formal charge to the symposium contributors. Each author received this document when he consented to take part in this venture with the instructions that he was free to use it as he saw fit in preparing his material. The charge is reproduced here, just as it was received by each participant in the winter and spring of 1966.

Cogitanda for Symposium Participants (January 14, 1966)

THE THEME:

"The essence of science lies in the fact that if a scientist holds something to be true he must verify it" (Page, 1965) and that "even unwelcome truth is better than cherished error" (Corklin, 1943).

If this is so, then anthropology as one scientific community in the tapestry of such communities must engage in continuous and open self-examination of its aims and methods.

A critical reassessment of what anthropology is and does is urgent if it is expected to continue to grow in its special place and proper role in the scientific community as a whole.

Such self-examination is all the more urgent if anthropology as a whole is to mature soundly in its increasing relations with and influence in the relevant neighboring sciences and disciplines.

THE TASK:

There exists a clear and present need for a concerted effort to weigh the philosophical and empirical foundations of the science of man in the neighboring sciences and disciplines.

It is a task which must embrace also the consideration of appropriate ways and means for improving the standards of education and training relevant to the future work of anthropologists in these fields.

THE ISSUES:

1. Is there, indeed, a "real" conflict between anthropology as the history or the science of man? If so, how can it be bridged?
    1.1 Has the traditional and legitimate anthropological interest in the question of how culture and society are possible led to an overconcern

with the structure and function of the situation of collective action — i.e., with "system": its prerequisites and order, its equilibrium and boundary maintenance?

1.1.1 If so, has this also brought about a temporary or premature closure about what we want anthropology to do?

1.1.2 In particular, has it led to an overemphasis of a type of analysis of data which tends to proceed "inward," breaking up a "system" into "subsystems," and then seeks to impute functions and interactions to these, rather than register the actions taken, or choices made by them in the face of a certain range of possible alternatives?

1.2 Has anthropology not also been vitally concerned with the question of how and why individual (and group) life is possible within a given environment and culture?

1.2.1 Has it not, therefore, given sustained attention to the range of alternative behavior open in each situation to collective action, as well as aimed at understanding the course or "process" of action actually engaged in?

1.2.2 At the same time, has it not been consistent in focusing on the problem of the nature of the relation between collective action and the range and change in particular choices of individual conduct?

2. Has anthropology not always aimed at being a *bridging science* between the neighboring sciences and disciplines which also deal with man's nature and his works as a biological and social animal?

2.1 Has it ever been enough for anthropology to stress the "mechanical" or "reactive" aspects of man's social nature by focusing on the external regularities of his being — his customs and institutions?

2.1.1 Has anthropology not been equally concerned with man's experiences, his "responding" and adapting, his becoming a certain kind of individual being in a particular culture or environment?

2.1.2 Has anthropology not striven to assess the evidence of man's endeavors and conduct as they are linked with his physiological needs and inner urges that biological experience implanted in his tissue and marrow?

2.2 Has anthropology not therefore sought to encompass as its primary objective not only the detailed description and systematic explanation of the regularities in the reactions and interactions of man, but also the "discovery" and interpretation of the different ways of man's experiences and responses?

3. Must the anthropological subject matter as it is studied and taught be "pure" to the extent that its content is primarily that which has been of intrinsic interest rather than extrinsic interest to anthropology?

3.1 Is the scientific necessity for the specification of the domain of the explainable for the field such that it precludes the anthropologists' exploration and adaptation of other frames of reference to the same observed human phenomena?

    3.1.1 If anthropologists do seek to "discover" and "explain" regularities in man's nature and his works, is it not sufficient to know that they can only be said to state something about regulative actions and behavior under certain well-defined conditions, and no claim can be made that they regulate all behavior?

3.2 To what extent has anthropology always been an "extrinsically motivated" science seeking to find answers to questions that were originally part of some other branch of science?

    3.2.1 Have the "important" anthropological questions not been more often posed from without rather than from within a narrower field of inquiry within anthropology?

    3.2.2 To what extent have the chosen problems been judged both important and soluble on the basis of the breadth of added understanding their solution would afford rather than on the grounds of their immediate practical utility or application?

        3.2.2.1 To what extent has the choice of problem-specialization been dictated by extrinsic forces such as inertia, fashion, employment opportunity, and administrative considerations?

4. Has anthropology been or become too "lopsided" as a technique for acquiring new knowledge by stressing the science of man as the search for new unitary, fragmented or "pure" symmetries?

4.1 If this is so, has it been achieved at the expense of emphasizing the science of man as the organization and codification (or synthesis) of existing knowledge?

    4.1.1 Has the institutionalized pressure for research, the increasing push towards area specialization, and the concomitant accumulation of more and more data accentuated the denial of anthropology as science in this sense?

    4.1.2 Has it reached a point where the transformation of its data into relevant information to neighboring fields is not keeping pace with developments in these fields?

4.2 Are anthropologists willing to live with the fact that this is a type of knowledge which is more often useful to the neighboring discipline than for the science of man where the codification must originally take place?

    4.2.1 What are anthropologists doing, or can they do, about continually condensing and concentrating their means for communicating the fund of anthropological knowledge?

4.2.2 If the answers to the above are clarifiable, how can they be used more effectively to enlarge and reinforce the professional ties between anthropology and the sciences and disciplines to which it is related, and from which demands are now being felt?

5. How "pure," indeed, must anthropology as a branch of science be as it is taught to and studied by members of neighboring disciplines and sciences?

5.1 What necessary changes or modifications will have to be made in the basic anthropological curriculum, both undergraduate and graduate, to more adequately prepare future anthropologists for work in and about the neighboring sciences and disciplines?

5.1.1 At what stage in the education and training of the anthropologist should materials and concepts from neighboring sciences be introduced to students? What kinds of materials, in what amounts, and in what form?

5.1.2 To what extent, if at all, should anthropology encourage more interdisciplinary "cross-overs" and "switches" of the student as he passes through the baccalaureate to doctorate to post-graduate educational sequence?

5.1.3 To what extent and in what way should the undergraduate major and postgraduate anthropology experiences with neighboring fields, particularly the natural or biological sciences, be put on a more explicit and formal basis to achieve a firmer grasp of and a lasting commitment to the skills and rigor of these fields?

5.1.4 How early should anthropologists urge the student to begin developing a particular expertise through formal educational experiences in neighboring sciences to promote a better understanding of their unique contributions to the various sectors of human behavior?

5.2 Should graduate anthropology education continue to be based on the assumption that at least one half of the doctoral candidates have not achieved a sufficient level of exposure or familiarity with the subject prior to graduate school, and that this deficiency has to be made up early in graduate training?

5.2.1 May it not continue to be more important to consider this issue on the basis of whether the graduate applicant demonstrates sufficient familiarity with the ways of science or had serious prior exposure to rigorous scientific study regardless of the particular subject matter of his concentration?

5.2.2 How, and in what ways, if at all, should the graduate education and training program in anthropology be standardized from department to department?

6. In the teaching and training of the anthropologist for work in neighboring fields, how important or relevant is it to define for him the ethical basis of science by making the obligations and responsibilities of the scientist as a man explicit to him through experience in appropriate contexts?

The Unity and Diversity of Anthropology

The rise of anthropology into a formal discipline and science has been a long and complex process (M. Harris, 1968), and new ground in anthropological research continues to be broken into many different interdisciplinary directions at an ever-increasing pace. Because of this and the nature of this book, we now present a brief, yet inclusive overview of the unity of anthropology in its diversity.

Anthropology is the study of the similarities and differences, both biological and behavioral, among the peoples of the world from the dawn of human history to the present day. Anthropology excavates and analyzes the remains of past civilization (archaeology); describes the evolution and present biological characteristics of our species (physical anthropology); traces the development and spread of customs and technologies over the face of the earth, showing how these forms, arts, faiths, and tools satisfy the psychological needs of individuals and keep societies together (cultural anthropology); defines the varieties of human speech and the relationship among the tongues of men (linguistics) (Kluckhohn and Kelly, 1945).

Anthropology is concerned with the comprehensive and comparative study of man and his works, of the human organism evolving, and of human society, whether preliterate, or literate. Anthropologists have investigated the biological, behavioral, and cultural characteristics of man from earliest times to the present: not man in isolation, but rather man in his environmental context. Traditionally, the field of anthropology has encompassed the four major specialties of physical and biological anthropology, archaeology, cultural anthropology (including ethnography, ethnology, and social anthropology), and linguistics.

Although only one or two generations ago an anthropologist could encompass the entire range of knowledge, today the knowledge explosion has been so extensive that we must consider the definition, problems, and work of each field separately.

Physical and Biological Anthropology

To understand "man's place in nature," physical anthropology originally focused on demonstrating human evolution, emphasizing the phenotypic description and phylogenetic classification of races of man on the basis of indirect evidence from fossil remains, the embryology and comparative anatomy of primates, and the anthropometry of living peoples. This emphasis has given way to the systematic analysis of the how and why of the process of evolution. The new synthetic theory of evolution which has emerged from a union of genetics, paleontology, and systematics (Huxley, 1942) has prompted the physical anthropologist to consider the complex pattern of interaction among adaption, behavior, and the fossil record. This approach also has brought about a progressively closer working relationship among archaeology, ethnology, and linguistics.

The evolution of physical anthropology into contemporary biological anthropology is illustrated by its changing concerns and controversies since Darwin's *Theory of Evolution.* The phenotypic division of human species into Caucasian, Mongolian, and Negroid is no longer taken seriously. These and other typological pragmatic thought models, like orthogenesis, were viable only so long as the physical anthropologist interpreted his primary task as looking for invariant properties — that is, to learn something about the races of man from the presence or absence of factors devoid of adaptive value.

Biological anthropologists are now trying to clarify the role of biochemical, genetic, and cultural factors in the development and continuity of *population,* rather than *racial* characteristics. Current biologic studies of morphology, genetic mutation, natural selection, differential reproduction, and adaptation draw on important theoretical and substantive contributions by biological anthropologists working on patterns of biosocial adaptation of different populations in diverse natural habitats around the world.

Four main areas of interest and technical specialty make up the field of biological anthropology: (1) *evolution* — long-term evolution of primates, paleontology, anatomy, and zoology; (2) *primate behavior* — psychology, ecology, and animal behavior within the natural habitat; (3) *fossil man* — geology and archaeology; and (4) *race and biosocial adaptation* — genetics, population dynamics, ecology, biometry, and biochemistry (Washburn, 1963).

No one anthropologist can master all of the complexities of this biological "subfield." As physical anthropology becomes more and more concerned with problems of adaptation, it can no longer be contained within its traditional boundaries. For example, interest in the individual organism adapting and behaving has led to the relatively new concentration on biometrical studies of the relationships among physique, growth, behavior, and environment, including contemporary and fossil man's susceptibility to various diseases. Another closely linked component of biological anthropology is the growth, development, and pathology of dentition.

Of all the branches of anthropology, biological anthropology has moved closest to the physical and health sciences in the probabilistic formulation of problems and conclusions. It not only employs many of their methods and techniques, but it also borrows such sophisticated tools as colorimeters, spectrometers, and radiographs in place of the traditional technique of bone measurement. In the process of making, "the study of the evolution of behavior . . . central to an understanding of the problem of man's origin" (Washburn, 1968), and in the course of refining its methods and techniques, biological anthropology also has come "closer to, not further from, a humanistic outlook" (Lévi-Strauss, 1966c).

Archaeology

Archaeology studies ancient remains, especially the technological and material handiworks of man. Formerly, it expressed the interest of the antiquarian and was a blend of fine arts, history, and the classics. Today archaeology stands midway between history and anthropology. As history, it uses the findings of ancient civilizations to describe the human past. As anthropology, it deals with . . . [the fossil remains of early man and] . . . cultural artifacts, and it contributes to the formulation of scientific generalization and warranted assertations of a cross-cultural character (Kurtz and Handy, 1963).

The techniques and methods used by archaeologists are largely adapted from paleontologists, paleobotanists, and paleoclimatologists. Stratigraphic excavations, chemical and geological analysis of soil and rock, and dating through radiocarbon-14 methods, as well as electronic measuring devices and assessment processes derived from atomic physics, are the most common methods of reconstructing the sequence of changes in man's biogeographical or ecological condition, his material culture and technology (Movius, 1949). Such information may then be used in making inferences about the social structures and social processes of prehistoric man.

A gradual convergence of archaeology and cultural anthropology has resulted in archaeology's making two major contributions to anthropology (Woodbury, 1963): (1) The demonstration of the antiquity of culture, its initial simplicity, and the complexity of its growth and diversification, and (2) an understanding of the extent to which our own cultural background can be traced back past the classical world of Rome and Greece to its much earlier Near Eastern beginnings.

Many concepts, such as cultural area, diffusion, invention, trait, and trait complexes, are basic to archaeology as well as to cultural anthropology, although some controversy still exists as to whether archaeology should be considered a social science, cultural anthropology, a humanity, a history subfield, or a bridge to all. The historical reconstruction of prehistoric and ancient civilizations would not have been possible without the large assemblage of data available through archaeological studies (Braidwood, 1964).

Archaeology has become the history of the peoples without written records. It is beginning to make important contributions to understanding the origin and growth of culture and its relationship to human evolution, adaptation, behavior, and subsistence technology. "American archaeology in a little over one hundred years, has come from the most uncontrolled speculation about the past, through an era of collecting and classifying, through another of chronological ordering, and now is attempting to explain and understand the past" (Willey, 1968). Old World archaeology is similarly aiming for a "complete chronicle of the remote past . . . and the interpretation of that chronicle by comparative studies" (Daniel, 1968).

Cultural and Social Anthropology

The study of culture is the central theme of both cultural and social anthropology. Clyde Kluckhohn has defined culture as:

[all the] historically created designs for living, explicit and implicit, rational, irrational and non-rational, which exist at any given time as potential guides

for the behavior of men. [Also,] a historically derived system of explicit and implicit designs for living, which tend to be shared by all or specifically designated members of a group (that is a society) (Kluckhohn and Kelly, 1945).

In studies of "primitive" societies and more advanced cultures, the social anthropologist seeks to grasp those "facts of general functioning" that have a high probability of being "universal" and of having "actuality," for man, groups of men, and their behavior (Parsons, 1966).

Cultural and social anthropology may be divided into three major subfields of inquiry (Murdock, 1954) consisting of bodies of theory and fact about (1) *cultural dynamics* — the processes by which cultures change over time; (2) *social structure* — personal interrelationships in social or institutionalized groups and status categories (such as family, kingroup systems, and the language of kinship; "sacred" and "secular" organizations and societies). A more recent development in this subfield, largely stimulated by the work of Lévi-Strauss, seeks to show that observable "organizations on the ground" (Leach, 1966) represent transformations of underlying *patterns* not immediately apparent to the observer. Hence, social structure is theoretically reducible to a limited number of covert "mental structures" (Lévi-Strauss, 1966a). (3) The third subfield is *culture and personality*—the transmission of cultural norms and values in behavior (including preferred, alternative, and idiosyncratic patterns of behaving), and the formation of personal, social, and national character through the process of socialization and individuation (including unconscious processes) in different cultural milieus.

"Social and cultural anthropology continues to be both a generalizing discipline and historical one — the tensions between history and science have not been resolved but the differences have become less important" (Eggan, 1968). A new organization of investigative effort is "emerging, centering on man and his works and providing a spectrum of specialized fields which interlock with those of the social and behavioral sciences" (Eggan, 1968).

Important related foci of research have arisen from studies of primitive or tribal life and have become more crystallized through work in larger, less homogeneous contemporary societies and their man-made problems and solutions. Some of these studies delve into the nature of the relationship between economy, technology, and social structure. Others are concerned with the linkages between man's beliefs (such as cosmology and religion), his institutions (such as law and form of government), and the expressive arts. Still others are dealing with problems of possible correspondences and distinctions between the Western tradition of materialistic science and the so-called natural perceptions and magical formulations of indigenous or primitive people. New emphasis on the study of social and economic change ("modernization") in tribal societies and increasing urbanization in "underdeveloped areas" has brought a sizable growth in the number of publications in this area during the last decade. These are summarized in recent bibliographies by Brode (1969), Frey (1969), and Knop (1967).[1]

Different anthropological emphases continue to characterize the study of the particular aspects of culture. However, as the various theoretical approaches are being formulated with increasing precision, the traditional formal gaps between them are viewed more and more in a scientific perspective. Above all, cultural and social anthropology continues to "aim at discovering invariant properties beneath the apparent particularity and diversity of the observed phenomena" (Lévi-Strauss, 1966b).

Anthropological Linguistics

Linguistics, as an organized body of theory and knowledge, goes back to the early nineteenth century when the comparative study of European languages first led to the postulated existence of a "social superorganic" (Grimm's Law).

[The] significance (of the sound correspondences between Germanic and other Indo-European languages) was overwhelming, since they showed that mass human action is not altogether haphazard, but may proceed with regularity even in the way that individual sounds are pronounced in the flow of speech (Bloomfield, 1933).

1. See John Brode, *The Process of Modernization: An Annotated Bibliography on the Sociocultural Aspects of Development,* Harvard University Press, Cambridge, 1969; Frederick W. Frey et al., eds., *Survey Research on Comparative Social Change: A Bibliography,* MIT Press, Cambridge, 1969; Edward Knop and Kathryn Aparicio, *Current Sociocultural Change Literature: An Annotated Classification of Selected Interdisciplinary Sources,* University of North Dakota, Grand Forks, 1967.

Although the study of comparative philology, as it is called, still is viable as a self-contained study, the wedding between linguistics and anthropology did not take place until the early years of this century.

Franz Boas, known as the father of American anthropology, was the first to examine preliterate languages systematically, studying languages of American Indians. He and his students insisted that the study of language is a central concern to the ethnologist. This trend of thought continued to the 1930's. During the 1940's and 1950's, interest in the study of language as a unique social phenomenon declined among social and cultural anthropologists, partly because only a handful of professionals and their graduate students practiced linguistics in anthropology on a full-time basis. During the past decade, a resurgence of interest in the social-contextual study of language has been taking place.

Having an organized body of comparative data, early twentieth century linguists were able to expand their field of interest to describe not merely sounds but other speech components. They rigorously distinguished between *la langue* and *la parole* (Saussure, 1959), a distinction which has been very productive, but which still haunts the modern anthropological linguist. Scholarly concentration since that time has been and continues to be on *la langue,* the "abstract linguistic system existing quite apart from the individual" (Waterman, 1963). On the other hand, *la parole,* the stream of verbal behavior, was assumed to be "psychological," and not subject to general rules.

The greatest step forward in descriptive linguistics was the explication of the *phoneme;* the significant sound unit. Until the 1920's considerable phonetic description, attempting to classify sounds, had been done in many different languages. The phonemic principle has been extremely important in studying preliterate languages since it permits the investigator to create an alphabet for *any* human language, which conforms to the way that native speakers react to their own sounds. It is a methodology for discovering a cognitive map of the sound structure of language, without using a priori observational schemes to merely classify sounds acoustically.

In addition to phonemics, descriptive linguistics also includes the study of morphemics and syntax. Morphemic questions include the relationship between the forms of a given verb, the derivation of nouns from verbs, and the different phonemic forms of affixes (Z. S. Harris,

1951; Hockett, 1958). Syntax, as a body of theory and knowledge, was generally neglected by linguists until the past decade (Chomsky, 1957, 1965, 1966). Two approaches are current. *Immediate constituent analysis* attempts to build up the sentence from its constituent parts. *Transformational or generative grammar* begins with phrase structures and shows how these are put together to form the layers of linguistic "competence" of the native speaker to create all possible sentences in any language. Although "the goal of discovering and defining the universal properties of all languages — or of writing 'general grammar' — has gained ascendency in linguistics and has motivated many students of aboriginal languages" (Lounsbury, 1968), its direct relevance to anthropological linguistics remains to be demonstrated.

Anthropological linguistic studies have varied largely as the central interests and energies of the discipline have changed. A pioneering and continuous focus of research has involved recording the indigenous languages of North America and other parts of the world for basic information and comparative analysis. The study of meaning also has been a central concern of anthropological linguistics and has become progressively linked with thorough descriptive structural studies (Bloomfield, 1933; Whorf, 1952). Another area of investigation has been the search for the origin of language and for the relationship between language and culture. So long as anthropologists continued to look at language as an abstract system rather than as a human activity, that is, a verbal behavior, this search remained little more than that.

At present, the traditional distinction between language and culture is giving way to the conception of language as a form of behaving which cannot be "insulated in character, content, and organization from other behavior" (Pike, 1954). Hence, for anthropology "the relevant problem is not that of the origin of language, but rather that of the origin of the capacity for language; and, along with the biological sciences, linguistics may be expected to contribute to the specification of this capacity" (Lounsbury, 1968). Anthropological linguists are becoming concerned with many "new possibilities for evidence and interpretation" (Lounsbury, 1968) in the study of such aspects of verbal behavior as speech development and vocalization, speech and social class, style, cognition, speech and personality, communication and interaction in man and animals.

A Summary

The range and variety of anthropology is such that wherever any form of human existence has been found or has been traceable, anthropologists of various persuasions and specialties have found subject matter and problems for study and reflection. It is perhaps the only behavioral science which has consistently sought to encompass the natural (biological) with the social science approaches while retaining many of the characteristics of humanistic disciplines. Anthropology "is both a science and a humanistic discipline, and it is concerned with both synchronic and the diachronic approach. It treats both man the physical beast and man the social animal, and it does so both historically and analytically" (Kluckhohn, 1962).

If we assess the work of most anthropologists against a historical perspective, we also understand why they try to grasp the whole of a complex "object" like culture and man and why, in the main, their work differs from that of economists, psychologists, and sociologists who are more concerned with the analysis and interpretation of partial behaviors.

[The anthropologist] must not only utilize other specialties but also look with a double perspective. He must be able to seize not only the other culture but also his own in the process of interaction with it. . . . Moreover, as anthropologists have approached more complex societies and more complex problems, they have tended to add other scholarly specialties to their own. Thus, most anthropologists can now claim as a specialty some discipline such as economics, political science, sociology or psychology (Parsons, 1966).

Regardless of the significant decline in extant so-called primitive peoples, anthropologists continue to find cultural enclaves of mind and behavior where man has sought refuge or at least temporary respite from onrushing civilization. Language, kinship and sex, ethnobotany and ethnozoology, ethnonutrition and medicine may serve as examples. Hence, for the anthropologist at least, "the importance of understanding how different peoples perceive external reality or selectively value only portions of the total potential of human behavior and perceptions is beyond dispute" (DuBois, 1963).

The anthropologist's task has been to "enlarge the scientific conception" or basis of systematic explanation of human nature. As a rule, he has tried to discover and explain regularities in man's works as well as in man's nature. In proceeding toward this analytical aim, the appropriate variables are identified and formulated during an extended period of viewing "events in all their richness and texture" (Wolf, 1964).

Anthropologists can only make particulate, and hopefully significant, statements about man's regulative actions and behavior under certain well-defined, culture-relevant contexts. Thus, every seasoned anthropologist is wary of letting his formulations of cultural and social realities and of man's place therein become prematurely entrapped by the blandishments of certain theoretical systems. He knows only too well that man in nature, society, and culture can operate by both the simplest and most complex mechanisms simultaneously and that no methodological convention can produce a fundamental revelation on the structure of man's universe.

The still small number of professional anthropologists together with the diversity of their particular training, skills, and interests may have led to the continued vitality and recent surge of interest in anthropology as a scientific endeavor. Anthropologists as a group have remained dedicated to the proposition that an optimum of diversity must prevail for humanity. They have also felt bound together by the underlying theme that many mansions must exist in the search for basic principles that govern man's physical and cultural origins, his development, and his continued existence within change.

Education and Training in Anthropology

With the recent sharp climb in graduate student enrollment, departments of anthropology are confronted with the major task of designing new tightly constructed and better articulated curricula. At the same time, specialty training and preceptorial instruction for each of the four major subfields must be reshaped, without jeopardizing the essential basic education in general anthropology. The equally recent demand at the high school level for bona fide instruction in anthropology has increased the sense of urgency in reappraising anthropological teaching methods and programs.[2]

2. A recent national manpower survey of anthropologists highlights many of the academic and professional issues involved. See U.S. Department of Health, Education, and Welfare, Public Health Service, *Sociologists and Anthropologists: Supply and Demand in Educational Institutions and Other Settings,* Publication No. 1884, Washington, D.C., 1969.

These educational pressures are taxing the limit of existing well-qualified anthropology teachers. To the professional anthropologist who completed his training as little as a decade ago, this rich demand for his field has become both a source of pride as well as embarrassment. In his moments of pride, he may well point to a commonly uttered sentiment of college deans that every undergraduate should acquire at least a general familiarity with some society other than his own. A few anthropologists have even claimed for anthropology the new status of a "supra-discipline," which "is destined to take over the role formerly occupied by the classics in a liberal arts education" (Casagrande, 1963).

Such optimism, however, is quickly tempered by the realization that most professional anthropologists have been trained to think of teaching anthropology as a graduate enterprise, closely connected with intermittent, prolonged field research. As a rule, many anthropologists feel ill-suited to do justice to the careful curricular planning expected of them, although they are gratified to know of the AAA-sponsored and NSF-funded *Anthropology Curriculum Study Project* in Chicago. Because of its mandate to develop instructional materials for the high school curriculum, this program is only indirectly concerned with the needs of graduate anthropology education.

To date, most of the existing graduate departments of anthropology (and university administrators) have been loath to ask their faculty to assume the arduous task of curricular reform on more than an informal or ad hoc basis. Despite major difficulties, however, an increasing number of junior and senior faculty members are addressing themselves to the reevaluation and reprogramming of the basic and special anthropology curricula. With growing government support for this purpose, and a more flexible attitude among university administration in regard to instructional needs, the successful outcome of these ventures is no longer in doubt. (Several recent AAA memoirs on the quality and scope of teaching in anthropology give a measure of the profession's concern with curriculum reform. See Mandelbaum, Lasker, and Albert, 1963.)

In the typical anthropology department, few junior and no senior staff members are expected to be available in an instructional capacity on a year-round basis. The staff member's continued professional standing among his colleagues, as well as his promotional opportunities, depend on his engagement in repeated and prolonged (e.g., one-year) research in the field.

Most universities and graduate departments have been eager to minimize the administrative, salary, and recruiting problems of a staffing pattern which has to provide for nearly one position in the field for every two anthropologists in residence. In addition, the great cost of establishing and maintaining the basic laboratory space and facilities required for *each* of the four subfields has lead to the custom whereby almost no anthropology department is willing to offer a high quality doctoral program in more than two or three of these fields.

As teachers of graduate students, anthropologists generally agree that the core of a three-year "residency" at the university consists of (1) didactic course work in each of the four subfields and at least one major ethnographic area; (2) theoretical and research problem-oriented seminars and proseminars; (3) at least one supervised "brief" practicum (usually three months) in naturalistic observations and interviewing in a supervised field setting; and, (4) demonstrated competence in two foreign languages and in elementary descriptive, analytical and sampling statistics. Today, some formal training in the application of computer programming to anthropological research is often recommended as an elective experience (Hymes, 1965).

Satisfactory completion of these requirements is requisite to formulating an original dissertation problem which has to be tested in field research for a minimum period of one year. Fieldwork has always been an integral, as well as obligatory, phase in training anthropologists. Broadly speaking, it is intended to inculcate certain professional attitudes of "empathy, curiosity, and objectivity" (DuBois, 1963) in every doctoral candidate.

In fact, field research, with which every anthropological career begins, is mother and nurse of doubt, the philosophic attitude *par excellence*. This "anthropological doubt" does not only consist of knowing that one knows nothing, but of resolutely exposing that which one thought one knew, and indeed one's very ignorance, to the insults and contradictions which are directed at one's most cherished ideas and habits by those who can contradict them to the highest degree (Lévi-Strauss, 1966c).

Taken as a whole, fieldwork training has four special objectives: (1) it cultivates a special regard for the informant on the basis of prolonged rapport-building prior to any formal research activity; (2) fieldwork aims at developing one's capacity for assimilating new representations of reality through communicating directly with individuals from another culture or ethnic group. Hence, (3) it represents a particular design for resisting the temptations of a naive rationalism. Acquiring "experience in the field" means learning to discover appropriate questions to ask (Paul, 1956) by exploring ideas which grow out of phenomena commonly considered "obvious" or purely "subjective." Finally, (4) prolonged fieldwork helps the anthropologist to uncover and control an observer bias which arises from unanalyzed perspectives of his own cultural heritage. This experience also serves as a motivating force for devising new ways of explaining man to man as the universal element of daily life on whatever continent or in whatever social order he chances to be born.

This unique training serves as a powerful corrective personal experience analogous to the one-year internship of the physician. Under optimal individual and supervisory circumstances, this experience may approximate the characteristic effects of the didactic analysis required of psychoanalytic candidates (von Mering, 1969).

In sum, graduate education in anthropology employs what has been called the "pyramidal" approach to specialization and makes fieldwork an integral part of professional training. Consequently, research based exclusively on library resources is not a permissible substitute for fieldwork. Although the focus of fieldwork may change to suit the changing investigative concerns of anthropologists, fieldwork as a training process for the student-apprentice is likely to remain a basic curriculum requirement and a vital learning experience to be repeated in the course of his professional career.

With the steadily growing emphasis on the interdisciplinary role of anthropology as a craft and profession, the traditional preconceptions about what an anthropologist is, and should know, are beginning to lose their hold on the established modes of education and training:

The understanding of human behavior is too complicated and too important to be hindered by departmental structures whose origin lies in the nineteenth century. If there is any lesson . . . it is that knowledge cannot be usefully divided along the traditional lines and that, perhaps even more than a synthetic theory of evolution, we need a synthetic theory of education (Washburn, 1968).

The preceding must be understood only as an opening statement on some of the basic issues that must be resolved if we wish to shake off the dross of our pedagogical past and reconsider the education and training needs for the "new anthropologist" amid the ever-changing behavioral and health sciences. To do more than this now would be an attempt on our part to oversteer rather than stimulate the development of free discourse on the best ways to build essentially new designs for acquiring basic anthropological-behavioral scientific knowledge.

We hope that the words of all the contributors to this book become an open invitation to forego the easy habit of restitching and stretching the old curricular wineskins. The anthropologist is not treading alone in resampling and tasting the choice grapes of the behavioral and health science tree. His many colleagues sitting on its branches also are recombining the body and flavor of the requisite learning content and experience into new designs for teaching and apprenticeship. For the anthropologist, the decision to join in this educational ferment is now.

Anthropology and the Behavioral and Health Sciences

General Trends

The increasing tendency for interdisciplinary efforts in the behavioral sciences is a post–World War II phenomenon, and parallels the trend in the natural sciences. Alongside this centripetal trend exist centrifugal forces which push each of the behavioral sciences toward departmental autonomy, and toward the further development of their core areas. Hence, the nature of the growing interrelationship among the behavioral sciences has not been so much of a meshing of people and their work as it has been a series of alliances based on the mutual borrowing of concepts and theories and the rise and fall of personal partnerships in research. Basic approaches, methods, and core content remain special to each field, and for the most part, the behavioral scientist still continues to be a sociologist, psychologist, anthropologist, economist, historian, or political scientist. In the main, such autonomy is thought to further, rather than to hinder, the possibility for lasting and fruitful cooperative ventures (Casagrande, 1963).

Differences in approach in the selection of subject matter and in the manner of obtaining and analyzing data have, of course, fundamental implications for the relationship between anthropology and its sister behavioral sciences. The same is true of its relations with the health sciences and, particularly, the field of medicine.

Broadly speaking, anthropology and medicine share common ground in the biological perspective on man and in the clinical or field approach to the analysis and interpretation of human behavior. Both fields also stress the salience of historical processes — individual and cultural — and the importance of the natural environment in relation to man's thought processes, feelings, and actions. In particular, anthropology has met medicine on the basis of its general perspective on evolution and the biosocial adaptation of man; the ties through physical anthropology with the biological sciences, especially anatomy, and more recently human genetics, have been intimate. Since the 1930's, psychoanalysis, psychiatry, and social anthropology have met and interacted continuously in the area of culture and personality or psychological anthropology.

Perhaps the best way of summarizing the basis of the growth of mutually rewarding working relationships between anthropology, the health sciences, and medicine is to state two related principles which seem to have emerged out of the papers and commentaries contained in this volume. These principles are as follows: (1) disease is nothing but life under altered conditions, and (2) all conditions of relative well-being or "health" are, in a sense, inseparable from other changes in the life of the community and society.

The Plan of the Book: An Overview

The papers and commentaries on anthropology and the behavioral and health sciences are divided into two parts. Part I, entitled "Anthropology and the Behavioral Sciences," focuses on the more traditional relationships with the social and psychological sciences as well as on patterns which are emerging with the rise of the new fields of communication and ethology and of the anthropology of education. Part II, "Anthropology and the Health Sciences," brings together six papers and discussions which, with the exception of those dealing with the place and function of biological and dental anthropology in the health sciences, present new developments in the orientation and work of anthropologists.

Each paper shows as much diversity of scientific inquiry and experience as that characterizing the related fields within which the different contributors have been working. And yet, the overall impression gained is one of the steady growth of unity of purpose and intellectual ferment amid a diversity of scientific endeavor.

The Contents of Part I

With the exception of Professor Wax's examination of the relationship between anthropology and sociology, all the papers in this section were written by anthropologists. Although Professor Wax was formally trained as a sociologist, his professional and research interests have led him to carry out extensive anthropological fieldwork among American Indians. In comparing and assessing contrasts and similarities between approaches, methods, departmental organization, and formal training in social anthropology and sociology, Professor Wax is concerned especially with the impact which the growing emphasis on methodological rigor and technique has in each field.

He discourses eloquently on the dialectic tension between "being committed, empirically and morally to the human drama" and the increasing pressure for scientific precision in research. He also raises and explores the issue of whether this pressure may not be leading to a sacrifice of accuracy in many current sociological endeavors as well as contributing to a relative decline in the diversity of important questions about human behavior and society that need to be asked from different points of view. The commentaries following his paper further explore these and other pertinent issues.

With the recent growth of abstract and rather formal methods of analysis — as represented by componential analysis or the contextless, statistical correlation of kin terms — the anthropologist will possibly have to face these perplexing problems in the near future to the same degree as the sociologist is doing today. On the other hand, most anthropologists still view their discipline primarily as a craft; and, as in the acquisition of any craft skill, personal characteristics and their development are most important. Thus, unlike their sociological colleagues, whose professional certification is not predicated on fieldwork, anthropologists continue to regard becoming an anthropologist as a matter of acquiring special information and techniques *and* as a passage through an apprenticeship (Epstein, 1967). This fundamental difference in training experience has recently been accorded special recognition by two prominent educational theorists:

In anthropology, "field work" in an alien culture is still regarded as having educational value above and beyond the data collected, but few other disciplines have comparable requirements. This has remained true despite the increasing availability of second-hand data, and is a tribute to the anthropologist's awareness that socialization of apprentices depends on what they have done as well as what they have read (Jencks and Riesman, 1968a).

The continuing debate between "formalists" and "substantivists" over the uses of Karl Polanyi's substantive economics in analyzing economic behavior in different social orders of the Western world is one of the basic themes of Prof. Richard Salisbury's paper on anthropology and economics. Also covered is the applicability of various derivative analytical schemata to tribal economic life. Both he and his discussants consider many of the ramifications of those issues in the work of contemporary anthropologists and economists.

Dr. Salisbury reviews the problem of the validity of generalizations based on the discovery of structural similarities in very different social systems as well as the significance of conclusions about economic behavior in comparative studies. He considers the consequences of analyzing, comparatively and functionally, particular features of several social systems apart from the context in which they exist. Even if the relative cross-cultural merits of several alternative formulations of rational economic man and of the supply and demand principle remain an open issue, the two fields are now firmly interlocked. They are trying to develop new paradigms that pose model problems and offer some solutions for every student of economic behavior.

In his paper, *History and Political Science,* Professor Bernard Cohn examines the nature of disciplinary similarities and contrasts on the basis of the major orientations and activities that characterize work in these fields. It leads him to discuss the extent to which the particular site and style of work determine the types of questions which are asked and considered significant, and how they have influenced the manner in which answers are sought.

Unlike Professor Wax, Professor Cohn explores the problem of relationship in terms of the question of *how* historians, political scientists, and anthropologists work. He is only indirectly concerned with the consequences of what they do. On the other hand, the relationship between the approach and the end product of their scientific efforts, and such issues as the consequences of recent trends in core curriculum building in these fields receive special attention in the three commentaries that follow Dr. Cohn's paper.

Professor Solon T. Kimball, in his paper on anthropology and education, raises a different set of cross-disciplinary problems. He is concerned with the relevance of anthropological approaches to the understanding of the contemporary educational system. Among other things, he considers the problem of social class in relation to the concept of "subculture," and the utility of the anthropological view of "social structure" and "transmission of culture" in analyzing the formal and informal structure of educational institutions within the larger society.

Both his paper and the commentaries suggest that a question of professional ethics is posed by the application of such analyses to policy decisions within the school system. Pertinent questions arise about the pedagogical consequences of the growing feedback of anthropological knowledge into the formal educational process and, in turn, into the general culture. New insights about these and related issues may result from more systematic anthropological studies of significant subcultural continuities and differences in the process of education.

Although Professor Jules Henry does not as such address himself to the cross-disciplinary relationship of anthropology and psychology, his paper on the normal and abnormal in human behavior is an important contribution to the long history of attempts to build a viable bridge between the scientific study of social man and that of psychological man. Instead of focusing on the variation found in different cultural traditions, he states the fact and explores the significance of certain universal underlying invariants, or intuitively perceived factors common to all cultures.

Professor Henry identifies and defines several of these invariants, and documents the special significance of some, such as "circumspection" and "contradiction" in ordinary everyday life. He also develops a mode of anthropological analysis which seems to hold great promise for conducting cross-cultural studies of human conduct which would go beyond the traditional relativistic approach of treating abnormality and normality primarily as an artifact of singular cultural traditions.

The commentaries evoked by his paper not only bring into focus the continuing theoretical and methodological controversies about this problem; they also mirror the special experiences and orientations, both explicit and implicit, of the individual discussants.

Professor Harvey Sarles traces the long and involved history of the study of human communication both within and outside of the field of anthropology in relation to the conceptual and methodological development of the new "interdiscipline" of ethology. He and his discussants provide a selective overview of the confluence of the major ideas and approaches from the behavioral science field which gave birth to ethology as a distinct field of scientific inquiry.

Among other matters, these contributors, as a whole, consider the relevance of the psychological approaches in the experimental study of animal behavior and recent research formulations in communications theory and in anthropological and general linguistics, including "Cartesian Linguistics," psycholinguistics, and the micro-linguistic and kinesic analysis of verbal behavior and gesture in man and animal. They do so within the broad perspective of new theoretical developments in the comparative study of man's biosocial adaptation to his environment and in terms of new insights arising from the systematic observational study of primate behavior in diverse natural habitats.

The process of conceptual and methodological cross-fertilization brought about by these comparative studies of human and infra-human behavior appears to form the basis for challenging certain traditional assumptions about the "basic human nature of man," both among anthropologists and other behavioral scientists. In particular, the ethnological approach, when wedded to communications theory, has led them to ask questions about modes of communication which, while they may be culturally patterned, are not overtly or directly accessible either to the members of the societies involved or to the analyst-observer. Thus, entirely new subfields of study, such as kinesics, are beginning to deal with the problem of non-verbal communication and are raising fundamental questions about the relationship between verbal and non-verbal forms of speech.

The Contents of Part II

In his paper on anthropology and constitutional medicine, Dr. Albert Damon discusses morphology, the traditional approach to constitutional medicine. To date, this field of study has generally involved the study of the physique and the application of these studies to normal and physiological measurements such as age-height standards for insurance, military, and industrial purposes. In a disease-oriented study, however, the major reasons for considering physique are (1) to be able to predict who is susceptible to disease and their probable response to that disease and to appropriate therapy; (2) to investigate the mechanisms underlying association between disease and its physiological, biochemical, and anatomical manifestation; (3) to elucidate the causes of disease through research and the relation of body form to function; and (4) to determine where, in the web of disease, intervention can help prevent disease.

After discussing the various methods for analyzing physique, Dr. Damon hypothesizes that constitutional research may eventually indicate how to prolong life by identifying group types which should avoid certain foods, drugs, or occupations. Indeed, recent, exhaustive reviews have concluded that real associations do exist in the body-behavior relationship for both normal and abnormal behavior. In summarizing research findings on the relation of constitution, particularly disease, to physique, Dr. Damon places special emphasis on the relation of physique to coronary heart disease as an example of a "confirmed association."

In response to Dr. Damon's paper, the value of combining the epidemiological view with the anthropological view of constitutional medicine is introduced. Further discussion focuses on the need to study genetic variations in man, how the various genic systems interact with environment to produce morphology, and the morphology-function-behavior relationships. Throughout, it is emphasized that the normal rather than the pathological should be the focus of concern.

Professor Bertram Kraus in his paper on anthropology and dentistry and oral medicine discusses the ramifications of the increasing interaction between dentistry and anthropology with respect to the past, and for the cycle of future growth and development in individuals. Discussants generally agree that the interdisciplinary nature of dental research has long been appreciated by anthropologists but not by dental schools. The unparalleled accomplishments in this field in the last ten years point to an equally promising future. The study of the development of face and dentitia opens a Pandora's box for research.

Professors Donald Hochstrasser and Jesse Tapp discuss the development and changes taking place in the relationship among anthropology, social medicine, and public health and the expanding professional opportunities for medical anthropology. Increasing evidence indicates that new patterns of social organization are needed for providing and delivering health and medical care services. Anthropologists are urged to play a significant part in collaborating with medical researchers, educators, and practitioners for the eventual integration of personal and social medicine within modern society. Such collaboration may eventually lead to improving man's cultural and biological circumstances through optimization of physical, psychological, and social sufficiency in health and meaningful living.

In ensuing discussion, the appropriateness of social medicine and public health as fields of study for the medical anthropologist is stressed, particularly since much remains to be done in both medicine and anthropology before knowledge now applicable to social areas can be applied to individuals.

Professor Wilton M. Krogman chose to discuss the place of physical anthropology in forensic medicine in his paper *Physical Anthropology and Forensic Medicine*. He provides a synoptic overview of the nature of this relationship with a discussion of duration of interment, examination of skeletal material, and the use of radiography for determining how long a person has been dead and for identifying the remains. In briefly covering various effects on skeletonization and evaluating the techniques of biochemical analysis, electron microscopy, specific gravity studies, or fluorescence, and conductivity for supersonic oscillation, he emphasizes the need for graduate anthropology students to study osteology extensively. Professor Krogman's emphases are continued and expanded by the discussants. Although the extent of anthropological involvement in forensic medicine is not clear, it obviously has not extended as far as it should in both teaching and research. There also appears to be a continuing need for a greater appreciation of the philosophical implications of the relationship of anthropology to forensic medicine.

In reviewing the formal relationship between anthropology and medicine begun over a hundred years ago, Professor Otto von Mering in his paper on anthropology and medicine and psychiatry considers the meaning and cause of disease within the interplay of disease condition, the complaint, the pattern of disease, and culture. While the study of ecology and etiology of specific or named disease will largely remain the province of the physician-researcher, the anthropologist will concentrate on specific, or nonspecific, manifestations of disease under local conditions and indigenous human responses. In his anthropological review of the problem of disease in man, Professor von Mering discusses the significance between the nature of a disease episode and its setting; the care process; and the Western approach toward organic disease, mental illness, and treatment as opposed to tribal and folk practices.

Following Dr. von Mering's review, the discussion centers on what anthropology can contribute to the study of life under altered conditions, especially in the study of disease patterns. Special emphasis is placed on adaptation and its implication, and again, on defining the pathological in contrast to the normal in a psychocultural environment.

Student education is a major concern of Professor Richard Snyder who laments the small number of anthropologists involved in aerospace sciences. He stresses the need for an infusion of aerospace sciences technology (in particular, the more advanced techniques for measuring human behavior) into the anthropology curricula, especially for graduate students. His critique is not directed solely at anthropologists, however, since aerospace researchers also lack knowledge of what the anthropologist can do.

Professor Snyder cogently argues that concurrent with the emphasis on specialization in most branches of science, the need exists for scientists who have an overall view of man. Indeed, the most important contribution the anthropologist can make to collateral aerospace efforts is his breadth of knowledge about man. As man has gained the ability to escape the environmental limitation of terrestrial ecology, so too has the study of man changed. Professor Snyder challenges anthropologists to use their knowledge of terrestrial man to investigate, among other things, the ramifications of the possibility of extraterrestrial life.

The discussants generally hold the view that anthropologists should move toward more active participation in the problem-oriented, multidisciplinary, academic departments which undertake "real-world" studies. However, the exchange must always be two-way: both aerospace research and development and the field of anthropology will benefit from the stimulation of the many scientific disciplines necessary for solving problems of human adaptation in the space age.

Concluding Remarks

It is fair to state that the essays and discussions are altogether a refutation of comforting views of science "predicated on the assumption that the scientific community knows what the world is like" (Kuhn, 1962). In a sense, the particular mix of reconsideration and advocacy of the anthropologist's work within the behavioral and health sciences is also an example of the kind of rethinking needed to bring about an academic revolution in cross-disciplinary fertilization of research and teaching (Jencks and Riesman, 1968b). We hope that the variegated interpretations about some of the relevant realities may move future anthropologists closer to this goal.

REFERENCES

Association of Social Anthropology. 1965—   . A.S.A. Monographs 1— . Tavistock Publications, Praeger: London, and New York.

Bloomfield, L. 1933. Language. Henry Holt: New York.

Braidwood, R. J. 1964. Prehistoric Man. Natural History Museum: Chicago.

Casagrande, J. B. 1963. Relations of Anthropology with the Social Sciences. The Teaching of Anthropology, eds. D. Mandelbaum, G. Lasker, and E. M. Albert, Memoir 94, American Anthropological Association, pp. 461–74.

Chomsky, N. 1957. Syntactic Structures. Mouton: The Hague.

———. 1965. Aspects of the Theory of Syntax. Massachusetts Institute of Technology Press: Cambridge.

———. 1966. Cartesian Linguistics: A Chapter in the History of Rationalist Thought. Harper and Row: New York.

Corklin, E. G. 1943. Man Real and Ideal. Scribners: New York.

Daniel, G. 1968. One Hundred Years of Old World Prehistory. One Hundred Years of Anthropology, ed. J. O. Brew, pp. 57–93, 89. Harvard University Press: Cambridge.

DuBois, C. 1963. The Curriculum in Cultural Anthropology. The Teaching of Anthropology, eds. D. Mandelbaum, G. Lasker, and E. M. Albert, Memoir 94, American Anthropological Association, pp. 27–38.

Eggan, F. 1968. One Hundred Years of Ethnology and Social Anthropology. One Hundred Years of Anthropology, ed. J. O. Brew, pp. 119–49, 145, 147–48. Harvard University Press: Cambridge.

Epstein, A. L., ed. 1967. The Craft of Social Anthropology. Social Science Paperbacks, Tavistock Publications: London.

Gluckman, M. 1964. Closed Systems and Open Minds: The Limits of Naivety in Social Anthropology. Oliver and Boyd: Edinburgh and London.

Harris, M. 1968. The Rise of Anthropological Theory. Crowell: New York.

Harris, Z. S. 1951. Methods in Structural Linguistics. University of Chicago Press: Chicago.

Hockett, C. F. 1958. A Course in Modern Linguistics. University of Chicago Press: Chicago.

Huxley, J. S. 1942. Evolution, the Modern Synthesis. Harper and Row: New York.

Hymes, D. H., ed. 1965. The Use of Computers in Anthropology. Mouton: The Hague.

Jencks, C. and D. Riesman 1968a. Where Graduate Schools Fail. Atlantic Monthly 51: 49–55, February.

———. 1968b. The Academic Revolution. Doubleday: New York.

Kluckhohn, C. 1962. Culture and Behavior: Collected Essays. Free Press: New York.

Kluckhohn, C. and W. Kelly. 1945. The Concept of Culture. The Science of Man in the World Crisis, ed. R. Linton. Columbia University Press: New York.

Kroeber, A. L., ed. 1953. Anthropology Today. University of Chicago Press: Chicago.

Kuhn, T. S. 1962. The Structure of Scientific Revolutions, p. 5. University of Chicago Press, Phoenix Editions: Chicago.

Kurtz, P. and R. Handy. 1963. A Current Appraisal of the Behavioral Sciences. American Behavioral Scientist 7, Supplement, pp. 1–144.

Leach, E. R. 1966. Rethinking Anthropology. Athlone Press: London.

Lévi-Strauss, C. 1966a. The Savage Mind. Weidenfeld and Nicolson: London.

———. 1966b. The Scope of Anthropology. Current Anthropology 7(2):112–23, 120.

———. 1966c. Anthropology: Its Achievements and Future. Current Anthropology 7(2):124–27, 127.

Linton, R., ed. 1945. The Science of Man in the World Crisis. Columbia University Press: New York.

Lounsbury, F. G. 1968. One Hundred Years of Anthropological Linguistics. One Hundred Years of Anthropology, ed. J. O. Brew, pp. 153–225, 159, 171, 173. Harvard University Press: Cambridge.

Mandelbaum, D., G. Lasker, and E. M. Albert, eds. 1963. The Teaching of Anthropology, Memoir 94, American Anthropological Association; see also Resources for the Teaching of Anthropology. 1963. University of California Press: Berkeley.

Movius, H. L. 1949. Old World Paleolithic Archaeology. Bulletin Geological Society of America 60:1448–49.

Murdock, G. P. 1954. Sociology and Anthropology. For a Science of Social Man, ed. J. Gillin, pp. 14–31. Macmillan: New York.

Page, I. H. 1965. Medical Research as I See It. Journal of the American Medical Association 194 (13):1355–62, 1361, December.

Parsons, A. 1966. Commentary. Current Anthropology 7(3):362–65, 363.

Paul, B. D. 1956. Anthropology and Public Health. Some Uses of Anthropology, Theoretical and Applied, eds. J. Casagrande and T. Gladwin, pp. 49-57. Anthropological Society: Washington, D.C.

Pike, K. L. 1954. Language in Relation to a Unified Theory of the Structure of Human Behavior, Part I. Summer Institute of Linguistics: Glendale.

Saussure, F. de. 1959. Course in General Linguistics, eds. C. Bally and A. Sechehaye, trans. from the French by W. Baskin. Philosophical Library: New York.

Tax, S., ed. 1964. Horizons of Anthropology. Aldine: Chicago.

Tax, S., et al., eds. 1953. An Appraisal of Anthropology Today. University of Chicago Press: Chicago.

U.S. Department of Health, Education and Welfare. Public Health Service. 1969. Sociologists and Anthropologists: Supply and Demand in Educational Institutions and Other Settings. U.S.P.H.S. Publication No. 1884. Washington, D.C.

von Mering, O. 1969. Behavioral Sciences in Medical and Psychiatric Education: With Special Reference to Anthropology and Sociology. Teaching Psychiatry in Medical School, ed. L. W. Earley. pp. 445–481. American Psychiatric Association: Washington, D.C.

Washburn, S. L. 1963. The Curriculum in Physical Anthropology. The Teaching of Anthropology, eds. D. Mandelbaum, G. Lasker, and E. M. Albert, Memoir 94, American Anthropological Association, pp. 39–47.

———. 1968. One Hundred Years of Biological Anthropology. One Hundred Years of Anthropology, ed. J. O. Brew, pp. 97–115, 98, 115. Harvard University Press: Cambridge.

Waterman, J. T. 1963. Perspectives in Linguistics. University of Chicago Press: Chicago.

Whorf, B. L. 1952. Collected Papers in Metalinguistics. Foreign Service Institute, Department of State. Washington, D.C.

Willey, G. R. 1968. One Hundred Years of American Archaeology. One Hundred Years of Anthropology, ed. J. O. Brew, pp. 29–53, 53. Harvard University Press: Cambridge.

Wolf, E. R. 1964. Anthropology, p. 88. Prentice-Hall: Englewood Cliffs.

Woodbury, R. B. 1963. Purposes and Concepts. The Teaching of Anthropology, eds. D. Mandelbaum, G. Lasker, and E. M. Albert, Memoir 94, American Anthropological Association, pp. 223–32.

Part I

Anthropology and the
Behavioral Sciences

Sociology

A. L. Kroeber once observed that it was not the human capacity for creative innovation that distinguished man from the other animals, but rather his ability to transmit from one generation to the next that which has been innovated, tried, and proven valuable. I have taken this thesis as my guide for the present paper. In reviewing two fields such as sociology and anthropology which have vast bodies of literature, I can hardly be significantly original within the compass of a few pages, nor can I hope to be complete or fair. My role is rather like that of the preacher who singles out in his sermon a few of the human truths already known to his audience and presents them in an unconventional context.

The Bureaucratic Ecology of Social Science

As a prologue to discussing social organization, let us remember that sociology and anthropology are institutional units within the system of universities and scientific societies. While there are sociologists and anthropologists laboring outside the university system, the significant shifts of policy, manpower, and organization still occur within the dual context of university and scientific society. This is true not merely in the United States, but also in many other nations where the study of sociology or anthropology is in progress.

Within the United States, and other nations which are moving along the same current of mass education, the university system has become increasingly bureaucratic. Knowledge is assumed to be divided into fixed quanta, marked by the course, class period, textbook lesson, and examination. These quanta are cumulative as credit hours and, when they sufficiently accrue to the individual, he is certified with a degree. Plainly, that knowledge which fits best into this iron framework is dead knowledge, fixed and finished, consisting either of a body of texts composed by scholars long deceased, or of a body of hard propositions forming a closed formal system, such as classical mechanics within physics.

Within anthropology, subfields such as physical anthropology and archaeology have often closely approximated the model of the body of texts, fixed and finished, and have fitted easily into the bureaucratic structure of the university. However, much of the rest of anthropology and much of the best of sociology have posed a more difficult exercise for the bureaucratic sergeants of the university organization. Indeed, from the viewpoint of a systematic and logical division of scientific labor, the very existence of the disciplines or sciences which are taken to constitute the social or behavioral sciences makes little sense. Sociology, anthropology, and the various other disciplines, such as economics and psychology, are not the outgrowths of a systematic division of social-scientific labor, but are, instead, the arbitrary consequences of particular social processes. In particular, the character of sociology in the United States owes a great deal to the fact that it had to push its way into the universities, elbowing room for itself against the more ancient disciplines of economics, political science, and history. Sociologists had to claim that they were concerned with something other than what their senior colleagues were doing. Most of them based this claim upon a concern with the social problems associated with industrialization and urbanization, particularly the problems of urban poverty, crime, and familial disorganization.[1] Such social problems were worthy of detailed empirical investigation and had been slighted by the existing disciplines; thus, they provided an intelligible field of specialization for sociology.

1. Sociology in the United States sees itself as filiated to the pioneer studies of urban poverty undertaken by the English investigators, Charles Booth, Beatrice Potter Webb, and Henry Mayhew. (See the historical review by Nathan Glazer in Lerner's *The Human Meaning of the Social Sciences* 1959). The sociological studies of poverty in the United States often have been given an ethnic focus, whether the focus is upon the Poles in Chicago (Thomas and Znaniecki, 1958) before World War I, or the Spanish in New York City after World War II (C. W. Mills, 1960).

From the point of view of a systematic division of social-scientific labor, however, this kind of differentiation among the disciplines has never made sense. How can we study crime without studying the political machinery that defines crime and labels men as criminals (Kitsuse and Cicourel, 1963; Erikson, 1962)? How can we study the State without studying the ways people resist the claims and authority of the State? Likewise, how can we study poverty without studying the labor is not that several different disciplines are studying the same subject matter (while giving different labels to their activities), but rather the obverse; namely, that the gaps between our disciplines are much too large. How can sociology or anthropology attempt to build a science of societies or review the history of mankind without giving the most serious consideration to political and economic power, production, and trade? The ethnocentric provinciality of much of political science and framework of production and trade in which people are poor? And how can we study the economy without studying how it is that people become, and live as, the poor?

In my opinion, there is no set of scientific disciplines whose interrelationships can be discussed as sociology and anthropology. Rather, I see a set of scientific societies, each of which, as a result of particular social processes, has managed to gain some mandate to study the body social.[2] In terms of a logical and systematic division of social-scientific labor, much of sociology and anthropology should be grouped together as one discipline. For example, social psychology, ethnopsychology, and psychological sociology are actually one field, and the attempts to justify their disparateness are almost comical.

Yet, as social scientists, we know that logic seldom organizes social relationships, and I think we all realize that, faced with departmental baronies, university monarchies, and multi-university imperiums, no edict from the pope of the Ford Foundation, nor even any decision of the "College of Cardinals" of all benevolent foundations could possibly bring into a logical table of organization our current system of university departments and scientific societies. Perhaps it is better as it is now for, given that scholars are human beings and not instruments of inquiry, it may be best that the social sciences are chaotically di-

2. The concept of "mandate" and the general orientation toward the social sciences and the place of sociology among them, have been adapted from Everett C. Hughes (1958, 1959, 1961, and elsewhere).

vided and that the various divisions are professional rivals for the same subject areas. The consequence often may be that a man unpopular with his fellow sociologists will receive among anthropologists the encouragement to continue his heretical endeavors. Likewise, a theory, such as psychoanalytic psychology, that infringes on the vested interests of one discipline and so is stamped as heretical, may find in a neighboring discipline the opportunity for employment and refinement. Fortunate developments like these, however, can only occur where there is a sufficient degree of overlap among the academic disciplines.

Assuming this to be true, the defect of our present division of labor is not that several different disciplines are studying the same subject matter (while giving different labels to their activities), but rather the obverse; namely, that the gaps between our disciplines are much too large. How can sociology or anthropology attempt to build a science of societies or review the history of mankind without giving the most serious consideration to political and economic power, production, and trade? The ethnocentric provinciality of much of political science and economics has been even more scandalous, but that is not my concern here. Nevertheless, considering the attacks that have so often been leveled against Marxism, it would only be fair for me to note that for a long period of time the principal banner raised against the artificial divisions among the social sciences was that of the Marxists who insisted on the interrelationship of the economic, the political, and the cultural.

The Little Community: A Natural Whole

For anthropology, the effects of the detachment from the more established sciences of economics and political science have been especially evident in the study of the little community (Redfield, 1955), the model for cultural investigation. The anthropologist has felt free, or even compelled, to describe every significant aspect of the life of his particular community, including its economy and political structure. In the most successful of these studies, the ethnographer described the life within his little community as a natural whole, and his mode of presentation predisposed him to steer a delicately balanced course between the abstract description of reified social forms and the novelistic rendering of human relationships. The anthropologist, however, was able to perform this *tour de force* only at a high cost, for the little community model and the research connected with it were built on a deliberate blindness — a blindness that appears very conspicuous in the accusing vision of the intellectuals of ex-colonial areas (Maquet, 1964). In his scholarship, at least, the ethnographer chose to ignore the politico-economic linkages between the little community of his research and the great societies encompassing it. When he could not accomplish this isolation in the present, the ethnographer retreated into an idealistic past, "the ethnographic present," so that the only linkages he needed to consider were those among little communities, rather than those between his little community and greater societies.

Had there been any real meaning to the social-scientific division of labor, it should have been here that colleagues in other disciplines, especially in sociology, rushed to reprove the errors of the anthropologist. By and large this was not so. Instead, a substantial bloc of sociologists were so impressed with the success of the little community studies that they hastened to emulate them. Some sociologists proceeded to study whatever within urban society was sufficiently small and isolable to have some of the form of a little community: a prison, an asylum for the insane, a small town, or an ethnic slum. Some of the results achieved by these sociologists were extraordinarily fine (cf., Vidich, Bensman, and Stein, 1964).

Meanwhile, other sociologists were attracted by the conceptual scheme — functionalism — that had been utilized by some of the more eminent anthropological students of little communities. These sociologists attempted to find ways by which they could apply functionalism to the study of the systems of modern, industrial, and urban societies (Brotz, 1961). But, in stretching and adapting the functionalist schema to cover such a systemic complexity, these theorists found it necessary to eliminate much of the capacity for insight and understanding that made the ethnographic study of the little community so appealing. Worse yet, some of these theorists committed the folly of attempting to treat a huge, modern nation-state (such as the United States or the Union of Soviet Socialist Republics) as if it was but an enlarged and elaborated version of a little community. They, therefore, had to insist upon a homogeneity of values and norms for the nation-state that was both false to the facts and freighted with a conservative political bias.[3] Here, anthropologists could be useful as critics by showing the frequency with which the nation-state is an ecological system, or system of societies. Also, cultural anthropologists are in an excellent position to remind sociologists of the multinational, international, and nonnational quality of so much of modern (and ancient) life.[4]

Ideologies of Sociology

Several times in this paper I have referred to the problem of a systematic division of social-scientific labor, but so far I have begged the question of what sort of sciences sociology, anthropology, and their companions actually are. Are they destined to follow the route of the natural sciences for which classical mechanics within physics has been the archetype? Or are they some other kind of enterprise — practical, humanistic, historical, moral, or philosophical (Evans-Pritchard, 1964; Wax, 1965a, 1965b; Winch, 1958; Seeley, Nisbet, et al. in Stein and Vidich, 1963)? Put genetically, the issue is whether the social sciences are simply the latest representatives of our endless human preoccupation with our own and our neighbor's conduct, or whether they really have sprung freshly into existence during the past century or so of Western society and, thus, mark the radical innovation of applying to the study of human society that master tool — scientific method.

The issue is not idle inasmuch as agencies such as the National Science Foundation and the American Association for the Advancement of Science (AAAS) have been steadily using their influence to

3. An interesting case in point is the contrast in the portraits of the Industrial Revolution in England as presented by the Parsonian sociologist, Smelser (1959), and by the social historian, Thompson (1964). Concerning the possibility of a minimum wage law, Thompson (1964) is forced to protest, "The difficulty lay, not (as Professor Smelser has it) in the 'dominant value-system of the day,' but in the strong opposition of a minority of masters and in the mood of Parliament (which Professor Smelser commends for its success in 'handling' and 'channeling' the weavers' unjustified disturbance symptoms)." Social system theorists are led to an over concern with "the problem of Hobbes" and a general slighting of the remainder of the great tradition of political philosophy.

4. At the beginning of this paper, I noted the international character of the system of universities and scientific societies and especially of the disciplines of sociology and anthropology. This was not an idle comment, but was made to emphasize the supranational values that adhere to the callings of these disciplines.

push social scientists into following the model of the natural sciences. The AAAS annually offers a prize of a thousand dollars in order "to encourage in social inquiry the development and application of dependable methodology analogous to the methods that have proven so fruitful in the natural sciences." This is quite significant because no agencies are offering prizes to natural scientists for research that uses dependable methodology; whatever prizes are being offered in their fields are for achieving particular results or for solving particular problems. Accordingly, it must be said that if such pressures are to be considered meaningful, they must betoken a corresponding resistance. After all, social scientists have been engaged in research for a considerable length of time and, if they persist in using those undependable methodologies of the "Brand X" variety, something critical must be wrong. Either the social scientists are stupid or they are traitors to pure science and are being seduced by well-known humanistic fleshpots.

More seriously, I should like to point out that, for well over a century, social scientists of one discipline or another have been trying to apply what they understood to be the methodology of the natural sciences to one or another area of human life. Pareto, Freud, Radcliffe-Brown, Watson, and others too numerous to mention each thought he was studying human behavior in a fashion akin to the way the natural scientist had been studying the nonhuman world. Each man cited thought he had been successful. Some of our contemporaries continue to think of these men as successful. If the scientist-critics of our disciplines believe that these efforts have, in fact, been so inconsequential and, if these investigators represented some of the most talented, energetic, and magnetic intellects of their time, then what properly ought to be concluded? I suggest the proper conclusion is that the social sciences cannot be transformed into the kinds of scientistic enterprises which have been enshrined in the ideology of our critics.

One clue to understanding the kind of science that social sciences are is in their genesis. Sociology arose in relationship to the Industrial Revolution, to the growth of new and peculiar social forms. The new military technology, the new systems of transportation and communication, combined with the increasing specialization and division of labor, meant that human beings were associated together in larger numbers and for more complex technical operations than ever before. At the same time, the quality of human associations were changing drastically

so that in more and more areas of their lives people were now dealing
— or linked — with others who were not their kith and kin. A significant index to these developments is provided by the rise of the modern
nation-state with its mass armies and its cult of patriotism.[5]

The emergence of sociology as an intellectual discipline was a reflex to these developments and has its parallel in the emergence of
classical economics. Let us recall that classical economics was predicated upon the most crude portrait of human nature and social interaction. As compared to the heritage of Western political and moral
philosophy, classical economics represented a genuine retrogression;[6]
yet, its very crudity was essential to its task, namely, that of describing
a particular institutional system based upon partial or degraded human
relationships. Much of sociology can be characterized in the same
fashion; the images of man and of social interaction are degraded in
order that the scientists can attempt to describe large populations organized in complex nets of partial or loose association. To say this is
not to derogate either classical economics or its sociological counterpart, but rather to warn ourselves that these models are necessarily
and inevitably untrue. The warning is necessary because there has been
a marked tendency to convert from heuristic models, useful for social
analysis, into ideologies and creeds. Let us remember that classical
economics was used to justify the most terrible and inhuman treatment
of the lower classes of England. The warning about the fallaciousness
of these models is also necessary because there is a tendency to regard
sociology and the other social sciences as representative of a revolution
in man's understanding of man. I would qualify this by saying that
the revolution is in actual human society — in the emergence of mass,
industrial, urban societies and, correspondingly, in our understanding of

5. In the sixteenth century, the élites who had controlled the European states
had become so detached from the local populations that they would not dare
arm them lest the weapons be used for rebellion. At that time, the national armies
were composed of imported mercenaries (Kiernan 1965), so that the integrity
of the national political unit was based almost exclusively upon the military force
of the elite and very little upon a social unity. The only groups that had solidarity were local communities of kith and kin or the religious orders.

6. In his *Theory of Moral Sentiments,* Adam Smith presented a far more
complex picture of man and a correspondingly more elaborate social psychology
than in his *Inquiry into the Nature and Causes of the Wealth of Nations.* In
Germany, this disproportion was so well recognized that it became known as *das
Adam-Smith-Problem.* This point is briefly reviewed in Truzzi (1966).

how these societies are possible. The development of sociology as a universal science of human societies has lagged far behind its development as a discipline devoted to the analysis of the national societies of the modern West.

If we turn from its genesis to its present, we will find that sociology, and, for that matter, anthropology, derives much of its character from a particular kind of intellectual tension which may be clarified by a religious metaphor. By its very essence, the Christian religion is torn between life according to the great traditional message of its scriptures and the religious function as asserted by Durkheim. On the one hand, Christianity bears a message that would be possible to heed only if men were saints liberated from mundane involvements. On the other hand, it is religion which embodies the moral solidarity of numerous actual communities. To be grasped as a real social phenomenon, Christianity cannot be considered as either the one or the other, but as being pulled between the two. I would like to argue similarly about sociology and the other social sciences. They are gripped by a tension between building a pure, if inhuman, science and being committed, empirically and morally, to the human drama. Crudely speaking, sociology is torn between the urge to abstract, even if the resultant abstraction says nothing of significance about human beings, and the urge to describe and understand human conduct, even if the resultant account fails to withstand the rigorous tests of a pure science. Researchers at the one extreme produce abstract, precise, and arid monographs, devoid of application to the human world, while those at the other extreme produce reports which are humanistic, novelistic, historical, or polemical in texture.

Although I could spend my time trying to analyze the fallacies inherent in attempting to transform sociology (or anthropology) into pure science, I think such an effort would be misguided because the tension between attempting to become both a pure science and to understand human existence may have been good for (and perhaps may have been the essential quality of) sociology. The same tension seems to have been even better for anthropology. Whether we agree or disagree with this analysis of sociology as a science, I think that, as anthropologists, we will have to grant the value of diversity. Sociology and anthropology are in a better state because they harbor individuals and factions of opposite opinion than they would be if they were characterized by greater unanimity. I fear, therefore, that we have to acknowledge the usefulness of having within our scientific societies bands of men who seem, on our blackest moments, to be the most egregious fools.

Moreover, I have to acknowledge that all manner of advantages accrue to sociology and anthropology because of the popular belief that these fields are striding firmly and determinedly along the high road to true behavioral sciences. Science is one of the sacred symbols of the United States and the modern world and, insofar as sociology and anthropology can claim to be creating a science, rather than writing history, cultivating the arts, addressing social problems, framing a social philosophy, or doing any other human and worthy activity, then to the degree, they seem to exercise a claim upon the resources of the community. Benevolent foundations and federal and local governments all rush to assist their cause. They gain not only funds for research, for teaching, and for teaching teachers, but also acquire social status. Hence, to use a theological metaphor once again, we may note that, even if the belief in a pure behavioral science is a fantasy akin to the belief in an afterlife in paradise, nonetheless, it does have its mundane utilities.

Accuracy and Precision: A Dialectic

Corresponding to the tension between the ideal of a pure science and that of an impure or humanistic or moral science, there is a conflict in social science between the search for precision and the search for accuracy.[7] Within the discipline of psychology there has been a

7. I have taken the notions of "accuracy" and "precision" from the natural sciences where it is clearly and frequently obvious that a "precision instrument" may be inaccurate unless continually recalibrated against a standard. Thus, a device for measuring length may give repeatable results to six or more significant figures but, unless the fiducial points of the instrument have been established exactly (at that place and occasion), the precisely measured readings may be so inaccurate as to be meaningless. "Accuracy" thus refers to the closeness with which the reading of the instrument approximates the true value (in statistical terms it is the closeness of $\bar{x}$ to u), while "precision" refers to the number of significant digits in the reading of one instrument as compared to another. It easily can happen that, of two instruments, one will be more accurate and the other more precise. I find the accuracy-precision dichotomy more congenial than the validity-reliability dichotomy, as to me, the latter connotes a concern with measurement rather than a discovery of the truth. For those who would prefer a discussion phrased in terms of validity and reliability, see Deutscher (1966a).

prolonged and extreme drive to achieve precision, almost regardless of accuracy or relevance. Frequently, it was not at all clear what it was that the experimental psychologist was able to measure, but the precision of his efforts conveyed the nimbus of natural science.

Within the discipline of sociology, the sample survey, for a long period of time, has represented the instrument of precision. The elegant statistical theories of sampling and tests of significance have developed about the sample survey so that, by these means, the researcher could know precisely the probability of his errors. The data acquired by the survey could be processed mechanically now, by computer, and this, too, conveyed the nimbus of natural science. Moreover, sample surveys have found practical applications in plotting the strategy of campaigns for political office, of campaigns for selling soap, cigarettes, and government bonds, as well as for reducing the frictions of life in the armed services. Yet, the ironical feature of the sample survey is that it is postulated on an image of man that is quite unsociological — an image of man that is markedly similar to that which is found in classical economics, for, in the sample survey, man is seen as a social atom, a self-contained individual (Deutscher, 1966b). The field interview situation is designed accordingly, with the respondent interviewed in isolation from family and friends by a person who is a stranger. The interviewer is instructed to minimize social interaction between himself and the respondent and, especially, not to discuss with the respondent the issues of the survey. Each respondent, thus suitably isolated, is asked to choose among a cluster of alternative responses. When the questionnaire schedules have been returned to the survey offices, the aggregates of individual choices are summed by machine and interpreted by a professional staff housed in these offices. By means of the sample survey, statements can be made describing the population as a whole, and these statements can be as precise as there are funds available to be expended. The limitation of the survey, however, is that, necessarily, it cannot provide a portrait of social interaction, nor of human group life, nor of social solidarity, nor any portrait of particular subgroups of societies. It is significant that the survey director has to assume that all his respondents speak, not only the same language, but the same dialect of that language; or, if he does not assume that, he assumes that languages are basically isomorphic so that any question can be translated precisely into any language. To some degree at least, such assumptions are self-confirming, as the sample survey has tended to accompany the spread of mass urban society with its systems of mass media, mass production, and mass marketing.

Yet, even where a mass urban society tends to exist, as within the United States, there remains considerable inaccuracy associated with the most precise survey results. Consider, for example, the opinion surveys on public support for United States involvement in Viet Nam, and the debate that has ensued about the meaning of the clusters of responses revealed in these surveys. Consider further that, for one family, the cost of supporting United States involvement may be the risk of death of a son serving overseas, while for another family it may be a decrease in the purchasing power of an annuity pension; for yet other families, involvement in the war may mean the opportunity for a better job or the opportunity for a rootless youth to find meaning in life by joining in the adventure of a national crusade. Converting these disparate human experiences into a series of numerical tabulation is the task of the sample survey, and it is this sort of operation which gives a bureaucratic quality to so much of the science of sociology.

It should be almost unnecessary for me to point out the extreme contrast between sample survey procedures and those associated with participant observation and ethnographic field research. Where the survey interviewer confronts an isolated individual, the ethnographer confronts a little community and, where the interviewer obtains only a set of verbal responses as data, the ethnographer learns about the community by participating in its life. Over a period of time, the ethnographer learns the language of the community, its world view and ethos, and so is able to see meanings in verbal comment and behavior which would quite escape the outsider. In general, the ethnographer can interpret particular actions within their social context. So accurate and detailed are the reports of a good ethnographer that we have little in the way of precise languages or frameworks to handle them.

In following this argument, we should realize that precision is not so much an abstract virtue in social science as it is a necessity for certain types of investigations within mass society. We should also realize that, so far, precision in social science has been acquired at the expense of accuracy and that this is a poor bargain. I think it is important to emphasize here the limitations of precision because, recurrent within the social sciences, fads emerge which are based on the appeal to precision, as if by being more precise the investigator were thereby being more scientific. In their insistence upon rigor as the supreme virtue and in their indifference to accomplishment, these fads call to mind the behavior of sectarians within Judaism and Christianity. Some sectarians argued that the Kingdom of God did not appear because the true believers were not sufficiently pious. When, in the succeeding months and years, the Kingdom of God still did not appear, they again insisted that the cause was lack of piety and they exhorted higher standards of conduct. At times, it appears to me that those who preach the creed of a pure science are being motivated by a similar chain of reasoning: we are failing to achieve the Kingdom of Behavioral Science because we have not been sufficiently rigorous in our methodology, but if we will only purify ourselves and put away those humanistic fleshpots, the prophecy will be fulfilled and scientific salvation assured.

Against the prophets and their methodological fads, I invoke the statement of Kroeber with which I began this paper: human progress depends less on novelty than on continuity. If we have social science today, it is not simply the consequence of an intellectual revolution of the past century but, more important, it is due to the outgrowth of the millennia during which man has been struggling to understand himself. During this time, human beings have set themselves progressively more difficult tasks by utilizing their previously acquired knowledge in order to construct ever more complex and intricate systems of societies. Our current difficulties in describing and analyzing these systems of societies are not a mark of our failure as social scientists, but are intrinsic to the paradoxes of human evolution.

COMMENTARY: Melvin Mednick
Arthur J. Vidich
Horace M. Miner

Melvin Mednick

Professor Wax suggests that the division of labor among the social sciences is neither orderly nor logical and that, for this reason, he is reluctant to discuss the interrelationships between anthropology and sociology. I may agree that in some well-ordered universe the social sciences might be arranged so that they operate without distortions, gaps, redundancies, and rivalries. But even in this less-than-perfect world good reason exists for discussing anthropology and the neighboring disciplines, for such discussion may help control and limit the disorder, although not eliminate it. Moreover, even in the existing disorder there are positive aspects. Professor Wax, himself, notes that this disorder permits scholars with heretical ideas in one discipline to take refuge in another.

I would make the suggestion that another advantage of disorder is well illustrated by American anthropology, where disparate interests have been brought into a relationship by historic accident. To some extent, however, the result illustrates Professor Wax's original point. American anthropology has been continually riven by arguments concerning biological and cultural interests within one discipline. However the present situation has provided some unexpected gains. For example, the study of primates moved beyond ethology and comparative anatomy when social anthropologists contributed their techniques and interests. Similarly, new dimensions opened up in social anthropology when structural linguists brought their methods of analysis to bear upon the study of kinship. I believe that the same may be true of the relationships between any two social sciences. Thus, the arbitrary and sometimes chaotic arrangements of which Dr. Wax complains contain possibilities for serendipity which would not exist, or perhaps even be sought, if the present relationships were considered the best possible.

I agree with Professor Wax that the social science disciplines, in gaining and maintaining a mandate for their work, have tended to segment human behavior and break down the natural interrelatedness of the whole as a consequence of the Industrial Revolution. I wonder if this could ever have been otherwise. Perhaps our current divisions are a product of our American culture rather than a phase of history. European social science does not completely share our divisions or goals. Thus, it is conceivable that a social science rising out of a distinctly different cultural background might segment human behavior in various, unexpected ways.

Even more important, this segmentation may not be completely arbitrary but, rather, a response to particular data. Dr. Wax notes that certain kinds of investigation within mass society may require that sociology take an atomistic approach, although he generally prefers the "natural whole" approach in anthropology. However, the natural whole approach did not arise from an abstract commitment to a particular kind of study, but emerged from an endeavor to look at simple societies as part of the "here and now" obviously interrelated character of the institutions being studied. Thus, for anthropologists to take pride in studying natural wholes, or for sociologists to take pride in quantifying while studying atomistic behavior in a mass society, is to make a virtue of necessity.

If a relationship between approach and material exists, then, insofar as the material is different, the approach also must be different; to this extent, at least, the boundaries between disciplines are real, not arbitrary. It is unlikely that anthropologists working in traditional societies will widely adopt the sophisticated survey techniques of the sociologist — not because they wish to avoid a degraded image of man, but because the sociologist's techniques have limited utility for anthropological data. On the other hand, preoccupation with only certain kinds of data can dull awareness of other possibilities. It is not by accident that anthropology arrived at a structural-functional mode of analysis earlier than sociology. It may be true, as Davis (1959) has suggested, that a functional approach is inherent in scientific method rather than an anthropological "discovery." (Apparently, sociologists like Moliere's gentleman had been speaking prose, i.e., in functional terms, all along but did not know it.) But it is also true that the interrelated character of anthropological data encouraged this mode of analysis earlier in anthropology than elsewhere in social science. When the functional approach emerged in anthropology, it brought with it assumptions about integration and equilibrium, again reflecting tendencies in the material from which the analysis was derived. But such tendencies are less apparent in the data to which sociologists address themselves and, as a result, sociologists have been increasingly dissatisfied with the structural-functional approach.

In recent years, sociology has developed an alternative, the "conflict" model, which while retaining a functional approach, sees change and conflict as inherent in a system and seeks to identify factors interfering with the normal process of change (Coser, 1956; Dahrendorf, 1964). Anthropologists, too, have been increasingly unhappy with the equilibrium model (Gluckman, 1963), but the problem arises as to how much they can increase their understanding through studies of societies in which conflict and change appear abrupt or incidental to larger continuing processes. In the societies studied by sociologists, however, change and conflict have a long history, and have long been matters of sociological concern; and it comes as no surprise to find a conflict model emerging within sociology. Sociology found it useful to adopt and rework the structural-functional model despite its origins in the "natural whole" approach of anthropology. Similarly anthropology may find useful such models as the conflict one, despite its origins in a discipline here accused of having an "atomizing" approach. (See Murphy, 1957, for one example of the explicit use of a conflict model within anthropology.)

Another question arises from Dr. Wax's paper concerning the concept of the "natural whole." Dr. Wax's use of the phrase and discussion of the concept implies that wholes exist in nature, awaiting discovery and proper evaluation, and that anthropology and sociology have erred insofar as they have fallen short of describing the "real" whole. It could be argued that social wholes above the level of a visibly interacting group never exist in nature, and that anything beyond this is an artifact of investigation. But, even if we accept the notion that entities such as tribes, communities, or societies are real and meaningful units for study, this does not make their delineation any less arbitrary. All wholes must somehow be defined and torn loose from their ultimate context if they are to be usefully studied; to some degree wholes must eliminate or obscure some of the fullness of human life.

Even Professor Wax realizes that what is truly important is not so much the nature of the whole, but the commitment to as rounded and full-bodied a view of human behavior as possible. The little community is merely a convenient device for this purpose. While sociology, by and large, lacks this commitment, there is, nevertheless, an overlap between sociology and anthropology concerning the small society. The small society is defined for anthropological purposes as the tribe or village and for sociological purposes as the gang or factory. It is debatable whether a study of a total institution can achieve the same understandings as the study of a simple society, but it should be noted that one sociologist, Homans (1950), found it possible to encompass such widely disparate small societies as slum gangs, factory teams, and the Tikopia within a single conceptual framework.

Sociological studies of the small society tend to emphasize the social-psychological dimension, although they are balanced by an interest in organization. Much of the study of complex organization in sociology is concerned with the flow and distribution of power and authority in a finite social system. However, complex organizations and total institutions develop their own symbols, values, customary understandings, and patterns of association which are not always immediately understood by reference to the stated goals of the organization or to the lives the participants lead outside the context of the organization. Such organizations are, in effect, simplified cultures and societies which, unlike true cultures and societies, have a definite starting point in time. The sociological version of the natural whole offers to students of culture a means of studying the manner in which shared understandings arise, diffuse, and become perpetuated, something which is often difficult to do within societies having a long and complex history.

So far I have been discussing issues peripheral to the major point of Dr. Wax's argument: the dialectical tension he perceives between the ideal of a pure science and a humanistic understanding of man, and the conflict between the search for accuracy and the striving for precision. The term "tension" is apt, for it suggests something that can be brought into balance, but not necessarily eliminated. The issue is not so much one of "either-or," as of "how much," "where," and "when." The study of man has its origins in the humanistic impulse, and the evidences of the impulse are to be found in sociology as well as in anthropology. Indeed, sociologists worry far more about the "image of man" than do anthropologists, as can be witnessed in a book by that name, edited by Mills (1960), a sociologist, or in a celebrated article by Bendix (1951), "The Image of Man in the Social Sciences," which reflects the same concern Professor Wax shows in his paper.

It need not be greatly feared that the humanistic impulse will be totally eliminated from sociology or anthropology. What is to be feared is the indiscriminate use of precision for its own sake. If good portion of modern sociological research seems irrelevant to larger understandings and problems, it is not because behavior has been broken down into meaningless segments through a passion for precision. Rather, the desire to be precise often limits the sociologist to the investigation of those things which can be measured, although the results may have little value beyond description. Indeed, I sometimes feel that sociological research is an old-fashioned ethnography, a hodge-podge description of customs and attitudes described to at least an .05 level of confidence, but not really saying much beyond this.

It is apparent that some mixing of precision and accuracy is called for in both social science disciplines and individual pieces of research. If sociology has too large a portion of precision, it may be said that anthropology has too large a portion of accuracy. Anthropologists are becoming more and more involved in cultures which can no longer be described as homogeneous, and are studying problems where measures of frequency, magnitude, and correlation could be useful. As knowledge of the non-Western world becomes more important, the other social sciences look to anthropology for hard data. Anthropological canons of proof (coherency and consistency) may suffice for the anthropological reader, but the non-anthropologist demands something more precise. I am not suggesting that precision be the goal of anthropology or that anthropology bow to interests other than its own but, if anthropology is to realize the values inherent in its data and its approach, it would do well to make judicious use of precision.

Arthur J. Vidich

By invoking the Kroeber dictum that "it was not the human capacity for creative innovation that distinguished man from the other animals, but rather his ability to transmit from one generation to the next that which has been innovated, tried, and proven valuable," Professor Wax seems to be saying two things. First, modern sociologists and anthropologists have forsaken their intellectual legacy by forgetting that progress depends on continuity and by responding to more enticing and lucrative contemporary fads. Taking advantage of the market opportunities presented by government, universities, foundations, and business, they have too quickly abandoned those problems of social inquiry which past generations have proved valuable. In short, by responding to the immediate and the novel, the intellectual sources of these disciplines have been violated. Second, he indicates that both fields have thoughtlessly merged their styles of inquiry to the requirements of the form of society in which they happen to be located. Both disciplines have allowed themselves to become organizationally and intellectually bureaucratized, just like any other agency or institution. This has led astray modern practitioners of the arts of social inquiry so that they no longer pursue those problems which were once the common starting point of both sociology and anthropology.

The main burden of Professor Wax's statements seems to be a plea for the recovery of a lost past, a time when social science analyzed the real and vital problems of social life. When he cites with dismay the AAAS, annual thousand dollar prize offer "to encourage in social inquiry the development and application of dependable methodology analogous to the methods that has proven so fruitful in the natural sciences," he is reacting against arid positivism. Instead of carrying his attack forward, however, Professor Wax merely notes that the social sciences are "gripped by a tension between building a pure, if inhuman, science and being committed, empirically and morally, to the human drama." In the last section of his paper, Dr. Wax rephrases this issue as the problem of a dialectic between accuracy and precision. He clearly opposes mindless positivism. However, instead of stating the significant problems of modern social science (irrespective of method), Professor Wax can only tell us that man will go on "struggling to understand himself." While this is true, I do not see how this conclusion resolves the issue.

I would argue that the issue of the relationship between anthropology and sociology must be discussed in terms of their common origins and problems. The common starting point for both disciplines was based on a reaction to events within the Western world. Specifically, early social analysis tried to make sense out of the social and intellectual upheavals brought about by the destruction of the "feudal" order under the impact of the emerging industrial, liberal, capitalistic society. Taking feudalism and capitalism to stand for dominant forms of social organization, the early thinkers tried to understand the revolutionary shift from the one form of society to the other.

In the early stages of social analysis, for example, Montesquieu, Rousseau and the thinkers of the French Enlightenment did not differentiate between what we would now call sociology and anthropology.

In their work, they merely responded to the dominant events of their time, both in their own countries and in the rest of the world. They studied the effects of the newly emergent order on their own society, and the consequences of the penetration of Western society throughout the rest of the world. At a later stage, this same approach was characteristic of German social thought, as exemplified by Marx and Weber whose analyses always assumed a dialectical relationship between the advanced industrial countries and the rest of the world.

In these foregoing traditions, anthropology and sociology were simply opposite sides of the same coin. Sociology focused on an analysis of the internal evolution of Western institutions while anthropology concentrated on a new social order "integrated" on a world-wide basis from the perspective of the last four hundred years. Thus, the anthropologists were not part of the world they studied but, by definition, were part of the dominant Western tradition which viewed the rest of the world from perspectives developed within Western society, rather than from perspectives indigenous to the primitive world.

The task of anthropology was more difficult than that of sociology. Not only did anthropologists have to study societies in the midst of change forced upon them from the outside, they also had to act as the historians of those societies with no written histories. How well anthropology discharged this formidable intellectual responsibility remains to be evaluated.

With the benefit of hindsight we all know that within a certain period of time the specialized branches of knowledge and academic jurisdictions known as sociology and anthropology emerged. It now appears that we no longer live easily with this academic bifurcation. Perhaps we shall have to cast the problems of social analysis into another mold by taking a fresh look at the newly forming institutions from the emerging world order and disorder.

The twentieth century has been one of cataclysmic events: wars, mass communications, world-wide corporate enterprises, and the competition of the great powers have destroyed the older nations of the small stable (or unstable) community, society, or nation-state. Everywhere primitives are becoming modern, and the traditional models and perspectives of anthropological analysis are no longer adequate for understanding the modern world.

Anthropology has not yet found a way to adapt to the new circumstances of the present world. Rather, it has developed an academic and professional lore and tradition of its own, which makes it a prisoner of its own occupational culture. Professor Wax understands this. In responding to his own instincts, he automatically returns to Kroeber's aphorism that "progress depends less on novelty than on continuity." He seems to be asking us to return to the theories of earlier and less corrupted thinkers.

No doubt we can learn much from the great social analysts of the past. However, we also must realize that past social and anthropological theory cannot cope with the novel problems posed by the modern world. The world has changed much faster than the capacity of social analysts to comprehend it, and a return to the older theories will certainly not rectify this deficiency.

Horace M. Miner

As an anthropologist by *rite de passage,* while also having been accepted by sociologists despite my lack of their tribal marks, I am sympathetic to Professor Wax's view of the institutionalized separation of the two fields. I too have noted that sociology has been more sensitive than anthropology to the possibility of borrowing theory and methodology. My anthropological colleagues are apt to explain this phenomenon by asserting that anthropology has more to offer, but this is probably an oversimplification.

It is noteworthy that Wissler acclaimed *Middletown* for establishing the new field of "social anthropology of contemporary life," although the Lynds, who conducted the study, were sociologists without prior anthropological experience. One may even doubt that Warner's subsequent *Yankee City* studies were as thoroughly anthropological in their approach, despite the author's Murngin background. My point is that all these studies, as well as those done by anthropologists on Irish and French-Canadian villages or Italian-American slums, have become a more integral part of the sociological than of the anthropological literature. The reverse was true, however, of most studies of Latin American villages, despite the profound Hispanic impact on the indigenous Indian cultures. It appears that it is subject matter, rather than methodological or theoretical approach, which establishes disciplinary relevance. Despite fundamental cleavage along lines of subject matter, the two disciplines do employ methodologies which are as distinctive as the objects of study themselves.

Consider three outstanding characteristics of urban industrial society: size, heterogeneity, and literacy. Minimally, the first two require the collection of demographic data, while literacy makes census-taking possible. Such data, which are the *sine qua non* of empirical sociology, are largely lacking in anthropological studies. Although anthropologists welcome and report available census data, few fieldworkers feel compelled to conduct a census when the data are unavailable. This apparent lack of interest is due partly to the fact that counting is less mandatory for adequate description in societies where most variations in lifeways correspond to sex and age groups. A more important reason, however, is that anthropological interest in "cultural" analysis leads to normative statements about the behavior of human groups, while the study of "society" places conceptual emphasis on the patterns of interaction among group members who need to be counted and categorized. The same distinctions are evident in the anthropologist's satisfaction with informed informants and in the sociologist's concern over the adequacy of samples.

Professor Wax's observations relate to the professional characteristics of anthropologists in America. In Britain, social anthropologists have considered themselves sociologists as well. Other varieties of sociologists were not evident until after World War II. In Africa, this dual mandate enabled British anthropologists to pursue tribal natives into town. Most American anthropologists, however, have been loath to study urban Africans, although there is growing evidence that urban anthropology will be much more common in the future. Probably, the traditional diffusion between anthropology and sociology will change as we face the problems of analyzing modernizing masses.

REFERENCES

Bendix, R. 1951. The Image of Man in the Social Sciences: The Basic Assumptions of Present Day Research. Commentary 11:187–92.

Brotz, H. 1961. Functionalism and Dynamic Analysis. Archives Européennes de Sociologie 2:170–79.

Coser, L. 1956. The Functions of Social Conflict. Free Press: Glencoe.

Dahrendorf, R. 1964. Out of Utopia Toward a Reorientation of Sociological Analysis. Sociological Theory, eds. L. Coser and B. Rosenberg, pp. 209–27. Macmillan: New York. (Reprinted from American Journal of Sociology 64:115–27.)

Davis, K. 1959. The Myth of Functional Analysis as a Special Method in Sociology and Anthropology. American Sociological Review 24:757–72.

Deutscher, I. 1966a. Words and Deeds: Social Science and Social Policy. Social Problems 13:235–54.

———. 1966b. Public vs. Private Opinions: The "Real" and the "Unreal." Syracuse University Youth Development Center, Mimeographed.

Erikson. K. T. 1962. Notes on the Sociology of Deviance. Social Problems 9:307–14.

Evans-Pritchard, E. E. 1964. Social Anthropology and Other Essays. Free Press: New York.

Glazer, N. 1959. The Rise of Social Research in Europe. The Human Meaning of the Social Sciences, ed. D. Lerner, pp. 43–72. Meridian Books: New York.

Gluckman, M. 1963. Order and Rebellion in Tribal Africa. Free Press: Glencoe.

Homans, G. C. 1950. The Human Group. Harcourt, Brace: New York.

Hughes, E. C. 1958. Men and Their Work. Free Press: Glencoe.

———. 1959. The Dual Mandate of Social Science: Remarks on the Academic Division of Labor. The Canadian Journal of Economics and Political Science 25:401–10.

———.1961. Ethnocentric Sociology. Social Forces 40:1–4.

Kiernan, V. G. 1965. Foreign Mercenaries and Absolute Monarchy. Crisis in Europe: 1560–1660, ed. Trevor Aston, pp. 117–40. Basic Books: New York.

Kitsuse, J. and A. V. Cicourel. 1963. A Note on the Uses of Official Statistics. Social Problems 11:131–39.

Lerner, D. 1959. The Human Meaning of the Social Sciences. Meridian Books: New York.

Maquet, J. J. 1964. Objectivity in Anthropology. Current Anthropology 5:47–55.

Mills, C. W., ed. 1960. The Images of Man. G. Braziller: New York.

Murphy, R. F. 1957. Intergroup Hostility and Social Cohesion. American Anthropologist 59:1018–35.

Redfield, R. 1955. The Little Community, p. 53. University of Chicago Press. Chicago.

Smelser, N. J. 1959. Social Change in the Industrial Revolution. University of Chicago Press: Chicago.

Stein, M. and A. Vidich, eds. 1963. Sociology on Trial. Prentice-Hall: Englewood Cliffs.

Thomas, W. I. and F. Znaniecki. 1958. The Polish Peasant in Europe and America, 2 vols. Dover: New York.

Thompson, E. P. 1964. The Making of the English Working Class, p. 300. Pantheon: New York.

Truzzi, M. 1966. Adam Smith and Contemporary Issues in Social Psychology. Journal of the History of the Behavioral Sciences 2:221–24.

Vidich, A. J., J. Bensman, and M. R. Stein, eds. 1964. Reflections on Community Studies. Wiley: New York.

Wax, M. L. 1965a. The Tree of Social Knowledge. Psychiatry 28:99–106.

———. 1965b. Some Limitations of "Science" in Sociology. Kansas Journal of Sociology 1:42–45.

Winch, P. 1958. The Idea of a Social Science and its Relation to Philosophy. Routledge & Kegan Paul: London.

Economics

An excellent summary of the relationship between anthropology and economics up to and including 1960 was written by Joseph Berliner (1962).[1] However, the state of the two disciplines has changed considerably since 1960, necessitating a stock-taking.

Berliner's major analysis showed that all social science data can be visualized as a matrix with rows representing particular societies and columns standing for such entities as economy and religion. Anthropology has involved mainly the comparison of all cells in a column (i.e., cross-cultural studies of single institutions) or of all cells in a row (i.e., studies of functional relationships between institutions of a single society). Berliner showed that the strength of economics, as a discipline, was in the intensity of its study of relationships within the single cell of "Western economies" and he called for more intra-cell studies of non-Western economies. The attempt to demonstrate that non-Western economies had the same institutions as Western economies had doomed earlier economic anthropology to sterility; Berliner felt that the suggested intra-cell studies might bring about a revitalized anthropology.

Berliner's predictions would seem to be borne out by the healthy

1. Stock-taking would have been easier if Nash's textbook (1966) had appeared before rather than after the writing of the present paper, as the lines of thought in both are parallel. The reader is referred to Nash for a fuller documentation of much descriptive material mentioned in the present paper, which presents a somewhat more developed stand on the nature of formal analysis and models than Nash might prefer. I wish to acknowledge that my thinking on this has developed in the course of discussions, not only with Nash, but with, among others, C. S. Belshaw, R. Crocombe, A. G. Frank, L. Hazlehurst, L. Kasdan, M. Sahlins, and Mrs. G. Sankoff.

state of economic anthropology at the present time (if economic anthropology was not already more healthy in 1960 than Berliner knew). Currently, the major issue in economic anthropology is not whether non-Western economies have different substantive economic institutions, for it is now accepted that they have, but to what extent different formal calculi of rationality or of "economizing" can be isolated in non-Western conditions. Before considering the anthropological work that has led to this point of development, let me review some changes in economic thinking that have taken place in the past decade.

The Economic Side

In 1960, Berliner could still generalize plausibly about what comprises the main trends in economic thinking — Marshallian (or classical) theory, Keynesian theorizing about cyclical changes in national economies, and institutional economics and economic history. However, by 1966, the unmentioned infant economic fields of 1960 seem to have effected a revolution in economics. Neo-Keynesian thinking no longer concerns regular cyclical fluctuations, but focuses on how to induce continued expansion and secular change. Development economics in 1960 was concerned with transplanting Western economics to underdeveloped areas; it now studies and generalizes about the form of developing economies in their own right and theorizes about sequences within the developmental process. "Structural transformation" is now a respectable term in economics and not merely a use of social-anthropological jargon. Even though economists focus on such readily quantifiable topics as changing patterns of income distribution and wage differentials between export and internal sectors, they are closely concerned with the same problem as anthropologists who study the breakdown of caste barriers in plural societies. In 1962, Hagen was avant-garde in proposing an individual psychological explanation of the emergence of entrepreneurship; in 1966, he is more concerned with how entrepreneurial behavior relates to (or is irrelevant in) the context of economic choice for peasant farmers. Economists, in short, are emerging from their private Western-economies cell. They are going up and down columns into different societies and along rows into other institutions, and are increasingly concerned with secular change.

Another related trend in economics has been the study of decision-making at the levels of individuals, business firms, and nations, and outside the classical context of supply-price-demand balancing. Von Neumann with his invention of game theory was one initiator of this trend. The use of computers for playing simulated economic "games" has been another. Linear programming is perhaps the most mathematically advanced branch of this type of study. The effort is not to disprove the maximizing assumption of classical economic theory, but to demonstrate how most rationally to maximize specific magnitudes under various conditions of risk where differing time spans exist or where one decision is contingent on other people's decisions. Economics has moved far from the classical *homo oeconomicus* position based too much on hypothetical Robinson Crusoes, ridiculed in anthropological literature from Malinowski to Polanyi.

Another closely related and expanding economic field is business administration. For the anthropologist this field is perhaps most accessible through the works of sociologists such as Mason Haire with his studies on the growth of business organizations (1959). Such works enable economists to conceive of alternative total organizations and to compare the efficiency of overall structures in terms of their ability to respond to particular environmental problems and their eventual outputs. In short, they enable economists to see organization and managerial skills as factors of production to be measured and considered in general analysis.

The Anthropological Side

Ethno-Economics

As economists escaped from their cell, anthropologists became more focused on the internal analysis of single cells. Starting with Bohannan's study of the Tiv (1955), several studies have been made of the economic categories used in non-Western societies, which are intra-cell studies of single economic systems. My own study of categories used in relatively affluent tribal societies (Salisbury, 1962) would serve as an example. Foster's (1965) discussion of the concept of "the limited good" is a major comparative summary of a form of conceptualization that would appear to be prevalent in many societies. This type of study has established an important new subfield, which may be labled "ethno-economics" insofar as it aims merely at the description of single economies. As description, it undoubtedly benefits from the refined methodology of the "new ethnography." I would maintain, however, that its major theoretical importance has been the advances it has permitted in the field of formal analysis. I will return to the topic of ethno-economics when I deal with formal analysis.

Substantivism

Achieving greater prominence in the period from 1957 to 1966, the so-called substantivist school generalizes about the channels through which goods flow in total economies. This school stems largely from Polanyi's seminal *Trade and Markets in the Early Empires* (Polanyi, 1957; Polanyi, Arensberg, and Pearson, 1957), which introduced a typology of societies "integrated by reciprocity, redistribution and market exchanges." Considering the lack of quantitative studies then available, this was a remarkable synthesis. Unfortunately, most of the subsequent work of the school has involved the application of labels from Polanyi's typology, rather than a detailed investigation of the underlying processes which generate the social types Polanyi discussed. The major finding of Bohannan and Dalton's (1962) eight hundred-page compilation of studies of African marketplace trade is that societies in which trade is imbedded in other institutions and in which cash is not used are different from societies which form some system of market exchange.

"Redistributive," as a label, has been applied to societies such as those in Polynesia and West African kingdoms. The use of this term seems indiscriminate in the light of quantitative studies. Nadel's excellent early study of the Nupe economy (1942) shows that only a small portion of the total flow of goods and services is channeled through the king and even where guilds nominally operate as agents for the king, the degree to which they organize production in terms of private customers is mainly determined by the size of the private market. Village self-sufficiency, trade partnerships, and open-market trading are more common. It seems as if substantivists have seized upon some rare, but distinctive, features — a court, guilds, tribute payments, and negotiated foreign trade between the court and foreigners — and have used a label based on these features to characterize the total economy.

Polanyi's own posthumous work on Dahomey (Polanyi and Rotstein, 1966) does indeed get away from the rigidity of regarding reciprocity, redistribution, and market exchange as mutually exclusive and as characterizing entire economies or integrating entire societies. He sees all three principles as operating together, each in a different domain within the single society. Yet, at the same time, he sees the main achievement of this book as the classification of institutions as "primitive" (i.e., found in reciprocative societies), "archaic" (i.e., characteristic of redistributive societies), or "market." Thus, Polanyi goes to great lengths (Polanyi and Rotstein, 1966: 141–69) to unravel the difficulties Europeans had in balancing their bookkeeping in the seventeenth- and eighteenth-century slave trade, resulting from empirically fluctuating and varied, but nominally fixed, units used in different areas and times in West Africa. After concluding that West Africa had "archaic" money, incompatible with a modern monetary system, Polanyi isolates the characteristics of "archaic" money in terms of its status-building function in the emergence of state systems (Polanyi and Rotstein, 1966: 192). To an audience that accepts the fact of "trade in equivalencies," mere classification appears sterile. The identification of what caused the changes in exchange rates — such as differences of power balance, numbers of slaves, or availability of manufactures — becomes the interesting problem.

In short, "redistribution" or "archaic economy" may be useful labels for summarizing the way emergent national polities centralize certain services and organize taxation and the production of specialized commodities by infant industries by providing stability in market, raw materials, and labor. But such concepts would appear equally useful for analyzing the actions of newly independent, but fully monetized, nation-states. These are not terms that characterize entire economies or modes of integration, nor are they terms which fit economies into a unilineal progression from primitive to archaic to market.

The same is true of the concept "reciprocity." Analyses of the actual working of societies crudely labeled "reciprocative" (Salisbury, 1960; Sahlins, 1965a, 1965b) have shown that inter-individual transactions are always unbalanced and involve a continual struggle to obtain as much advantage over an "opponent" as possible, short of breaking off the relationship and establishing new relationships with another partner. Each relationship between a pair implies a series of other relationships by each of them, and the terms of trade between one pair can be understood only against a background of their other relationships. The same generalization could be made about exchanges between partners in a monetary economy. The differences between reciprocal and market exchanges are not sufficiently clarified by attempts to characterize total systems of which they are parts. Rather, they are better understood through closer analysis of the specific situations in both monetary and tribal societies where it is mutually advantageous to use recurrent rather than isolated exchanges, or where imbalances in volumes tendered can be, or must be, tolerated for long periods. Such studies consider markets as general economic phenomena, not as the peculiar institution of localized "marketplaces." The recent proliferation of such studies indicates the decline of the "anti-market mentality" (Cook, 1966).

Specific Institutional Studies

In practice, most descriptive anthropological work has been more specific in its aim. An impressive literature has been emerging regarding the types of exchange and marketing behavior found under different conditions of risk, volume of the total market, relative numbers of buyers and sellers, knowledge of the market, and the power positions of parties to the exchanges. This has been extensively summarized elsewhere (e.g., Belshaw, 1965: Salisbury 1968), and further review of the findings is not needed here. It will suffice to mention, as outstanding examples, Dewey's lengthy discussion of *Peasant Marketing in Java* (1962), and Nash's analyses of the calculations involved in the marketing of pottery in Chiapas (1961). In terms of the trends in economics, there has been a convergence of interest with both disciplines focusing more precisely on how the context of economic choice can influence the nature of the choices actually made.

Spheres of activity other than marketing have not received such close scrutiny. Ethnobotanists and geographers have encouraged anthropologists to record how far considerations of plant varieties, soil types, or micro-climatic variation enter into the calculation of bush-fallow agriculturalists (Conklin, 1961). Also, agricultural economists often have done studies that could be considered anthropological in the same way. Edwards' (1961) study of why Jamaican small farmers often rejected the advice of agricultural officers led him to ask for peasant evaluations of land types and crop species. Returning later to the area, he found that peasant evaluations, initially at variance with agronomists' orthodoxy, often had become orthodox after research led agronomists to change their minds.

A relatively small number of anthropologists have collected labor input figures for different crops or techniques of cultivation and have investigated the extent to which agriculturalists make choices on this basis. But these few studies — for example, Pospisil (1964) comparing labor inputs and yields for field and mound cultivation of sweet potatoes in New Guinea, and Nash (1965) comparing them for various crops and techniques in Burma — indicate the value of investigating this variable. Such studies also need to be linked to a treatment of how variations in labor demand correlate with different patterns of choice in production — of how, for example, different labor demands affect deep-sea and in-shore fishing.

The use of capital, and its accumulation in peasant societies, has been the focus of less analysis than would appear from the publication of Firth and Yamey's *Capital, Savings and Credit in Peasant Societies* (1964). Most of the authors in this volume were social anthropologists who proudly vaunted their ignorance of economic analysis and merely described how different social groupings accumulated cash in particular societies. Little attention was devoted to the use made of such accumulations or to the nature of capital. One exception to this general criticism was Barth's (1964) analysis of the capital needs and flows among South Persian nomads, and of the ways in which needs are related to the arrangements for meeting them. Also, Firth's own classic study of Malay fishermen (1946) still stands out as an examination of the relation of credit to production.

Again, agricultural economists have contributed to this subfield of study. Besides Edwards' previously cited study, Hills' (1956, 1963) discussions of how Ghanaian cocoa farmers accumulated capital and land, and of how different organizational forms were used to facilitate investment at different stages in the growth of the cocoa industry are outstanding. Many anthropologists in the South Pacific have similar interests. Belshaw's study of Fiji (1964, 1965), studies by the Australian National University's New Guinea Research Unit (e.g., Crocombe and Hogbin, 1963), and my own study of the New Britain Tolai (1969) could be cited. The focus in all of these studies is on the forms of organization used in capital-holding groups.

Entrepreneurship is another aspect of economic process that has been studied. Many descriptive studies of social change have listed the forms of cash-earning businesses that have emerged in formerly subsistence agricultural societies, and have classed all such businessmen as entrepreneurs. Relatively few studies (e.g., Hazlehurst, 1966) have gone back to theoretical treatments of entrepreneurship, notably to Schumpeter (1949), to consider the various roles focal to the concept. These roles include risk-taking, the middleman bringing together production factors, and the organizational innovator who exploits technological innovations made by others by bringing together new groupings. Yet, the study of such roles would seem to be of primary interest to classical anthropological theory. It would seem that consideration of the nature of organizational innovation would be a major area where new developments within economics could parallel and fructify developments in formal organization theory and in economic anthropology.

Organization theory regarding both entrepreneurship and capital use constitutes a common thread to the studies mentioned above. Organization of production, generally, needs to be given greater consideration. In 1959, Udy surveyed cross-cultural anthropological evidence on production organization, comparing such activities as "hunting, fishing, collection, animal husbandry, construction, and manufacturing." He concluded that technological demands were highly significant up to a certain level of social complexity with a widely varying range of organizational types thereafter. This conclusion demands closer analysis to explain the residual variance in organizational forms.

The ethnographers' laboratory of variant forms and variant social and physical environments should be exploited to provide information on the relative efficiency of particular forms. On the one hand, existing ethnographic descriptions need comparison and analysis in terms of a consistent theoretical viewpoint; Barth (1963) analyzed a series of field studies in Norway in this way, and Sankoff (1965) began such work using published sources. On the other hand, more ethnographic studies are needed in which investigators trained in organization theory can ask appropriate questions about organizational efficiency in both traditional and cash activities. Such studies, as Erasmus' (1956) early study of the advantages and disadvantages of work bees and hired labor in Mesoamerica, should give much greater insight into the process of economic development than do analyses couched in terms of all-or-nothing "value changes."

Model-Building

Anthropological economic studies have not been confined entirely to specific institutions and increasingly detailed studies of relationships between smaller segments of social and economic activity. Just as input-output economists have interested themselves in constructing models of total economies, seeing the total system as the outcome of the flows and transactions between sectors, so some anthropologists have begun to visualize entire economies as the resultant effects of flows between particular sectors. Development economists have proposed models of economic change which involve phase sequences. For example, infrastructure development at one phase leads to increased profitability of later industrial investments, and so to mass marketing. So anthropologists (and ethno-historians) have proposed models of local economic development in terms of phase sequences and have looked for the causative relationship between phases.

The difference between the models of the economist and the anthropologist has largely been in the range of included phenomena. The economist tends to include such factors as demography, technology, organizational techniques, or political controls only as boundary conditions for his models, making such simplistic assumptions as "they remain constant," or "they increase at steady rates." These assumptions are often disguised. A simple statement as "it is assumed that the marginal product of labor is positive" or "it may be assumed that in a period of growth there is some organizational slack," implies questionable assumptions about the nature of technology or organization. However, making such assumptions, the economist can clarify the logic of his model and can proceed immediately to quantification.

The anthropologist is more concerned with building relationships between technology, organization, or politics and the economic activities *into* his models. Thus, Geertz' (1963a) model involves technology as a major variable in the interactions of labor-intensive monocrop agriculture in Java with foreign exchange-earning, cash-cropping, and multicrop bush-fallow agriculture in outer Indonesia. The model shows the long-term prospect of impoverishing and "peasantizing" the outer islands. In my own model (1962, 1969), organization is the major vari-

able. It shows how, in New Guinea, surpluses are created by technological change funneled into the creation of more complex political
organizations and how such political change permits the organizational
change for the establishment of new types of productive activity.

It could be argued that such models represent a return to many of
the fundamental concerns of anthropology — the problems of social
evolution and cultural change. Leslie White pioneered the return to interest in these problems, but his unidimensional scheme relating social
development to the availability of energy sources was too simplistic. It
may now be hoped that general models of a Leslie White type may
become increasingly available. In such models technology levels, communication technology levels, and organizational variables may be given
quantitative forms, visualized as forms of entropy (Adams, 1960), in
order to consider types of society in terms of evolutionary dimensions.

Such a utopian idea would see anthropologists returning closer to
the traditional interest of their own discipline. But then, where does
the future for a relationship between anthropology and economics lie?
Here I would return to my earlier analysis of substantivism and of current trends in economic anthropology. As I see it, where the substantivists attempted to classify total economies and came up with static
models, more recent workers have tried to see the low-level relationships
which generate the eventual form of total economies. The models they
build inevitably include a dynamic element. Yet, to arrive at the relationships occurring at low levels, they have used the *tool* of economic
analysis which substantivists scorned — that is, formal analysis.

Formal Analysis

The formal approach of economists involved seeing economic magnitudes as the primary data and, by comparing magnitudes, demonstrated inductively the relationships among numbers of variables, each
of them impinging at a low level on vast numbers of economic choices.
Only when the formal analyses have been undertaken and the variables
isolated have dynamic models of the interplay of multiple variables
been constructed.

Ethno-economists may take a shortcut. Instead of isolating variables by the mathematical analysis of quantitative data, they may consider the economic concepts given them by informants as close approxi-
mations to the operating variables. But, they then should consider de-

ductively how the systematic use in the society of such concepts would give rise to overall patterns. They should construct models based on ethno-economic concepts. While it may be untrue to say that goods are absolutely limited in peasant society, it may be useful to consider what would happen if all (or many) members of a society believed that life were a zero-sum game. Game theory (or formal economic theory) could then be used to make predictions about such matters as the size of coalitions or the degree of tolerance of income inequalities. Anthropologists have been generally averse to such "as if" deductive theorizing, preferring to "stick to the facts." Exposure to economists and their methods could be invaluable in correcting this bias and in making deductive model-building familiar.

As an ethno-economic description of the principles of choice verbalized by informants leads to the formulation of ideal or hypothetical models, behavioral analysis also must progress. It must determine principles of choice from a consideration of transactions actually occurring, and test the fit of hypothetical models against quantitative reality. Here, too, anthropologists have much to learn by working with economists and their tools. In the 1950's, Gluckman (1964) argued that it is better to remain naive about other disciplines, even when intruding in fields which they cover. I do not feel that this is true for anthropology and economics in the 1960's. Anthropologists should study economics and vice versa, not to make the anthropologist an economist, but a better anthropologist. Given economic tools, he will improve anthropology. Give an economist the anthropological tools of sensitivity to what people say and of readiness to try to see order in different conceptual systems and he may improve economics.

COMMENTARY: George Dalton
Cyril Belshaw
Leonard Kasdan

George Dalton

The theoretical and methodological questions of what the scope of economic anthropology is and whether anthropologists should incorporate the conceptual language of conventional economics into their analyses of primitive and peasant economies have been issues since Firth's survey of economic anthropology in 1939, Goodfellow's book in the same year, and Herskovits' work a year later. The issues raised in these works were never resolved and fell dormant until 1957 when Polanyi's symposium, *Trade and Markets in the Early Empires* (Polanyi, Arensberg, and Pearson, 1957), touched off the second round of disputes which continue to the present. I would like to discuss here the underlying reasons for the persistence of these disputes.[1]

The complexity of economic anthropology and the extremely wide scope of its subject matter are often insufficiently recognized. Economic anthropology is concerned with the structure and the performance of thousands of primitive and peasant economies studied at different points in time, in all parts of the world, and under static and dynamic conditions. By structure I mean the organization of the economy: The transactional modes used to allocate land and labor, to arrange work, and to dispose of produce; in short, the processes of production, marketing, external trade, and money use. Structure also refers to the connections between economic and social organization which Polanyi calls "the place of economy in society." Performance refers to the quantifiable results of economic process, the quantity of subsistence and prestige goods produced, and the degree of equality of income distribution, as well as the productivity of labor, land, and other resources.[2]

I define primitive economics as the Trobriand and Tiv types, whose principal modes of economic transactions are socially obligatory gift-giving (Mauss' presentation and Thurnwald's reciprocity), and redistribution of labor, land, tools, and produce through political or religious leaders. These are economies in which the bulk of transactions involving resources and produce are carried on in non-market spheres.

1. For a more complete statement on this subject, see George Dalton, "Theoretical Issues in Economic Anthropology," *Current Anthropology*, Vol. X, No. 1, 1969, pp. 63–102.

2. No equivalent seems to exist in the conventional subjects of anthropological inquiry, such as kinship, religion, and polity, to the quantifiable performance of the economy. The closest equivalent is simple enumeration, e.g., frequency of murder, theft, or divorce. The distinction between economic organization and the quantifiable performance of the economy applies to all economies, whether studied by anthropologists, economists, or historians.

By peasant economies, I mean those in Latin America described by Tax (1963) and Wolf (1955) and in Asia by Firth (1946), where commercial (market) transactions for resources and produce are quantitatively important and where cash transactions, the pricing of land and tools, and wage labor are common.

In addition, two basically different sets of conditions exist under which anthropologists analyze primitive and peasant economic structure and performance. The first is the relatively static or slow-changing set of conditions before modernizing activities take place. Anthropologists sometimes call this traditional economy. Malinowski (1921) describes the traditional internal and external economy of the Trobriands, although the European-organized commercial activities of pearl fishing and plantation agriculture were present. The second focus for analysis is economic change, growth, and development: the enlargement of production for sale, the adoption of Western technology and applied science, and other modernizing activities (Geertz, 1963b; Epstein, 1962). For the most part, we are only at the beginning of systematic analysis of these aspects of primitive and peasant communities.

Despite the complexity and diversity of the subject matter, several writers are searching for a universally applicable theory of economic anthropology as though it were a Holy Grail which, once found, would shed the grace of understanding on all economies. "What is required . . . is a search for the general theory of economic process and structure of which contemporary economic theory is but a special case" (Le Clair, 1962).

Such views betray not only an insufficient appreciation of the complexity of economic anthropology, but also gross misunderstanding of conventional economics which, until recently, was concerned exclusively with industrial capitalism. Economics contains no notion of a general or universal theory which may be applied to widely different processes and problems. Price theory is concerned with the determinants of price under different market conditions. Aggregate income theory considers what determines national income for one year. Different concepts are employed for different processes even within a single economy. When other economies are analyzed, such as those of the Soviet Union or the underdeveloped nations of India or Nigeria, new theoretical concepts must be invented to deal with what is special to their structures and performance.

In the same way that economists need several sets of theoretical concepts to study different kinds of economies and various problems within each economy, I suggest that economic anthropologists also require several sets of theoretical concepts because they, too, are concerned with different structures, processes, and problems.

Richard Salisbury's paper and much of the recent literature of theoretical contention in economic anthropology (Le Clair, 1962; Burling, 1962; Cook, 1966) describe the anthropologist's idea of conventional economic theory and urge anthropologists to base their analytical approach on the concepts of conventional economics, as though this would provide all the tools of analysis needed in economic anthropology. I am repeatedly told by anthropologists that what they mean by economic theory is applicable to the economies anthropologists study. I will consider the question of exactly what anthropologists mean by applying conventional economics to primitive and peasant economies after I describe some pertinent features of economics and anthropology.

Disputes about the relevance of economics to economic anthropology are not likely to be resolved until more economists who have worked in the same parts of the world as anthropologists are brought into symposia to address themselves directly to the issues. The only economists who have written directly on the organization of traditional economies and the relevance of economies to anthropology are Polanyi (1944), Neale (1957, 1962), Pearson (1957a, 1957b), Fusfeld (1957), and myself (Dalton, 1961, 1962, 1965a, 1965b) — the group associated with Polanyi. Economists such as Hagen (1962), Lewis (1955), Myrdal (1957), Berliner (1962), Adelman and Morris (1965, 1967), Deane (1953), Yudelman (1964), and McLoughlin (1964, 1967) have worked in underdeveloped economies or, like Berliner, have become concerned with the relation of economics to social organization. Their views on the relevance of economics to economic anthropology should be sought.

Of all the social sciences, economics and anthropology are least alike in their traditions, methods, and emphases. The mainstream of economics relates almost exclusively to our own kind of economy. Price theory, income theory, money and banking, and public finance are concerned with the processes of large-scale, nationally integrated, industrialized capitalist economies. With the exception of writers such as Veblen and Galbraith, economists relegate institutional matters relating to social organization and culture to industrial sociology and business administration. Even the few economists concerned with economic history and comparative economic systems usually focus on the post-industrial period in Europe and America. Economics has no tradition of detailed fieldwork, area studies, or concern with small-scale communities. Nor has it any concern with folkviews or human behavior. Economists almost never incorporate the work of sociology and psychology, except in the recent work on institutional aspects on economic development (Hagen, 1962).

There are two positive traditions in economics. The first is the creation of formal abstract theory which increasingly is expressed in mathematical models. The second is a pragmatic concern for policy-making, a sensitivity to current problems such as depression and inflation. Keynes' work is a clear example of formal analysis designed to make policy. A more recent example is the creation of economic development theory in response to the problems of developing the national economies of Africa, Asia, and Latin America.

In most ways anthropology has a radically different tradition. Theory in anthropology is not highly abstract or mathematical. The empirical knowledge of anthropologists derives from societies and cultures other than our own, and fieldwork is an important part of training and research. Most frequently, the unit of analysis is a small community rather than a nation-state. Anthropology's concern with human behavior and folkviews and its interests in culture and society make it closer to sociology and psychology than to economics. Finally, only a slight pragmatic tradition exists in anthropology; policy-making has not been a principal interest in theory-building.

When anthropoligists argue that conventional economics is applicable in economic anthropology, they have three things in mind (Le Clair, 1962; Burling, 1962). The first is peasant economies (Tax, 1963; Firth, 1946) where market dependence for livelihood is important, cash transactions are frequent, and commercial activities are familiar. Where there is wage labor and purchase and sale of land and produce, the conceptual categories of conventional price theory are obviously applicable, and the economic generalizations about price and income formation are relevant. But these theories are not applicable to primitive economies whose main sectors are not organized by the market mode of transaction.

Conceptual categories of conventional economics are also adaptable to measuring economic performance. In peasant economies one can measure the money value of income generated (output produced) in the commercial sectors of production and distribution (Firth, 1946) and arrive at the local community equivalents of national income and gross national product sums and their components, as conventionally measured for the United States. For primitive economies, measurement of community output is possible in terms of quantities of each kind of goods produced, but not in national income accounting terms because of the absence of cash transactions. The same applies for attempts to measure productivity of resources, such as output per man hour or per acre (Salisbury, 1962).

A third way anthropologists "apply" conventional economics is simply to use the terminology of economics, such as "maximize," "economize," "scarcity," and "rational choice," to describe whatever economic processes and activities they find in primitive and peasant societies:

The elements of scarcity and choice, which are the outstanding factors in human experience that give economic science its reason for being, rest psychologically on firm grounds. . . . Our primary concern in these pages is to understand the cross-cultural implications of the process of economizing (Herskovits, 1952).

It is a misunderstanding of terms to assume that what economists mean by scarcity, choice, and economizing in our own economy is present in all economies. To apply these concepts to primitive economies lacking market organization is to equate all purposeful activity with "economizing," and then to conclude that the apparatus of economic theory is applicable because economizing activities have been identified:

From this point of view we are "economizing" in everything we do. We are always trying to maximize our satisfactions somehow, and so we are led back to the notion that economics deals not with a type but rather with an aspect of behavior. This economic view of society becomes . . . one model for looking at society. It is a model which sees the individuals of a society busily engaged in maximizing their own satisfaction — desire for power, sex, food, independence . . . (Burling, 1962).

This is a distortion of the meaning of economic activities in primitive societies. Priests become stockbrokers maximizing piety instead of profit. Bridewealth becomes the price one pays for sexual and domestic services. Indeed, when market language is used to describe all activities, the distinction between marriage and prostitution disappears, because both are being regarded as ways of purchasing services for a price (Dalton, 1966).

I should like to conclude by clearing up some misconceptions about Polanyi's analytical framework. Polanyi's categories do not describe entire economies. No economy is organized exclusively by one transactional mode. One can identify the dominant transactional mode of an economy by determining how the basic resources of land and labor are allocated to users. In the United States national economy, market exchange is the dominant mode of transaction, but governmental provision of welfare services and military spending have increased the quantitative importance of redistributive transactions; gift-giving remains the smallest set of transactions, confined to ceremonial occasions such as Christmas or birthdays.[3]

Reciprocity, redistribution, and market exchange refer not only to the disposition of produced goods, but also to the disposition of labor, land, and tools. It is a mistake to regard exchange systems apart from production processes. The disposition of a produced item, such as yams in the Trobriands, is simply the last part of a production process which begins with the acquistion of land to grow the yams (land tenure) and of labor to do the farming. Even in the same economy, each of the several production lines (yam-growing, house-building) may use a different transactional mode. In the United States, labor for most production lines is acquired by market purchase for a money wage. But some labor for military service is acquired by the draft, and small amounts of labor are given as gifts, as when parishioners build their own church or when friends help each other to move to new houses. The market

---

3. The great philanthropic foundations, such as Ford, Carnegie, and Guggenheim, may be characterized as devices of "private redistribution." Like governments, they use their income to provide social services. A special characteristic of transactional modes in United States economy is that they all make use of the same money and markets. Gifts are first purchased on the market by givers. Governments use their tax receipts to purchase the buildings, equipment, and the services of personnel, to provide education, defense, etc.

transacts labor in the first case, redistribution in the second, and reciprocity in the third.

Finally, Polanyi's critics give the impression that he was concerned exclusively with the putting of economies into one of three pigeonholes labeled reciprocity, redistribution, and market exchange, and with arguing that conventional economics has nothing to do with the economies studied by anthropologists.[4] These are crude caricatures of his work. His analysis of ports of trade adds to the understanding of devices (like silent trade and border markets) used to facilitate trade between alien cultures and also adds to the knowledge of the West African slave trade (Polanyi and Rotstein, 1966). His analysis of primitive and archaic money is broadly applicable in anthropology and archaeology and allows fitting the many kinds of monies, valuables, and treasure items described in the literature into a theoretical framework linking money with organizational forms.[5] His detailed analysis of the social consequences of nineteenth-century European industrial capitalism is applicable to present-day welfare states as well as to the social and cultural implications of economic change in underdeveloped areas (Polanyi, 1944).

The theory of economic anthropology is in its infancy despite its copious, rich, and diverse literature of case studies. Even the obvious connections between preindustrial economies studied by anthropologists and those studied by historians of preindustrial Europe and Asia have scarcely been touched (Goody, 1963; Beattie, 1964). Only in the last few years have we begun to construct a theoretical framework which, in systematically comparing traditional economies with our own, yields in-

4. *Primitive, Archaic, and Modern Economies: Essays of Karl Polanyi* (Polanyi, 1968) brings together those of Polanyi's essays of most interest to anthropologists. It consists of three chapters from *The Great Transformation* (1944: ch. 4, 6, 13); three chapters from *Trade and Market in the Early Empires* (Polanyi, Arensberg, and Pearson, 1957: ch. 5, 12, 13); three chapters from *Dahomey and the Slave Trade* (Polanyi and Rotstein, 1966: ch. 3, 10, 11); three journal articles ("Our Obsolete Market Mentality," "Ports of Trade in Early Societies," "The Semantics of Money Uses"); two unpublished papers, and an expository introduction to Polanyi's work by myself. Also forthcoming is one or more volumes of Polanyi's unpublished lectures and papers in economic anthropology and economic history.

5. Compare Polanyi's analysis of primitive, archaic, and modern money (Polanyi, Arensberg, and Pearson, 1957; 1968; also, Dalton, 1965a) with the analytical statements on money in Malinowski (1921), Firth (1929), Einzig (1966), and Quiggin (1949).

sights of the sort obtained by analyzing traditional kinship, polity, and religion. The second large branch of the subject — processes of socio-economic change, growth, and development as small communities modernize and become integral parts of nation-states — is even less developed.

Like economics, economic anthropology borders at one end on historical description of economies that have long since been transformed and, at the other, on quantitative measurement of dynamic processes of change and development. There is ample room for different theoretical approaches because of the many structures, processes, and problems that comprise economic anthropology.

Cyril S. Belshaw

It is very difficult to comment on Professor Salisbury's competent paper because I agree with most of his points. The best I can do is underline one or two of these points. We are concerned with economic anthropology because it has become one of anthropology's controversial areas. The reason for this is related to two main trends.

First, because of our association with economists who use levels of abstraction remote to us, we are confronted with the nature of model-building and of abstraction in our discipline. Second, because we are dealing with societies that are undergoing very rapid change in a highly technological and sophisticated institutional age, we find ourselves in the position of having to become predictive as well as of trying to see society as a whole. We can no longer explain what happens in village society simply by looking at village society, but also must consider what happens in the surrounding social area. This means either that economic anthropologists are becoming sociologists or that we are beginning to move from micro-models into macro-models. In either case, strains are being placed upon our tools and the ways in which we handle them.

A number of gaps exist in our approach to economic anthropology. Some of these seem curious, although they are perhaps simply reflections of the small amount of anthropological labor which is directed toward these ends. For example, anthropologists, as well as economists, tend to be ethnocentric when considering the line of development or the direction of change in emerging economies. Neither consistently inquires into the potential alternatives, nor systematically follows the institutional and technical imperatives. We know that if one is going to establish a steel mill or an institution of commerce, certain consequences will result. But nowhere in anthropology do I see economic issues of this kind examined systematically from the point of view of both the constraints and choices that are offered to the societies which are changing.

The problem of model-building is being contrasted with institutional comparisons, giving the impression that we have both a formalistic and a substantive school. I do not think this is a very good way of putting it because, in both instances, we are concerned with formal models and with substantive evidence; what differs is the nature of the models and their applications.

The substantive school has revealed a great deal that we were somewhat unaware of and that we underplayed about the regularities and the nature of social conditions under very different circumstances. For example, one of Polanyi's great contributions was the descriptive and analytic attention he gave to port of trade enclaves. We could multiply this example many times. At the same time, I find it difficult to use polytypologies of this kind for predictive purposes and to translate them into anything approaching universal comparative models. If our only objective is to concentrate upon analysis of individual societies for their own sake, we will be losing some of the potentialities for comparison which most of us are hoping to demonstrate. The so-called substantive models will have to be turned into models which permit continuous examinations of a range of factors in relation to different societies. This is not too difficult a task and Professor Salisbury has shown the way. But it has to be done deliberately as an adjunct to something over and above typologies.

Economic man has taken a tremendous beating. I do not think that we can afford to leave him bloody and battered on the field — we must try to put life, objectives, and values back into him. There are ways of doing this; one way is simply to consider man in a particular culture at at a particular time and place and to analyze descriptively the goals he is working toward and the ways he makes his choices through reference to value systems. Although this will help, above all we must seek to develop a micro-model of economic behavior and try to rethink "economic" man in a way different from the economist.

Again, this is not an impossible task, but we must look at the models in a way that can be examined and applied cross-culturally. For example, we could ask of the maximization principle — How can this be broken up, and how can this be linked with the elements which are comparable from one society to another? If we attempt to do this formally, we also will have to examine differing minimization principles. In this way, perhaps, we can get away from the old form of economic man and produce a more abstract, though not wholly satisfying, kind of anthropological man.

Thus, we will have to move from the micro-model to a macro-model. Unfortunately, at this point we will find that our theoretical tools for universalistic comparison are not very well developed. Although we talk of value systems, we do not readily link these with concepts used in economics. We must somehow extend the effective demand principle across society and perhaps develop a concept, such as a behavioral profile of culture, which would be to the anthropologist what the demand schedule would be to the economist. We must think of future possibilities in terms of societal goals, particularly when trying to explain the various paths development takes. From this, we will consider the potential profile of culture which lies somewhere between the effective profile and the ultimate value system.

Anthropologists can make a substantial contribution to economics. However, this is not at all a one-way street. One of the most provocative and useful studies in this field comes from sociology: Peter Blau's book, *Exchange and Power in Social Life* (1964), represents the direction in which economic anthropology might well move. It provides an abstract model for cross-cultural use and forces the economist to consider some of our more abstract notions.

Leonard Kasdan

I am living proof of Gluckman's dictum concerning necessary naivety among anthropologists when dealing with other disciplines. I have no formal training in economic anthropology and my interests in it developed from an attempt to understand the traditional Ottoman state before the impact of industrialization on the peasant market economies in the Middle East. My initial interest was not primarily in economics at all, but rather in political systems, although, of course, I was interested in the connections between the two.

While examining my field data and the historic material I gathered, I was struck by the fact that, for extended periods, the villages of the Middle East have participated in market activities only marginally, although the Middle East is supposedly an area in which markets have played a vital role for thousands of years. In fact, in the particular village I studied, I found the total amount of capital available per family per year to be approximately one British pound, ten — a discovery which led me to suspect that perhaps this was not a market-oriented economy at all. I was then faced with the problem of finding categories which would help me better describe the "universe" I was examining. At this juncture I came across Polanyi's *Trade and Markets in the Early Empires* (Polanyi, Arensberg, and Pearson, 1957) and tried to apply these concepts, hoping to solve my problem. However, the concepts of redistribution and reciprocity, aside from being handy names, failed to tell me what to do once I had observed such behavior.

I discovered that in this sort of economy, people play a rather elaborate and circular game with prestige as a primary goal. Through personal generosity, and with the backing of a strong patrilineal lineage, a person with political aspirations could build a power base which could extract patronage from the larger society. This patronage ultimately could be translated into higher economic status for the particular individual involved. This, however, is the end product and not the beginning or central part of the process. Rather, the individual begins by accruing power which derives from a particular kind of solidarity in the political realm. Only subsequently does the individual translate this kind of gain into improved economic status and, even when he does this, it is to assure the solidarity of followers.

I further discovered that the concept of "the limited good" also had only limited utility when applied to this society. The limited good seems to be one point in a developmental cycle, rather than a general principle to which all members, simultaneously hold. Although this could be further elaborated upon, I would prefer to get to my major point of departure, which is the relationship between power and economics. This is an area which, until Richard Salisbury's work, has been relatively neglected and which "naive" anthropologists have not grasped, but actually have studied without developing the sophistication of economists.

Professor Salisbury mentioned the contribution of economics in the development of game theory. It is surprising that there has been no follow-up in the extremely stimulating work that Fredrik Barth initiated in his paper, "Segmentary Opposition and the Theory of Games" (1959). Game theory has a definite relevance for anthropologists, particularly for those who are studying social and political change where factionalism is an important aspect. Yet, as far as I know, Barth's article remains an isolated instance of its application and anthropologists continue to ignore this helpful tool which economists have developed.

I would like to conclude with a brief discussion of entrepreneurship. I have been working on an explanation of entrepreneurship from a structural point of view. What are the factors which motivate people to take the kind of risks that we call entrepreneurial activity? What are the channels which limit the choices which they do take? My study of a Druze village leads me to conclude that, at least in this instance, a close linkage exists between the political arena and this particular aspect of economic activity.

The ubiquitous Middle East trader can be found all over West Africa and South America. Yet, looking at the villages from which many of the traders derive, we would probably conclude that these are the last people who would become entrepreneurs. I would hypothesize that these people, in learning to "maximize" in the factional political realm, have developed skills easily transferable to the economic realm when placed in a different context and when given different channels of opportunity than those found in the village. I suggest that when dealing with the motivation to participate in a particular kind of economic activity, we should not deal with it purely in terms of the economic experience of the peoples being studied. We may find it more fruitful to examine such unrelated factors as decision-making and alignments within the political sphere (Southall, in press; Swartz, in press). These factors may, indeed, teach us much about entrepreneurial activity which a focus on the economy, however well-defined, could not do.

REFERENCES

Adams, R. N. 1960. Energy and Expanding Systems. Paper presented at the American Association for the Advancement of Science meeting, December 31, 1960. New York.

Adelman, I. G. and C. T. Morris. 1965. Factor Analysis of the Interrelationship Between Social and Political Variables and Per Capita Gross National Product. The Quarterly Journal of Economics 79:555–78.

———. 1967. Society, Politics, and Economic Development. Johns Hopkins University Press: Baltimore.

Barth, F. 1959. Segmentary Opposition and the Theory of Games. Journal of the Royal Anthropological Institute 89:5–21.

———. 1963. The Role of the Entrepreneur in Social Change in Northern Norway. Norwegian Universities Press: Oslo.

———. 1964. Capital, Investment and the Social Structure of a Pastoral Nomad Group in South Persia. Capital, Savings and Credit in Peasant Societies, eds. R. Firth and B. S. Yamey, pp. 69–81. Allen and Unwin: London.

Beattie, J. H. M. 1964. Bunyoro: An African Feudality? Journal of African History V, 1:25–36.

Belshaw, C. S. 1964. Under the Ivi Tree. University of California Press: Berkeley.

———. 1965. Traditional Exchange and Modern Markets. Prentice-Hall: Englewood Cliffs.

Berliner, J. 1962. The Feet of the Natives are Large: An Essay on Anthropology by an Economist. Current Anthropology 3:47–77.

Blau, P.M. 1964. Exchange and Power in Social Life. Wiley: New York.

Bohannan, P. 1955. Some Principles of Exchange and Investment among the Tiv. American Anthropologist 57:60–70.

Bohannan, P. and G. Dalton, eds. 1962. Markets in Africa. Northwestern University Press: Evanston, Illinois.

Burling, R. 1962. Maximization Theories and the Study of Economic Anthropology American Anthropologist 64.802–21.

Conklin, H. C. 1961. Shifting Cultivation. Current Anthropology 2:27–61.

Cook, S. 1966. The Obsolete "Anti-Market" Mentality: A Critique of the Substantive Approach to Economic Anthropology. American Anthropologist 68: 323–45.

Crocombe, R. G. and G. R. Hogbin. 1963. The Erap Mechanized Farming Project. New Guinea Research Unit Bulletin No. I. Australian National University: Canberra.

Dalton, G. 1961. Economic Theory and Primitive Society. American Anthropologist 63:1–25.

———. 1962. Traditional Production in Primitive African Economies. The Quarterly Journal of Economics 76:360–78.

———. 1965a. Primitive Money. American Anthropologist 67:44–65.

———. 1965b. Primitive, Archaic, and Modern Economies: Karl Polanyi's Contribution to Economic Anthropology and Comparative Economy. Proceedings of the 1965 Annual Spring Meeting of the American Ethnological Society, pp. 1–24. University of Washington Press: Seattle.

———. 1966. Bridewealth versus Brideplace. American Anthropologist 68:732–37.

Deane, P. 1953. Colonial Social Accounting. National Institute of Economic and Social Research, Economic and Social Studies, 11. Cambridge University Press: London.

Dewey, A. G. 1962. Peasant Marketing in Java. Free Press: Glencoe.

Edwards, D. 1961. Report on an Economic Study of Small Farming in Jamaica. University College of the West Indies, Institute of Social and Economic Research. Glasgow.

Einzig, P. 1966. Primitive Money in its Ethnological, Historical and Economic Aspects, 2d ed. (1st ed., 1948.) Pergamon: Oxford.

Epstein, T. S. 1962. Economic Development and Social Change in South India. Manchester University Press: Manchester.

Erasmus, C. 1956. Culture Structure and Process: Occurrence and Disappearance of Reciprocal Labour. Southwestern Journal of Anthropology 12:444–69.

Firth, R. 1929. Currency, Primitive. Encyclopedia Britannica, 14th ed.

———. 1946. Malay Fishermen: Their Peasant Economy. Routledge Kegan Paul: London.

Firth, R. and B. S. Yamey, eds. 1964. Capital, Savings and Credit in Peasant Societies. Aldine: Chicago.

Foster, G. M. 1965. Peasant Society and the Image of Limited Good. American Anthropologist 67:293–315.

Fusfeld, D. B. 1957. Economic Theory Misplaced: Livelihood in Primitive Society. Trade and Market in the Early Empires, eds. K. Polanyi, C. M. Arensberg, and H. W. Pearson, pp. 342–56. Free Press: Glencoe.

Geertz, C. S. 1963a. Agricultural Involution. University of California Press: Berkeley.

———. 1963b. Peddlers and Princes: Social Change and Economic Modernization in Two Indonesian Towns. University of Chicago Press: Chicago.

Gluckman, M., ed. 1965. Closed Systems and Open Minds. Aldine: Chicago.

Goody, J. 1963. Feudalism in Africa? Journal of African History IV:1–18.

Hagen, E. E. 1962. On the Theory of Social Change: How Economic Growth Begins. Dorsey Press: Homewood, Illinois.

Haire, M., ed. 1959. Modern Organization Theory. Wiley: New York.

Hazlehurst, L. W. 1966. Entrepreneurship and the Merchant Castes in a Punjabi City. Duke University Press: Durham.

Herskovits, M. J. 1952. Economic Anthropology, rev. ed., pp. 3, 4. Knopf: New York.

Hill, P. 1956. The Gold Coast Cocoa Farmer: A Preliminary Survey. Oxford University Press: New York.

———. 1963. The Migrant Cocoa Farmers of Southern Ghana. Cambridge University Press: London.

Le Clair, E. E. 1962. Economic Theory and Economic Anthropology. American Anthropologist 64:1179–1203.

Lewis, W. A. 1955. The Theory of Economic Growth. Allen and Unwin: London.

McLoughlin, P. F. M. 1964. The Policy Relationship Between Individual Rights to Land and Migrant Labor Systems in Africa. Civilizations No. 1–2.

———. 1967. Some Technical Research Problems for Agricultural Development in Tropical Africa. Development Digest V (1):123–32.

Malinowski, B. 1921. The Primitive Economics of the Trobriand Islanders. The Economic Journal XXXI:1–16.

Myrdal, G. 1957. Rich Lands and Poor: The Road to World Prosperity. Harper and Row: New York.

Nadel, S. F. 1942. A Black Byzantium: The Kingdom of Nupe in Nigeria. Oxford University Press: London.

Nash, M. 1961. The Social Context of Economic Choice in a Small Society. Man 61:186–91.

———. 1965. The Golden Road to Modernity. Wiley: New York.

———. 1966. Primitive and Peasant Economic Systems. Chandler: San Francisco.

Neale, W. C. 1957. The Market in Theory and History. Trade and Market in the Early Empires, eds. K. Polanyi, C. M. Arensberg, and H. W. Pearson, pp. 357–74. Free Press: Glencoe.

———. 1962. Economic Change in Rural India: Land Tenure and Reform in Uttar Pradesh, 1800–1955. Yale University Press: New Haven.

Pearson, H. W. 1957a. The Secular Debate on Economic Primitivism. Trade and Market in the Early Empires, eds. K. Polanyi, C. M. Arensberg, and H. W. Pearson, pp. 3–11. Free Press: Glencoe.

———. 1957b. The Economy has no Surplus: Critique of a Theory of Development. Trade and Market in the Early Empires, eds. K. Polanyi, C. M. Arensberg, and H. W. Pearson, pp. 320–39. Free Press: Glencoe.

Polanyi, K. 1944. The Great Transformation. Farrar and Rinehart: New York.

———. 1947. Our Obsolete Market Mentality. Commentary 3:109–17. (Reprinted in Polanyi, 1968, ch. 13.)

———. 1957. The Economy as Instituted Process. Trade and Markets in the Early Empires, eds. K. Polanyi, C. M. Arensberg, and H. W. Pearson, pp. 243–70. Free Press: Glencoe. (Reprinted in Polanyi, 1968.)

———. 1968. Primitive, Archaic and Modern Economics: Essays of Karl Polanyi, George Dalton, ed., pp. 175–203. Anchor Books, Doubleday: New York.

Polanyi, K., C. M. Arensberg, and H. W. Pearson, eds. 1957. Trade and Markets in the Early Empires. Free Press: Glencoe.

Polanyi, K. and A. Rotstein. 1966. Dahomey and the Slave Trade. American Ethnological Society, Monograph No. 42. University of Washington Press: Seattle.

Pospisil, L. 1964. The Kapauka Papuans of West New Guinea. Holt, Rinehart and Winston: New York.

Quiggin, A. H. 1949. A Survey of Primitive Money. Methuen and Co.: London.

Sahlins, M. D. 1965a. On the Sociology of Primitive Exchange. The Relevance of Models for Social Anthropology, A. S. A. Monograph No. 1, gen. ed. M. Banton, pp. 139–227. Tavistock Publications, Praeger: London and New York.

———. 1965b. Exchange Value and the Diplomacy of Primitive Trade. Proceedings of the 1965 American Ethnological Society Spring Meeting, pp. 95–129. University of Washington Press: Seattle.

Salisbury, R. F. 1960. Ceremonial Economics and Political Equilibrium. Proceedings of the 6th International Congress of Anthropological and Ethnological Sciences 2:255–60. Paris.

———. 1962. From Stone to Steel. Australian National University: Camberra.

———. 1968. Trade and Markets. International Encyclopedia of the Social Sciences, XVI, pp. 118–22. Free Press: New York.

————. 1969. Vunamami: Economic Transformation in a Traditional Society. University of California Press: Berkeley.

Sankoff, G. 1965. The Organizational Factor in the Economic Development of Traditional and Peasant Societies, M. A. Thesis, McGill University.

Schumpeter, J. A. 1949. Economic Theory and Entrepreneurial History. Change and the Entrepreneur, Harvard University, Research Center in Entrepreneurial History. Cambridge.

Southall, A. In press. Orientation in Political Anthropology. Canadian Journal of African Studies.

Swartz, M. J. In press. Processual and Structural Approaches in Political Anthropology: A Commentary. Canadian Journal of African Studies.

Tax, S. 1963. Penny Capitalism. University of Chicago Press: Chicago. (First published in 1953, Government Printing Office, Smithsonian Institute, Institute of Social Anthropology, Publication No. 16, Washington.)

Udy, S. H. 1959. Organization of Work: A Comparative Analysis of Production Among Non-Industrial People. Yale Human Relations Area Files Press: New Haven.

Wolf, E. R. 1955. Types of Latin American Peasantry. American Anthropologist 57:452–71.

Yudelman, M. 1964. Africans on the Land. Harvard University Press: Cambridge.

CHAPTER **3** Bernard S. Cohn

History and Political Science

The Changing Character of the Social Sciences

The social and behavioral sciences once again are entering an accelerated period of rethinking and reorganization. Such periods have been common since the disciplines emerged from social philosophy in the eighteenth century and from history and political economy in the nineteenth century. We have perhaps reached the point when the organizational structure of the disciplines essentially formulated in the late nineteenth century will be changed. These disciplines include sociology, history, political science, psychology, economics, geography, and anthropology, even though the latter still seems to be in a militantly nativistic phase in which ideas are arising from within. I believe this nativism is largely an artifact of the growing numbers of anthropologists and the expanding number of departments of anthropology. This demographic and departmental expansion has produced several changes. Our social-intellectual life more than ever revolves around colleagues who have been socialized in the same traditions, who have read the same monographs, who have similar work styles, and who have shared the same rite of field work.

With a larger faculty, the number of specialized courses have proliferated and students are often obliged to take many anthropology courses simply because the courses are there to be taken. The feeling seems to be that more substance has been added to the central "core" of anthropology than has characterized our discipline fifteen or twenty years ago. There is a paradox here however, because as our specialization has increased, often with doubling and tripling of the number of

89

sub-specialists in larger departments, we think more and more in terms of training our students in the core and sub-specialties of our discipline. This only adds to our nativism.

The current expansion has also affected the demography and social structure of our sister disciplines. While graduate programs in anthropology have become longer and more militantly anthropological with more courses and more specialties to be learned, related disciplines have developed in the same way. This internal focus makes discipline-jumping all the more difficult for students.

Departmental core programs for the training of professionals make it difficult for outside students to penetrate the field of anthropology. The day when students could take one or two courses to get the feel of related disciplines seems to be over. To learn something about political science or sociology, the student must take five or six courses to understand the core which these disciplines have developed. The converse is true for the student of political science, history, or sociology who wants to learn something of anthropology. Although the faculty is painfully aware of the dangers of intellectual parochialism and warns students to learn the techniques and methodology of other disciplines, increasingly, this necessary broadening is being done through "capture and incorporation" of hyphenated specialists from other fields. For example, people who are essentially survey-research sociologists are teaching research methods to political scientists; mathematicians are teaching in economics departments and business schools; social psychologists in law schools; political scientists and economists in history departments; physical geographers and biologists in anthropology departments, and statisticians and psychologists everywhere.

Increase in size is not only bringing us to intensive professional concern with our disciplines as disciplines and with the increasing number of incorporated specialists trying to add breadth to our departments, it is also reflecting the accelerating rate of radical transformations through which many of the social sciences have gone. In recent years many social science disciplines have accepted new paradigms, "universally recognized scientific achievements that for the time being provide model problems and solutions to a community of practitioners" (Kuhn, 1964). Without going into the knotty and crucial questions of whether social scientists' paradigms are the equivalent of the natural scientists', I feel that the impact of Keynes on economics, of the Learning Theorists on psychology, of Boas and his followers on American anthropology, or the impact of Radcliffe-Brown and the British structuralists on British and much of American anthropology is akin to Kuhn's paradigms.

The widespread acceptance of radical new frames of reference within communities of practitioners and the coincidental new methodology and techniques have also contributed to the problems of cross-discipline borrowing. Anthropologists are finding increasing difficulty in understanding post-Keynesian economics, although older styles of institutional economics are accessible. Modern economics and model construction are beyond many of us; much the same can be said for experimental psychology. Contemporary sociology seems to be heading in the same direction in its attempt to apply mathematical models. Although political science still seems to be at a preparadigmatic stage, older historical and normative-oriented theory and research are rubbing shoulders increasingly with behavioral and mathematical approaches. Anthropology is in similar development; new ethnography, cross-cultural methodology, and arguments about whether we are studying ideal models or reality in the field coexist with older styles of work and thought.

One function of this present emphasis on cross-discipline borrowing is to make more hybrid or hyphenated types of social scientists available. The institutional economist finds a home with anthropologists and historians; the sociologist, whose stock and trade is grand sociological theory, has a wide audience in anthropology, political science, and history. I find that my concerns with simple structuralism, theories about the nature of peasant societies, and anthropological work concerned with the social-structural interpretation of symbol and myth have considerable resonance among my historian colleagues. Some of us find ourselves "interdisciplinary" because we are the emigrees from an ancient regime, driven off by Kuhnsian revolutions or the latest fads. I would point out that the emigrees play a vital role, much as their political counterparts have done in bringing social and economic changes in world history.

Two types of borrowing seem to be occurring among disciplines. One might be termed retrospective, or the selective application of concepts from one discipline to thought in a related field. For example, some political scientists have recently found anthropology's concept of culture to be extremely useful and have begun to apply it to the relationship between socialization and authority and the nature of the political system found in societies, although this type of study is declining in anthropology itself.

In addition to the retrospective, hyphenated social scientist, a second type of borrowing involves men who have mastered the latest methodology and/or theory of another discipline and see how to apply this knowledge to another discipline. In the natural sciences, these men are unflatteringly called "skimmers," but they are the founders of the interstitial disciplines which have proliferated in the natural sciences in the last few generations into such combinations as biochemistry and astrophysics.

It is not surprising that the methodologists are the most likely candidates among the social scientists for bringing recent or emerging methods and theories to other disciplines. Survey research methods have proved successful and useful in political science, social psychology, law, and anthropology, as well as in a wide variety of quasi-academic fields like market research. A specialized variant of survey research — the study of voting behavior through quantitative methods — is having an increasing impact on the study of American political history. The econometricians are rapidly affecting research in economic history and may be the first to develop testable diachronic theory.

Looking at the relationships between disciplines from my split vision as an anthropologist and historian, particularly from the standpoint of training future professionals, I think the disciplines are more rigid than ever while, at the same time, departments are incorporating specialities from other disciplines to try to bring breadth to their activities. As the disciplines within the social sciences widely accept new frames of reference, they provide more and more common methods and problems. The "old-fashioned" practitioners then move to other areas often outside of their original disciplines, providing one type of link for retrospective borrowing. At the same time, the "new breed" who are in the forefront of their fields also may affect sister disciplines. Increasing professionalization, which is partially a function of the affluence and growth of departments, vies with the intellectual necessity of breadth and a knowledge of other disciplines.

The social sciences may begin to spin off new departments, just as the natural sciences have been doing. Social psychology may be the first to achieve departmental status within universities, if it has not already done so, followed by political sociology, economic history, and biological anthropology. Other than our own discomfort at this kind of growth, the only barrier is the famed reluctance of those controlling university budgets to finance additional departments. One alternative to proliferation exists, however, in the continuation of what we have today, with some formalization. Social science departments can continue to grow not only in size, but also in complexity by developing a conscious federated structure within each department.

In some ways the larger departments have already become federal systems as a result of their growth. In history departments, for example, formal and informal departments are functionally divided, for most purposes, into three groups: European, American, and "exotic." The latter includes the study of history outside the Euro-American context, such as Indian, Chinese, and African history, as well as the history of science. Political science departments generally have two organizational divisions: the first, geographic and the second, functional. The first divides those concerned with American politics into one grouping, European into another, and non-Western into the third. The functional division separates behaviorists and institutionalists, as well as those interested in comparative law, political theory, and other such fields. In anthropology departments, divisions generally separate subject matter specialists, including the archaeologists, interested in the recovery of information about past societies from uncovering physical remains; the physical anthropologists, interested in man basically as a biologically being; the anthropological linguists; and the social and cultural anthropologists, concerned with contemporaneous societies and cultures which can be studied in the field. Each of the ways of dividing history, political science, and anthropology is different, but the splits tend to be derived from the subject matter and only partially from the methodology. In recent years, similar subject matter has formed the basis of our cross-disciplinary explorations, with area studies being one of the primary links of cooperation with other disciplines.

These links, based on area or problem, have emerged in the last twenty years and are probably enduring. However, my point is that, in addition to this kind of tie, broad-scale methodological groupings in the social sciences will develop which may prove even more enduring. I label these mathematical, behavioral, and historical-comparative. The distribution of these three methodologies in any one of the given disciplines is uneven. For example, there are only a few mathematical-behavioral historians, e.g., Lee Benson, William Adyollote, and Robert Fogel. A new economic history which utilizes economic methods and models may be the first product to emerge from an organized grouping of mathematical-behavioral historians.

While a few mathematical anthropologists vigorously label themselves as such, it is only a short step from componential analysis and modern linguistics to the specialty of mathematical anthropology. Behavioral anthropology has been with us for a long time in the form of intensive observation and fine-grained study of individual behavior, sometimes with statistical treatments. A similar patterning of methodological emphasis has emerged among political scientists. Like most anthropologists, however, they are generally in broad-scale historical-comparative work which treats whole societies and cultures in terms of how they have developed and changed.

In a real sense, I believe that the historical-comparativists are beginning to feel themselves under siege. By their purposefulness, steely-eyed confidence, and the assurance that marks our more behavioral mathematical colleagues, they are telling us that Science is on their side.

History and Anthropology

Against my perception of ambiguous trends in all developments in the social sciences, I will consider the relationship of history to anthropology with particular reference to teaching, research, and interdisciplinary cooperation.

Historians consider themselves members of a scholarly tradition going back to Herodotus and Thucydides. Identified with the major philosophical-educational strand of Western civilization, and with "old-fashioned" philosophers and literary scholars, historians see themselves as the main interpreters of our past. Given the depth of historical range and the sense of being participants in and contributors to the great traditions of our civilization, the historians think of wisdom, mature judgment, and style as being central to their training and development. Combined with the fact that historians seem to improve with age, acquiring more knowledge and more experience, the profession takes on an "age grading" to some extent lacking in anthropology. Athough the historian's tradition is an old one, his profession, including many of his techniques and methods, is relatively new. The methods and techniques which are the mainstay of the modern historian, involve attention to validity and reliability of sources, elimination of overt bias from these sources, and the monographic tradition. These methods date from the beginning of the nineteenth century and the founding of critical historiography associated with B. G. Niebuhr (1776–1831) and Leopold von Ranke (1795–1886). The advent of academic historians is relatively recent dating only from the 1870's in this country.

Until recently, when anthropologists seem to be desperately searching for ancestors, most anthropologists thought of their discipline as a very young one indeed. They tended to think that their field was founded by an act of genius by Lewis Henry Morgan and E. B. Tylor, and that professional anthropologists really only date from the turn of the century when Franz Boas began to teach at Columbia and C. G. Seligman was appointed at the London School of Economics. This reputed newness of the field helped to make age grading quite a secondary consideration in organized anthropology. Anthropologists also tended to feel that many of the significant advances in the field came from direct experience of a conversion type such as Boas was supposed to have had with the Eskimo and Malinowski with the Trobriand Islands. This has led to the almost mystical belief that the anthropologist learned his craft in the field and obtained his ideas gathering field data. Hence, almost anyone who had done fieldwork could contribute to the discipline.

The folk hero of the anthropologist was unconventional in his dress and his personal life and was in rebellion against his own society. He was seen as an individual finding glory in his assumed task of cutting Western civilization down to size by pointing out the similarities in behavior and culture between ourselves and the primitives. Indeed, a great many anthropologists have made a virtue of personal idiosyncrasy and professional separateness.

In contrast, the historian's folk hero was the "establishment man" in dress, manners, and behavior. My impression is that historians, until about thirty years ago, were largely recruited from dominant social and economic groups in American society. Ethnicity and separateness were neither valued nor encouraged. The most valued characteristics were maturity, sensibility, and a good narrative writing style, rather than analytical skills. Since the establishment of the American Historical Association (AHA) in 1884, two presidents of the United States,

Theodore Roosevelt and Woodrow Wilson, have been AHA presidents. While historians have long served as high government officials and representatives of the United States overseas, anthropologists had to wait until the rise of the "new nations" before serving as ambassadors.

Both place and style of work differ radically for the anthropologist and historian: the field and the archive represent two very contrasting environments; an anthropologist in the field creates his own data, while the historian must find his data. In the field the anthropologist constantly builds his observations into hypotheses about the culture of the people he is studying, and continually revises these hypotheses. He can always generate data on questions which interest him. The historian, on the other hand, works deductively from assumptions about past events based on the course of those events. No matter how good his questions or hypotheses, however, the historian cannot create the data he needs to describe the course of events if they are not there.

Although both the historian and the anthropologist work with general theory, concepts, and categories of analysis, the anthropologist develops his concepts, categories, and theories self-consciously and, consequently, presents his research findings in the form of hypothesis testing. The historian tends to use "native categories" from his society and culture based on what he thinks of as common sense; he organizes his monographs in these common sense terms.

The major overall difference between historian and anthropologist lies in their conception of a system. The anthropologist tries to present his material in systematic terms, to integrate the bits and pieces of data into a system which he builds up and fits together.

[The writing of an anthropological monograph] involves breaking up the vivid, kaleidoscopic reality of human action, thought, and emotion which lives in the anthropologist's note books and memory, and creating out of the pieces a coherent representation of a society, in terms of the general principles of organization and motivation that regulate behavior in it (Fortes, 1963).

Since the anthropologist assumes order in the world, the creative act of anthropological research is to demonstrate the nature of that order with data from a particular society.

Most historians are less convinced than anthropologists about the systematic nature of society; historians are more likely to stress the random behavior of society and to see the organizing principle in terms of successive events which, at times, seem to be governed by chance.

I think cooperation should begin with a recognition of existing differences. Although I have presented anthropologists and historians as polar types in their working environments and in their personal and professional styles, their intellectual constructs do overlap and areas of true interpenetration occur in the two fields. I will briefly try to show where some of the methodological and theoretical overlaps occur through a quick review of the relations between the two fields.

Certainly from the beginning of history as a professional tradition, a few historians have been aware of the need for conscious theory; over the years more have moved to develop techniques for testing hypotheses. Ever since James Harvey Robinson's *The New History* (1965), published in 1912, historians have looked to economists, sociologists, psychologists, and anthropologists for methodological and conceptual help in framing and studying historical problems.

In the pre-professional periods of history and anthropology during the nineteenth century, the activities of anthropologists and historians were not as rigidly separated as they are today. During this time, some historians engaged in the systematic study of the origin and history of institutions. Fustel de Coulanges, Robertson Smith, Maitland, Pollock, and Vinogradoff were equally valued as scholars by anthropologists and historians, although not always for the same books. Similarly, McClennan, Maine, Morgan, and Lubbock seemed to think of themselves as historians along with their incipient identification as anthropologists.

The hard and fast distinction which anthropologists make between anthropological and historical studies paradoxically reached a climax with a generation of anthropologists who thought they were doing historical research: Boas, Wissler, Sapir, Kroeber, and Lowie. Convinced about the lack of what they thought constituted bona fide historical source material in their data, they tried to develop methods different from the historian's. In Sapir's "Time Perspective in Aboriginal American Culture: A Study in Method" (1916), only two of eighty-seven pages are devoted to the use of oral tradition and documents for writing the history of American Indians. Kroeber (1923) believed that for the study of "poor dateless primitives . . . we do not possess even one document before our day." In an attack on Swanton and Dixon's attempt to study the history of American Indian migrations on the basis of oral traditions and documents, Lowie (1920) utterly denied "that primitive man is endowed with historical sense or perspective."

Since the American historical school, or the distributionists, denied the use of either oral or documentary direct source material, they tried to develop indirect methods of studying history through plotting distributions of traits. Although some members of the school, such as Kroeber and Goldenweiser, were interested in European or world history at a macro-level, they did little direct historical research and used historical examples only to illustrate general cultural processes. Even during the distributionist period, roughly from 1910 to 1930, some American anthropologists did considerable amounts of direct historical work, such as Swanton (1905, 1917) and Speck (1915, 1935) on American Indians, and Laufer (1938) on the distributions of crops and material culture. At about the same time on the Continent and in England, "historical schools" concerned with distribution studies also developed.

American historians in the early twentieth century took E. A. Freeman's dictum "history is past politics" seriously and tended to emphasize monographic political and biographical studies. This tendency was confirmed in the twenties as a result of the revulsion which many historians had for their propagandistic role during World War I. One way they felt they could redeem themselves was to reaffirm the narrow monographic tradition which devoted itself primarily to political events, without any attempt to relate their work to explicit theory or wider problems.

Even from 1900 to 1930, however, counter tendencies should not be overlooked among historians such as Beard who used economics to explain the American constitution; James Harvey Robinson (1965) who called for a new history which "will avail itself of all those discoveries that are being made about mankind by anthropologists, economists, psychologists, and sociologists — discoveries which during the past fifty years have served to revolutionize our ideas of the origin, progress, and prospects of our race." In the twenties, Harry Elmer Barnes (1925) tried to make historians aware that anthropology

has supplied history with the most perfect of analytical techniques for the interpretation of cultural processes and complexes, that it has worked out in an admirable manner the laws and processes of cultural development, that its wealth of comparative data should furnish the best imaginable antidote for chauvinism, bigotry, and conservatisms, that it has destroyed the racial basis of national arrogance, and that it will prove progressively more valuable as an auxiliary science to history, as the latter comes to be more and more concerned with the explanation of cultural development and less and less absorbed in the narration of political events.

This kind of brave statement about the power of anthropology continues to be made by historians and exhorters of historians to mend their ways. It also illustrates one of the difficulties inherent in cross-discipline borrowing. The outsider often overestimates the coherence and power of the anthropologist, frequently leading to the assumptions that anthropological technique, method, theory, and outlook are readily packageable and applicable; that a book, or course, or conversation will provide the historian with the philosopher's stone.

Since the twenties, under the impact of functionalism, many anthropologists in Great Britain and some on the Continent and in the United States have worked explicitly on the assumption that history and anthropology are two completely different kinds of intellectual activities. From the early twenties until the fifties, Radcliffe-Brown (1952) consistently argued this position, based on the observation that "conjectural history," as produced by both European and American distributionists, was a hopeless waste of time since there were no documents, as Sapir, Lowie, and Kroeber had argued, and since history was, after all, based on a study of documents. He was wrong in this as ethnohistorians are increasingly demonstrating. An enormous number of documents, usually generated by Europeans, can be utilized by anthropologists to write the history of specific tribal societies. In addition, a historian of Africa, Jan Vansina (1965), has brilliantly demonstrated that oral traditions can be collected, collated, verified, and used as conventional historical documents. When recorded oral traditions are used with European documents and interpreted in the light of contemporary fieldwork, they provide substantial material for building the history of the so-called poor, dateless primitives.

One of Radcliffe-Brown's assumptions about history is serious and important from the standpoint of contemporary anthropological and historical studies. Drawing on the dichotomy first developed in linguistics between diachronic and synchronic study, Radcliffe-Brown argued that synchronic study leads to scientific generalization while the diachronic leads to particularistic non-generalizable study. This dichotomy is still widely held by both anthropologists and historians. According to Radcliffe-Brown, historical study promotes "ideographic inquiry, the purpose of which is to establish . . . certain particular or factual propositions or statements . . . nomothetic inquiry, on the contrary, has for its purpose to arrive at acceptable general propositions" (Radcliffe-Brown, 1952). Social anthropology was to be a nomothetic study.

The belief that historians are interested in the unique and that social anthropologists are interested in the findings of general laws is still with us today; in fact, stereotypes of this kind help to separate the practitioners of these disciplines. While some validity to this belief exists, neither field is monolithic; rather, members of these scholarly communities range along a continuum from those who are interested only in understanding a particular situation and see causality in terms of the succession of events, to those who claim they study particular situations or compare particular cases to arrive at general laws of human behavior. In quantitative terms, the majority of practitioners in both fields seem to be interested in uniqueness. Most anthropologists, however, strive to relate particular cases to some general theory, and most anthropological works are implicitly or explicitly comparative since the authors usually report on societies other than their own.

A growing number of works by historians consciously set out to find general laws in the study of particular places through time, to test hypotheses, and to come to conclusions which are further testable. Merle Curti's, *The Making of an American Community* (1959), Sam B. Warner's *Streetcar Suburbs* (1962), and Sumner Powell's *Puritan Village* (1963) read somewhat like anthropological studies; they demonstrate the feasibility of applying social science theory directly to historical study and general findings to the unique. Similarly, a growing number of social scientists have turned to direct historical study to test theory developed from synchronic study. Charles Tilly, in *The Vendée* (1964), relates broad theories of urbanization to political action and social change. James Sterling Young's *The Washington Community, 1800–1828* (1966) looks at the development of social groups in early Washington as a community and demonstrates how the social and ecological arrangements, the boardinghouses in particular, affected political behavior. Evans-Pritchard's *Sanusi of Cyrenica* (1949) clearly demonstrates the process by which an acephalous political system based on lineages can turn into a state system. Lloyd Fallers (1964) and his associates have demonstrated in their study of Buganda how stratification theory can be utilized to study modernization through time. Fred Eggan, since the publication of his paper on Choctaw kinship in 1937, has time and time again effectively demonstrated that diachronic and synchronic study can be closely related in the development of kinship theory.

In the face of so many examples of historians using social science and, conversely, of so many social scientists using history, can we really set history and anthropology on opposite ends of some continuum between idiographic and nomothetic? I do not think so. Since the thirties, the anthropologist has been increasingly interested in peasant societies, the process of social and cultural change, and, paradoxically, in what the "natives" are like today, not what they may have been like in some aboriginal state of nature. These interests have drawn a significant number of anthropologists to the archives for historical study. The increasing involvement of the historian in the study of non-European societies, the growth in the number of specialized monographs which enables the historian to ask synthesizing questions, and the realization on the part of some historians that the "historical imagination" can be aided directly by comparative and cross-disciplinary work has led the historian to the systematic study of the social sciences.

Conditions for Cooperation

Although programmatic statements by historians and anthropologists still abound in the literature and at annual meetings of professional societies, many quietly accept the importance of work from other disciplines and utilize what they can. Do we need institutionalized programs to further the mutual interpenetration of anthropology and history? If certain conditions which already exist in many graduate schools continue to exist and are developed further, I do not think this will be necessary. These conditions include the following:

1)   The federated structure of departments, which I already discussed, should continue to be the style. A federated structure allows both faculty and students to move more freely across boundaries.

2)   After the initial exposure to other disciplines and materials, we should recognize no shortcuts to learning other bodies of theory, method, and technique. As professionals or students, there is no substitute for the hard work of learning and applying knowledge from

another field. More might be done to structure the opportunity for exposure; once this has been accomplished, however, it is up to each individual to obtain the specialized training he needs in other fields. In short, there is no substitute for the historian's reading of anthropology or the anthropologist's reading of history.

3)   The anthropologist must do the same work with manuscripts and documents that the historian does, although he must ask his own questions in his own way. Conversely, more historians must get into the "field." R. H. Tawney perceived this when he stated, "What the historian needs is not more documents but stouter boots." Marc Bloch (1939, 1940) long ago demonstrated that even a medievalist can directly observe some of the things which he knows only from documents by careful selection of his place, specifically the observation of the three-field systems in northern Sweden. There may not be a direct relationship even in a genetic sense between what a historian observes and what he studies in his documents; the experience of seeing that the bits and pieces of behavior can be systematic is crucial in utilizing modern anthropology. Historians have already begun to assign their students to do fieldwork as preliminary to, or part of, archival work. H. Stuart Hughes has had some students in the field in France; students in the Pacific History Department at Australian National University also have done a piece of heuristic fieldwork as a part of their training, and many historians of Africa do field work as anthropologists.

In other words, not only must we grasp the ideas or methods of our colleagues but, to properly utilize these ideas or methods, we must work to some degree in their environments. J. M. Wallace-Hadrill (1959), a medievalist of the University of Manchester, states in his discussion of the blood feud among the Franks:

Vendetta may be studied, even today, in almost any quarter of the globe, in Arabia or Africa, for instance, or nearer home among the patriarchal societies in the mountains of Albania, Sicily, Sardinia and Corsica; and it is so studied by the sociologist. We can learn from him and afterwards look with a new eye to the more particular study of the feuding in medieval Europe.

Thus, the historian under certain circumstances should, like the anthropologist, go into the field himself.

In turn, for the anthropologist interested in a wide range of questions, problems, or theories — including the impact of industrialization on family structure, the relationship between technological innovation, the problem of integration in new states and how it changes through time — all have a historical counterpart available with hard work and imagination. A brief survey of the secondary literature is not a substitute for relating questions of change through time or for using well-ordered documentary studies in depth.

A call for the anthropologist to study social change through direct historical study is not new. Even Radcliffe-Brown recognized in 1935 that the study of the relationship between structural change and the changing nature of functions of institutions in a society "can be studied in the development of the legal and political institutions, the economic systems, and the religions of Europe through the last twenty-five centuries."

COMMENTARY: Lloyd Fallers
Richard L. Park
Sylvia Thrupp

Lloyd Fallers

I have much sympathy for Professor Cohn's general theme that anthropology and history are not at opposite ends of a continuum between the "ideographic" and the "nomothetic"; that we often overlap in the same kinds of intellectual work; and that we are ultimately indispensable to each other. He also says that our work methods, or the craft aspects of our disciplines, are quite different. Those differences are important and must be respected. The anthropologist cannot properly double as historian so long as he uses documents in a pre-professional way, and, of course, the reverse is also true. However, I should like to take mild issue with Dr. Cohn on a few points.

First, his intellectual history of the two disciplines seems to me too parochially American and too influenced by the boundaries between present-day academic disciplines. The ancestry of systematic history stretches back well beyond the time of Beard and James Harvey Robinson, even if American historians were too preoccupied by the supposed uniqueness of the American experience to recognize this. That American historians in this century have had to look to anthropology for systematizing ideas is a revealing commentary on the discipline of history in this country. It suggests American historians had cut themselves off from the earlier sources of such ideas within the historical tradition itself. Burckhardt's (1878) work contains a sense of the interconnectedness of cultural and social elements which today appears strikingly "anthropological." Even older is the notion that history had a plot, a systematic, directional movement.

The Enlightenment view of history as the progress of reason was perhaps best exemplified by Kant's essay entitled, "A Proposal for a Universal History," by which he meant evolutionary history. Other views included Hegel's notion of a strain toward coincidence between culture and the state, a notion to be regarded as hypothesis, however much it also has been considered an ideology. Marx's dialectical theory of classes certainly left a residue in social scientific thought, whatever one may think about his concepts and hypotheses. His theories also stimulated much empirical research by persuading both historians and social scientists to seek social and economic data below the elite levels of society.

Much of the work I have cited is not now regarded as being in the main-line ancestry of history as an academic discipline. However, the point is that an interaction between systematizing ideas and the developing data-gathering craft has a long ancestry, particularly in the nineteenth century, which forms part of the intellectual history shared by historians and anthropologists, as well as by political scientists. Many of our current issues were debated by those nineteenth-century ancestors of our modern disciplines and we ignore these debates at the peril of wasting time through useless repetition. Perhaps this unhistorical lack of attention to our intellectual past accounts for the circular motions in our thought in anthropology and the other sociocultural disciplines, an effect a colleague recently called "the whirligig of time."

Second, I think we can say something more about the similarities and differences on the craft level. Gathering sociocultural data through close and continuous interaction with persons of another culture is indeed a special and harrowing kind of data-gathering. The mystique of anthropological fieldwork is perhaps justified as a means of attracting people into a different line of work.

However, most anthropologists — perhaps not Dr. Cohn — tend to think of intercultural understanding as such as something peculiarly anthropological. I think it is inaccurate to say that historians have generally worked through the "native" or "folk" categories of their own cultures. I even doubt the justice of accusing Western historians of Western societies of this, although their task of intercultural understanding is less difficult than that of other historians. In fact, historians worried about and debated the problem of cultural relativism before anthropologists, as Burckhardt illustrates. Naturally, historians did not face the problem of understanding preliterate cultures since they did not study them. However, it is common to find historians otherwise sensitive to the problem. The interpretation of documents from other times and places often presents problems of intercultural understanding quite as radical as those involved in the interpretation of behavior and utterances occurring before our eyes.

In illustration, let me quote briefly from F. W. Maitland's *Doomsday Book and Beyond* (1897), an account of the author's attempts to analyze one of the great documents of English history. The *Doomsday Book* was complied by the Norman government after its conquest as a kind of survey of the human and natural resources it had acquired. It is a treasure house of data, but the conceptual categories used by its compilers are not readily understood by a modern reader and, without such understanding, the document becomes unintelligible or, at best, misleading. At one point, Maitland writes:

As regards the legal ideas in which feudalism is expressed, a general question may be raised. If we approach them from the standpoint of Roman law [the body of ancient legal concepts most familiar to Maitland's generation], they are confused ideas. In particular, no clear line is drawn between public and private law. Ownership is *"dominium,"* but government power, jurisdictional power, these are also *"dominium."* Office is "property," taxes are "rent," governmental relationships are "contractual." [The question then arises, says Maitland,] whether we are right in applying to this state of things such a word as "confusion," a word which implies that things that were once distinct have wrongfully or unfortunately been mixed up with each other, a word which implies error or retrogression.

Maitland is struggling here to understand "in its own terms," as anthropologists like to say, the contextual meaning of a key concept in medieval political and economic life. What he is doing is very similar to Evans-Pritchard's (1937) effort to understand and explicate the concepts central to Zande magic and witchcraft. The sense of wonder and discovery in the presence of strange ideas that these passages of Maitland's clearly embody a feeling of intellectual challenge very similar to that experienced by anthropologists observing behavior or overhearing utterances similarly strange.

In this sense, I think anthropologists and historians do similar work, although it is as difficult to imagine Maitland patiently working out the intricacies of Sudanese spells as it is to visualize Malinowski spending his life in archives. (I do not contrast Evans-Pritchard here because he *did* train himself to do historians' work.)

Anthropologists and historians do similar work, then, but by means so different as to require radically different skills, and perhaps even different temperaments.

Richard L. Park

Without drawing a careful set of relationships between political science and anthropology as Professor Cohn did for history and anthropology, let me say that we in the social sciences and history are growing together in one respect: we are concerned either with political phenomena directly or others consider our work "political." We are brought closer by forces of external suspicion.

Professor Cohn has stressed the gradual growth of cooperation among those scholars called "behavioral scientists," which include political behavior specialists, students of comparative politics and political development, political sociologists, political anthropologists, and social and political historians. Although behavioralism is a method rather than a discipline, persons from various behavioral fields read much the same literature, examine the same theories, and, to a certain extent, talk the same academic language.

In the early 1950's, a so-called behavioral revolt in political science started at the University of Chicago, led by Charles Merriam and others. The behavioralists have won the battle; consequently, many of the rest of us have had to move to the outer ramparts, safeguarded by tradition.

This behavioral revolution has transformed political science by adding selected theories, methodologies, and techniques from mathematics, sociology, and social psychology, and, to a lesser extent, from social and cultural anthropology.

The new political science is devoted extensively to collecting and analyzing empirical data using increasingly sophisticated techniques of data manipulation and aggregation, such as simulation and survey research. We often study methodologically oriented problems which lend themselves more to computer manipulation than to what might be considered the most important questions. Fortunately, there is sometimes a coincidence of technique and relevance.

While behaviorists and others in political science now coexist, the isolates can retreat to other departments (including history) if the heat of resentment from mathematically inclined colleagues becomes too great.

For mundane and practical reasons, political scientists and anthropologists working in the field often meet in mid-career because of a curious reversal in their research histories. The young anthropologist usually does his first research in a village or a tribal area; in later years, he may take on somewhat more complex situations, such as a town or city. Some anthropologists are even attempting holistic studies. The political scientist's pattern is nearly the reverse: the political science graduate student often approaches a large theme, even if on a small scale, and produces a narrow study of a large problem. After more experience, he may study a region, town, and village; this is common in Asian and African studies. Somewhere along the line the political scientist meets the anthropologist. It is at this point that mutual interest begins to grow between the two.

Thus, in my own interests in modern Indian studies, I find the work of F. G. Bailey on Orissa, of Bernard Cohn on Banaras, of Harold Gould on Uttar Pradesh, or of Adrian Mayer on Indore directly relevant to my work. Many other political scientists have had the same experience. Although we speak slightly different languages, we usually talk about the same subject matter.

As for training in political science, despite the behavioral revolution, political scientists interested in all levels of local government of many societies of the world have been provided totally inadequate methods of investigation. In this regard, I am in complete sympathy with the point made by Professor Cohn. While it is difficult to train non-professionals in anthropological techniques, it is essential to devise methods for training students of local government. Although anthropology can offer much in this respect, our curricula for disciplinary graduate study have become so professional in the core subject requirements that an "outsider" has considerable difficulty getting systematic training in any field other than his own. One really has to be eccentric, fight the system, and, in effect, teach and prepare oneself.

A dangerous trend is arising in political science. We have moved into the survey research field in sufficiently sophisticated ways to deal with single cultures, for example to analyze elections and to conduct binational studies supported by the simpler form of comparative analysis. Now, however, several massive cross-national studies are nearing completion. These massive studies bother me, because, in such situations, the analyst must depend upon data banks of materials, none of which he has collected. Consequently, studies may compare fifty or eighty modern cultures, involving a vast number of social variables. Yet the analyst has little cultural or historical restraint over the data and, thus, may be unable to ascertain its validity.

Sylvia Thrupp

A few points from a paper I have been preparing called "Cannibalism by Candlelight" will explain why I agree with Professor Cohn's conclusions, while disagreeing strongly with some of his reasoning. It seems to me that interdisciplinary borrowing follows much the same path as intercultural borrowing. A distinguished historian of the Near East, Sir Hamilton Gibb (1964), has offered a tentative formulation of laws for intercultural borrowing. Gibb holds that creative borrowing from the outside is essential to maintain the vitality of a culture. Mere imitating and borrowing of techniques are not considered creative. According to Gibb's first "law," before a culture can borrow creatively, some activity related to the elements to be borrowed must occur within the borrowing culture. This parallels the premise of my argument: in the academic world, social relations are cannibalistic; no one takes an interest in anyone else's work unless he can tear something out of it and incorporate it into his own.

The historical profession is so highly differentiated that Dr. Cohn's attempts to generalize about it as one whole are misleading. What he sees as a continuum is really a series of subgroups. Some of these always have oriented their work around concepts of system and structure. Economic historians, legal historians, and historians of science, art, and religion did so from the start. We historians have a common professional sense that our ways of dealing with time and change are indispensable, and that we must look for a synthesis of human experience. Yet, we do not get very far with this synthesis. When our different groups meet at world congresses, they tend to meet separately and to come together only for the pleasures of music, wine, and sharp disagreement over philosophy and methods.

Most historical specialists creatively borrow concepts and ideas from the outside, mostly from the older social sciences (law, economics, political science) or from philosophy but to some extent from the newer social sciences. By Gibb's first law, they would rate a high vitality score.

Borrowing falls into a variety of patterns. For example, the classical historians, who for a time did little but amass materials, have begun to conform to Gibb's law. They have entered into new communication with political scientists over such matters as voting practices and they have discovered that cultural anthropology can illuminate the Homeric world. American historians similarly are borrowing concepts from sociology, not to imitate, but because they so frequently encounter sociological problems. In Europe, similar encounters occur, but non-Marxist sociology developed there in competition with Marxist sociology, and the latter has a continuing attraction.

Non-Western historians have naturally borrowed from anthropology, and European historians have begun to do the same as they become more conscious of the many peculiarities of their history through comparative study. Some history departments even have an anthropologist available for consultation with students.

Why then are the clichés about historical method so often repeated? It is puzzling to social scientists and quite baffling to analytical philosophers that historians seem so uninterested in going beyond the conventional emphasis on factual accuracy and narrative ordering. Political historians pass this off as representative of historical methods. In their case, accuracy of fact is extraordinarily important and never to be taken for granted because most of their work is still recent enough for the basic facts to be distorted by dishonesty or partisanship. Consequently, the political historian's conscience in the matter of critical sifting of evidence is as important as the principle of the free press. This fight against political falsification goes back to the more courageous of the medieval chroniclers. The fact that both unbiased history and free press are suppressed in times of war or totalitarian influence proves my point.

In reviews of each other's books, historians habitually commend a writer for "throwing light" on a matter. Now where can one "throw light"? Only in the dark. Lévi-Strauss is said to have remarked in a press interview[1] that social science is at about the same stage as natural science was in ancient Assyria. However, there have been many new developments in historical work; among these, comparative studies are of particular interest to anthropologists. A few years ago a small group of anthropologists and medievalists founded a journal called *Comparative Studies in Society and History, An International Quarterly* (Cambridge University Press), which has become a forum for communication among historians and social scientists. As we face new problems, and we borrow from common sources, communication between disciplines becomes easier. None of our disciplines is so enlightened as to be above benefiting from some give-and-take relationship with another discipline.

1. As cited by Paolo Caruso in "Exploring Lévi-Strauss," *Atlas,* 11:4 (April, 1966), pp. 245–46. (Trans. from *Il Contemporaneo,* Rome, n.d.).

REFERENCES

Barnes, H. E. 1925. The New History and the Social Studies, pp. 305–06. Century Co.: New York.

Bloch, M. L. 1939. La Societé féodale: La formation des liens de dépendance, A. Michel: Paris.

———. 1940. La Societé féodale: Les classes et le gouvernment des hommes, A. Michel: Paris.

Burckhardt, J. C. 1878. The Civilization of the Period of the Renaissance in Italy, authorized translation by S. G. C. Middlemore, 2 vols. C. K. Paul & Co.: London.

Curti, M. E. 1959. The Making of An American Community. Stanford University Press: Stanford.

Eggan, F. 1937. Historical Changes in the Choctaw Kinship System. American Anthropologist 39:34–52, January.

Evans-Pritchard, E. E. 1937. Witchcraft, Oracles and Magic Among the Azandi. Clarendon Press: Oxford.

————. 1949. Sanusi of Cyrenica. Clarendon Press: Oxford.

Fallers, L. A., ed. 1964. The King's Men: Leadership and Status in Buganda on the Eve of Independence. Published for East African Institute of Social Research. Oxford University Press: London.

Fortes, M. ed. 1963. Social Structure: Studies Presented to A. R. Radcliffe-Brown. Russell and Russell: New York.

Gibb, H. 1964. The Influence of Islamic Culture on Medieval Europe. Change in Medieval Society: Europe North of the Alps, 1050–1500, ed. Sylvia L. Thrupp, pp. 155–67. Appleton-Century-Crofts: New York. (Bulletin of the John Rylands Library, 1955.)

Kroeber, A. L. 1923. Anthropology. Harcourt, Brace: New York.

Kuhn, T. S. 1964. The Structure of Scientific Revolutions. Phoenix Books: Chicago. (Originally published 1962, p. 10. University of Chicago Press, Chicago.)

Laufer, B. 1938. The American Plant Migration. Field Museum: Chicago.

Lowie, R. H. 1920. Primitive Society. Liveright: New York.

Maitland, F. W. 1897. Doomesday Book and Beyond: Three Essays in the Early History of England. Cambridge University Press: New York.

Powell, S. C. 1963. Puritan Village: The Formation of a New England Town. Wesleyan University Press: Middletown, Connecticut.

Radcliffe-Brown, A. R. 1935. On the Concept of Function in Social Science. American Anthropologist 37:394–402.

————. 1952. Introduction. Structure and Function of Primitive Society, p. 1. Free Press: Glencoe.

Robinson, J. H. 1965. The New History: Essays Illustrating the Modern Historical Outlook, p. 24. Free Press: New York. (Originally published 1912, Macmillan, New York.)

Sapir, E. 1916. Time Perspective in Aboriginal American Culture, A Study in Method. Canada Geological Survey, Memoir 90, Anthropological Series No. 13. Government Printing Bureau: Ottowa.

Speck, F. G. 1915. The Family Hunting Band as the Basis of Algonkian Social Organization. American Anthropologist 13:289–305.

————. 1935. Naskapi. University of Oklahoma Press: Norman, Oklahoma.

Swanton, J. R. 1905. The Social Organization of American Tribes. American Anthropologist 7:663–73.

————. 1917. Some Anthropological Misconceptions. American Anthropologist 19:459–70.

Tilly, C. 1964. The Vandée. Harvard University Press: Cambridge.

Vansina, J. 1965. Oral Tradition: A Study in Historical Methodology, trans. by H. M. Wright. Aldine: Chicago.

Wallace-Hadrill, J. M. 1959. The Bloodfeud of the Franks. John Rylands Library Bulletin 41(2):461, 459–87, March.

Warner, S. B. 1962. Streetcar Suburbs — The Process of Growth in Boston, 1870–1900. Harvard University Press–MIT Press: Cambridge.

Young, J. S. 1966. The Washington Community, 1800–1828. Columbia University Press: New York.

Education

Any appraisal of the relation between anthropology and education should first specify the areas of common concern. From the anthropological perspective, the most inclusive concept is the transmission of culture (Kimball, 1966) which encompasses not only what is taught and learned, but also the organization, pattern, and processes of education in their social and cultural settings. Professional educators usually would agree that the transmission of culture also is their major concern, but they would then insist that, as practitioners, their orientation is primarily programmatic. They would say that their job is to know what to do and how to do it, although some might add that they could use assistance in developing new understanding of their problems and in learning how changes in current practices could produce improved results.

The sharpest differentiation between educator and anthropologist is likely to appear in the perspective, definition, and solution of educational problems. Teachers, school administrators, and other educational specialists are primarily trained for and engaged in activities subsumed under instruction. In contrast, the anthropologists, proceeding from the perspective of his discipline, seeks to describe the social system and cultural behavior within the educational institution and to place it in the context of the community. By ordering this accumulated knowledge, the anthropologist may suggest modifications in organization or procedures that will increase the effectiveness of the educational system. When he works with educators, he functions primarily as a consultant and refrains from direct intervention in the responsibility of those trained to operate the system, the professional educators. Anthropologists who have worked in applied anthropology are aware of the connection between preliminary, traditional field research on a problem, and the preparation of innovative proposals based upon the findings of this research. They also are aware that they must resist becoming practitioners since this responsibility belongs to those whose training, experience, and aptitudes have prepared them for this role.

I should draw attention to another fundamental distinction between educators and anthropologists, since they may view such specific problems as those of school dropouts, under-achievement, or discipline from quite different perspectives. The cross-cultural and holistic perspective of the anthropologist permits him to interpret the data from specific research in a wider context than the educator who usually is concerned with one specific situation. Furthermore, some aspects of behavior which educators may ignore, treat casually, or even be unaware of, such as informal groupings or induction of new personnel or students, may strike the anthropologist as of major significance. In particular, the anthropologist's perspective gives him a strategic view of the relationships among schools, the educative process, and the community. His knowledge of cultural continuity and comparative analysis also should prove advantageous in understanding cultural change.

These differences in outlook and procedure need to be examined in the context of purposes and their associated values, although it is difficult for me to phrase or specify them, except in the most general terms. Let us assume that American anthropologists and educators are equally committed to the principles of democracy. Although no attempt will be made to enumerate these principles in any detail nor to assess the congruency between ideal and practice, for illustrative purposes, I shall mention representative government, cultural pluralism, equality of opportunity, and protection of individual dignity. The immediate problem is of another kind: to examine the extent to which democratic tenets influence the American anthropologists, first, in his analyses of the school system operation either as implicit or explicit assumptions, and, second, in the solutions he recommends for an educational problem. Can we, as anthropologists, claim some deeper and more universal insights about human nature, culture, and social groupings than those implicit in the democratic creed and, if so, do these contribute to a dilemma by contradicting the validity of some goals which we readily accept?

Presumably, few educators need to be confronted with the doubts which I suggest face anthropologists. Although thoughtful educators are distressed by the gap between ideal and practice, the pressure of daily responsibility leads many to do their job without a sufficient understanding or questioning of the system and makes them largely insensitive to its inconsistencies. For example, the once prevalent belief that the United States was free of social class was supported by contrasting the United States to Europe where a hereditary aristocracy barred the advance of the capable and ambitious. It was believed that in the land of the free any man could rise to great heights, as had Lincoln, Edison, and Ford. When the community studies of the early thirties began to provide evidence for the existence of social class distinctions in the United States, some labeled both studies and researchers as un-American. Later, Warner, Havighurst, and Loeb in *Who Shall Be Educated* (1944), showed how children of different social levels were differentially treated in the schools. Subsequent studies in Chicago by students of Everett Hughes and in Detroit by Patricia Sexton (1961) confirmed the disadvantages that children of the working class faced through unequal distribution of educational resources and personnel.

The assumption that equitable distribution of resources ensures equal educational opportunities or results is, of course, fallacious. Class biases appear in subtle and unconscious ways, even among those who profess ardent support of democratic equality. In Spindler's (1959) research, the teacher so stereotyped class behavior that he was unaware of the differences between his rating of students and their actual performances. Jules Henry (1963) has shown the subtle and automatic rewards and punishments which teachers mete out to those students who conform to, or violate, their class-oriented sense of proper behavior. Ruth Landes (1965) reported that Mexican-American students in California rejected certain aspects of schooling which threatened their cultural identity. Thus, boys who took part in athletic programs were accused by their peers of becoming "Anglicized," and cultural values of Mexican girls were violated by what they considered the immodest exposure they suffered when they were required to shower in open stalls in physical education classes. Landes further reported that when these ethnic-based behaviors were understood by the teachers and efforts were openly made to accommodate to them, much of the unwittingly created tension disappeared. Perhaps stress generated by violations of class identity might also disappear given the same treatment, although traditionally subcultural variations expressed in social class have not been accorded the same dignity and respect sometimes given autonomous cultures.

In other words, the American acceptance of cultural pluralism and the anthropological value of respecting cultural antonomy are fairly well in accord. But the problem gets sticky when we view social class as a subcultural variant while adhering to a relatively uniform educational approach expressing only middle-class values. In the extension of middle-class values in education, we witness an attempt to bring children of the lower class into the orbit of middle-class behavior. Many attempts are made to justify this procedure, but this might also be construed as an example of social class, or cultural imperialism. The recent spot announcements on television which urge continued education, predicting a dismal future for the unheeding, are obviously intended to reach working-class youth and, regardless of the validity of the exhortation, those who respond to the message serve middle-class values.[1]

It is generally accepted that the schools which serve the slums of the big cities are relatively unsuccessful in their educational efforts when judged by, and compared with, middle-class standards.[2] One problem that plagues educators in slum sections is the inability to keep older children enrolled in school. There are several ways in which this high dropout rate may be interpreted. The school program may be so inept and the school environment so punishing that they may contribute to the high attrition rate. Perhaps those who withdraw or are rejected represent the intellectually marginal. Perhaps they withdraw because they equate a given age with adulthood and see school as only for children. Or perhaps all three ideas possess some validity as explanations of the situation, although educators are less likely to look to the social and cultural setting for explanations than to purely pedagogical ones.

From time to time some educators have had the temerity to suggest special curricula for the so-called culturally disadvantaged, but such

1. A strict application of this interpretation would view schooling for middle-class children as a form of age-status imperialism.
2. Whether educational programs are any more or any less effective than other social betterment efforts in these areas is a moot point.

propositions are repugnant in a democracy unless they carry a magical label such as "enrichment." Even these labels can be political dynamite. Nevertheless, differential schooling already is in effect. The "track" system is justified on the basis of vocational interests and aptitudes, while in reality it divides students on the basis of class background. A further separation appears with the special treatment accorded the mentally retarded and the emotionally disturbed, most of whom are recruited from the poorer classes, as exemplified in the "600" schools in New York City.

This brief excursion into aspects of social class and education is primarily intended to show some of the complications facing both educators and anthropologists in a society where practices and ideals are not, and cannot be, in accord, and where the complexities of a culturally diverse society create conflicting values.

If the problems confronting educators seem difficult, those facing anthropologists who attempt to analyze the educational system and to work with educators seem even greater. For example, should the degree of objectivity maintained when observing initiation ceremonies among Australian aborigines be any different from that maintained when observing a school monitor system, where students selected for their size use force to punish other students who have violated school rules? Is not the principle of cultural congruency demonstrated by the discovery that physical prowess is the basis for a pattern of dominance and submission among the same students outside the school? What should be the basis for intervention in either case? As anthropologists, we have not been overly sympathetic with missionary or governmental suppression of native custom. Is it possible that we have a double set of values when confronted by behavior we label offensive in our own culture? Instead of protesting the danger of going native, should we not recognize that we are already one with the natives when we make judgmental evaluations based on their values? If our perspective and method are to be useful to American education, we must learn to keep our analysis free of culture bias to the same degree demanded in our work elsewhere. Otherwise we had better steer clear of advocating educational reform since its practitioners are far more competent than we are in their spheres.

Perhaps the distinctive role and contribution of the anthropologist in the field of education can be further clarified if we examine some specific area of research. Consideration of the informal group system of a high school student body can well serve this purpose. These groups are not areas of great concern to either school administrator or teacher, and I know of no books on school organization or curriculum, excepting those written by sociologists, which even mention the subject. From such evidence I think we are justified in concluding that educators do not consider informal grouping among students, or its absence, to be of any great relevance to the educative process. Some years ago, student peer group choices were explored when sociometrics made quite a splash; however, the interest continued for only a brief period. Like so many other innovations, the mechanics of determining student preference and rejection were adopted to serve the needs of teachers and administrators, but the flesh and blood of theory and the therapeutic goals of the method were never assimilated. Actually, small group theory in anthropology is genetically unrelated to sociometrics, although the techniques of the latter have some utility.

Three major reasons manifest the importance of informal or small group studies. First, we know that in many societies much of what a child learns is acquired from his peer group. Where education is institutionalized under the control of adults, the official knowledge of textbook and lecture must contend with the unofficial and possibly contradictory lore which children teach each other. Furthermore, knowledge and experience always are assimilated through a perceptual screen which includes the criteria for discrimination and evaluation.

The relationship between the student's informal system and that of the community and of the institutional structure of the school provides the second reason for the importance of small group studies. Hollingshead's (1949) study in Elmtown, for example, shows that the high school clique system reproduces the parental status and value systems. There are many intriguing problems in this area, such as the relationship between student and teacher cliques and the evaluations which each group makes of the other; it is obvious that we need several studies to provide us with comparative data. Research on the school has not yet established the correspondences between formal and informal systems, but the results of studies in hospitals, factories, and prisons have demonstrated such relationships.

A final reason for the importance of small group studies is covered by such rubrics as morale, organizational health, job satisfaction, and productivity. Other ways of describing these phenomena include participation and involvement, organization and communication, or executive function. Here again we must turn to industrial research to provide us with the clues to what we might expect to find. Mayo's (1933) report on the consequences of changed conditions in the textile plant upon worker behavior seems particularly relevant. In this plant, it will be remembered, the general malaise which afflicted all workers gradually disappeared as they were brought into a meaningful relationship to their environment. Arensberg's (1951) analysis of numerous such studies supports the same conclusion. A vitally important area of study is the extent and the ways in which student peer groups mediate a meaningful and participant relationship between students and the school environment.

The student system is much more than informal grouping as Gordon (1957), Coleman (1961), and Burnett (1964) have told us in their major studies of high schools. It also includes the extracurricular programs organized around student government, athletic, literary, dramatic, musical, and club activities. Events associated with these activities are highly visible and involve varying degrees of faculty assistance and control and parental participation. Extracurricular activities provide a meeting ground between school and community that is not provided in any other fashion. In addition to being viewed as an extension of the academic program, these activities represent the varied social and cultural interests of the community and, as such, serve as a training ground for them. This, however, is not the perspective emphasized by educators. Although they are well aware of this phase of school life, with some misgivings I may add, they are more concerned with program and supervision than they are with the social and cultural implications. This narrow emphasis of the educator provides the anthropologist with the opportunity, even the responsibility, to bring the systematic approach of social science analysis to this aspect of the educational system. Here the anthropologist can exercise his competency in describing the relationship between social structure and culture pattern in an institutional and community setting.

Thus, the student system is a social science problem with relevance for education, while its programmatic aspects remain the responsibility of professional educators. With this distinction, we can avoid distorting our results through culture bias. For example, the discovery that lower-class children opt for adult values and behavior at earlier ages than do middle-class children is a consequential scientific finding for educators who are programmatically concerned about dropouts. As applied anthropologists, however, we also have the right to evaluate or recommend procedures designed to change the situation in one or another direction. The ethics involved in offering such advisements have already been clearly stated by the Society for Applied Anthropology (1963–1964) and need not be elaborated here.

In order to broaden the scope of this inquiry, I will designate divisions for grouping specific problems of education, and discuss relevant anthropological theory for each of them.

There are six major areas which are broadly inclusive of the enterprise of education. These are (1) training of school personnel, (2) organization and management of schools, (3) the specification of curriculum and preparation of materials, (4) pedagogical practices, (5) the relations between school and community, and (6) philosophy of education. In no sense should these categories be considered mutually exclusive units for study. Obviously, the activities of a teacher and students in a classroom have relevance for all these, but for research purposes these items, singly or in combination, must be viewed as primarily topical. Although this does not invalidate them as appropriate research subjects, we should try to find some alternative or complementary arrangement, some frame of reference, which provides a more insightful conceptualization and serves the goals of social science as well as those of education. To do so we must turn to anthropology.

Anthropology utilizes an inductive, empirical, natural history method through which it seeks to describe the structure, pattern, and process of human behavior. It shares with other sciences the ordering of data as systems which reflect the qualities and relationships of individual items in their activities. From anthropological operations and from the results of analysis, we theorize about the connections between patterns of behavior and the forms of human grouping in stable or changing environments. We have developed theoretical formulations for many aspects of behavior. The problem here is to decide which of these areas of theory are most appropriate to educational research.

Earlier I suggested that the transmission of culture, inclusive of developing cognitive capacities and technical skills, should be the primary objective of an educational system. But the strict application of such a view would neglect the implicit, and often intended, socialization and growth of affective, evaluative capabilities, to say nothing of the purely physiological aspects. Obviously, all of these must be considered in framing research. Other ingredients in the teaching-learning process include the institutional setting, the traditional practices of school and classroom, and the relationships with other institutions in a specific community environment. Together, these items suggest four areas of applicable theory: learning theory, culture theory, theory of organization, and theory of change.

Learning theory, thus far, has not been a major concern to anthropologists. Wallace (1962) has been interested in this problem and has called attention to the contrast between stimulus-cue-response and cognitive learning. In an earlier period, Mead, Hallowell, Linton, Kardiner, and others produced useful and exciting studies of child-rearing practices which helped us understand how personality is formed in a cultural environment. Their theory, however, borrowed mainly from psychoanalysis, gave much greater emphasis to psychomotor and affective learning and behavior than to cognitive or intellectual learning. Among both anthropologists and psychologists, the implicit acceptance of the stimulus-response paradigm and of the conditioned reflex as basic neurological processes may help to explain the neglect of the distinctly human, symbolic aspects of behavior, and the processes of their acquisition. If the study of culture transmission is to be truly comprehensive, it also must be concerned with the cognitive, symbolic structure, the cultural behavior, and the social groupings within which learning occurs.

The realization of such an objective requires that we broaden our area of inquiry considerably beyond the traditional description of child-rearing practices and specification of personality formation. We must look for the congruencies between culture pattern, social grouping, and the logics of mythology and language and their relationships to the cognitive screen through which experience is received and organized.

Once this objective has been realized, we are in a better position to seek solutions to some perplexing problems, such as defining the relationships between psychomotor, affective, and cognitive learning. What consequences will ensue in the results we obtain if we shift from treating directed learning as stages in development to focusing on transition or, alternatively, to viewing learning as pattern embellishment and expansion? Can we establish cultural levels of cognitive complexity and relate these to culture and community? It seems to me that learning theory based on solutions to these problems is directly applicable to curriculum materials and pedagogy, as well as to teacher training and the philosophy of education. Actually, the inductive, natural-history approach contains a powerful learning tool and implicit learning theory.

Culture theory, in contrast, has general applicability for all aspects of education. In particular, those understandings of continuity and persistence and of pattern and congruency will be useful in tracing the origin and development of custom and in explaining their function. Education has much to learn from specific research utilizing the time and space formulations of Hall (1961) and the studies of body socialization and movement by Birdwhistell (1952). In international and cross-cultural education, many of the difficulties accompanying attempts to transfer educational systems from one culture to another without taking into account the distinctive culture patterns of the recipient culture could be alleviated or eliminated if these anthropological concepts were available.

Theory of organization has particular relevance for the training of administrators, for school organization and management, and for relations between school and community. Studies in industry can contribute both method and theory to this area of interest which is shared with some sociologists and social psychologists. The contributions of many individuals in these several fields are worthy of close study, specifically Arensberg, Richardson, Whyte, Hughes, Becker, Rossi, Sanders, and Sayles. Atwood (1964) has already demonstrated the utility of interaction theory in school organization. One significant question, of course, is the extent to which custodial or supervisory practice facilitates or impedes the learning process. When we examine the dimensions of school and community relations, we encounter a much broader and less clearly defined area, but the technique of event analysis should help to place schools in the institutional setting of the community.

Theory to deal with problems of educational innovation and change comes from anthropology's long-standing interest in culture growth and spread, and from its more recent concern with the forms of human groupings and their dynamics, as well as with the relationship between culture and community. Anthropology's natural-history approach leads us to the processes of transformation, either those affecting the individual as they may be observed in rites of passage, or those of group and community as seen in stress or in the stabilizing rites of intensification. From this perspective, we seek to understand the process of group formation, modification, or dissolution, as well as what happens with individual induction or expulsion. The notable accomplishments of applied anthropology in the theory and procedure of innovation and change should give us confidence that the principles and procedures we have already tested also are applicable to educational problems and processes.

These, then, are the areas of anthropological research competence and theoretical concern which seem to have special relevance for education. The insistence upon framing problems in social science terms does not negate the importance of problems as they are seen and described by educators. It is our task, however, to translate these into research problems where our theory and techniques can apply. Also, the perspective and inductive methodology characteristic of our discipline can make additional and unanticipated contributions.[3]

COMMENTARY: Malcolm Collier
       Elizabeth Eddy
       William P. McLure

Malcolm Collier

I would like to discuss two points made by Professor Kimball which have relevance to my recent preparation of anthropological materials for high school social study courses. The points to which I refer involve (1) the question of students having a meaningful relationship to their environment (although Kimball meant total environment, I am referring to the educational environment only), and (2) the question of con-

---

3. Although I have given no attention to the introduction of anthropology as subject matter in school curricula, this omission is not an oversight. In my opinion, it is not the content of class materials, as much as the manner in which they are organized and presented, that is important. If materials about the American Indian are taught in the traditional fashion, it is history and nothing more.

tinuity between the world of the school and the world outside the school.

It has occurred to me recently that undergraduate anthropology courses tend to be taught as if the students were to become anthropologists. Thirty years ago this was almost invariably the case, and these courses provided the groundwork for future learning in greater depth. My materials for high school students, on the other hand, assume that the teacher and the students in some sense already are anthropologists. While there are a number of ways in which this assumption is manifested in the materials, I will mention only a few. The students are given casts of stone tools and fossil bone materials and, although not able to examine actual archaeological sites, they do scrutinize site maps, read translations of tablets, and encounter ethnographic materials rather than syntheses of them. Perhaps this is an exceptional approach for high school students, but it is a useful one. After four years, we are beginning to see effects which are more than just initial reactions to an experimental situation in the schools.

The use of these curricular materials helps to create a meaningful relationship to the educational environment by allowing the students to act as if they were already anthropologists. It docs this by changing their environment; that is, learning becomes meaningful to life because it is something the student does rather than something that happens to him. Conceivably, it even becomes something to do outside of school. Also, when students and teachers both behave as anthropologists, a continuity is established between the school and the outside world, which is the continuity or discontinuity to which Professor Kimball refers. It seems to me that this is the only kind of link between the school and the world which does not mean bringing the world into the school. The latter is what really happens in extracurricular activities. No extracurricular program disguised to simulate the real world can take the place of a student's understanding of knowledge as an actual process and an understanding that this process is the same inside the school as it is outside. It would be difficult for students to make the connection between these two worlds if this kind of learning were not allowed to take place in the schools.

Although I have concentrated on the pedagogy of these curriculum materials, the anthropological content of the materials also serves to reinforce the relevancy of these points. Anthropological materials impart a particular sense of daily life and of common humanity which is relevant to the student's relationship to his educational environment and to his establishment of continuity between the school and the outside world.

As Dr. Kimball stated, education and anthropology are both concerned with the transmission of culture. To anthropologists, this notion automatically includes the perceptions of what culture is; for educators, I think that the perception of culture is sharpened by an acquaintance with anthropological curricular materials, which may increase the educator's effectiveness in transmitting culture.

Elizabeth Eddy

In responding to Professor Kimball's paper, I will try to state and expand its primary contribution to anthropology and education and will indicate some of its implication for new training approaches in the combined fields of anthropology and education.

Essentially, Dr. Kimball discusses a number of problems of concern to educators and redefines them in anthropological terms, so that anthropologists can work on them in a manner meaningful to both the educator and the anthropologist. When the educator knocks on the door of the anthropologist, he has a specific problem or problems. Usually, these have to do with school personnel training, school organization and management, curriculum materials, pedagogical practice, school-community relations, and educational philosophy and practice.

What is implied is that the educator comes not only with problems but also with a proposed solution — that of employing an anthropologist to alleviate or solve his problems. Usually, the anthropologist is requested to teach a course or two in a training program for educators or to serve as a consultant to educators seeking to understand the cultural aspects of a particular problem. Less common, although growing in importance, is the request for research on the educational system. It is important to add that the educator may view the anthropologist as a new educational technique to make students or others more sensitive to cultural factors relevant to education.

If anthropologists are to make a real contribution to education, they need to redefine educational problems, bringing to educators an understanding of theories of culture, organization, and cultural innovation. Anthropologists must work as anthropologists and, in their relationships with educators, uphold the traditions of their discipline. Of these, objectivity is a particularly difficult problem for, in effect, the anthropologist is studying his own educational system. In addition to the potential biases Professor Kimball mentioned, biases arise both consciously and unconsciously as a result of being a graduate of the system and of having long-standing attitudes toward schools and school personnel.

If those anthropological insights discussed by Dr. Kimball are to be diffused in our educational system, the work of applying anthropology to education must be done at the grass-roots level — not by anthropologists, but by classroom teachers and school administrators with sufficient anthropological training to change the manner in which they define and attempt to solve educational problems.

From the past experience of other social sciences, notably psychology and sociology, we can anticipate that educators will choose those elements of anthropology which seem to best fit their traditions. It also seems likely that educators increasingly will ask for specialized courses and departments in educational anthropology. Even if anthropology is given a place in the school or department of education, most students in the immediate future will take only one or two of these courses, and only a few will do advanced work. Effective training is further hindered by the fact that these courses are frequently given early in the student's career and are separated in time from "methods" courses and student teaching.

The question is whether or not anthropologists can develop and use more fully other kinds of institutional settings for the training of students whose specialty is education rather than anthropology. One possibility is the department of anthropology with a good percentage of undergraduates majoring in anthropology who go on to careers as classroom teachers in our public schools. Traditionally, the anthropology department is separated from the teacher education program. Yet it offers courses taken by students in the teacher education program. These students frequently fail to see any relationship between anthropology and the work for which they are preparing. An anthropologist's training should enable him to perceive more fully the social and cultural settings within which these students will teach and to ask questions about the relevance of anthropology to these settings. What, for example, *does* the anthropology major need to know and experience in a department of anthropology to enable him to make the transition into the professional corporate world where he becomes a teacher or, for that matter, a doctor, nurse, or social worker? As educators, do anthropologists need to define their own educational problems and, if so, can this create a basically anthropological perspective? Can we not only introduce courses in urban anthropology, but also develop departments of anthropology which are attuned and responsive to the needs of an urban world and to the needs of students in our courses who will not become anthropologists?

My purpose in raising these questions is not to underestimate the importance of present work with educators, but to ask whether those who are educators and anthropologists can be a source of educational innovation and change within their own departments to influence and to develop education in new ways. If so, we might have a far greater influence on educational development in the modern world than we now anticipate.

William P. McLure

I believe Professor Kimball defines educators as the professionals who comprise the organized school system. If so, he is indirectly talking about government, because educational systems represent government. Education is, therefore, more than the public school system; it includes other institutions closely associated with the formal schools, such as universities involved in the preparation of teachers. While school systems may be described as gate-keepers of society, they have many open doors to social controls, perhaps too many, resulting in some irrelevances and interferences.

In this context, is a promising sign that disciplines such as anthropology are interested in making contributions to education, although not all members of a discipline need to be directly interested in anthropological interpretations in education. The unique mission of any discipline is to advance knowledge, and it is the job of education to glean whatever knowledge it can use. If disciplines such as anthropology tend toward bureaucratic expansion for purposes other than advancing knowledge, jurisdictional quarrels might develop, but it would be interesting to see if such a trend might provoke education to become more interested in anthropology.

As education increases in complexity, more and more specialists trained in a variety of disciplines will enter the educational sphere for research purposes and related roles. Anthropologists and others also may make unique contributions to education within their own disciplines.

REFERENCES

Arensberg, C. M. 1951. Behavior and Organization: Industrial Studies. Social Psychology at the Crossroads, eds. John H. Rohrer et al. Harper & Brothers: New York.

Atwood, M. 1964. Small-Scale Administrative Change: Resistance to the Introduction of a High School Guidance Program. Innovation in Education, ed. Matthew B. Mills Teachers College Press: New York.

Birdwhistell, R. L. 1952. Introduction to Kinesics. Department of State, Foreign Service Institute: Washington, D.C.

Burnett, J. H. 1964. A Participant Observation Study of a Sociocultural Sub-System of the Students in a Small Rural High School. Unpublished doctoral (Ph.D.) dissertation. Columbia University.

Coleman, J. S. 1961. The Adolescent Society: The Social Life of the Teenager and its Impact on Education. Free Press: Glencoe.

Gordon, W. 1957. The Social System of the High School. Free Press: Glencoe.

Hall, E. T. 1961. The Silent Language. Premier Book: Greenwich, Connecticut.

Henry, J. 1963. Attitude Organization in Elementary School Classrooms. Education and Culture, ed. George D. Spindler. Holt, Rinehart and Winston: New York.

Hollingshead, A. B. 1949. Elmtown's Youth. Wiley: New York.

Kimball, S. T. 1966. The Transmission of Culture. The Body of Knowledge Unique to the Profession of Education, pp. 45–70. Pi Lambda Theta: Washington, D.C.

Landes, R. 1965. Culture in American Education. Wiley: New York.

Mayo, E. 1933. The Human Problems of an Industrial Civilization. Macmillan: New York.

Sexton, P. C. 1961. Education and Income. Viking Press: New York.

Society for Applied Anthropology. 1963–1964. Statement on Ethics of the Society for Applied Anthropology. Human Organization 22 (4).

Spindler, G. 1959. The Transmission of American Culture. Harvard University Press: Cambridge.

Wallace, A. 1962. Culture and Cognition. Science 135:351–57.

Warner, W. L., R. Havighurst, and M. Loeb. 1944. Who Shall Be Educated? Harper & Brothers: New York.

CHAPTER **5**   Jules Henry

Normal and Abnormal Behavior

My many encounters with the singular problem of deciding what is
normal or abnormal behavior in families of psychotic children[1] have
led to the present reconsideration of the major issues involved.[2] While
analyzing detailed daily observations of such families, I found it almost
too difficult to make judgments with confidence. Consequently, I confined myself largely to describing behavior and interpreting it in relation
to family history and interaction. Although little difficulty exists in evaluating gross symptoms of psychosis, we sail without a compass under a
dead sky when evaluating other behaviors (Henry, 1947, 1949, 1966b,
1967).

In my daily clinical observations and research, I have become aware
that I intuitively refer behavior to certain "invariants" (Henry, 1953,
1954, 1958). This paper is an attempt to elucidate some of these
clinically derived constants with little regard for such existential problems as what decent human behavior is; whether an entire civilization
can be sick for four thousand years; or whether the so-called sick are
often in better mental health than the so-called normal.[3]

1. This study was made possible by a grant from the Sonia Shankman Ortho-
genic School of the University of Chicago.
2. This paper was prepared during the author's tenure as Fellow of the Center
for Advanced Study in the Behavioral Sciences.
3. For a further discussion of these and related issues, see von Mering and
Mulhare, *Anthropological Perspectives on Socialization*, ch. 3, in E. James Anthony and Therese Benedek, eds. *Parenthood — Its Psychology and Psychopathology*, Little, Brown & Co., Boston, 1970.

A clinical report, oriented toward the pathognomic significance of action, suffers from serious epistemological limitations. In the interest of clarity on empirical issues, other issues which still belong in the realm of social criticism rather than clinical judgment must momentarily be set aside. Regardless of how we abhor the expression "clinical judgment" and regardless of how it seems to exclude the existential, clinical judgments must be made so criteria must be explored.

In any culture, the normal is assumed to be what is culturally acceptable and the abnormal is what is not acceptable. The criteria for determining when a transgression has occurred are culturally determined and largely intuitive. I know that absolute power bestows the right to transgress all criteria and that such a thing as a "socially patterned defect"[4] is an ambiguity characteristic of our culture. I also am aware that my relativistic distinction between normal and abnormal begs the issue of generalized human suffering and mental health. However, since this paper must be limited, I shall address myself solely to the criteria of normal and abnormal.

Invariants

While all cultures establish their own criteria of the normal, judgments of normality are intuitively based on certain factors found in all cultures (Henry, 1963, 1966a). I call these universal factors invariants, although they lack the constancy of invariants in the exact sciences and cannot be given rigorous definition. Since it probably is impossible to identify all of them, and since such an effort would carry me beyond the limits of this paper, I will discuss only the following: (1) circumspection; (2) circles of approval, affection, and communication; (3) perception; (4) communication; and (5) contradiction.

Circumspection

All cultures link people together systematically in relations of time, space, motion, and objects. Work is performed at certain times, at a certain pace, and with certain people who handle certain objects and not others. Another expression of the linkage of time, space, objects, and people is living together in one house or living far apart during

4. We owe this useful expression to Erich Fromm. See his *The Sane Society,* Holt, Rinehart & Winston, Inc., New York, 1956.

certain times of the year or during certain periods of the life cycle. At certain ages, children need to be close to their mothers while, at other ages, they can be separated. At certain ages, children can be high off the ground while at others they cannot. People must appear at certain times at certain places in order to perform certain tasks or obligations.

Circumspection has been called the inherent characteristic of the human mind that enables it to put things together. While circumspection is an inherent capacity of *homo sapiens*, it is expressed in different ways in different cultures. Every culture makes demands on circumspective capabilities and failure to meet these demands is considered abnormal. When people lack circumspection, they are "pathogenic" in that particular culture.

Circles of Approval, Affection, and Communication

All cultures offer the individual an inviolable series of concentric circles[5] of approval and affection. In our culture, under normal conditions parents and children are the center of the series; usually one seeks approval and affection first and foremost from within the nuclear family. Then come friends and, as one gets older, friends may become more important than family. Beyond the circle of friends may lie school acquaintances or teachers. Associated with each circle is a convention of communication: vocabulary, forms of discourse, and content.

Other cultures have different dispositions of approval, affection, and communication. Whatever the culture, "normal" people understand the limitations of each circle: they do not seek affection in circles where it is not expected; do not communicate inappropriately; do not seek affection from those expected only to approve; do not seek approval or affection from those normally indifferent; and they do not seek conversation with or information from the wrong people. "Abnormal" people violate the circles.

Perception

Perception is culturally determined within certain limits. Those perceptions not culturally determined are apodeictic — perceptions from which certain inferences necessarily follow. A boomerang is a stick, *culturally defined* as a throwing stick. But the perception of its

5. Other images may be more suitable to other cultures.

rigidity, hardness, weight, and extension is apodeictic perception, from which certain inferences necessarily follow and which, therefore, are perceived by normal people. That a throwing stick is heavier than a feather is a perception not affected by culture; the fact that it is to be thrown is culturally defined. Normal people infer from its rigidity that it cannot be bent, that it will not lose its shape if placed in water, that it cannot be poured, that it can compress soft material like flesh, and so on.

The ability to perceive an object in its apodeictic state and relations is normal. If a throwing stick is perceived to be rubbery, perception is disturbed or abnormal. Apodeictic inference is least vulnerable to abnormal communication. Disturbance in apodeisis, such as perceiving solids to flow or seeing a rigid surface as rubbery and then acting accordingly is probably the most ominous symptom of abnormality.

The ability to grasp and act on the *denotative* qualities of objects is another sign of normality. To be able to perceive a bow and arrow or a gun as a weapon is normal. To perceive these things as food would be abnormal. To be able to perceive food as such is another mark of the ability to grasp common denotative significance; not to be able to is abnormal.

The ability to accept *connotative* meanings characteristic of one's culture is also normal. To perceive a person as a man is a simple denotative perception, but to perceive him as "sacred" is to accept a culturally defined connotation. In the Southern states, for a white man to perceive the Negro as a human being is a serious violation of culturally-determined connotative meaning and is abnormal.

It is impossible to make a rigorous distinction between perception and communication, since perception usually takes place in a social context. This overlap is particularly important in parent-child relations, where the normal parent endeavors to clarify culturally defined perceptions for his child and does not scramble, distort, or disallow the child's perceptions. He does not insist that things are there when by cultural definition they are absent; he does not negate the child's perception when it is correct; and he does not distort apodeictic configuration.[6]

---

6. We understand that "thereness," *das da es gibt,* is culturally determined and tends to be a rubbery category in some cultures.

The fundamental invariants of perception — the apodeictic, the denotative, and the connotative — are universals and form a basis for intuitive judgments of normality and abnormality.

Communication

Communication involves not only the ability to speak, to understand the language, and to adopt the kinesic system, it also includes the ability to put the required amount of redundance into each utterance; ability to comment on one's own utterance in culturally prescribed ways — by intonation, facial expressions, etc.; and ability to suit the amount and character of discourse to the occasion. In our culture, we do not make jokes at funerals or speak of death at weddings, nor do we talk too long to persons placed higher than ourselves. A book could be written on the subject of universal requirements of normal discourse. Every culture has rules for the relative emphasis of subjects and predicates in particular situations, as well as limits on how frequently one subject may be shifted to another subject.[7] Violation of these rules leads to the judgment of abnormal.

Contradiction

Contradiction is present when two mutually incompatible propositions are held to be true. It enables us to bridge the gap between propositions related to cognition and the experience of being a feeling human, and the gap between objective analytics and existential analytics.

Although all human beings can perceive contradiction, the culture determines which contradictions shall be perceived, which propositions shall be asserted as contradictory, and which contradictions shall be admitted to be contradictory. Every culture establishes areas in which contradiction may be recognized, and only an abnormal person would assert a contradiction where the culture sees none. For example, the government of the United States officially defines our role in the war in Viet Nam as peace-maintaining and nation-building; it is somewhat "abnormal" to perceive it as war-maintaining and nation-destroying. At

7. On the general issue, see E. von Domarus, "The Specific Laws of Logic in Schizophrenia," in *Language and Thought in Schizophrenia,* edited by J. S. Kasanin, University of California Press, Berkeley, 1944.

the same time, the relative tolerance accorded such abnormal opinions illustrates that cultures vary in the extent they allow the perception of contradiction. An extension of this is sham, which exists where contradiction is perceived but denied.

A main factor in the etiology of illnesses called emotional is the presence of contradiction within a family when members, particularly children, are compelled to deny the existence of any contradictions. Most obvious of such contradictions is the verbal assertion of love, but its denial in action, for the child is forced to act as if he were loved, and is denied the right to act as if he were not. Thus, in our culture, the complex of such pathogenic contradiction is affirmation in words and denial in action which compels the object of the contradiction to act as if the affirmation were reality. The compulsion to act as if the affirmation were not denied is an indispensable element in the development of pathology from contradiction. Under these circumstances the object of the contradiction, such as a child, survives best either by pretending or learning not to see it. In Albee's *Tiny Alice,* Brother Julian was finally shot for not recognizing sham as reality.

There are many other circumstances within a family or within a social system where patent contradictions must be denied. For example, a parent does something for his own good, affirms that it is for the child's good, and then insists that the child act as if he did not see that it was for the parent's good. A confused parent is unclear in what he says, but insists that the child act as if he had been clear. A parent is tyrannical, but insists that the family act as if he were gentle and permissive. The most pathogenic effects are achieved when the child is severely punished for failing to act as if the contradiction did not exist. For example, a mother seduces a child by insisting that he come to her regularly to have his penis washed gently with soap and warm water, but beats him for being an "animal" if he attempts to masturbate against her, the implicit denial being that she is not seducing him.

All cultures define areas where contradictions are denied and areas where they may be admitted, where sham is the basis of social interchange, and where truth is permitted. Failure to observe the conventions of contradiction is usually punished, the severity depending on the culture, the convention violated, and who perpetrated it. In tribal social systems the phenomenon most commonly denied is fear;

that is to say, *A* fears *B* but must act as if he did not. The moment he starts acting as if he fears *B*, *B* might kill him.[8]

In our culture the most lethal form of contradiction involves love — probably because of its serious self-reinforcing circular effects. Mrs. X prefers her son Johnny to her other son Billy, but insists she loves them equally and reacts violently to Billy's perceptions and statements of truth. She then humiliates Billy while insisting she loves him, and punishes him for reacting against this humiliation. The dialectic consequence of this tension brings Johnny and his mother closer together and thus alienates Billy still further. Such a vicious circle is seriously destructive to Billy, who is torn between his rage, grief, and hatred on the one hand, and his need to dissemble on the other. At the same time, Mrs. X perceives that he is dissembling and punishes him for it — in her eyes he has become a fake.[9]

Close scrutiny reveals the pathogenic sequence in action. For example, equal love for all children, which is culturally valued, is denied by favoritism: gentleness is denied by tyranny and violence; and the linguistic criterion of redundancy is denied by scrambling. While cultural values are cancelled in the interaction, the negation cannot be admitted. Consideration of the universal human capacity to perceive and to deny contradiction opens the pathway to an examination of such concepts as repression, dissimulation, denial, and reaction formation.

Illustrative Situations

My clinical observations made during specific case studies of families of psychotic children illustrate the problems of interpreting behavior in relation to the invariants of circumspection, communication, and contradiction. Generally, I reserve judgment as to whether the behavior described is normal or abnormal.

Circumspection
Second day:
On the second day of my visit, Mrs. Jones and I were sitting on the front porch steps. Harriet, her sixteen-and-a-half-month-old baby, was playing

8. This situation existed among the Kaingang, for example. See Jules Henry, *Jungle People: A Kaingang Tribe of the Highlands of Brazil*, J. J. Augustin, New York, 1941 (out of print). Reprinted by Random House, New York, 1964.

9. These phenomena of affirmation, denial, compulsion and punishment are related to the double bind, yet more exists in contradiction, including the dialectic, than the double bind.

nearby. Harriet would run down to the edge of a walk leading to the road, whereupon Mrs. Jones would run after her in a jolly way and catch her just before she got into the road. The baby would laugh joyously, taking it as a game, and Mrs. Jones had to run after her two or three times to prevent her from running into the road.

Sixth day:

Our backs were turned only for a moment before Harriet was almost in the middle of the road. A huge oil truck came tearing around the corner, missing the baby by about ten feet. When we returned to the porch, the chasing game between Harriet and her mother began again. After Mrs. Jones had chased the baby twice, I asked her, "Do you like this?" She first said "No," but changed it to "I do." When the baby ran off a third time I asked, "Would you like me to chase her?" And she said with apparent relief, "Oh, please do!" When I chased the baby, she extended her arms to be picked up. That was the end of her running because the real fun was to be picked up by her mother.

Tenth day:

Dr. Jones, who is a dentist, and Mrs. Jones and I were talking to neighbors. Suddenly we looked around, and Harriet was again in the road. The Joneses have a peculiar faith that Reggie, their dog, can bring Harriet back. When they sent Reggie after Harriet, the dog obviously did not understand his mission. He ran barking in Harriet's direction, but passed the baby and did nothing to head her off. Twice this afternoon the baby went into the middle of the road where cars were passing, and both times they sent Reggie after her before they went tearing after her themselves.

It might be too much to expect an ordinary mother to understand that when she makes running toward the road a warm and jolly game, she is teaching her baby to court danger. But one can expect an ordinary mother to prevent her very young child from running toward the road, and it also seems reasonable to expect even a stupid mother to stop playing such a game after her child has narrowly escaped from being hit by a truck. Consequently, we may infer that Mrs. Jones lacks the kind of circumspection that enables her to connect running toward, and getting into, the road with possible death. The most bizarre expression of this absence of circumspection is sending Reggie after the baby in the presence of a clear and visible danger. Here, husband and wife, in the *folie à deux,* stereotype dogs as faithful, intelligent, all-knowing savers of human beings.

In another example, Mrs. Jones seemed to believe that it would be easier to get Harriet to eat if she did not fill her up at meal times but, because Harriet often seemed to be hungry, Mrs. Jones constantly gave her bits of food between meals. This is useful to bear in mind, although not crucial to the understanding of the complex of observations that follow.

Fifth day:

Mrs. Jones had to give some medicine to Harriet, who had diarrhea for several days. Dr. Jones thinks Harriet has a "bug." It wouldn't surprise me if it was picked up right in the Jones household, because Mrs. Jones never puts the butter away, saying it gets so hard in the refrigerator that it becomes too difficult to use. She butters Harriet's toast with butter that is almost liquid. She is almost as careless with the milk, which she lets stand uncovered in the summer. She puts everything else imaginable in the refrigerator, making it difficult to get things in and out.

At any rate, Mrs. Jones mixed Harriet's medicine with the uncovered, unrefrigerated milk. Harriet was supposed to get the medicine six times a day but, although I was in the house until 8 P.M., Harriet received her medicine only once, at 2 P.M. This seems to be evidence of Mrs. J's sloppiness rather than anything else, for she appears to be mad about the kid: she constantly smiles at her and puts her forehead to the baby's, and the baby responds warmly.

When I saw Mrs. Jones give medicine to Harriet the next day, I asked her whether she had been able to give the baby her medicine regularly; she replied that she had given Harriet the medicine the prescribed number of times the day before.

Harriet still has diarrhea. Mrs. Jones fed her at lunch time and then suddenly remembered that she had completely forgotten to give the baby her "cocktail," by which she meant her milk mixed with medicine. When Dr. Jones asked her at lunch whether she was giving the baby skimmed milk she said yes, although the milk she was using was actually homogenized. On the eighth day of my stay, Harriet still had diarrhea.

Comment on this situation is scarcely necessary except, perhaps, to underscore the fact that, even as Mrs. Jones was making disorganized attempts to care for Harriet's diarrhea, she might have been promoting it by using milk that had been standing around and by using homogenized milk instead of the skimmed milk her husband had instructed her to use. Thus, lack of circumspection again led to biologically inappropriate behavior and the courting of death.

Those influenced by psychoanalytic theory might impute the "death wish" to these parents yet, after observing Mrs. Jones closely for nine days from morning to night, I became convinced that she loved and even doted on Harriet, but in her own way. The fact that the baby sought her mother in a relaxed and joyous way is the best proof one can have that the baby loved her mother in return.

Communication

The following are examples of scrambling perception through communication. Mr. Wilson confused his six-year-old daughter as to what television program she was watching. In this way he scrambled signals coming to his child from the outside world.

When Mr. Wilson came into the livingroom, Norma, who was half watching *Robin Hood,* became absorbed in her doll, and wandered off into another room. Her father turned to a horse opera, which he likes very much. When Norma came back, she asked whether *Robin Hood* was on; her father told her it would be over in ten minutes. Norma became confused. She didn't know whether or not she was looking at *Robin Hood.* Of course, *Robin Hood* was on and would be over in ten minutes, but on a different channel, not now visible on the screen. Mr. Wilson kept Norma thinking she was looking at *Robin Hood* and at the same time not looking at it. I found the whole thing very confusing. After ten minutes, Mr. Wilson said, *"Robin Hood* is all over; now it's time to go to bed." Norma looked completely nonplussed and befuddled; I admit that I was befuddled too.

In the next example, four-year-old Georgie Ross was ill and running a fever. I slept in Georgie's room. At 5:55 A.M. his mother came in.

. . . He was complaining of pain in his ear and stomach, but she kept telling him, "your ear and stomach don't hurt, but your neck hurts. . . ." She said he had a lot of congestion in his chest, and was warm. Whenever he said that some part of his body hurt, such as his ear, stomach, teeth, or head, she would say it didn't hurt. At 9:07, she said, "Your head can't hurt because I gave you aspirin."
Georgie woke up at 10:15 A.M. He started to whimper and his mother went in and asked him, "What is the matter, darling?" She touched him and said that his temperature had gone up, and she called Dr. Koch.
Several times today Georgie wandered around pitifully, saying, "I have a cherry in my tummy." Mrs. Ross tried to get him to explain what he meant by a cherry: she asked him its shape, and its roundness, making a circle with forefinger and thumb, and he said, "Yes." Then she asked him if it was this shape, crossing her fingers, and he said, "yes." She asked him how big it was, and he indicated with his hands it was a rectangle about six inches

by two. Although he did not seem distressed about it, she did. Twice when he said that he had a cherry in his tummy she picked him up, held him tenderly, and kissed him. Georgie asked her to take the cherry out.

What is most striking in this case in Mrs. Ross's rejection of Georgie's reasonably probable accurate inner perception of his own physical condition, and her fascination with the improbable — the cherry in the tummy.

Contradiction

The final extracts from field notes taken of the Lewis family in whose house I lived for a week, illustrate the problem of contradiction.

Irving Lewis is thirteen-and-a-half years old; his brother Ben is twelve. Ben is acquiescent and is his parents' favorite; Irving is resistive and is, at best, only second in their affections. Both parents frequently spoke belittlingly of Irving, but always praised Ben. The following is a conversation with Mrs. Lewis on the subject.

Mrs. Lewis said that Irving says his parents like Ben better than him. She wondered why he said this, and I said. "Don't you like Ben better than Irving?" Instead of answering this question she proceeded to tell me what a nice boy Ben is and how selfish Irving is, saying Ben always does things for people and lets things slide, while Irving is always kicking up a fuss. She can't figure out how Irving knows they like Ben better. It puzzles her and Mr. Lewis tremendously. "What do we do," she wonders, "to let Irving know we like Ben better than him? After all, don't we treat them both alike? Anything we do for Ben we also do for Irving." When pressed she would not say directly that they like Ben better, but she kept on saying how you can't help but like Ben because he is such a nice boy.

Affectionate physical contacts between the Lewis parents and their children are rare and both boys shrink from them when offered. Neither boy approaches a parent except when he wants something material. Ben, however, does what he is told and never flies into rages; Irving has frequent rages. Below are some notes bearing on Irving:

Mr. Lewis yelled angrily at Irving. After a while Irving went upstairs and his father yelled after him. One of the things he said was, "Who are you?" In the context, it was belittling, and Irving answered back. Then Mr. Lewis said, "You don't respect your parents." Irving answered, "You don't respect me." This, of course, is the crux of the matter, and was followed by a dead silence.

On the following day Irving and Ben had one of their usual fights and, although Ben was obviously winning, Mr. Lewis interfered angrily, blaming Irving. Irving flew into a rage, struck his father, locked himself in the bathroom on the lower floor, and proceeded to have some mild respiratory trouble. His parents, in rage and anxiety, fearing suicide, tried to persuade Irving to come out.

A great deal of conversation took place between Irving and his parents, particularly between Irving and his mother. Mr. and Mrs. Lewis mixed efforts at appeasement with hostile comments on Irving's behavior. We had originally decided to go to the park that evening, and Mrs. Lewis said to Irving, "We're going now, and you'll be left behind." Irving shouted, tearfully, "Go ahead!" His mother kept telling him to come out. I cannot remember very much of what was said as the parents stood outside the bathroom door, but it was mostly inadequate to the situation and continued to enrage Irving, even after his coughing had quieted down. His tearful voice could be heard through the door. One of the things he kept saying was, "You cause me so much heartache in this house. I have nothing but heartache in this house. You blame everything on me. You are doing to me what you did to Abe."[10]

Mrs. Lewis promised Irving he could stay up as long as he wanted, watching his favorite TV show. She said, "Come on out, Irving, you'll miss your favorite TV show," but Irving clamored back, "You never do anything for me." She protested how much she had done, and this was mixed with hostile rebuttals of his accusations. Mr Lewis's statements were mostly hostile rebuttals of what Irving had said. Every time his mother reminded him of what she had done for him, Irving became sarcastic and told her how great she was. Mr. and Mrs. Lewis spoke of their love for him, and Irving ridiculed them. When Mr Lewis accused Irving of wanting to cause the family pain, Irving said they caused him a great deal of pain.

This family situation seems to illustrate the following: (1) the existence of the vicious cycle described in my discussion of contradiction; (2) the consequences; and (3) differing results of a virtuous cover-up, as in Ben's case, and of frankness, as in Irving's.

Conclusion

The preceding has been a discussion of the nature of certain types of universal invariants which underlie intuitive judgments of normal and abnormal behavior. Singled out for special scrutiny have been the invariants of circumspection, contradiction, and communication. This

10. Abe was a very severely emotionally disturbed brother in an institution.

discussion strongly supports the argument that the dynamic interrelationship of these invariants constitutes the structural underpinning of culture.

Many other such invariants are identifiable and their workings in everyday life can be analyzed in the same way. Thus, all cultures have rules for "dependency behavior." Similarly, in any culture there are established conditions under which people must make themselves available to others. All cultures have evidential criteria of truth and mendacity. Moreover, every culture formulates the criteria for emotional expression, thereby ordering its content on such bases as age, sex, class, and occasion. Indeed, wherever man has lived, the total content of culture is apportioned by such variables so that no one group bears the entire cultural burden. These rules and criteria are the conventional bases for the judgment of normality.

All cultures have some measure of tolerance for deviation. These tolerances vary, depending upon which rules are transgressed, the number of rules transgressed, and the extent and frequency of violation. Gross abnormalities, called psychoses, are probably a combination of several transgressions and their mutually reinforcing circular interlocks. Thus, massive environmental interventions which seem to attack the underlying structures of culture appear to be of paramount significance in producing individual psychotic behavior. When these structures are attacked in this way, there is no reason why the metabolization of adrenachrome should *not* be disturbed. At the very least, they constitute the triggering mechanism of such gross forms of human aberration.

In sum, this formulation of the evidential bases of normality goes beyond simple pragmatics, stating that "normality is what the culture says it is," as well as beyond Karen Horney's qualitative and quantitative criteria (1939, 1945). It points to structures underlying all culture and thus broadens the idea of an inherent, biocultural underpinning for human existence; it also points to ways in which gross interferences with these structures can produce "abnormal" behavior in man.

COMMENTARY: John Whiting
Ari Kiev
Anthony F. C. Wallace

John Whiting

Dr. Henry pointed out the false dichotomy between assuming that mental disorder is the same in all respects and recognizable throughout the world, independent of culture, and of assuming that mental disorder is entirely culturally determined with no way of defining mental illness in one culture compared with another. Dr. Henry touched only briefly on the question of whether there are differences in the psychiatric problems or in the conflicts from one culture to another. I would like to present some evidence to support the hypothesis that different cultures have different problems. It would help to understand the complex relationship between culture and the deviant individual by recognizing cultural differences. Knowing what the problems are in dealing with any member of a different culture or society will provide a shortcut to understanding the individual.

The values study in the Southwest published by Vogt and Albert (1966) gives some evidence for this hypothesis. Sometime in the history of three of these cultures some kind of social crisis, e.g., continuous intrusive contact with the dominant white population, led to drastic action, particularly in shifting the social structure, the household, and family organization. Such exaggerated demands were made on the children to meet this crisis that many members of the culture would have been in serious trouble without a culturally acceptable outlet.

Let me reify and almost humanize culture for a minute. To defend its members from the conflicts it has engendered, each culture sets up some defenses that, if manifested by individuals in some other culture, would be defined as neurotic and deviant. These defenses are not only accepted, but often ritually required by the culture in question; the culture provides a permitted form of neurosis that is an outlet and defense for the individuals under conflict. A member of this culture can accept this neurosis and not be considered a deviant; however, if he chooses another neurosis, he will be called a deviant.

One example exists in the Zuni culture. Archaeological evidence indicates that the Zuni lived in scattered homesteads in about A.D. 1,000. The dwelling size suggests that the families were independent and the households were nuclear and probably monogamous. Then, within a very short period of time, these small scattered homesteads disappeared and were replaced by the condensed pueblos found in the Southwest today. The independent nuclear family had been replaced by the extended matri-local family and household characterizing the present Zuni culture.

The worst thing a modern Zuni can be is mean. This value is expressed by the well-known method of child-rearing, the "Scare Katchina." A Zuni, dressed in mask and regalia to represent a god, knocks at the door with a basket and a knife in his hand and says, "Are there any naughty children here? Children who have been mean?" The mother looks around and says, "No-o-o, I don't think so. Anyway, they'll be good after this." He says, "But I'm hungry," and the children run behind their mother and, protected by her, are led off from this punishing spirit. Cross-cultural evidence suggests that these strong feelings against aggression are the consequence of some crisis which took place about A.D. 1,000. In cultures which have extended family households, child-rearing practices are found to be severe in order to control the expression of aggression, since the children cannot fight or be mean if they are going to live in close quarters.

It is my hypothesis that this demand puts such severe strain on the individual that some cultural defense must be provided. Witchcraft, one cultural defense for the Zuni, works in the following way. Since meanness is bad and harmony is good, it is believed that if a person is not harmonious, he cannot be a Zuni. So a non-harmonious or mean member of the society must be a witch and not a true Zuni. If he is clearly mean be may be executed in a hostile and expressive way—he is hung by his heels and clubbed to death.

My theory is that when a culture requires the hostility that is part of human nature to be completely inhibited, that culture must provide a culturally acceptable outlet for those who cannot comply. To be able to diagnose a Zuni, one should know that witchcraft is the permitted defensive system of this culture. Knowledge of the dynamics and meaning of the culturally permitted beliefs and expected ritual, such as witchcraft, is quite important for understanding the individuals within that culture.

Let me illustrate the use of permitted defense or outlets in our own culture. A group of Texans living next door to the Zuni were also a part of this values study of the Southwest. They also have undergone a change in family structure, but a change almost directly opposite to that of the Zuni. They came from England with an extended Elizabethan family where aggression was not permitted and obedience was required. When they moved to this country, the extended family broke up into nuclear families and the young men went West. The taboo on independence and aggressiveness was replaced by the dominant and essential value of success. Where the Zuni must be harmonious and is a deviant if he is mean, the American must be successful and deviates if he fails.

What does our culture give us as permitted defenses? The Texans moved during the time of the Dust Bowl to the desert of New Mexico where they tried to raise pinto beans, although they rarely had a good crop. Their characteristic reaction was, "It was a particularly bad year, we haven't had such a bad drought in years." Whether this, in fact, was the case is beside the point. Shifting the blame from self to the environment, denying personal failure and attributing it to the weather was their defense. It is permitted for them and for us to shift the blame for failure.

Another type of defense was indicated by a large sign over the Post Office at the center of town in which the Texans lived. The sign read, "Fence Lake, Bean Capital of the World." It was inconceivable that this was the bean capital of anything, let alone the world; yet the affirmation was quite acceptable. So another permitted defense is boasting. I would say that our culture demands success above and beyond the ability of many individuals to achieve it. Our culture, therefore, permits defenses against failure, such as shifting blame and boasting. Knowledge of these defenses is useful in diagnosing people raised with success as a dominant value.

Ari Kiev

It is most difficult to determine what constitutes psychopathology when studying people from other cultures. For this reason an operational definition of abnormality is used rather than an absolute standard against which the patients' symptoms are viewed as distressing either to him or to the group. According to this view, it is not the content of a delusion, but the way the content is used by an individual, the nature of this use, and the distortion of belief relative to the standards of the group which are the crucial determinants of a psychopathological label. The practical value of such a relativistic approach, however, obscures the fact that certain behavioral phenomena are universally judged to be abnormal, as Dr. Henry has indicated. Some features of psychiatric disorders are independent of social labeling.

A more valuable step than deciding what is normal and abnormal from culture to culture is distinguishing between the essential aspects of specific psychiatric disorders and their culturally conditioned aspects. Cross-cultural studies can be valuable to psychiatry in helping to make these distinctions, as with cross-cultural differences in the symptoms of schizophrenia. In a worldwide questionnaire survey conducted by Wittkower and Murphy of McGill University, catatonic rigidity, negativism, and stereotyped movements were commonly reported in Indian schizophrenics, while aggressiveness and expressiveness were common in southern Italian patients. African patients were generally quieter than patients in the Western world. The withdrawal of Indian schizophrenics was related to the formal hierarchical nature of Indian culture, with its high regard for introversion and emotional control. The barrenness of the clinical picture in preliterate Africans was tied to the paucity of their culture and intellectual resources and their difficulties in dealing with abstractions. While these recorded differences suggest a tie-in between symptoms and culture, four out of twenty-six symptoms and signs were very common in schizophrenia: social and emotional withdrawal, auditory hallucinations, illusions, and flatness of affect. These findings suggest that there are nuclear features of schizophrenia other than the culturally determined symptoms which usually are used to distinguish various illnesses from culture to culture.

Recent evidence obtained from studies on the effects of different hospital environments on psychiatric patients suggests that much of the disability associated with chronic psychiatric disorders is the result of faulty management. Many symptoms of social deterioration, such as withdrawal, negativism, self-destructiveness, and apathy, are not characteristics of schizophrenia or chronic psychiatric disorders, but are secondary symptoms grafted onto the underlying disorder by social and interpersonal factors in certain hospital settings.

Dr. Henry's remarks are particularly significant for cross-cultural study of such secondary behavioral patterns, which may be more disabling than the basic disorder. He has considered specific distortions in behavioral areas which connote abnormality within specific contexts.

Judgments on two of these criteria, perception and communication, require intimate knowledge of the cultural subtleties as well as careful study of a respondent by a member of the culture. Perceptual disturbances are especially difficult to assess since they depend on subjective accounts. The other criteria cited by Dr. Henry lend themselves more readily to simple observational techniques which can be scored against a scale describing the affected pattern in a culture. Social functioning in work, families, and social and recreational roles are useful and readily obtainable indices of psychological functioning, as are the dimensions of circles of approval and communication. It is important to know how these criteria are defined from culture to culture, for if such patterns could be specified from culture to culture, they might be applied usefully in international comparative studies. An example from my own work will help clarify this point.

I am engaged in a pilot follow-up study of several thousand people who have had psychiatric hospital experience during the past several years. My associates and I are interested in determining the prevalence of a severe social breakdown syndrome among these people, manifested by distortions of personality functions through patterns of withdrawal, anger, and hostility which are associated with more or less severe destruction of the affected person's social relationship. Evidence has been found that these maladaptive patterns develop as a result of disturbances in personal processes, as in the double bind that Dr. Henry illustrated, and that these patterns are preventable.

Severe social breakdown is determined by judgment of patterns of behavior such as conversation. In our study we attempt to assess the individual's behavior in the seven days prior to his interview. We ask whether the individual responded only on one day or did not speak at all; whether the individual had control of his own money, was given an allowance, or was forbidden to have money at all; whether he was free to leave the house and free from observation. These and other criteria can be useful indices of severe social disability in our society. However, to study severe disability in other cultures we must know the equivalent behavior in these cultures with regard to such matters as initiating conversation or handling money. Each individual's performance of these functions relative to the normal patterns of his own culture is most significant.

Dr. Henry has outlined a number of dimensions of behavior which seem most suitable for application in my work which seeks to understand more about the natural history and characteristics of specified disorders in different cultures and contexts.

Anthony F. C. Wallace

Let me begin my comments by paying tribute to a word which Dr. Henry uses and which serves a very useful function, one that was not familiar to me: the term *apodeictic,* which refers to that type of perception which correctly assesses the true nature of some object in the outside world. Since there are various circumlocutions available for referring to primary, and perhaps biologically determined, failures in perceptual and cognitive processes, this term provides me with a convenient short cut through such phrases as "nuclear processes" and "primary thought disorders."

The crux of Dr. Henry's paper is a distinction between apodeictic disorders or apodeictic abnormality, and cultural abnormality. While this distinction is valid, Dr. Henry does not carry his analysis far enough. It seems to me that some simple equations are possible. First, where there is a fundamental apodeictic disorder as well as a cultural abnormality, the conclusion of society will be that the individual is, in some radical sense, not in possession of his faculties (i.e., "sick" or "possessed") and the sanctions imposed will take this into account. Second, where the behavior is abnormal but the disorder is not considered apodeictic, the definition will be that the abnormal behavior is criminal, or contrary, or an insult or attack on other persons. In this circumstance, retaliation is likely to occur. What Dr. Henry points out is that, whenever there is a serious apodeictic disorder, there almost certainly will be a cultural abnormality, regardless of the nature of the culture, but that it is also possible for culturally abnormal behavior to occur without apodeictic disorder.

Even when it is accepted that there are apodeictic disorders, it is extremely difficult to define them. Seeing double when only one object is present is a readily recognizable disorder in perception, but a great many other failures of perception are not so easy to recognize. A given perceptual error may occur as a function of either or both an apodeictic disorder or a cultural disorder.

Part of Dr. Henry's paper contained excerpts from field notes describing interactions between mothers and children. These field notes contained an example of a mother's behavior which was disorganized and, in a sense, a failure. The mother was expected to give her child eight doses of medicine in the course of the day, and actually only provided the child with two. If this is abnormal behavior, what kind is it? Is it a cultural abnormality? Is it an expression of hostility against the child? I do not believe the two categories Dr. Henry offers, the apodeictic and the cultural, are adequate for the analysis of failure to do what one is told or expected to do. There is a third kind of abnormality involved here which we might call "normal" abnormality. The Army called it "snafu" (situation normal, all fouled up). A good deal of human experience takes place in situations which are fouled up in the sense that ideal cultural expectations are not being fulfilled, but this is so common that imputations of abnormality to the individuals involved are made at some risk.

Furthermore, the very use of the abnormal, in the context of a dichotomy between normal and abnormal, obscures a number of important distinctions. Is the "abnormal" behavior of a non-bigoted Southerner who sees Negroes as human beings or of a protester against the Viet Nam War in fact an abnormality similar to those about which we have been speaking? Does this kind of behavior really belong in the same terminological class? I would say that, in these instances, we are discussing a difference of opinion about policy. At the present time, both the means and scheduling of racial integration processes, as well as the role of the United States in Southeast Asia, are matters for legitimate public policy debate. This is the cultural situation, and those who take a minority position are not violating cultural norms. The use of a simple dichotomy makes such misconstrual of a policy disagreement situation much more difficult to avoid.

There also are serious problems of research design implicit in the discussion of "double bind" and other supposed situational determinants of pathological responses which are not discussed. It is very easy to say that children who grow up in households where they are subjected to double bind develop personality disorders in order to cope with the ambiguities of communication imposed on them. Most sick children do grow up in such households, but a great many children who are not sick also grow up in such households. Attention to problems of control groups, sampling, and the mechanics of statistical research design is essential here.

Finally, I would like to see more discussion of the "chicken-or-the-egg" problem: the interplay between emotional (psychological) stresses and disorders, and disorders in body chemistry. This is a giant research problem currently being investigated on many fronts. I know that Dr. Henry is interested in the role of physiological mechanisms in mental disease, and I wish this interest were more explicity related to a discussion of apodeictic disorders and to the whole problem of the genesis of mental illness, not just to abnormality.

REFERENCES

Henry, J. 1941. Jungle People: A Kaingang Tribe of the Highlands of Brazil. J. J. Augustin: New York (out of print). Reprinted, 1964. Random House, Vintage Book: New York.

———. 1947. Environment and Symptom Formation. American Journal of Orthopsychiatry 17:628-32.

———. 1949. Cultural Objectification of the Case History. American Journal of Orthopsychiatry 19:655-73.

———. 1953. Toward a System of Socio-Psychiatric Invariants: A Work Paper. Journal of Social Psychology 37:133-61.

———. 1954. The Problems of Invariance in the Field of Personality and Culture. Aspects of Culture and Personality, ed. Francis Hsu, pp. 139-71. Abelard-Schuman: New York.

———. 1958. An Anthropological Approach to Cultural, Idiosyncratic, and Universal Factors in Behavior. Progress in Psychotherapy, eds. Jules H. Masserman and J. L. Moreno, 3, pp. 199-203. Grune and Stratton: New York.

———. 1963. Culture Against Man. Random House: New York.

———. 1966a. A Theory for an Anthropological Analysis of American Culture. Anthropological Quarterly 69:90-109.

———. 1966b. The Study of Families by Naturalistic Observation. Psychiatric Research Report No. 20. American Psychiatric Association: Washington, D.C.

———. 1967. My Life with Families of Psychotic Children. The Psychosocial Interior of the Family, ed. G. Handel, pp. 33-54. Aldine: Chicago.

Horney, K. 1939. New Ways in Psychoanalysis. W. W. Norton & Co.: New York.

———. 1945. Our Inner Conflicts. W. W. Norton & Co.: New York.

Vogt, E. Z. and E. M. Albert, 1966. Peoples of Rimrock. Harvard University Press: Cambridge.

von Mering, O. and M. T. Mulhare. 1970. Anthropological Perspectives on Socialization. Parenthood: Its Psychology and Psychopathology, eds. E. J. Anthony and T. Benedek, ch. 3. Little, Brown & Co.: Boston.

Communication and Ethology

Both communication research and human ethology are multidisciplinary in practice, theory, and history. The field of human ethology now is developing into a new sub-discipline of anthropology. This development encompasses a number of approaches to the construction of process models of human interactions, their development, and change. Ethology views man as a biosocial animal whose life is built around shared methods of signaling and communicating within the context of his particular cultural background.

A particular approach to the study of social aspects of man's communicative behavior may be noted. This approach is problem-oriented and includes searching out subject matter and utilizing numerous recording methods to study the interaction process. It varies according to its practitioners and from pure natural history and description (studying previously neglected aspects of man's behavior) to theoretical model construction (tying verbal and non-verbal behavior into the wider construct of communication). This field may be broadly characterized as human ethology, or the study of man in his natural setting: how he moves, alone and with respect to others; what he feels, smells, sees, and hears; how others see him as he interacts; and whether he matures by direct growth or in spurts, perceiving and receiving different models of growth depending on how he himself is perceived. It is the study of space and territory; the occupation, use, and dynamics of the body in relation to other bodies and to the geometry of the "surround." It is the study of a particular view of nature, one organized and structured by man.

For the second time in a century, students of man's behavior are strongly involved in the study of other animals. Earlier, Darwin pointed out the similarities between the biostructural parts of man and animals (1958). Now, ethology, which is largely an outgrowth of Darwin's neglected *The Expression of the Emotions in Man and Animals,* (1965) is influencing our changing views of man's nature and ways of studying it. Through naturalistic studies of primates and other animals, we have discovered new parallels of social structure, development, territory, and rhythmicity between man and animals (Blauvelt, 1956; Blauvelt and McKenna, 1960, 1961). Much exchange already has occurred in this area.

Although this definition of man's communicative behavior or "communication" as an all-embracing term may seem too broad, there are several reasons for breadth, not the least of which is an attempt to avoid premature closure. However, communication obviously cannot be everything and still make sense.

Historical Antecedents

Early Western explanations of both man and language were generally couched in supernatural terms. Both man and language were assumed to be created whole (Genesis 11:1). The assumption of supernatural causation, kept alive through the Middle Ages as an extension of Aristotelian influence, leaves us with the residue of the Cartesian duality of mind (i.e., soul) and body (Boring, 1950). Even up to Darwin's time and beyond, man was assumed to be the animal (or perhaps the non-animal) with a "free," willful soul (Simpson, 1966). The practical result of this assumption was, for a long time, lack of observation of many aspects of human behavior, particularly in matters associated with the mind.

Within classical Western thought, the Platonic model of mind and language as "given" (Waterman, 1963) persisted until the Leibnitz influence in the early eighteenth century and the beginning of the German tradition in psychology. The mind was seen as a storehouse containing a set of "ideas," one for each name and its corresponding object. Language in this view meant vocabulary, and each individual word was accompanied by the corresponding "idea." This was a theory of meaning which held its data to be known and explainable in the mind without observation or knowledge other than that which each person had "by nature." Although Aristotle expressed the notion that language and meaning were derived from convention and agreement, the Platonic view persisted and still underlies most "common-sense" notions about language (Waterman, 1963).

Not until the introduction of printing with movable type in the sixteenth century was it possible to study vernacular languages. Until this time, classical languages, particularly Latin, were the vehicles for all scholarly thought. The printing of vernacular descriptions and dictionaries facilitated comparisons between languages, and the studies of language relationships and structures then began (Waterman, 1963).

The scholar of Leibnitz' time did not distinguish between philosophy, mathematics, the mind, or language. The concern of scholars was the nature of being and reality, with definite focus on adult, quiescent man as the sole model to inspect, account for, and explain. Leibnitz introduced the problem of development, holding that activity and interaction with the outside world is essential to man's being (Boring, 1950). He postulated an internal world and a separate external world, thus refuting Plato's preformed world of "ideas." It was also Leibnitz who first realized that "scholars would have to abandon their sterile practice of trying to relate all languages to biblical Hebrew," and who proposed that all Eurasian languages were "derived from a common, prehistorical ancestor" (Waterman, 1963).

The British pre-psychological tradition breaking with the early notions of the "free" or unstructured mind-soul began with the conceptualization of mind as inherently interacting with nature. It continued with the Berkeleyan attempt to locate reality in the mind and extended into the middle of the nineteenth century through James Mill's elaboration of "mental mechanics" and J. S. Mill's "mental chemistry." During much of its history, it paralleled the development and establishment — through essentially separate traditions — of linguistics, experimental psychology, and evolutionary biology. The century and a half following Leibnitz, an era of rapid geographical discovery and increased knowledge of physiology with the consequent breakdown of earlier conceptions, set the stage for a changing climate of thought and for the new sciences of man. The accumuation of evidence for the antiquity of earth, life, and man implied not only biological evolution, but contributed to evolutionary theories which paved the way for nineteenth-century ideas in areas such as language, where notions of original language were disappearing.

During this period several statements were formulated and subsequently considered "laws." Among these were the Bell-Magendie Law in physiology and Grimm's Law in language. The first stated that the body is composed of two different kinds of peripheral nerves, motor and sensory, which directly implied a differentially constructed brain. Grimm's Law stated that "there is a principle uniting, underlying, and lending pattern to sound changes" (Waterman, 1963).

The significance imputed to these so-called laws is as much due to the term "law" as to their scholarly basis. "Law" implies "always," in effect directing the investigator to seek answers in a particular manner. Traditionally, the linguist must search for a good, plausible, predictively correct explanation for sound change. One cannot have it both ways: questions must be answerable, or the investigator must revise his questions and enlarge his field of observation.

During the second half of the nineteenth century, Helmoltz established the central importance of perception and Wundt split it into complexes of elements. With this, the experimental, psychological, and historical study of man's mental functioning established a new investigative tradition. It represented a step away from linguistic-type determinism since most psychologists no longer considered how people structured their worlds, but rather how each human perceived certain attributes the observer called variables, as compared with the perception of others.

Wundt's ideas of apperception opened the door to a more sophisticated view. Instead of a mind in which all parts contributed to a singular perception, he posited two degrees of consciousness: focus or attention, and field. The idea that a mind could operate simultaneously along different lines, in essentially separate modes, was crucial to modern conceptualizations of mental functioning.

Opposition to the strict experimentalists developed through Brentano (Boring, 1950), who posited a system organized around the "psychical act," rather than only the sensate mind. Basically, the notion of "act" presupposes that human (and other organisms) organize the stream of behavior, of life, into effectively separate collections or bundles of momentary events. The assumptions underlying the concept of the psychic or symbolic act have long influenced observations of interactions and are still crucial.

Experimental Approaches and the Study of Communication

In the development of experimental psychology, the practice of controlled laboratory observations, especially of animals, became a predominant basis of theoretical psychology. Partly as a reaction to this, a few psychologists and zoologists (Carpenter, 1934) in the 1930's moved away from controlled laboratory situations and rediscovered ongoing nature. Building on this background as well as experience in examining social insects (Frisch, 1965), naturalists (Southwick, 1963) began making field observations of various animals, particularly primates. It soon became obvious that we were as myth-bound concerning the behavior of our anatomical relatives as we had been earlier concerning "natural man." As a result of the laboratory situation, restricted selection of "favorite" variables has been self-perpetuating within an increasingly narrow range of problems.

The new trend, which developed slowly, has become increasingly popular under the name ethology (McGill, 1965), and has resulted in the formation of the Animal Behavior Society. This area of study is a significant countervailing force to controlled laboratory manipulation of the individual organism away from his natural context.

Ethologists look at the nature of things without prejudging whether that nature should be divided into traditional categories and academic compartments. They treat biostructural-social properties such as space and territory as if they were unitary. Ethologists pose questions relating to similarities of form, structure, and process, such as the universal properties of communication among social animals and methods for exchanging messages within a species and compared to other species (Frings and Frings, 1964).

The second major influence on the present approach to communication has been the development of the assumption that behavior is organized. This took place along the lines of the two primary modes of sensation: sound and vision. Descriptive linguistics and Gestalt psychology developed as two distinct traditions, but with a great deal in common. Both were limited attempts to handle ongoing events, and each chose to select only some parts of the total stream. Each assumed some organization in the material it examined, and both were "mental chemistry" approaches, inductive and empirical by choice.

The idea that the stream of behavior is naturally broken up into separate, usually linear, acts strongly influenced linguistics. The classical and persuasive S–R type of model was nurtured in linguistics by Saussure and made central by Bloomfield. The Saussurian form states: "In order to separate from the whole of speech the part that belongs to language, we must examine the individual act from which the speaking-circuit can be reconstructed" (Saussure, 1959). The assumption that an encoder-decoder act is the natural unit in which language occurs underlies most modern linguistic developments.

Also implicit in this model is the assumption of a prior knowledge of how language evolves. "Act" psychologies tend to proceed from this knowledge rather than from search methodologies. Within this framework, arguments, such as introspectionism versus behaviorism, seem mainly concerned with location of data and techniques of data collection and reduction, rather than with arguments about the nature of the data.

In a different intellectual tradition, the study of linguistic phenomena within the deterministic framework of the "neogrammarians" (Waterman,1963) produced a new approach and methodology. The underlying assumption of basic linguistic units on which this theory rests is at least as old as the alphabet in Western thought.

The propensity to break up the sound stream into parts has long been noted by phoneticians (Saussure, 1959). The study of sound in speech also led the linguist to postulate the idea of significance of the acoustic events which make up speech; only some are "important," although many others are heard in everyday talk.

The apparent proclivity of speakers for classifying some parts of the sound stream as significant led the linguist to rephrase some problem areas. The major concern is that two or more interactors appear to impute the same order of significance to particular sound occurrences. This shifts the arena of data location to shared behavioral-cognitive mappings and implies that the problem area is not merely in the ahistorical individual. It also implies that the study of human nature depends not only on the observer's methods of classification but also on the interactors' models of the world. The study of the organization of behavior would be directed toward areas where the flow of data is treated in some shared, agreed-upon fashion.

Although the tendency to treat behavior as either static or composed of acts in some linear order has prevailed in this country, it is not the only approach that has been discussed. The changing point of view in an Einsteinian universe has undoubtedly influenced thinkers to consider the ongoing nature of man's world. Whitehead's (1957) philosophical examination of the fact that ability to observe is dependent on change is a constant reminder that notions of time and space are many-sided.

Linguistics early chose to restrict its subject matter. Saussure excluded *la parole*: "The flow of living speech . . . personalized language— your speech and my speech" (Waterman, 1963). Descriptive linguistics treats only a certain part of ongoing verbal behavior — that part called *la langue* by Saussure (1959) which forms a highly organized, relatively abstract system. The type of model developed in this tradition is necessarily committed to dealing with a certain kind of process and cannot relate a static world to a sensate mind. Instead, it implies a mind which can in some way handle the ongoing phenomena of sound, perhaps by making it into linear events.

The concept of the phoneme implies an essentially whole cognitive set or map which the interactor brings to any situation. It is a theory which holds that the large variety of sounds which occur in the already organized contexts of language — the sentence, the phrase, the word — are classified into restricted sets of sounds. Since it was developed from pre- restricted contexts, this particular theory will probably not account for the total sound stream. It was nonetheless a big step in the development of theories attempting to deal with the organism as an organized entity, rather than merely as a collection of disparate sensory modalities.

The sense of sight makes the outside world appear to be static. It often has led to the overly simple atomic-analytic theories of mental functioning. The major change implied in Gestaltist theory was merely a shift in assumption. As Köhler (1947) states: "The 'togetherness' of several stimuli . . . is the condition which has . . . specific effects in a sensory field." Therefore, organization is not a summational, mechanical process. To the extent that different modes of an organism are differently organized, a single model or point of view will never be able to account for all observed behavior. This further implies that behavior must be observed and described in the multiple ways in which it might be manifested, a problem we are just beginning to face.

The third major theme contributing to the present development of the study of communication is that of the inherently social nature of behavior. In the early views of social psychology, self only becomes self as as entity emerging from the interactional world in which it develops from birth and early infancy (G. H. Mead, 1956).[1] If these ideas are extended to human ethology, it is not meaningful to say only that a man exists or that an individual exists; they can and do exist only because of their societal structure. Man, as a personality or self, gains his sense of identity only as he becomes accustomed to being treated as if he is an individual.

The study of communication as human ethology is developing as an extension of these themes, as an outgrowth of studies of natural history and of social, organized behavior. The basic locus of data is in the ongoing interaction of these themes.

In this context, the point of view of each interactor differs in many senses. Each sees a body, a changing configuration of facial muscles, moving eyes and lips within a shared, delimited space. The interactors say things directly pertaining to the moment and within that shared spaced, but each also successfully talks about and describes things which the other might not have experienced. Each comes into an interaction with a different history: the member of an ethnic group, whose first division is between his people and others; the nubile female whose first thought is to get an engagement ring; the sick person who wants relief. The observer of interactional behavior must be aware that the data which occur at a given moment might result from points of view not inherent in the immediate situation.

The development of linguistic methodologies derived from interactional speech in its natural context is central to the study of communication. Studies of grammar as pure structure, whether transformation (Chomsky, 1957) or immediate constituent (I.C.) analysis (Trager and Smith, 1951), do not seem relevant in this context, since they assume a restricted model of speech acts. Instead, it seems certain that much presignaling and cross-referencing must occur continually within speech signals. A single mode examination of speech, such as that inherent in *la langue,* is insufficient to handle interactional speech in which the speaker and listener do not have the same kind of access to the same information (Sarles, 1966).

1. Natural studies of domestic animals show very clearly that an infant goat who is non-communicating will not survive and, indeed, is lethal in the technical sense of the word (Blauvelt, 1954). The literature on social insects indicates clearly that the individual ant or bee cannot exist independently (Frisch, 1965).

Some possible rules of organization in verbal behavior have emerged from attempts to relate structure and context. From previous observations of the relationships between questions and response-set answers in Tzotzil (Sarles, in press), an approach has emerged which deals with the dynamic relationships among parts, rather than merely with parts or units themselves. Problems relating to the understanding and intelligibility of speech are crucial to the study of interaction (Sarles, 1967).

Examination of oscilloscopic speech data suggests that ongoing repetitive information is available within the sound stream alone.[2] On the basis of this work, it appears that purely phonemic models will be insufficient to explain the subtleties of interactional speech.

The historical implications of the proposed models demand a study of ontogenetic development. Do children learn one model or are they presented modified models as they become competent with previous ones? How do mothers handle, touch, speak to, and react to their infants? Are all babies born with the same facial muscular abilities, or are they already different at birth? The amount and variety of movement observed in a four-day-old infant is amazing: nose-flaring, ear movement, synchronous limb movement.[3] Do children then learn to use only certain muscular complexes as they adopt their particular parental models, and does this shape the skeletal *anlage* to make them look like their parents? These are now testable questions cross-culturally as well as across species (Sarles, 1969).

Finally, a full array of recording and analyzing devices contributes to the viability of the dynamic study of ongoing interaction. From a pre-synchronized movie or videotape we can look at two or more interactors in any way we desire. Motion can be "stopped" or body movements altered in time relationships. For example, we can look at how the hands of two interactors join in a complex dance, or see how one person's sound stream is related to a listener's lip and eye movements. We can determine the limits in space and duration of ordinary movement and

2. For example, it often suggests length of the sentence to come, the location of words within phrases, and whether present context has an implied history outside the data itself.

3. A slow-motion movie (48 fps) of a normal, sleeping four-day-old infant was made by Dr. Donald Coleman at the Western Psychiatric Institute and Clinic (University of Pittsburgh). The study was done by two graduate students (Marilyn R. Cummings and Davydd Greenwood) in the context of my course in kinesics (1966).

we can now systematically examine differences in walking and in stance around the world. Since *mechanical* limitation on our ability to make detailed observations no longer exists, we do not have to speculate about movement.

Ethology and Anthropology

Anthropology and ethology seem similar in a number of ways. Primarily, they share a strong commitment to field observation. Problems of description, observer-introduced distortion, natural context, and social relations are central to both. Given these common bases, an anthropologist might consider looking across fields to ethology by comparing the study of different species to doing field work in different cultures. Through culture shock, we gain insight into our own culture and culture in general. Similarly, through culture shock across species, human problems become more apparent. For example, the study of proxemics derives directly from studies of animal territoriality. The fact that animals organize space makes it easier to see that human space also is organized. Similarly, an ethologist might hope that more active elicitation and participation procedures among anthropologists would yield useful insights for the study of other animals.

It would be misleading to imply that no significant differences exist between the two fields since, in fact, several differences cause difficulties in communication between the disciplines. For example, most ethologists become experts on the behavior of one or two species, and are hesitant to carry their observations over to other types of animals, much less to humans. A second problem is that, in ethology, an evolutionary theory provides a *raison d'être* and a partial closure for the field. In particular, a behavioral unit or component is largely defined in terms of phylogenetic reconstructability. Despite some early beginnings in this direction, anthropology has tended to shy away from the use of an evolutionary model. A third problem is that reading and training in the two fields are not thoroughly shared, which is due in part to the non-overlapping prestige reference groups for the two fields.

Ethologists tend to be species relativists and, although they study each species in its own terms, man as a social animal does not fall within their purview. Consequently, many ethologists who are tough-minded about animal behavior are willing to accept assumptions about human language and do not question the Cartesian separation of man (mind) and animal (body). This is currently exemplified in Chomsky's *Cartesian Linguistics* (1966) and in Hockett and Asher's *The Human Revolution* (1964). Animal language studies by ethologists utilize the instrumentation of human phoneticians, but few ethologists have had training in the assumptions and methodologies which underly the work of linguists. Even in the study of territoriality and use of space where one might expect a nearly complete transfer of study technique, few ethologists have studied the human species. Finally, some of the major concepts of anthropologists, such as culture and social structure, are not included in the conceptual framework of ethology.

In discussing the relationship between the two fields, it seems more useful to outline prospective interdisciplinary subject matter than to catalog what has been done. The following outline attempts to list problem areas of potential common interest with emphasis upon the areas of present interest. I would prefer to leave the question of differences between man and animal and concentrate on similarities, allowing residual categories of difference to emerge from study (Sarles, 1969).

Shared Problem Areas between Anthropology and Ethology

Classification

Classification includes the history of taxonomy, the evolution of the assumptions and procedures in the naming of entities which is an effective part of the disciplines. For example, the assumption that primates are behaviorally more like humans than other kinds of animals appears to derive not from behavioral studies but from morphological similarities. While this may be a sound assumption, it is based on taxonomic procedures which are taken for granted. Problems of language and dialect boundaries and definition seem to be practically identical to problems of species relationships as presently conceived, and may be a useful analogy to study. The problem of isolating and labeling behavioral units on the basis of the natural history of their occurrence is another aspect of classification which should benefit from a comparison between the procedures and experiences of anthropology and ethology.

Nature versus Human Nature

Anthropologists and most ethologists traditionally think that animals, not man, belong in nature, which is another instance of the Cartesian legacy. As a result, ethologists have concentrated principally on "innate" or "instinctual" behavioral patterns such as courtship rituals, threat displays, and call systems. Anthropologists primarily have looked at "learned" behavior such as language, ceremony, and child-rearing practices. The nature-nurture dichotomy has been accepted in practice, rather than questioned, and is largely responsible for the differences in conceptual frameworks and research practices between the two fields.

Anthropologists and ethologists, however, seem to share a particular sense of concern about their subject matter, which tends to set them apart from other related disciplines. Most linguistic anthropologists and cognitive mappers view their task as studying the already organized social-cognitive world of a culture to discover how its members see the world. Similarly, ethologists view animals as born into a preformed social-cognitive context which is effectively the world as they see it. Possible communication between species presumably would depend on man's acting as if the animal world represented nature, although nowhere in this process does a concern for "true" nature enter in. We can of course beg this question and yet gain valuable insights into the social-behavioral-perceptual worlds of all animals (Sebeok, 1965). While this may seem to be a purely theoretical exercise, it has very practical implications. The character of anthropological and ethological views of animal nature deserve careful consideration as an alternative to reductionist strategies and interests.[4]

Pathology

The consideration of pathology in the context of ethology effectively forces a discussion of normality across species and leads to questions of viability at all levels of social structure. Questions for consideration include who diagnoses pathology and how, what sorts of deviation always appear, which kinds are tolerated or changed, and what is meant by the idea of "cure."

Behavior

Ethologists and anthropologists agree that behavior is best studied in the natural setting. Probably the greatest contribution of both fields has

4. For a further discussion of these and related issues, see Harvey B. Sarles, "The Study of Language and Communication Across Species," *Current Anthropology*, 1969, 10:211-21.

been the insistence that, to study human nature, we must look at all human societies and, to look properly at animal nature, we must look at all animal societies. It is not sufficient to extrapolate from a man or some men to Man, or from laboratory, domestic, or zoo animals to Animal. Our observations must always extend to the natural world of the subject being studied. The question is what is characteristic of behavior *in situ* rather than what an organism can be induced or forced to do. A being may be born with many potentials; what he becomes and how he sees the world is primarily a statement about his parents, his society, his experience, and his shared or social nature. What he can do under given circumstances is of interest primarily for broader insights.

The difference between a "stream" of behavior theory and an "atomized" ("eventized") behavior theory is a matter for discussion. Presumably, no one has ever satisfactorily handled the "stream" of behavior, but the pitfalls inherent in atomism are generally insurmountable. An attempt to return satisfactorily from an atomistic description to actual behavior almost always is unsuccessful. The best safeguard against prematurely adopting an ultimately unproductive view is additional careful and tough-minded observation.

Perhaps the most important consideration in studying behavior is the concept of context. Now that videotaping is economically available and the mechanics of the systematic variation of context are greatly simplified, hopefully the search for behavioral units which has characterized so much of the work of anthropologists and ethologists will acquire increased sophistication. Similarly, the question of the nature of the in-behavior organization of these units should be reexamined.

Communication and Social Structure

The process of communication can be conceptualized from two almost opposite points of view: (1) communication is a continuous function in social terms or (2) existentially separate organisms need to learn to communicate. In the second, more popular, view, each organism is seen as a physically bounded entity which grows up to be more and more complex. The first, or "community," conceptualization sees the organism as part of a communication system in which he must be a good communicator at all points in his development to survive.

It is worth discussing these two points not only because of their implications, but also because they lead to different questions and observations. The "existential" view approaches the basic nature problem in adult terms, while the "community" view sees the constant interaction between adult and child as potentially crucial to species viability. In the latter case, parent perception of age grades is perhaps even more important than the actual size or age of non-adults.

Shared social structure determines, in a sense, social morality — the social judgments in terms of which adults see their children as, for example, pretty enough, smart enough, or well enough at each point in their development. If the adult does not see his child this way, he will constantly correct, forbid, or tacitly disapprove. Concentration on these aspects of social orders might be fruitful in comparative ethology at this point in the field's development. Because these aspects lead to seeking similarities rather than differences, they might lead to shared methodologies between ethology and anthropology.

COMMENTARY: C. R. Carpenter
Henry W. Brosin
Suzanne Ripley

C. R. Carpenter

Commenting effectively on Professor Harvey Sarles' paper is certainly a difficult task. Communication and ethology are described by Professor Sarles as a multidisciplinary field that is a sub-discipline within anthropology. After offering this complex thought, he suggests that the study of communications is a study of the "interaction process." Observers, from the practitioner to the natural historian, construct theoretical models and make direct observations of the communication process in a contextual situation.

I believe that wherever the word "process" is used to refer to a very complex net of phenomena, chances are high that the subject is being oversimplified. I think Professor Sarles is attempting to define a new sub-discipline in anthropology as "human ethology" and thus extend the old order sub-discipline of ethology in the biological sciences to the human level. I am sure that the originators of ethology in Europe would be delighted at this extension.

Human ethology is defined as a field which includes the systematic study of human behavior, interaction, sensory perception processes, growth, and adjustment in space, including territory and broad organizations of natural phenomena. Professor Sarles applauds a recent resurgence of interest in the study of animal behavior as an approach to the study of "human nature." He seems to approve the broad naturalistic approach to the study of communications but, when communications are defined this broadly, he is clearly concerned about the diffuseness, and therefore the adequacy, of the definition. He defines his problem in such a way that delimits the areas of communication and ethology by showing that they are an outgrowth of the concepts that lead to the present ideas. An interesting description follows of the changing and developing concepts of man, his experience, and his behavior from the eighteenth to the twentieth century. Dr. Sarles emphasizes the dilemma of analysis and synthesis. He indicates when separate disciplines were formed and concludes that, a century and a half after Leibnitz, modern linguistics, experimental psychology, and evolutionary biology all became well-established disciplines through essentially separate traditions. He then states that these conditions set the stage for the new sciences of man.

This raises the question of whether there is a convergence of lines of thinking, or whether the overall systematic conception of a field is not progressively differentiated so that the special fields evolve from the more general field. I would point to the way in which curricula in American universities have developed a progressive differentiation toward specialization, rather than toward special fields converging into Professor Sarles' new sciences of man.

Dr. Sarles describes conditions which advance the new sciences of man: evidence for the antiquity of the earth; language and implicated progression in language as involved in biological evolution; development of laws; the rise of the concept of natural selection; development of experimental psychology and the concept of human variability; and emergence of the part-whole controversy and alternative solutions proposed by "Act" psychology and later by Gestalt psychologists.

Sarles argues that the new sciences of man developed from three dominant themes: natural history, organization, and the social nature of behavior. A position with which I concur holds that these themes frequently cross-cut each other and that there has developed a myth of primitive man in relation to a myth of anatomical realities that has confused our conceptions of the origin of man.

The present rise in ethology seems to be a reaction to overcontrolled laboratory manipulations of individuals out of their natural contexts. I would agree with Professor Sarles that, to properly understand any development, study in the biotic context is necessary. However, setting contextual studies over and above laboratory studies goes too far in not recognizing the complementary nature of the two methodologies. Human ethology entails studying animals in their context, observing objectively for categories and traditions, stressing similarities, and attempting to discover the nature of life within its natural context. Communications and human ethology are developing from these themes.

Professor Sarles observes that "general systems theory" leads to the expectation of something useful. He also observes that the listener in communications interactions is not merely a passive decoder but has a reciprocal relationship to the speaker. He agrees that significant developments in apparatus and equipment allow for a much more systematic, detailed, and scientific study of communications processes than previously possible.

Dr. Sarles has emphasized some important characteristics of the communications network, such as study in context to determine the various interacting organisms and interactions with environmental situations to interpret how communications processes fit into the more broadly perceived field of animal activities. He has shown that this is an interdisciplinary activity and, although he has drawn heavily on the history of psychology to make this point, he has omitted much that has occurred in psychology that relates to understanding and properly describing the development of human communications and speech.

Professor Sarles substitutes many technical terms for a more direct and simple behavioristic approach to understanding the complex interactional behavior of animals, which I think of as the signaling system in these non-human organisms. The study of animal communication does not indicate a high degree of continuity from the level of animal signaling systems to human communication, and we are warned by Professor Sarles to guard against making such assumptions of continuity without adequate proof.

Henry W. Brosin

My first reaction to Professor Sarles' review of the history of ideas which preceded current work in communication (linguistics) and ethology is that linguistics deserves mention by friendly observers because it is probably the first of the behavioral sciences to show considerable strength as a systematic study.

Grimm's Law (1822), a statement about orderly transitions or principles of relationships in Indo-European languages, opened the door to comparative philology and related subjects, and far-reaching implications concerning the development of man. The philosophical works of Sir William Jones (1746–1794) identified the branching tree of Indo-European societies and prepared us for a concept of the evolution of societies before Darwin.[1]

Saussure and many others carried forward the comparative study and reconstruction of the Indo-European languages. These languages, with their regularities, may not have a psychological and sociological basis, but have given us a basis for examining many other fields. Regularities of ongoing, continuous, organized or patterned behavior are of immense value to enlarged concepts of human behavior having both biological and sociopsychological roots and, therefore, are of crucial importance to the clinician in the study of human interaction.

Similarly, the ethologists have brought dignity as well as intriguing data to the natural history method. An essay on method by Robert Hinde (1959) contains convincing evidence of the soundness of the data and concepts for examining complex phenomena in contextual and non-contextual matrices or forms of animal behavior. It is curious that this should be true, since there are many examples of fruitful medical discoveries resulting from natural observations, but the ascendancy of the laboratory currently has tended to obscure the usefulness of the natural history method when it is much needed.

I have always been impressed by the fact that, though Charles Darwin (1965) published his *The Expression of Emotions in Men and Animals* in 1872 when he was already a world-famous figure, his recommendations for studying animals in their natural habitat (for which he is con-

1. I would like to call attention to a two-volume work published by Professor Thomas Sebeok (1966), which is a compilation of historical and crucial contributions to linguistics beginning with Sir William Jones.

sidered the Father of ethology) were not followed for nearly thirty years. Charles Otis Whitman and Oskar Heinroth are cited by K. Lorenz (1952, 1966) as pioneers who rediscovered the "starting point of ethology." Similarly, Darwin's recommendations to study communication in child development and in psychoses were not taken seriously by most workers until World War II.

It may be useful to recall that "teleology" in any form was descried in biology until the combinations of physics and mathematical concepts called cybernetics (1947) made it respectable to speak of "purpose" because it could be seen as it was built into a machine.

Fortunately, we need not limit ourselves to a historical discussion. Although the data are not easily come by, there now are numerous studies, beyond those envisioned by Edward Sapir (1949a, 1949b, 1949c) in the thirties and McQuown (1957) and Hockett (1958, 1968) in the mid-fifties, which demonstrate the feasibility of interaction studies in the clinical setting (Brosin, in press). I will mention a few projects completed in Pittsburgh.

E. J. Charney (1966) observes consistent consonant postural behavior (postural harmony) with changes in lexical production in a film of a patient and a therapist. This has also been observed by A. E. Scheflen (1966, 1968) at the Temple University Department of Psychiatry. Two types of postural consonance were revealed in this film: (1) mirror image and (2) identical image. Each was significant in its own way to the thematic pattern of the interaction as a whole.

Condon and Ogston (1967b) demonstrate that linguistic units cannot be divorced from kinesic units and that aural and visual investigations of the streams of human communication do not constitute separable areas of study. Demonstration of the presence of synchrony sequences at the micro-level satisfies the crucial need for definable interactive units in the multi-level, continuous process of information exchange transactions (communication) between two persons. They have defined minimal and higher order movements of body parts (head, eyes, eyebrows, mouth, and fingers) which recur isomorphically with units of speech, establishing units which are truly linguistic-kinesic, rather than linguistic and kinesic. Also, there is a hierarchy from minimal units through syllabic to verbal, phrasal, and larger communicational forms. This can be better observed with film at 48 frames (double-speed) and 64 frames per second than at the conventional 24. "Self-sychrony" (internal harmony of an individual's communicative behavior) is more clearly seen at 64 frames per second.

Condon and Ogston (1967a) have found synchrony and dissynchrony in the higher primate in a film made by Professor Harry Harlow (1957, 1963) of Wisconsin. Preliminary study suggests that such synchrony can also be observed in pulse rate and rhythm, and in electroencephalographic patterns. Not only were synchronous wave forms observable, but a phrase, repeated subvocally by one of the two subjects in the interaction, appeared to give an identifiable EEG trace. However, because of technical difficulties, this work must be carefully verified.

In a 33-minute film of a patient talking to a therapist at various levels of lexical, linguistic, and kinesic activity, Condon and Ogston (1966) identified 41 units of behavior. They found that the linguistic and kinesic units tended to occur in specific lexical and/or "meaning class" contexts. Linguistic units (phonemes, morphemes, and larger units of speech) were found to begin and end simultaneously (down to 1/24th of a second) with the beginning and ending of kinesic units. Referring to several related body movements to be studied in detail, Loeb (in press) worked on a gesture called "S_2" consisting of a specific pattern of movement which resembles a grasping movement. This gesture (S_2) occurs with the words "in," "out," or "off," and in every case with the meaning class "something or someone getting 'off' (out) away from the patient or her mind," or with the meaning class "someone or something getting 'in' close to her or her mind." This was verified in another film of the same patient in another context, as well as in yet another film where a psychiatrist from a different subculture used the same gesture in the same meaning class. Since the differences in the lexical contexts may be regional or characterological, more comparisons must be made, together with explanations to relate this gesture to various manifestations of the grasp reflex seen in infants and even in other mammals such as cats and dogs. It may be, in humans, a signal revealing unconscious activity which has remained remarkably free from modification by experience or ego control.

In addition to the work cited above, Dr. Sarles, an anthropologist-linguist, has been concerned with obtaining more focused issues and better contrastive data now available with new tools for studying such phenomena as pitch, stress, and tempo (1969). Under specified experimental conditions, using a precisely sound-synchronized film taken at "double-slow motion" (48 frames per second), Sarles finds that information concerning the shape of the total sentence to come, at least with respect to the number of words, is already established after the first one or two items; that many pitch and stress phenomena seem to be related to the listener's reactions to contrasts; and that pitch and stress relationships partially overlap, as far as the speaker of English is concerned. The apparent speed (perceived difference) of a speaker often may be a matter of the spacing of silences, rather than differences in terms of larger units such as the phrase or sentence. The use of oscilloscopic microtechniques for more accurate and systematic observations is proposed to uncover a new body of knowledge concerning language structure.[2]

Dr. Jane Lancaster at the University of California, Berkeley, has been working on studies of monkey communication, and also communications of infants and of very young children. Dr. Norman Geschwind, a neurologist at Boston University, works with neurosurgeons on patients with aphasia and is laying the groundwork which will provide more useful "models for mind," which genuinely combine linguistic communication studies and ethology. A thorough theoretical and methodological review of these and other studies, as well as the results of long-term researches by Gregory Bateson, Ray Birdwhistell, Charles Hockett, and myself on verbal and gestural behavior in the interview process will soon appear in a volume entitled *The Natural History of An Interview* (McQuown, in press). These and other studies lead me to believe that we are on the threshold of a renaissance in this area like one envisioned by Edward Sapir over thirty years ago.

Suzanne Ripley

From the contrasting ideas of nominalism, dualism, empiricism, ahistoricism, atomism, and rationalism, Dr. Sarles conceptualizes a putatively new sub-discipline of anthropology — human ethology — which is characterized by a total contextual approach, is rooted in systems theory and linguistics, and is focused on social interaction in natural surroundings.

First, when Dr. Sarles uses the word "historical," he mentions it only in the context of the "study of ontogenetic development." I would reserve the term "historical," at least in the context of culture, to refer

2. See my "Mental Status Examination Aided by Microanalysis of Sound Film," in *Evolving Concepts in Psychiatry*, Grune & Stratton, New York, 1969.

to a biologically meaningful time-depth in humans of a minimum of three successive generations, or those alive together at any one point in time. The implications of this point have been well developed in Margaret Mead's recent book, *Continuities in Cultural Evolution* (1964).

Second, the approach that Dr. Sarles calls human ethology is not new, but is a venerable one to which new vitality and a new label have been added. It is the study of social interactions as a set of phenomena requiring special investigational techniques and analytic concepts, apart from the analysis of the structure, functional relations, and history of sociocultural groups. Consequently, in presenting the pedigree of this area of study, I would stress the work of sociologists such as Cooley, Mead, Simmel, von Wiese, that of Hughes, Goffman, Becker, Strauss, and many others currently much influenced by their work, as well as the work of Arensberg, Chapple, Whyte, Richardson, and others in applied anthropology. It is this tradition of the study of the interaction process allied with the newer sociobiological studies of animal behavior and the various strains of communication studies, anthropological linguistics, decision and game theory, and military strategy that is significant and revitalizes an old approach.

This is the second time in a century that the study of animal behavior has been considered pertinent to the study of human beings. The first was at the time of Darwin and his adherents. This period is separated from the present by the submergence of interest in animal parallels and evolutionary questions among anthropologists because of Boazian criticisms of large-scale interpretations from small-scale evidence.

The study of animal behavior now is a sophisticated science, grown from its beginnings in the work of Heinroth, Fabre, Craig, Howard, Lorenz, Tinbergen, Wheeler, and many others. Until recently, research efforts primarily in Europe were devoted to the analysis of display behavior, particularly to courtship and threat, within closely related taxonomic groups by reference to stereotyped movements assumed to be motivated by action-specific energies. The study of animal behavior has burgeoned, especially in the analysis of endogenous biological rhythms and the external mechanism of their calibrations; also in the study of sense perception and filtering gates — both central and peripheral — particularly in the olfactory and auditory channels. There also has been growth in the study of early learning, especially imprinting phenomena; anatomical structure and behavior; physiology and behavior in stress and reproductive research; and ecological energy exchange systems. Most of this work has been done on animals other than primates. These new emphases are reviewed and illustrated in recent publications (Ellis, 1965; Klopfer and Hailman, 1967; Marler and Hamilton, 1966).

While the volume of data has increased, there remain profound problems in making comparisons of behavior among animals. One problem is assessing the role of intelligence in evolutionary selection for information processing and storage schemes on the one hand, and the relative development of social organization on the other (Eisenberg, 1966; Marler and Hamilton, 1966). The problems are correspondingly magnified in comparisons between non-primates.

The origin of human language is one area on which it is hoped that animal behavior data will shed light. There has been great interest in any systematic, and perhaps meaningful, production of sound by animals, on the assumption that speech is the major vehicle of communicative behavior in humans. This interest has centered on birds, insects, bats, fish, and sea mammals rather than on land mammals, thus broadening the attention of anthropologists beyond primates. Primates are vocally dumb but visually voluble, and therefore are of less interest in enlightening us about the structure of vocalization in early human language. However, the question of code structure, apart from considerations of channel, remains to be explored. It is possible that contrast, complementarity, arbitrariness, structural level, and context markers will be found in primate visual and tactile signaling systems. On the other hand, the structure of social interaction might prove that language emerged in humans without even modest antecedents in primates.

It is unfortunate that, since Saussure, students of linguistics have concentrated on only the verbal part of human communicative behavior. Such grappling with other aspects has been attempted by Smith (1960), Trager (1958, 1966), Bateson (1958, 1959), McQuown (1957, 1964), Birdwhistell (1956, 1959, 1963, 1964), Pike (1945, 1967), Hall (1959, 1966, 1968), Chapple and Chapple (1954), Scheflen (1964, 1967), Argyle and Kendon (1967), Kendon (1967), and others. Part of this uneven weighting of significance in favor of the verbal in human communication stems from an underestimation of the significance of so-called emotional modifiers on communicative behavior. Emotional modifiers have been known to alter totally message relations, particularly at a meta-communicational level.

Speech also is central in the recent development of interest in socio-cultural contexts of communication, as developed in the publications of Hymes (1964) and in the special issue of the *American Anthropologist* edited by Drs. Gumperz and Hymes (1964). This type of research is done on sound variance, lexicon size, dialect usage, and language selection as influenced by characteristics of speakers, audience, or situation. Nevertheless, these studies do reach a level of analysis at which other forms of communicational data can assume greater significance. More important, this type of research underscores the patterned, repetitive, non-novel construction of successful human communication. However, the overall absorption with one function obscures the role of language as an important, but additional, sub-system in human communication, its significance varying with context.

For example, one of Hockett's (1958) major distinguishing features of human language, displacement, is presented in terms of its value to a hunting people preparing for a hunt. Yet, to my knowledge, we have no good studies of the extent and manner in which speech is used in the coordination and planning of such an enterprise or in post-hunt discussion. Nor have we empirical studies of the degree to which speech is a factor in child learning of other cultural materials such as child-care, cooking, and housekeeping to compare with the studies of child language learning. We need to know more about the role of language in social processes and of the role of the novel message in speech situations. The recent study by Hendrix (1960) of the relative effectiveness of mathematics teachers indicates that paralanguage and kinesic signaling of phrase structures is of first importance in successful transmission of material that is abstract, rational, and novel. These data should be examined in the context of the effectiveness of mathematics classes and of schools in general in the supporting society.

I would like to relate this problem of context and novel content of messages to primate studies. A problem to primatologists is the reconciliation of the high degree of intellectual prowess of which monkeys and apes are capable in laboratory studies with the relative simplicity of their social organization in the wild. Primates learn to learn, they learn from each other's successes and especially from each other's mistakes, which is a very high order of learning. In the wild, what is learned must be accessible to the least among those on whom the continued viability of their society depends. Primates reduce responses in their young to those few characteristic of their group, presumably so that behavioral conformity can be relied upon when necessary. There is a low tolerance for ambiguity and multiple interpretation. One is forced to inquire, then, into the nature of the special social environment in which communicational novelty can be tolerated while the basic business of society is accomplished. The contemporary research laboratory creates circumstances in which the exploratory and innovative capacities of most wild, youthful higher primates are revealed and retained into adulthood. They thus provide some insight into the sustaining conditions which were required for the proliferative emergence of culture and its vehicle, language.

REFERENCES

Argyle, M. and A. Kendon. 1967. Experimental Analysis of Social Performance. Advances in Experimental Social Psychology, ed. L. Berkowitz, 3, pp. 55–98. Academic Press: New York.

Bateson, G. 1958. Language and Psychotherapy — Frieda Fromm-Reichmann's Last Project. Psychiatry 21:69–100.

———. 1959. Cultural Problems Posed by a Study of Schizophrenic Process. Schizophrenia: An Integrated Approach, ed. A. Auerback, pp. 125–46. Ronald Press: New York.

Birdwhistell, R. L. 1956. Kinesic Analysis of Filmed Behavior of Children. Conference on Group Processes, Josiah Macy, Jr., Foundation, ed. B. Schaffner, II, pp. 141–44. New York.

———. 1959. Contributions of Linguistic-Kinesic Studies to the Understanding of Schizophrenia. Schizophrenia: An Integrated Approach, ed. A. Auerback, pp. 99–118. Ronald Press: New York.

———. 1963. The Kinesic Level in the Investigation of the Emotions. Expression of the Emotions in Man, ed. P. H. Knapp, pp. 123–39. International Universities Press: New York.

———. 1964. Communicational Analysis in the Residency Setting. International Psychiatric Clinics 1:389–402.

Blauvelt, H. 1954. Dynamics of the Mother-Newborn Relationship in Goats. Conference on Group Processes, Josiah Macy, Jr., Foundation, ed. B. Schaffner, pp. 221–58. New York.

———. 1956. Neonate-Mother Relationship in Goat and Man. Conference on Group Processes, Josiah Macy, Jr. Foundation, ed. B. Schaffner, 2, pp. 94–140. New York.

Blauvelt, H. and J. McKenna. 1960. Capacity of the Human Newborn for Mother-Infant Interaction. Psychiatric Research Report 13:128–47.

———. 1961. Mother-Neonate Interaction: Capacity of the Human Newborn for Orientation. Determinants of Infant Behavior, ed. B.M. Foss, pp. 3–35. Methuen: London.

Boring, E. G. 1950. A History of Experimental Psychology, 2d ed. Appleton-Century-Crofts: New York.

Brosin, H. W. in press. Implications for Psychiatry. The Natural History of an Interview, ed. N. A. McQuown, ch. 4. Grune and Stratton: New York.

Carpenter, C. R. 1934. A Field Study of the Behavior and Social Relations of Howling Monkeys. Comparative Psychology Monograph 10 (48):1–168.

Chapple, E. D. and M. F. Chapple. 1954. Behavioral Definitions of Personality and Temperament Characteristics. Human Organization 13:34–39.

Charney, E. J. 1966. Psychosomatic Manifestation of Rapport in Psychotherapy. Psychosomatic Medicine (28):305–15.

Chomsky, N. 1957. Syntactic Structures. Mouton: The Hague.

———. 1966. Cartesian Linguistics: A Chapter in the History of Rationalist Thought. Harper and Row: New York.

Condon, W. S. and W. D. Ogston. 1966. Sound Film Analysis of Normal and Pathological Behavior Patterns. Journal Nervous and Mental Diseases 143:338–47.

———. 1967a. A Method of Studying Animal Behavior. Journal of Auditory Research 7:359–65.

———. 1967b. A Segmentation of Behavior. Journal of Psychiatric Research 5:221–35.

Darwin, C. 1958. The Origin of Species. New American Library: New York.

———. 1965. The Expression of the Emotions in Man and Animals. University of Chicago Press: Chicago.

Eisenberg, J. F. 1966. The Social Organizations of Mammals. Handbuch der Zoölogie, Band 10, pp. 1–92. Walter de Gruyter: Berlin.

Ellis, P. E., ed. 1965. Social Organization of Animal Communities. Symposium of the Zoological Society of London, No. 14. Academic Press: London.

Frings, H. and M. Frings. 1964. Animal Communication. Blaisdell Publishing Company: New York.

Frisch, K. S. von. 1965. The Dancing Bees. Harcourt, Brace: New York.

Gumperz, J. J. and D. Hymes, eds. 1964. The Ethnography of Communication. American Anthropologist 66 (6).Part 2.

Hall, E. T. 1959. The Silent Language. Doubleday: New York.

———. 1966. The Hidden Dimension. Doubleday: New York.

———. 1968. Proxemics. Current Anthropology 9:83–108.

Harlow, H. F. 1957. Experimental Analysis of Behavior. American Psychologist 12:485–90.

———. 1963. An Experimentalist Views the Emotions. Expression of the Emotions in Man, ed. Peter H. Knapp, pp. 254–65. International Universities Press: New York.

Hendrix, G. 1960. Non-Verbal Awareness in the Learning of Mathematics. Research Problems in Mathematics Education, pp. 57–61. Cooperative Research Monograph No. 3 United States Department of Health, Education, and Welfare, Government Printing Office: Washington, D.C.

Hinde, R. A. 1959. Some Recent Trends in Ethology. Psychology: A Study of a Science, ed. S. Koch, 2, pp. 561–610. McGraw-Hill: New York.

Hockett, C. F. 1958. A Course in Modern Linguistics. University of Chicago Press: Chicago.

———.1968. The State of the Art. Mouton: The Hague.

Hockett, C. F. and R. Asher. 1964. The Human Revolution. Current Anthropology 5:135–68.

Hymes, D., ed. 1964. Language in Culture and Society. Harper and Row: New York.

Kendon, A. 1967. Some Functions of Gaze Direction in Social Interaction. Acta Psychologica 26:22–63.

Klopfer, P. H. and J. P. Hailman. 1967. An Introduction to Animal Behavior: Ethology's First Century. Prentice Hall: Englewood Cliffs.

Köhler, W. 1947. Gestalt Psychology, p. 102. Liveright: New York.

Loeb, F. F. in press. The Fist: A Microscopic Film Analysis of the Function of a Recurrent Behavior Pattern. Journal of Nervous and Mental Diseases.

Lorenz, K. 1952. King Solomon's Ring. Crowell: New York.

———. 1966. On Aggression. Harcourt, Brace: New York.

McGill, T. E., ed. 1965. Readings in Animal Behavior. Holt, Rinehart and Winston, Inc.: New York.

McQuown, N. A. 1957. Linguistic Transcription and Specification of Psychiatric Interview Material. Psychiatry 20:79–86.

———. 1964. Discussion. Approaches to Semiotics, eds. T. A. Sebeok, A. S. Hayes, and M. C. Bateson, 222 pp. Mouton: London.

———, ed. in press. The Natural History of an Interview. Grune and Stratton: New York.

Marler, P. and W. J. Hamilton. 1966. Mechanisms of Animal Behavior. Wiley: New York.

Mead, G. H. 1956. The Social Psychology of George Herbert Mead, ed. A. Strauss, p. 212. University of Chicago Press: Chicago.

Mead, M. 1964. Continuities in Cultural Evolution, 471 pp. Yale University Press: New Haven.

Pike, K. L. 1945. The Intonation of American English. Linguistics, No. 1. University of Michigan Press: Ann Arbor.

———. 1967. Language in Relation to a Unified Theory of the Structure of Human Behavior, 2d rev. ed., 762 pp. Mouton: The Hague.

Sapir, E. 1949a. Language. Selected Writings in Language, Culture and Personality, ed. D. G. Mandelbaum, pp. 7–32. University of California Press: Berkeley.

———. 1949b. Communication. Selected Writings in Language, Culture and Personality, ed. D. G. Mandelbaum, pp. 104–09. University of California Press: Berkeley.

———. 1949c. Why Cultural Anthropology Needs the Psychiatrist. Selected Writings in Language, Culture and Personality, ed. D. G. Mandelbaum, pp. 569–77. University of California Press: Berkeley.

Sarles, H. B. 1966. The Dynamic Study of Interaction as Ethnoscientific Strategy. Anthropological Linguistics (8):66–70, November.

———. 1967. The Study of Intelligibility. Linguistics 34:55–64, August.

———. 1969. The Study of Language and Communication Across Species. Current Anthropology 10:211–21.

———. In press. An Examination of the Question-Response System in Language. Semiotica.

Saussure, F. de. 1959. Course in General Linguistics, eds. C. Bally and A. Sechehaye, translated from the French by W. Baskin, p. 11. Philosophical Library: New York.

Scheflen, A. E. 1964. The Significance of Posture in Communication Systems. Psychiatry 27:316–31.

———. 1966. Natural History Method in Psychotherapy. Research in Psychotherapy, eds. L. A. Gottschalk, and A. H. Auerbach, pp. 263–89. Appleton-Century-Crofts: New York.

———. 1967. On the Structuring of Human Behavior. The American Behavioral Scientist 10:8–12.

———. 1968. Human Communication: Behavioral Programs and Their Integration in Interaction. Behavioral Science 13:44–55.

Sebeok, T. A. 1965. Animal Communication. Science 147:1006–14.

———. 1966. Portraits of Linguistics. University of Indiana Press: Bloomington.

Simpson, G. G. 1966. The Biological Nature of Man. Science 152:472–78, 475, April.

Smith, H. L., Jr. 1960. Linguistics: A Modern View of Language. An Outline of Man's Knowledge of the Modern World, ed. Lyman Bryson. McGraw-Hill: New York.

Southwick, C. H., ed. 1963. Primate Social Behavior: An Enduring Problem. Selected Readings. Van Nostrand: Princeton.

Trager, G. L. 1958. Paralanguage: A First Approximation. Studies in Linguistics 13:1–12.

———. 1966. Language and Psychotherapy. Research in Psychotherapy, eds. L. A. Gottschalk and A. H. Auerbach, pp. 70–82. Appleton-Century-Crofts: New York.

Trager, G. L. and H. L. Smith, Jr. 1951. An Outline of English Structure. Studies in Linguistics, Occasional Paper No. 3, 91 pp. (7th printing, 1966.) American Council of Learned Societies. Columbia University Press: New York.

Waterman, J. T. 1963. Perspectives in Linguistics. University of Chicago Press: Chicago.

Whitehead, A. N. 1957. The Concept of Nature. University of Michigan Press: Ann Arbor.

Part II

Anthropology and
the Health Sciences

CHAPTER **7**   Albert Damon

Constitutional Medicine

Unlike clinical scientists, who focus on pathological individuals, physical anthropologists generally study man in groups. In recent years, some anthropologists have become interested in the individual as well as the group — one of the meanings of "constitution" is "anthropology of the individual." Most research on constitution has resulted from medical problems, and the majority of its applications have been directed toward disease. Accordingly, this paper will be primarily disease-oriented, although many other applications of constitutional medicine will be mentioned.[1]

The notion that the proper study of mankind may encompass individuals as well as groups, and practical application as well as description and theoretical reconstruction or projection, has received little support from the profession. Applied physical anthropology, also called human engineering or biotechnology, has been termed "an academic stepchild, untaught by university anthropologists and largely unavailable to their students" (Damon, Stoudt, and McFarland, 1966). The same may be said for constitutional anthropology. Few anthropologists know the status of constitutional anthropology as a scientific discipline with currently vigorous research activity and solid accomplishments. For this reason, my exposition will be largely factual. Speculation and polemics based on too little evidence have resulted in stereotyped attitudes which should be reexamined in the light of the facts.

1. This work was done in part during the tenure of an established investigatorship of the American Heart Association and with the support of a research grant from the same source.

179

Definitions

"Constitution" is the sum of a person's innate and relatively fixed biological endowment. Draper (1924) regarded the individual as a four-sided pyramid resting on a base. The four sides ("panels") represent the morphological, biochemical, immunological (i.e., disease-diathetic), and psychological aspects of the person; the base represents his genetic make-up. The interrelationships of these aspects of the individual are the subject matter for the discipline of constitution.

Morphology is only one of several constitutional approaches and is probably less important than age, sex, race, biochemical and genetic make-up, blood group, and disease diathesis. Morphology has been the traditional approach, however, largely because physique can be correlated with other characteristics of the individual, partly for historical reasons, and partly because physique is obvious and easily described. In these respects physique resembles demographic variables in epidemiology which include age, sex, race, marital status, income, occupation, and residence. Since these variables are usually at hand, if not always directly relevant to a given problem, they are almost always investigated. So it is with physique.

Constitution means different things to different investigators: to the clinician it means the patient's biological individuality; to the epidemiologist, host factors in disease; to the immunologist, tissue specificity; and to the serologist, it means transfusion reactions. To physical anthropologists, psychologists, and behavioral scientists generally, constitution means physique in relation to environmental adaptation, disease, or behavior. As such, constitution is one application to man of the structure-function relationship, the central concern of physical anthropologists. I shall concentrate here on the morphological aspect of constitution (physique) without implying thereby that the genetic or biochemical aspects are less important.

The Study of Physique in Constitutional Medicine

Physique is relevant to the medical sciences, both preclinical — chiefly anatomy and physiology — and clinical. Normal variation in body build can be correlated with other structural and functional characteristics to help account for the variety of the latter among normal persons, and to set up standards of normality. In relation to abnormal functions, or disease states, we study body form for the same reasons that we study age, sex, race, and other personal or "host" characteristics. These reasons include the following.

1)   Body form is studied to predict in advance who is susceptible to disease and who will respond in what way to disease or therapy. Response to therapy can be as important as who gets the disease in the first place. Prediction can help in prevention, diagnosis, and therapy. To take an example, the identification of persons who have a high risk of developing coronary heart disease (i.e., those with a family history of cardiovascular disease, with elevated blood pressure and serum cholesterol, and those who are overweight and heavy smokers) can indicate who needs frequent examinations and who should be advised to change those pathogenetic features of their environment which are alterable. Again, the decision to begin steroid therapy in connective-tissue diseases rests on a balance between the unknowns of irreversible tissue damage versus potential hazards of medication and of "rebound" after withdrawal. In both examples, further knowledge of constitutional or host factors associated with the disease in question would assist the physician and his patient by improving the accuracy of prediction.

2)   Body form is studied to obtain clues to mechanisms underlying any associations found. Such clues may be sought in biochemical and physiological correlates of disease; in anatomical relationships such as the distribution and structure of organs, tissues, and cells correlated with external body form; or in genetics, via linkage or pleiotropism.

3)   Laboratory research suggested by the associations found between body form and function may help to elucidate the causes of disease. It is obvious that body build does not cause disease. What then is the factor common to both the characteristic body build and the disease in question?

4)   Finally, this process can disclose several places in the web — not the chain — of causation at which intervention can help prevent disease. For example, now that many stages of cholesterol metabolism have been demonstrated, we can intervene at many points to prevent coronary heart disease.

Of course, it is possible to intervene in an attempt to prevent disease without understanding all the causal mechanisms. As we have just seen, the identification of high-risk individuals and groups, using constitutional and other available criteria, permits environmental manipulation. Even where virtually nothing is known about the underlying etiology, as with endometrial carcinoma, identification of the obese nullipara with impared glucose tolerance or frank diabetes as being particularly prone to this disease (Damon, 1960) should result, at the least, in frequent examination of those women who are high risks to detect possible malignancy in its earliest and most curable stages.

Background of Constitutional Medicine

The history of constitutional medicine (Tucker and Lessa, 1940) is an interesting combination of folklore, literature, and science. Its scientific ancestry includes clinical observation (beginning with Hippocrates and continuing through Hutchinson to Pearl and Draper in recent times), psychiatry and psychology (Kretschmer, Sheldon, Parnell, Eysenck), and criminology (Lombroso, Goring, Glueck), as well as anthropology (Hooton, Dupertuis, Seltzer, Tanner). In addition to scientists, constitution also has attracted more than its share of charlatans; such as the "mantics" and phrenologists (Lessa, 1952). A fascinating project in intellectual history and irrational behavior would be an examination of the reasons why constitutional studies currently are held in low esteem by the behavioral sciences in contrast to their high regard among the medical sciences. The patent correspondence of structure and function is acknowledged and studied in the chemical molecule, the cell, and in organisms below man, but in the study of man, ostensibly an area for rational investigation, the notion of such correspondence arouses violent emotion and is heatedly denied in some quarters.

If we grant the relevance of human body form to function, we may then assess the utility of the various techniques for delineating body form: classical anthropometry, indices, factor analysis, body tissue and component analysis, and general ratings of body form. Each of these techniques has advantages and limitations.

Methods of Analyzing Physique

Classical Anthropometry

Classical anthropometry is concerned with body measurement. Height, weight, and their relationship are still the most important measurements of physique, not only for describing body form but also for relating body form to function. Such functions include growth (as in percentile norms and the Wetzel grid used by pediatricians), nutritional status, and effects of disease. Also useful are specific body dimensions, such as stature and chest dimensions to correlate with pulmonary function and disease (Damon, 1966); limb length in relation to stature, altered in endocrinopathies and chromosome anomalies; and limb circumferences as guides to thrombophlebitis or to neuromuscular, bone, or joint disease (Damon and McFarland, 1953).

The drawbacks of classical anthropometry are (1) its limited armamentarium, devised a hundred years ago and oriented toward the skeleton and evolutionary and racial problems; (2) the training required to achieve technical and professional competence; and (3) the multiplicity of possible measurements and the difficulty of interpreting results.

Disproportions

Disproportions are extreme values of a ratio of one measurement to another, and were devised by Seltzer (1946). Disproportions reduce the many possible measurements to a few presumably key ratios. Seltzer's (1946, 1950, 1951) reports that superior performers within an occupation had fewer disproportions than average performers were confirmed among military flyers (Damon, 1955), but not among civilian bus and truck drivers (Damon and Crichton, 1965).

Factor Analysis

Factor analysis attempts to find a small number of independent or correlated factors, which account for the correlations between many body measurements, taken in pairs. Men who have done work with factor analysis include Burt (1947), Thurstone (1946), McCloy (1936), Sills (1950), Howells (1951, 1952), Hammond (1957a, 1957b), and Tanner (1964). Factors of human physique identified to date include one for general size and one for linearity versus laterality of build, but beyond these, there is little agreement. Moreover, the identified factors of physique have rarely been correlated with any aspect of behavior. Sills (1950), to my knowledge the only worker to attempt this, found that physical factors correlated no more closely with athletic performance than did somatotype ratings.

Disproportions and factor analysis, both highly sophisticated research tools still under development, have had limited success so far. By no means do they fill the need for a simple, clinically feasible method for describing physique.

The three preceding methods (classical anthropometry, disproportions, and factor analysis) can easily identify a linear-lateral, or lean-stocky axis of physique, and have proved useful in correlating with behavior. The following two techniques — body component analysis and general ratings or "types" — attempt to refine stockiness of build further by distinguishing between the fat and the bony-muscular components of body build.

Body Composition

Body composition, or tissue analysis, attempts to partition the body into its precentages of water, fat, and lean body mass — bone, muscle, and connective tissue. Skinfold measurement, densitometry, volumetrics, radiography, and dye or isotope dilution and distribution are among the techniques used. Leading workers in this field include Stuart, Behnke, Brozek, Garn, and Keys. While all of these methods involve appreciable error, the use of two simple skinfolds fortunately permits prediction of total body fat among young men to within 2 percent, which is equal to the densitometric range of error (Damon and Goldman, 1964). Body composition analysis has been applied in medicine to evaluate nutritional status, to quantitate obesity, and to estimate the severity of disease after it has occurred. Except for skinfolds, an anthropometric technique, body composition remains a laboratory exercise rather than a clinical or field science.

Ratings of Body Form

The rating of body form has had a long history, beginning with the Hippocratic phthisic and apoplectic habitus. Hippocrates' two physical "types" gave way to Kretschmer's (1925) three types: pyknic, athletic, and asthenic. Sheldon, Stevens, and Tucker (1940) and Sheldon, Dupertuis, and McDermott (1954) retained these three components, which they call endo-, meso-, and ectomorphy, and added a fourth, gynandromorphy, or morphological masculinity-feminity. Later, Tanner (1951a) as well as Osborne and De George (1959) devised other systems for rating gynandromorphy. Sheldon's fifth axis of variation, dysplasia, or disparity among five bodily regions, has not yet proved useful. However, he did make two major contributions. He replaced polar "types" with continuously varying dimensions of physique, and introduced objectivity with standardized photographs and an age-height-weight basis for rat-tings. Despite many unanswered questions concerning the stability of somatotype with age and under varying conditions of nutrition, and the biological interpretation of the components, Sheldon's somatotype system has provided a useful description of physique. Current technical develop-ments in somatotyping attempt to increase the objectivity of body build ratings by planimetry (Sheldon, 1963), by extending the age-height-weight and somatotype scales (B. H. Heath, 1963) or by substituting measurements on the living body for photographs (Lindegård, 1953; Parnell, 1958; Damon et al., 1962; Damon, 1965).

All the current efforts to establish relationships among the various anthropometric techniques seek a simple (non-photographic), clinically feasible and understandable (non-immersion, non-radiographic, non-injection), objective battery of external observations which will describe body form, correlate with body composition, and relate to behavior, physiology, and disease. Since all the systems now in use, including stand-ard anthropometry, have shown associations with some human function, the multiplicity of methods for describing physique should not obscure the fundamental fact that such associations do exist.

Applications and Results

Normal Standards and Disease Precursors

What have been the results to date of all this activity in constitution? First, in application to normal anatomical and physiological standards, such as age-height-weight standards for insurance, military, and indus-trial purposes, increasing note is being taken of differences in body build as modifying the so-called "normal" or "desirable" weights. Insurance companies now qualify their recommendations in terms of large, medium, or small "frames." Through their rejection of many outstanding athletes as "overweight" in World War II, the military services learned that weight can reflect muscle and bone as well as fat. We may hope that skinfold measurement will become a standard part of the examining physician's routine.

Anatomically, correlations have been established between external and cellular morphology by Bjurulf (1959). He reported that the number of fat cells is mainly genetic, and varies with the amount of chest hair, whereas the size of fat cells is mainly environmental, varying with age, biceps girth, and state of nutrition. Bjurulf is extending this work to a study of correlations between gross and microscopic anatomy in muscle.

Physiologically, external body form has been correlated with specific gravity, a measure of fat. Correlations have ranged between 0.70 with skinfolds (Brozek and Keys, 1951) and 0.85 with endomorphy (Dupertuis et al., 1951). Blood pressure varies with laterality of build, that is, stockiness or mesomorphy, rather than with obesity (Robinson and Brucer, 1940b). Extreme somatotypes were reported to be less variable in blood volume and cardiac output than mid-range physiques (Gregersen and Nickerson, 1950). Pulmonary function is independent of somatotype, but vital capacity is closely correlated with stature — oddly enough, more closely than with sitting height or chest expansion (Damon, 1966). Forearm strength has a correlation coefficient of 0.57 with forearm girth (Lindegård, 1953), so that forearm girth becomes a useful index of strength and muscularity. In respect to growth, mesomorphs reach maturity — dental, skeletal, and sexual — earlier than ectomorphs (Tanner, 1962).

Genetically, a twin study of physique (Osborne and De George, 1959) shows that the variance of body lengths is chiefly genetic in origin, whereas that of breadths and girths is mainly environmental. Heritability is also relatively large in body build or somatotype, particularly ectomorphy, and in certain measures of muscle (upper arm girth), bone (wrist breadth), and possibly skinfolds.

Biochemically, serum cholesterol, implicated as a risk factor in coronary heart disease, has been variously reported as correlating with physique. Tanner's (1951b) early findings of moderately high coefficients (0.32 to 0.39) with weight, endomorphy, and skinfolds among forty-six students have not been confirmed among other students (Thomas and Garn, 1960) or older men (Acheson, Hemmens, and Jessop, 1958; Oberman et al., 1965). The height/$\sqrt[3]{\text{weight}}$ index, however, is significantly and negatively correlated with serum cholesterol, 0.18 to 0.31 in various series. Stockily built men have higher serum cholesterol levels, as would be expected from their increased risk of coronary heart disease. An association has been shown between linearity of build and serum pepsinogen level, another disease precursor (Niederman, Spiro, and Sheldon, 1964; Damon and Polednak, 1967). Both men of linear build (Robinson and Brucer, 1940a; Wretmark, 1953) and those with elevated serum pepsinogen (Weiner et al., 1957; Niederman, Spiro, and Sheldon, 1964) have an increased risk of developing peptic ulcer.

Tanner et al. (1959) have reported high coefficients of correlation between other biochemical constituents such as creatinine, which is an index of muscle mass, and weight (0.76), surface area (0.63), skinfolds (0.47), and somatotype (0.44 to 0.49). They have also reported modest correlations, 0.22 to 0.31, between 17–ketosteroids, an adrenal cortical product, and weight, surface area, and somatotype. Androgens and estrogens are reportedly independent of somatotype (D. M. Spain, personal communication). I plan to explore the correlations between sex hormones and somatotype and gynandromorphy as part of the Framingham Heart Study of the United States Public Health Service.

Behavior

Apart from folklore and literary interest, there has been a long-standing scientific interest in the body-behavior relationship. Recent exhaustive reviews by Rees (1961) and by Domey, Duckworth, and Morandi (1964) conclude that real associations exist for both normal and abnormal behavior. In other studies Sheldon and Stevens' (1942) correlations of 0.7 to 0.8 between somatotype and temperament were not confirmed at such high levels. Child (1950), Cortés and Gatti (1965), and von Zerssen (1965) found moderate correlations (0.31 to 0.47) between mesomorphy and somatotonia, and lower r's or none at all between endomorphy and viscerotonia, and between ectomorphy and cerebrotonia. Cortés and Gatti (1966) obtained associations between somatotype and motivation. Associations of somatotype have been reported with occupational selection and success among military pilots (Damon, 1955), soldiers (Hooton, 1959), industrial workers (Garn and Gertler, 1950), bus and truck drivers (Damon and McFarland, 1955), lumberjacks (Eränkö and Karvonen, 1955), and students (C. W. Heath, 1945; Tanner, 1954; Parnell, 1954). The relationship of occupation to disease, particularly coronary heart disease, is pertinent here in that the same physical types prone to coronary heart disease, the stocky endo-mesomorphs, predominate among bus and truck drivers, a high-risk occupational group (Morris et al., 1953). Delinquent boys were found to be more mesomorphic than non-delinquent boys by Sheldon, Hartl, and Mc-Dermott (1949), Seltzer (1951), and Cortés (1961). As previously mentioned, Seltzer's (1946) "disproportions" have been applied to occupational groups, with positive findings for military pilots (Damon, 1955), but negative ones for civilian bus and truck drivers (Damon and Crichton, 1965). The preponderance of evidence from properly controlled studies of behavior has overcome the objection that Sheldon and Stevens' (1942) first-reported correlations between somatotype and temperament were not based on independent ratings of the two sets of variables.

Independently of food intake (Damon, 1961) and even before beginning to smoke (Seltzer, 1963), smokers were reported to differ physically from non-smokers. In these two studies and in others, however, the direction of physical difference was opposite among young men and adults; young smokers were heavier in build than non-smokers, whereas adult smokers were lighter and leaner than non-smokers. The interpretation of the reported associations is therefore obscure. Alcohol consumption seems to be independent of physique (Damon, 1963).

It is possible that constitutional research may eventually disclose which persons should avoid certain drugs, foods, or occupations. One purpose of a current longitudinal study of World War II veterans is to determine who, in constitutional terms, can smoke heavily, and who cannot.

A final application of constitution to behavior is in the area of reproduction. Among some twenty-six hundred Harvard men with completed families, the fathers' ponderal index (height/$\sqrt[3]{\text{weight}}$) was associated with sex ratio of offspring — stockier men had more sons — but not with fertility. While the fathers' baldness was unrelated to sex ratio of offspring or to fertility, tall men had more children than short ones (Damon and Nuttall, 1965; Damon, Burr, and Gerson, 1965; Damon and Thomas, 1967).

Disease

We are now able to summarize research on constitution, and particularly on physique, in relation to disease. Findings are presented in tabular form (Table 1). It should be noted that the "confirmed" associations for tuberculosis and hypertension are based on prospective studies, the most satisfactory kind of proof. In these studies, physical observations are made on healthy persons who are followed until they do or do not develop a specific disease. Work is currently under way in several studies to test prospectively the association between physique and coronary heart disease.

TABLE 1

Physique and Disease

Disease	Susceptible Physique	Author
No Association		
Acne vulgaris	None	Damon, 1957
Polycythemia vera	None	Damon and Holub, 1958
Disputed Association (probably real)		
Peptic ulcer	Linear	Robinson and Brucer, 1940a; Draper et al., 1944; Wretmark, 1953
Gallbladder disease	Stocky, lateral Fat	Draper, Dupertuis, and Caughey, 1944; Van der Linden, 1961
Psychoses: schizophrenia	Asthenic	Kretschmer, 1925; Betz, 1942
Psychoses: manic-depression	Pyknic	Kretschmer, 1925
Reported Association (unconfirmed)		
Poliomyelitis	Mesomorphic	Draper, Dupertuis, and Caughey, 1944
Meniere's disease	Mesomorphic	Damon, Fowler, and Sheldon, 1955
Otosclerosis	Ectomorphic	Damon, Fowler, and Sheldon, 1955
Breast and cervical cancer	"Hyperfeminine"	Damon, 1960
Uterine fibroids	Mesomorphic	Damon, 1960
Hypertension, malignant	Lean	Perera and Damon, 1957
Confirmed Association		
Tuberculosis	Tall, thin	Berry and Nash, 1955; Palmer, Jablon, and Edwards, 1957

Table 1 *continued*

Disease	Susceptible Physique	Author
Confirmed Association (cont'd)		
Diabetes: juvenile	Tall	White, 1959; Nilsson, 1962
Diabetes: adult	Obese	Lister and Tanner, 1955; Marks, 1956; Nilsson, 1962
Cancer, endometrium	Obese	Corscaden and Gusberg, 1947
Cancer, endometrium	Obese	Garnet, 1958; Damon, 1960
Hypertension, essential	Stocky, lateral	Robinson and Brucer, 1940b; Society of Actuaries, 1959
Coronary heart disease	Endo-mesomorphic	Gertler et al., 1954; Spain, Bradess, and Huss, 1953; Spain, Bradess, and Greenblatt, 1955; Spain, Nathan, and Gellis, 1963; Forssman and Lindegård, 1958; Bjurulf, 1959; Shanoff et al., 1961; Pomerantz, 1962.

The present evidence that physique plays a part in coronary heart disease is summarized below as an example of a "confirmed" association.

In 1959, a Conference on Methodology in Epidemiological Studies of Cardiovascular Diseases was held in Princeton, New Jersey, under the auspices of the American Heart Association and the National Heart Institute. The published report (Conference on Methodology, 1960) summarized the state of knowledge up to that time and provided standardized definitions and techniques in order to establish comparability among investigations. In addition, guidelines were offered for future studies in areas deemed important. One section of the report (pp. 59–64) concerned body form and summarized its relationship to cardiovascular diseases, particularly coronary heart disease and hypertension.

At that time, evidence for an association between body form and coronary heart disease came from two studies by American investigators who used Sheldon's somatotype technique for describing body build (Sheldon, Stevens, and Tucker, 1940) and from two studies by Swedish investigators who used Lindegård's (1953) anthropometric system. Lindegård's system attempts to ascertain the major factors in body build without the photography and subjective judgment inherent in the somatotype. In the United States, Gertler and his colleagues (1954), working with clinical material, characterized young coronary patients — those who sustained myocardial infarction under the age of 40 — primarily as mesomorphic (bony and muscular) and, secondarily, as endomorphic (round and fat). Spain, Bradess, and Huss (1953), working with autopsy material, confirmed the predominant mesomorphy of men who died of coronary occlusion under the age of 46. Furthermore, among 73 apparently healthy white men of similar age who died by violent means, the degree of coronary artery atherosclerosis was definitely greater in the dominant mesomorphs than in the dominant ectomorphs. In a later study, Spain, Bradess, and Greenblatt (1955) reported that coronary sclerosis paralleled serum beta-lipoprotein levels among endomorphs and mesomorphs, but not among ectomorphs, who are linear and fragile in build.

In Sweden, Forssman and Lindegård (1958) reported that 55 male post-coronary patients fell into two sub-types. The bony, muscular, and fat type had a high serum cholesterol level, but the opposite (lean) type did not. Bjurulf (1959) reported that, among 110 virtually consecutive autopsies on males over the age of 25, most of whom were elderly, the grade of coronary atherosclerosis correlated ($r = 0.31$) with subcutaneous fat thickness and ($r = 0.24$) with the biceps girth corrected for labile fat.

Up to 1959, American workers had identified mesomorphic males as particularly prone to early coronary heart disease, whereas the Swedes had implicated both fat and muscularity among older men with coronary heart disease.

Since 1959, confirming reports have appeared in several countries. In Canada, Shanoff et al. (1961) reported that men with coronary heart disease had a higher ratio of chest circumference to stature than controls. Pomerantz (1962) noted the same for large wrists. Both these physical measures are characteristic of mesomorphy. In the United States, Albrink, Meigs, and Granoff (1962) have directed attention to weight gain since age twenty-five, rather than to current weight, as a possible prognostic tool for cardiovascular disease, particularly coronary heart disease. Investigators in the Framingham Heart Study have been thinking along similar lines (W. B. Kannel, personal communication, 1966). In a longitudinal study, Harlan, Osborne, and Graybiel (1962) actually found that, when endomorphs and mesomorphs gained weight over an eighteen-year period, they had a significantly greater rise in blood pressure than did ectomorphs who gained weight.

To date, the most conclusive evidence relating body build to coronary heart disease has been supplied by Spain, Nathan, and Gellis (1963), and is based on a study of five thousand Jewish men in the New York City area. Here, the risk of coronary heart disease for endo-mesomorphs was about three times that for ectomorphs, whether or not hypertension was present. The magnitude of risk within this relatively homogeneous group is similar to that reported for the major known risk factors in coronary heart disease among other populations — heavy smoking, hypertension, a left ventricular "strain" pattern on the electrocardiogram, or high serum cholesterol levels. A 3:1 risk ratio is greater than that between men and women of all ages, greater than the largest contrasts reported among ethnic groups or geographic regions in the United States, and greater than any occupational differences observed between sedentary and active workers. It should be emphasized that any association established within a group so homogeneous, biologically and culturally, takes on added meaning in view of the restricted range of variation within that group. One might anticipate even greater risk within a more general population.

My own current work indicates that, among the Framingham subjects, somatotype ratings derived from body measurements by multiple regression equations can identify, on a prospective basis, middle-aged men who develop coronary heart disease before age fifty. Such identification is less accurate for myocardial infarction than for the other manifestations of coronary heart disease — angina pectoris, myocardial ischemia, and sudden death.

We may conclude, therefore, that body form is, indeed, related to coronary heart disease.

Current Research in Constitutional Medicine

Constitutional medicine did not begin and end with Sheldon, as many anthropologists seem to think. Current research in constitution is active along three major lines: (1) seeking better technical methods for describing physique (Lindegård, Parnell, Tanner, Heath and Carter, Haronian and Sugerman); (2) establishing associations or the lack of them between physique and physiological, pathological, and behavioral functions; and (3) investigating the mechanisms which underlie the associations found. I will discuss each of these trends.

1) The development of techniques which lead to better description of physique is desirable, but I feel that such an effort would be better directed toward establishing associations with the tools already available, and toward exploring associations already found, since possible associations are unlikely to be strong enough to permit prediction when used alone. I estimate correlation or contingency coefficients to range between 0.2 and 0.4. This by no means diminishes their theoretical or even practical importance if they are used in conjunction with other measures, as physicians always do. Further refinement of technique is unlikely to disclose strong associations otherwise occult. Such statistical developments as multiple regression and discriminants make it possible to predict directly from body measurements the dependent variable of interest, disease, or behavior, bypassing the intermediate step of determining body build or "type," which causes so much trouble.

2) The associations or lack of them between physique and function found by conventional methods, which have been cross-sectional and correlational, should be validated and quantitated by longitudinal studies. These associations should be tested further cross-racially and cross-culturally to determine the extent to which they are biological or reflect other, primarily cultural, differences.

3) We now know enough to investigate mechanisms underlying the associations already found between physique and disease. Here is the greatest challenge and reward. Some of the possibilities, which are by no means mutually exclusive, include morphology, biochemical or physiological correlations, and genetics. One promising lead is the association between gross and microscopic anatomy, as pioneered by Bjurulf (1959) and Jeanneret (1960).

Training in Constitution

In my view, medical training is essential for students of constitution — medicine provides the best available education in human biology. The combination of medical education with physical anthropology, including statistics, lays a solid foundation for work in constitution. Good work has been done by investigators who lack this combined background, but it is no accident that the leading figures in the field have both types of training.

Few institutions will be able to offer training in constitution, however. Despite the great demand for research collaboration, there are few institutions that offer appointments in constitutional medicine. Persons with this training have found careers in faculties of arts and sciences, schools of medicine, dentistry, and public health, or in research establishments. Departmental affiliations have included anthropology, anatomy, epidemiology, genetics, medicine, nutrition, preventive medicine, and pediatrics. Unfortunately, the constitutionalist usually finds himself on the periphery of any of these departments. While interdisciplinary sciences are encouraged in the abstract, institutions are still organized by traditional disciplines. Students should be advised, therefore, on both scholarly and practical grounds, to acquire solid competence in a traditional discipline as a base from which to branch out into constitutional medicine.

Constitutional Medicine in Anthropology

Constitution spans the widest spectrum of any anthropological subfield: its intellectual areas extend from biology, biochemistry, and medicine to the behavioral sciences; its objectives range from describing associations and predicting outcome for individuals or groups to probing underlying mechanisms. It deals with units from cells, tissues, and organs to individuals and populations. From a different perspective, constitution, the study of the individual, bears the same relationship to physical anthropology, a group or statistical science, as clinical medicine does to epidemiology, or as individual psychology does to social psychology or cultural anthropology.

In addition to its intellectual contribution as a descriptive, historical, and integrating science, physical anthropology has a practical value for mankind in its applications to medicine, equipment design, and personnel selection. For medicine, the physical anthropologist can establish physical and functional norms; for forensic medicine he can identify remains or assess race and paternity; and, as a student of constitution, he can relate physique to normal and abnormal function.

The preparation for a career in constitution — whether it is called constitutional medicine or anthropology — is long and the reward uncertain but, for a biological antropologist, I know of no area which better combines intellectual challenge with the possibility of helping mankind.

COMMENTARY: Roy M. Acheson
Paul T. Baker

Roy M. Acheson

As an epidemiologist, I make measurements in the mass; measurements which identify the healthy and, more important the sick and the diseases from which they suffer. An epidemiologist also must attempt to measure the environment in all its complexity: the social and physical, animate and inanimate, meteorological and geological, microbial and zoological; for, in the long run, most of the determinants of disease in man are found in his environment. Moreover, to assess precisely the risk man runs, these determinants must be quantitated.

There is, however, more to it than that. No two men react to the same risk factors in the same way, since the degree and nature of their reaction depend in part on their constitution. Dr. Damon defined "constitution" for the epidemiologist as "host factors in disease," and for the anthropologist as "physique in relation to environmental adaptation." Although I am an epidemiologist, I have had the pleasure of being a member of the American Association of Physical Anthropology for over ten years and have taken particular interest in environmental effects on the skeletal development of children. Thus, I personally combine these definitions by using the classification of physique in the quest for host factors in disease.

In general, epidemiology is a science of compromises. It is a well-known fact that the most precise and repeatable measurements in any study are those made by a single, highly skilled observer and that the larger the sample studied by an epidemiologist, the more likely his results are to be meaningful. Obviously, these facts are incompatible. A single skilled observer cannot measure hundreds or thousands of people; indeed the larger the sample, the greater the number of observers required and, therefore, the greater the error component in the variance of any measurement. Among the most difficult measurements are those of body width such as bi-acromial or bi-iliac diameter.

Dr. Damon spoke of the paradoxical situation in which the use of multiple regressions might permit the prediction of host liability to disease before a satisfactory system for describing physique is evolved. He may be right, but a necessary preliminary step is the development of accurate and repeatable methods for making appropriate multiple physical measurements in large populations. The Kaiser-Permanente health plan is taking steps along these lines. However, because the necessary equipment is elaborate and expensive, such work is beyond the reach of the majority of individual investigators in constitutional medicine who operate from fixed laboratory premises. Adaptation of the Kaiser-Permanente technique for fieldwork must, moreover, lie a good many years ahead. Therefore, in my view, the immediate future for meaningful epidemiological research in constitutional medicine involving measurements lies with those privileged scientists who have access to large funds.

A simpler approach, which gives us more limited data, separates the bulky from the lean on an interval scale. Obviously, body weight alone cannot be used because it is too dependent on stature. In one attempt to overcome this difficulty, researchers, in the Framingham Heart Study held stature constant and used the range of height-specific weights within the study population as a basis for comparison (Dawber et al., 1959). The major problem with this approach is that it provides no absolute way of judging physique. To put it crudely, "relative weight," as judged at Framingham, Massachusetts, cannot be expected to bear any relationship at all to "relative weight" as judged in Madras, India, because most Americans are overfed and most Indians are underfed. For an index of bulk to be used extensively in comparisons between different populations, as with stature and weight, the index must be derived from measurements of each individual in the population and not from comparisons among people from a given study population. The most sophisticated, and probably the most meaningful, index of this kind has been worked out by Epstein and his group in the University of Michigan's Tecumseh study (Epstein, et al., 1965). However, since this index has been calculated in a static laboratory from several measurements, some of them troublesome widths, it also presents the aforementioned difficulties.

I am naive enough to believe that the simplest of all indices, those based on height and weight alone, still have a great deal to tell us. Many of these indices are available and each can be converted to the other by correction with a constant. The ponderal index, calculated from standing height divided by cube root of weight, is the most popular in those parts of the world where people measure in pounds and inches. It ranges in adults from about ten for the bulkiest of people to something over fourteen for the very lean. It has two glaring disadvantages, the most important of which is that it fails to differentiate the bulky fat man from the bulky muscular man. Billewicz, Kemsley, and Thomson (1962) have drawn attention to a second difficulty — ponderal index is height dependent. Previously, it was believed that the ponderal index offered a perfect correction of weight for height within the normal adult range. However, Fowler's (1965) extensive analysis of a population much larger and more varied than the wee Aberdeen fishwives studied by Billewicz and his colleagues has shown that the extent of this height dependence in adult males is negligible, although it was confirmed by Fowler (1965) in women.

The ponderal index has two great advantages: (1) it depends upon the two anthropometric observations which probably can be made more accurately than any others, even by persons of limited training; and (2) these two observations are the most widely available. The ponderal index is also of great practical importance to the epidemiologist since he can calculate it from data available in routine hospital records.

This index has been shown to be related to a variety of chronic diseases. One finding indicates that, in college students, it can be a predictor of their liability toward coronary heart disease in later life (Paffenbarger et al., 1966). It is also related to present coronary heart disease in middle-aged (Gertler et al., 1954) and old men (Acheson, 1961). In one survey, men with a high ponderal index and glycosuria (lean men) had a low renal threshold for glucose, while men with a low ponderal index and glycosuria (bulky men) had diabetes (Fowler, 1965). Another study has shown that men with a low ponderal index also have a high serum uric acid and, presumably, an exaggerated liability to gout (Gertler, Garn, and Levine, 1951). Strangely, however, in a current survey in New Haven (Acheson and O'Brien, 1966) the ponderal index is predicting uric acid better than weight or body surface areas in males, while weight alone is the best predictor of serum uric acid in females — the ponderal index is significant, but second as a predictor (Gertler, Garn, and Levine, 1951).

The ponderal index is faced with three immediate challenges in this small corner of constitutional medicine. One, which has appeal because of its complexity and cost, is to take as many measurements as possible and use the largest available computer and the most incomprehensible statistics to see what can be made of them. The second challenge, which is cheaper, more difficult, and, therefore, less likely to be done, involves working out standards which will permit one single, simple measurement, such as skinfold, to separate those with a low ponderal index who are bulk-fat from those who are bulky-muscular and from those who are both.

The third and ultimate challenge is to answer the question "Why?" Why are people with certain physiques or constitutions liable to certain diseases? I agree with Dr. Damon that a solution to this third question is most likely to be reached by someone who has medical training. I believe, however, that anthropologists and other scientists will be as likely as any to answer the first two challenges successfully.

Postscript

Two studies undertaken since this paper was given, one by Khosla and Lowe (1967) and the other (shortly to be published) by Dr. Charles Florey working in my laboratory, have helped to establish further the value of simple height and weight indices. Florey's work is based on two large American population samples and Khosla and Lowe's (1967) on male industrial populations from Britain. Both confirm that the ponderal index within the usual ranges of physique in Caucasian Westernized populations is height dependent, and both indicate that this is less true of indices such as weight/height or weight/height^2. Florey goes on to develop models which will be helpful in the choice of the suitable height-weight index which according to the physique and sex of the population under consideration should be the most efficient in selecting the bulky from the lean; he shows that this efficiency can be considerable.

Paul T. Baker

I strongly agree with Dr. Damon's general thesis that physical anthropologists or, as I would prefer, "human biologists," must be concerned with the links between morphology, function, and behavior. I would go further and say that, if human biology is to contribute significantly to the general field of anthropology, it must study the genetic variations in man, shown how the various genic systems interact with the environment to produce morphology, and then study the morphology-function-behavior relationships. The study of these relationships and interactions is the basis of much of modern physical anthropology. Consequently, I would prefer to change Dr. Damon's emphasis on the interaction of morphology and disease, even though this emphasis is appropriate in the context of our relationships to medicine.

For human biology, the links of morphology to normal functioning and behavior within human groups are more important than those to disease. Although a large number of these relationships are now known, I am quite sure the anthropologist's basic research in human biology must remain concentrated on the "normal" rather than the "pathological."

Because of my special obligations as a teacher, the following remarks concern doctoral students in physical anthropology. About ten years ago, some leaders in the field pointed out that we could no longer hope to train a competent human biologist to have the previously expected depth of information in archaeology, cultural anthropology, and linguistics. Since then there have been two developments in graduate training. A number of schools have increased biology-related training for graduate students in physical anthropology, usually at the expense of education in archaeology, linguistics, and even cultural anthropology. I think this is the healthier trend. Some departments, however, have retained the requirement for general-depth knowledge and, consequently, have produced few, poorly trained human biologists. In rebellion against this, separate interdisciplinary groups have developed special graduate programs in human biology. Although the latter development may be the wave of the future, at present it seems premature and runs counter to the theoretical threads which are now tending to reunite some aspects of cultural and physical anthropology.

However the formal structure of the degree is resolved, it is quite apparent from symposia on such topics that more biology must be introduced into the training of the human biologist and that the number of professionals in this field must be increased. Some anthropologists have denounced the shortage of anthropologists engaged in applied research and the lack of biological training of those available. Others have stressed that the physical anthropologist needs to know anatomy, embryology, growth, microscopic analysis, and sex and race variability. Finally, Dr. Damon suggests that the only way to provide adequate background is for the student to obtain both a Ph.D. and an M.D. Such degree requirements necessitate, at a minimum, a ten- to twelve-year program. We need human biologists now and it is unrealistic to expect students to pursue non-paying or poorly paying training programs for such a long period of time. Surely, in the interest of keeping our field alive, it is better to sacrifice depth training in linguistics, archaeology, and even some aspects of cultural anthropology, than to run the risk of evolutionary death in the form of non-reproduction.

REFERENCES

Acheson, R. M. 1961. The Aetiology of Coronary Heart Disease in Old Men. British Journal of Preventive and Social Medicine 15:49–60.

Acheson, R. M., W. F. Hemmens, and W. J. E. Jessop. 1958. Serum Cholesterol in a Population Sample of Males Aged 65–85 Years. Gerontologia 2:357–71.

Acheson, R. M. and W. M. O'Brien, 1966. The Dependence of Serum-Uric-Acid on Haemoglobin and Other Factors in the General Population. Lancet 2: 777–78.

Albrink, M. J., J. W. Meigs, and M. A. Granoff. 1962. Weight Gain and Serum Triglycerides in Normal Men. New England Journal of Medicine 266:484–89.

Berry, W. T. C. and F. A. Nash. 1955. Studies in the Aetiology of Pulmonary Tuberculosis. Tubercle 36: 164–74.

Betz, B. 1942. Somatology of the Schizophrenic Patient. Human Biology 14:21–47, 192–234.

Billewicz, W. Z., W. F. Kemsley, and A. M. Thomson. 1962. Indices of Adiposity. British Journal of Preventive and Social Medicine 16: 183–88.

Bjurulf, P. 1959. Atherosclerosis and Body-Build. Acta Medica Scandinavica, Supplement 166.

Brozek, J. and A. Keys. 1951. The Evaluation of Leanness-Fatness in Man: Norms and Interrelationships. British Journal of Nutrition 5:194–206.

Burt, C. 1947. Factor Analysis and Physical Types. Psychometrika 12:171–188.

Child, I. L., 1950. The Relation of Somatotype to Self-Ratings on Sheldon's Temperamental Traits. Journal of Personality 18:440–53.

Conference on Methodology in Epidemiological Studies of Cardiovascular Diseases. 1960. American Heart Association and National Heart Institute, Princeton, New Jersey (1959). American Journal of Public Health 50 (10), Supplement: 59–64.

Corscaden, J. A. and S. B. Gusberg. 1947. The background of Cancer of the Corpus. American Journal of Obstetrics and Gynecology 53: 419–31.

Cortés, J. B. 1961. Physique, Need for Achievement, and Delinquency. Unpublished Ph.D. dissertation, Department of Social Relations, Harvard University.

Cortés, J. B. and F. M. Gatti. 1965. Physique and Self-Description of Temperament. Journal of Consulting Psychology 29:432–39.

―――. 1966. Physique and Motivation. Journal of Consulting Psychology 30: 408–14.

Damon, A. 1955. Physique and Success in Military Flying. American Journal of Physical Anthropology 13: 217–52.

―――. 1957. Constitutional Factors in Acne Vulgaris. Archives of Dermatology 76:172–78.

―――. 1960. Host Factors in Cancer of the Breast and Uterine Cervix and Corpus. Journal of the National Cancer Institute 24:483–516.

―――. 1961. Constitution and Smoking. Science 134:339–41.

―――. 1963. Constitution and Alcohol Consumption: Physique. Journal of Chronic Diseases 16:1237–50.

―――. 1965. Delineation of the Body Build Variables Associated with Cardiovascular Diseases. Annals of the New York Academy of Sciences 126:711–27.

―――. 1966. Negro-White Differences in Pulmonary Function (Vital Capacity, Timed Vital Capacity, and Expiratory Flow Rate). Human Biology 38:380–93.

Damon, A. et al. 1962. Predicting Somatotype from Body Measurements. American Journal of Physical Anthropology 20:461–74.

Damon, A., W. A. Burr, and D. A. Gerson. 1965. Baldness of Fathers and Number and Sex Ratio of Children. Human Biology 37:366–70.

Damon, A. and J. M. Crichton. 1965. Body Disproportions and Occupational Success in Bus and Truck Drivers. American Journal of Physical Anthropology 23:63–68.

Damon, A., E. P. Fowler, Jr., and W. H. Sheldon. 1955. Constitutional Factors in Otosclerosis and Meniere's Disease. Transactions of the American Academy of Ophthalmology and Otolaryngology 59:444–58.

Damon, A. and R. F. Goldman. 1964. Predicting Fat from Body Measurements. Densitometric Validation of Ten Anthropometric Equations. Human Biology 36:32–44.

Damon, A. and D. A. Holub, 1958. Host Factors in Polycythemia Vera. Annals of Internal Medicine 49:43–60.

Damon, A. and R. A. McFarland. 1953. Difference in Calf Circumference as Diagnostic Guide to Thrombophlebitis. Journal of the American Medical Association 153: 622–25.

―――. 1955. The Physique of Bus and Truck Drivers: With a Review of Occupational Anthropology. American Journal of Physical Anthropology 13:711–42.

Damon, A. and R. L. Nuttall. 1965. Ponderal Index of Fathers and Sex Ratio of Children. Human Biology 37:23–28.

Damon, A. and A. P. Polednak. 1967. Physique and Serum Pepsinogen. Human Biology 39: 355–67.

Damon, A., H. W. Stoudt, and R. A. McFarland. 1966. The Human Body in Equipment Design. Harvard University Press: Cambridge.

Damon, A. and R. B. Thomas. 1967. Fertility and Physique: Height, Weight, and Ponderal Index. Human Biology 39:5–13.

Dawber, T. R. et al. 1959. Some Factors Associated With the Development of Coronary Heart Disease: Six Years' Follow-Up Experience in the Framingham Study. American Journal of Public Health 49:1349–56.

Domey, R. G., J. Duckworth, and A. Morandi. 1964. Taxonomies and Correlates of Physique. Psychological Bulletin 62:411–26.

Draper, G. 1924. Human Constitution: A Consideration of Its Relationship to Disease. W. B. Saunders: Philadelphia.

Draper, G., C. W. Dupertuis, and J. L. Caughey, Jr. 1944. Human Constitution in Clinical Medicine. Hoeber: New York.

Dupertuis, C. W. et al. 1951. Relation of Specific Gravity to Body Build in a Group of Healthy Men. Journal of Applied Physiology 3:676–80.

Epstein, F. H. et al. 1965. Epidemiological Studies of Cardiovascular Disease in a Total Community: Tecumseh, Michigan. Annals of Internal Medicine 62: 1179–87.

Eränkö, O. and M. J. Karvonen. 1955. Body Type of Finnish Champion Lumberjacks. American Journal of Physical Anthropology 13:331–44.

Forssman, O. and B. Lindegård. 1958. The Post-Coronary Patient. Journal of Psychosomatic Research 3:89–169.

Fowler, G. B. 1965. Physique, Blood Glucose and Glycosuria in Population Samples. Unpublished doctoral dissertation, University of London.

Garn, S. M. and M. M. Gertler. 1950. An Association Between Type of Work and Physique in an Industrial Group. American Journal of Physical Anthropology 8:387–97.

Garnet, J. D. 1958. Constitutional Stigmas Associated With Endometrial Carcinoma. American Journal of Obstetrics and Gynecology 76: 11–19.

Gertler, M. M., S. M. Garn, and S. A. Levine. 1951. Serum Uric Acid in Relation to Age and Physique in Health and Coronary Heart Disease. Annals of Internal Medicine 34:1421–31.

Gertler, M. M. et al. 1954. Coronary Heart Disease in Young Adults. Harvard University Press: Cambridge.

Gregersen, M. I. and J. L. Nickerson. 1950. Relation of Blood Volume and Cardiac Output to Body Type. Journal of Applied Physiology 3:329–41.

Hammond, W. H. 1957a. The Constancy of Physical Types as Determined by Factorial Analysis. Human Biology 29:40–61.

———. 1957b. The Status of Physical Types. Human Biology 29:223–41.

Harlan, W. R., R. K. Osborne, and A. Graybiel. 1962. A Longitudinal Study of Blood Pressure. Circulation 26:530–43.

Heath, B. H. 1963. Need for Modification of Somatotype Methodology. American Journal of Physical Anthropology 21:227–33.

Heath, C. W. 1945. What People Are: A Study of Normal Young Men. Harvard University Press: Cambridge.

Hooton, E. A. 1959. Body Build in a Sample of the United States Army. United States Quartermaster Research and Engineering Center. Technical Report EP-102. Natick, Mass.

Howells, W. W. 1951. Factors of Human Physique. American Journal of Physical Anthropology 9:159–92.

———. 1952. A Factorial Study of Constitutional Type. American Journal of Physical Anthropology 10:91–118.

Jeanneret, O. 1960. Essai d'Analyse du Type Constitutionel Dit Sous-Méso-blastique chez l'Homme Adulte. Archives Suisses d'Anthropologie Générale, 25.

Khosla, T. and C. R. Lowe. 1967. Indices of Obesity Derived from Body Weight and Height. British Journal of Preventive and Social Medicine 21:122–28.

Kretschmer, E. 1925. Physique and Character. (English translation). Harcourt, Brace: New York.

Lessa, W. A. 1952. Somatomancy: Precursor of the Science of Human Constitution. Scientific Monthly 75:355–65.

Lindegård, B. 1953. Variations in Human Body-Build. Acta Psychiatrica et Neurologica, Supplement 86.

Lister, J. and J. M. Tanner. 1955. The Physique of Diabetics. Lancet 2:1002–04.

McCloy, C. H. 1936. Appraising Physical Status: The Selection of Measurements. University of Iowa Press: Iowa City.

Morris, J. N. et al. 1953. Coronary Heart Disease and Physical Activity of Work. Lancet 2:1053–57, 1111 20.

Niederman, J. C., H. L. Spiro, and W. H. Sheldon. 1964. Blood Pepsin as Marker of Susceptibility to Duodenal Ulcer Disease. Archives of Environmental Health 8:540–46.

Nilsson, S. E. 1962. Genetic and Constitutional Aspects of Diabetes Mellitus. Acta Medica Scandinavica, Supplement 375.

Oberman, A. et al. 1965. The Thousand Aviator Study: Distributions and Intercorrelations of Selected Variables. United States Naval Aerospace Medical Institute Monograph 11. Pensacola, Florida.

Osborne, R. H. and F. V. De George. 1959. Genetic Basis of Morphological Variation. Harvard University Press: Cambridge.

Paffenbarger, R. S. et al. 1966. Chronic Disease in Former College Students: Early Precursors of Fatal Coronary Heart Disease. American Journal of Epidemiology 83:329–37.

Palmer, A. E., S. Jablon, and P. Q. Edwards. 1957. Tuberculosis Morbidity of Young Men in Relation to Tuberculin Sensitivity and Body Build. American Review of Tuberculosis 76: 517–39.

Parnell, R. W. 1954. Physique and Performance: Honours Class at Oxford. British Medical Journal 2:49–66.

———. 1958. Behaviour and Physique. Edward Arnold: London.

Perera, G. A. and A. Damon. 1957. Height, Weight, and Their Ratio in the Accelerated Form of Primary Hypertension. Archives of Internal Medicine 100:263–65.

Pomerantz, H. Z. 1962. Relationship Between Coronary Heart Disease and Certain Physical Characteristics. Canadian Medical Association Journal 86:57–60.

Rees, W. L. 1961. Constitutional Factors in Abnormal Behavior. Handbook of Abnormal Psychology, ed. H. J. Eysenck. Basic Books: New York.

Robinson, S. C. and M. Brucer. 1940a. The Body Build of the Male Ulcer Patient. American Journal of Digestive Diseases 9:365–73.

———. 1940b. Body Build and Hypertension. Archives of Internal Medicine 66: 393–417.

Seltzer, C. C. 1946. Body Disproportions and Dominant Personality Traits. Psychosomatic Medicine 8:75–97.

———. 1950. A Comparative Study of the Morphological Characteristics of Delinquents and Non-Delinquents. Unraveling Juvenile Delinquency, S. Glueck and E. Glueck. Commonwealth Fund: New York.

———. 1951. Constitutional Aspects of Juvenile Delinquency. Cold Spring Harbor Symposia on Quantitative Biology 15: 361–72.

———. 1963. Morphologic Constitution and Smoking. Journal of the American Medical Association 183: 639–45.

Shanoff, H. M. et al. 1961. Studies of Male Survivors of Myocardial Infarction Due to "Essential" Atherosclerosis. I. Characteristics of the Patients. Canadian Medical Association Journal 84:519–30.

Sheldon, W. H. 1963. Constitutional Variation and Mental Health. Encyclopedia of Mental Health. Franklin Watts: New York.

Sheldon, W. H., C. W. Dupertuis, and E. McDermott. 1954. Atlas of Men: A Guide for Somatotyping the Adult Male at All Ages. Harper & Brothers: New York.

Sheldon, W. H., E. M. Hartl, and E. McDermott. 1949. Varieties of Delinquent Youth. Harper & Brothers: New York.

Sheldon, W. H., and S. S. Stevens. 1942. The Varieties of Temperament. Harper & Brothers: New York.

Sheldon, W. H., S. S. Stevens, and W. B. Tucker. 1940. The Varieties of Human Physique. Harper & Brothers: New York.

Sills, F. D. 1950. A Factor Analysis of Somatotypes and of Their Relationship to Achievement in Motor Skills. Research Quarterly 21:424–37.

Society of Actuaries. 1959. Build and Blood Pressure Study. Society of Actuaries: Chicago, Illinois.

Spain, D. M., V. A. Bradess, and I. J. Greenblatt. 1955. Postmortem Studies on Coronary Atherosclerosis, Serum Beta Lipoprotein, and Somatotypes. American Journal of the Medical Sciences 229:294–301.

Spain, D. M., V. A. Bradess, and G. Huss. 1953. Observations on Atherosclerosis of the Coronary Arteries in Males Under the Age of 46: A Necropsy Study With Special Reference to Somatotypes. Annals of Internal Medicine 38: 254–77.

Spain, D. M., D. J. Nathan, and M. Gellis. 1963. Weight, Body Type, and the Prevalence of Coronary Atherosclerotic Heart Disease in Males. American Journal of the Medical Sciences 245:63–68.

Tanner, J. M. 1951a. Current Advances in the Study of Physique: Photogrammetric Anthropometry and an Androgyny Scale. Lancet 1:574–79.

———. 1951b. The Relationship Between Serum Cholesterol and Physique in Healthy Young Men. Journal of Physiology 115:371–90.

———. 1954. Physique and Choice of Career. Eugenics Review 46:149–57.

———. 1962. Growth at Adolescence, 2d ed., pp. 94–104. Blackwell: Oxford.

————. 1964. Factor Analysis of Physique. Human Biology, G. A. Harrison, J. S. Weiner, J. M. Tanner, and N. A. Barnicot. Oxford University Press: New York.

Tanner, J. M. et al. 1959. The Relation of Body Build to the Excretion of 17-Ketosteroids and 17-Ketogenic Steroids in Healthy Young Men. Journal of Endocrinology 19: 87–101.

Thomas, C. B. and S. M. Garn. 1960. Degree of Obesity and Serum Cholesterol Level. Science 131:42.

Thurstone, L. W. 1946. Factor Analysis and Body Type. Psychometrika 11:15–21.

Tucker, W. B. and W. A. Lessa. 1940. Man: A Constitutional Investigation. Quarterly Review of Biology 15: 265–89, 411–55.

Van der Linden, W. 1961. Some Biological Traits in Female Gallstone-Disease Patients. Acta Chirurgica Scandinavica, Supplement 269.

von Zerssen, D. 1965. Eine Biometrische Überprüfung der Theorien von Sheldon über Zusammenhänge zwischen Körperbau und Temperament. Zeitschrift für Experimentelle und Angewandte Psychologie 12: 521–48.

Weiner, H. et al. 1957. Etiology of Duodenal Ulcer: Relation of Specific Psychological Characteristics to Rate of Gastric Secretion (Serum Pepsinogen). Psychosomatic Medicine 19:1–10.

White, P. 1959. Diabetic Children and Their Later Lives. The Treatment of Diabetes Mellitus, eds. E. P. Joslin et al. Lea and Febiger: Philadelphia.

Wretmark, G. 1953. The Peptic Ulcer Individual. Acta Psychiatrica et Neurologica Scandinavica, Supplement 84.

Physical Anthropology and Forensic Medicine

The graduate student of physical anthropology, in training to become a teacher and a researcher in the field, must be taught that the mastery of the practice of his science is as much a major objective as the mastery of theory and techniques. His goal is to learn about physical anthropology at work as well as in the laboratory. The practicing physical anthropologist, in both teaching and research, may be of great service to dentistry, medicine, law enforcement, and aeromedical and industrial research: wherever the human body or its parts are to be interpreted in form, in function, in the dynamics of variability, and in the age processes of pediatric growth and geriatric decline. As a member of a biobehavioral research team, the physical anthropologist has much to offer.

The graduate student in this field, therefore, must be well-grounded in such basic skills as the static morphometric and dynamic measurement and description of the total human body and its components under circumstances of adjustive and purposive functional movements. First and foremost, however, he must be well-trained in both comparative and human morphology. As a comparative anatomist, I would demand that general vertebrate anatomy serve as a prerequisite for more intensive study of mammalian embryology and classification, with particular emphasis upon osteology and odontology. As a human anatomist, I would demand that the student become competent in gross and microscopic anatomy, once more focusing on skeleton and dentition, but now encompassing the broad spectrum of the growth of earlier decades and the age changes of later decades. To round out his training, I also would require that he study sex and racial variability.

It will be noted that I have stressed the study of bones and teeth. I do this because these are the structures of mortal man that persist after his death; they are the tangibles that aid in identifying an individual long after his tissues and organs have become dust. Of course, skin and skin color, hair, eyes, muscles, vessels, and organs also testify to sex, race, age, circumstances of daily living, and health status. In fact, all of these may well be part of the reconstruction of a total individual and total life pattern. However, I am going to limit myself here to a discussion of osteology. Bones, in my experience, can articulate a story of individuality, and individuality is the key word in an identification process which presumes a focus upon one person out of a potential thousand or more.

I believe that the graduate student must be trained in the evaluation and understanding of the total range of human skeletal variability. For this training, access to and study of large collections of human skeletons, preferably of known origin (e.g., the Todd Collection at Western Reserve, the Terry Collection at Washington University, the Cobb Collection at Howard University, and materials at our great museums in New York, Washington, D.C., Cambridge, Chicago, and Berkeley), are the major avenues by which graduates learn to cope with the many variables involved in identification and description of the osteo-odontological remains of the individual.

In this paper, I will discuss three areas of osteology which students should master to prepare themselves to become physical anthropologists: duration of interment, examination of skeletal materials, and radiography.

Duration of Interment

Duration of interment, by which I mean, literally, how long an individual has been dead, is a very complex problem and one of great importance to forensic medicine and archaeology. It involves the study of soil structure and composition, seasonal and climatic factors, the composition of bones, and the nature and extent of change with time under varying circumstances. In forensic medicine, recency is critical, since identification for a law enforcement agency is usually involved with a relatively recent death. In a purely time-linked archaeological context, horizon or period is the issue. In this paper, I am interested in identification for legal purposes.

My own experience in problems of duration of interment has been quite empirical. I have excavated Indian mounds and observed bone preservation under varying conditions of inhumation. I have been present when cemetery remains were exhumed in order to make way for an expanding urban community. I have studied material uncovered in excavating house sites and in digging trenches for sewage and drainage systems and for gas and electric lines. I have worked with many sets of bones, turned over to me by the police from the bodies of the very recently dead. In most of these cases, details of inhumation and exhumation were secondary. I have read and studied carefully F. Wood Jones's *Archeological Survey of Nubia* (1910). From these experiences and studies I have learned to look for and evaluate certain basic and pertinent factors.

Skeletonizing, or reduction of the body to osteo-odontological remains, requires consideration of such physical circumstances as location of the body — on or in the ground or in water; types of soil; climate; and season. A body exposed to the air will decompose more rapidly than one under ground; cold will slow decomposition, heat will accelerate it, although dry heat produces mummification. Soft tissue will decompose completely within three to five years, but destruction of such tissues by animals also must be considered. Season is an important factor: bodies on the ground in late autumn and through the winter will show little change over a four- to five-month period. A body in the water will show the formation of adipocere, more so in warm water than in very cold water. In inland water, the bones will deteriorate faster than they would on the ground, but adipocere will last from ten to twenty years. In a river, the body will be skeletonized in about two years. For lakes and rivers, environmental factors to be considered in skeletonizing are the depth and current of water, temperature, and the presence of flesh-eaters, such as fish and crustaceans.

Inhumation, or location of the body in the ground, involves attention to the nature of the soil and circumstances of its makeup. For example, deep humus in a wooded area, moist clay, or clay-loess are not favorable to good bone preservation because inorganic intracellular substances are present, whereas lime-soil is favorable to bone preservation. The nature of the soil should be carefully appraised and soil samples taken to determine degrees of moisture or aridity, acidity, and lime content. In dry soil, e.g., in a sandy humus, sand-gravel, clay-gravel, or loess-clay, decomposition will not be complete for six or seven years; in moist soil, which is impervious to water, the time factor may be increased two- or threefold.

The foregoing generalizations are pretty well within the ken of anyone who has ever had to work with recovered skeletal material. However, I would add one admonition: the researcher should try to establish good rapport with local law enforcement agencies so that he is called in before exhumation. Thus, he will be in a position to determine, at firsthand, all the conditions associated with recovery of the remains, be they on or in the ground, or in a lake or river.

If it is accepted that bone is a lamellated fibrillary connective tissue, with calcium phosphate as its major constituent, then the structural decomposition of bone must be studied.[1] In acidic marshy soil the rate of decalcification is accelerated; the bones are pitted, fissured, scaly, and crumbly, especially at articular ends. In sandy, gravelly soil with a high lime content, the mineral content of the bone is converted to carbonate. The fibrillae contract, as can be seen under microscopic examination which reveals alveolar crumbling of the Haversian system.[2] A relatively simple method for assessing structural decomposition is testing bone for carbonate by using a 20 percent solution of HCl. The bone will foam if there has been a porous carbonate infiltration.

Using electron microscopy, Shackleford (1966) has shown that fossil bones, as old as nine thousand years, "contained considerable amounts of well preserved organic and inorganic materials"; that age, soil, and drainage factors "undoubtedly affect the integrity of ossified matrices"; and that, hence, biochemical analyses should supplement morphological

1. The rest of this paper is based almost exclusively on an excellent summary by Berg (1963).

2. I have noted that flat bones break down faster; this is probably also true of both very young and very old bones. Bones that are very light, friable, and breakable, as well as those in which the compacta can be scraped or incised by the fingernail are very old; Berg says 1,000 years+. However, in some cases, the action of rootlets may cause the outer cortex of a bone to become quite friable. The rootlets seem to penetrate small foramina (other than the nutrient) or to seek the margins of tuberosities or other irregular contours. Also, insects, especially beetles, probably feeding on the soft tissues, may get at the sub-periosteal bony substance and once more induce a degree of friability. Such possibilities reinforce my point that bone experts should be present at the time of recovery, especially in cases of exhumation.

studies. Since collagen becomes more cross-linked with age in the living animal, Shackleford believes that a study of "the molecular stability of collagen with geologic age" would be of considerable interest.

Tests for specific gravity and for color under ultraviolet fluorescence also may be useful in determining a bone's age. After the bone piece is weighed and its volume determined by water displacement, the density can be determined as "g/cm³ × 15°C." Recent bones will be valued at a density of 1.7—2.2; fossils may have a value as high as 1.2. The value of 1.7 or below may be used as a cut-off point between fossils and non-fossils. Ultraviolet fluorescence will indicate age cut-off at about one hundred years. Up to this age, bones will give off a decreasingly intense blue-violet color under fluorescence. Associated with this declining fluorescence is the bone's affinity for indophenol and Nile blue: with increased bone age, there is a decrease in the former and an increase in the latter, as shown in Table 1.

TABLE 1

Bone Age in Years (Dated Finds)	DEGREE OF STAINING	
	Indophenol	Nile Blue
9	+++	(+)
10	++	+
14	++	++
20	+	+
36	++	+
54	+	++
90	++	++
200–500	+	++++
1,200	(+)	+++
2,000	−	++++
4,000	−	++++

Source: Berg, 1963.

The conductivity for supersonic oscillation, employing an echoscope, can be useful. Velocity of the supersonic oscillation in the bone substance (longitudinal velocity $= V_L$) is determined "by measuring the interval between the outgoing/returning impulses on the radiograph" (Berg, 1963). Values for V_L in fresh bone range between 2,000 and 3,000. As the bone breaks down, sound transmission decreases and the V_L is smaller. Berg gives V_L values ranging from 2,700 to 2,200 in bones from 0 to 20 years old, to 1,250 in bones 1,000 years old, and 700 in bones from 4,000 to 6,000 years old.

Histologically, recent bone shows a connected lamellar system with typically actinomorphic birefringence of the osteon area. In contrast, old bone shows an encrustation or alveolar decomposition, with progressive loss of optical activity.

Vestiges of fat transgression in the Haversian system are useful criteria of time elapse. The marrow becomes adipocere, or decays and mummifies into shapeless, irregular black-brown fragments. The marrow may diffuse into the bone; this is visible and determinable for several decades. Total filling of the medullary cavity of the femur with adipocere will occur within twenty or thirty years. In ultraviolet light, adipocere has a weak, yellow fluorescence; in polarized light, it has a very strong birefringence.

Soft tissue remnants also must be recorded. The brown-black remnants in the medullary cavity may persist for from fifty to sixty years. Soft tissue on the external bony surface will last twenty years or less. Sulfuriron compounds of broken-down blood pigments cause a spotty discoloration of the bone surface or of the walls of the medullary cavity which may last several decades. (See Table 2.)

TABLE 2

Findings in the Examination

Duration (yrs.)	Consistency	Ultraviolet fluorescence	Adipocere remnants	Medullary cavity content	Soft tissue remains	Fat impregnation
0–10	+	+	+	+	+	+
10–20	+	+	+	+	+	−
20–30	+	+	+	+	−	−
30–50	+	+	+	−	−	−
50–100	+	+	−	−	--	−
100–500	+	(+)	−	−	−	−
500–1,000	(+)	−	−	--	−	−
1,000 +	−	−	−	−	−	−

Source: Berg, 1963.

Berg (1963) concludes, "The optical-morphological procedures are unequivocally superior to the chemical-physical methods for bone age determination."

In recent years, widespread use of the contraceptive pill suggests that there may be certain estrogen-mediated changes in the female skeleton. I wrote to several drug firms who marketed such pills, asking for information. Victor A. Drill, M.D., director of biological research, Searle and Company, replied (letter of April 4, 1966) as follows:

The oral contraceptives are, of course, not employed until after puberty has occurred and ovulatory cycles have been established. Thus, from this standpoint alone, one would not expect any effect of the oral contraceptives on bone age. Secondly, the oral contraceptives act to inhibit the pituitary output of gonadotrophins so that ovarian function is temporarily suppressed. The amount of estrogen supplied by the oral contraceptives is approximately the same, or slightly less than, the amount of estrogens elaborated by the ovary during a normal ovulatory cycle. Thus, no added effect of the oral contraceptives on the bone of the postpuberal woman would be obtained.

John B. Jewell, M.D., of Ayerst Research Laboratories (letter of June 2, 1966) sent a summary of "The Effect of Conjugated Equine Estrogen on Epiphyseal Changes in Adult Rats," by A. Hajdu, M.D., and G. Rona, M.D., Ph.D., F.R.C.P. (Can.), of the Ayerst Research Laboratories. According to this summary, in 120 female rats from 40 to 52 weeks of age who were given 0.4 mg/kg conjugated equine estrogen (Premarin) S.C. three times a week for 10 weeks, the dosage "promoted epiphyseal ossification and strengthened the structure of bone lamellae in the subepiphyseal region." These changes are a part of the anabolic (anticatabolic) properties of estrogen effect on bone metabolism.

As a result of this information, I think it is safe to conclude that "the Pill" will not significantly influence the registration of biological age in the female human skeleton.

The Examination of Skeletal Material

The examination of skeletal material requires a study of (1) centers of ossification, (2) suture closure, (3) the pubic symphisis, (4) sexing, (5) reconstruction of stature, (6) racial characteristics, and (7) certain residual aspects of individuality. The first three are criteria for registration of age at death.

Since I have thoroughly covered this material in *The Human Skeleton in Forensic Medicine* (1962), I shall evaluate rather than expound.

Centers of Ossification

There is no shortcut to a complete knowledge of human osteology. The phenomena of the appearance and union of the epiphyses, as well as of maturity indicators in carpals[3] and tarsals, must be mastered by the student. The center of bone growth of each bone — long, flat, or round — should be known precisely, as should the morphology of each bone, so that fragmentary material can be recognized. With this information, the expert — if he is present at exhumation — will know precisely what to look for in immature cases, i.e., those below twenty years or so. Furthermore, there should be familiarity with the appearance of the reciprocal relationship of epiphyses and diaphysis in terms of degree of osteological relationship and in terms of the "billowing" of the surfaces of un-united epiphysis and diaphysis. If a bone is brought in without an articular end, it should be possible for the expert to state whether it is broken off, normally un-united, or pathologically un-united.

The student should know the time of appearance and of union. These are determined according to sex (with the female, they occur a bit earlier); race (different races have slight differences in sequence and in time); intrinsic variability in terms of "early" and "late" maturers; and extrinsic variability, with dietetic, health, and endocrinic factors to be evaluated. So-called race differences may fall into the extrinsic category; however, "in every individual case the bones must be carefully studied to see if they give any clue to an extrinsic modification. Then interpretation must take cognizance of both intrinsic and extrinsic variability: not racial, but individual" (Krogman, 1962).

Depending upon completeness of skeletal recovery, a statement of age at time of death in the first two decades of life should be at a given year ± six months in the first decade and at ± one year in the second. For example, age at death might be stated as "4 years ± 6 months," or "14 years ± 1 year."

Suture Closure

As far as we know, no significant race, sex, or side (right [R] or left [L]) differences occur in closure of vault and circum-meatal sutures,

---

3. See Greulich and Pyle (1959) on the carpals; also Pyle and Hoerr (1955).

either ecto- or endo-cranially. Because of "lapsed union" in ectocranial closure, only endocranial suture closure should be evaluated.

Sutures are the least reliable of all age criteria in the skeleton and, therefore, should be estimated only within a decade, as from thirty to forty years. "If the skull is the only part present then this . . . age evaluation is the best that one can do, and the statement is then diagnostic. If other bones are present, then suture age may become, at best, partially corroborative" (Krogman, 1962).

Other so-called criteria of aging in the skull, including texture, lineae, and depression, are too subjective to be reliable.

The Pubic Symphysis

I believe that the pubic symphysis "is probably the best single criterion of the registration of age in the skeleton" (Krogman, 1962). In his classic studies, Todd (1920) set up ten "phases" of pubic symphysis and principally focused upon five osteological criteria: symphyseal surface, ossific nodules, ventral margin, dorsal margin, and extremities (superior, inferior aspects of symphyseal face). His age periods for each phase are shown in Table 3.[4] In 1955 Brooks shifted phases V–VIII about three years downward (see Table 4).

TABLE 3
Age Determination According to Todd's Ten Phases of Pubic Symphysis

I.	18–19 years	VI.	30–35 years
II.	20–21 years	VII.	35–39 years
III.	22–24 years	VIII.	39–44 years
IV.	25–26 years	IX.	45–50 years
V.	27–30 years	X.	50+ years

Source: Todd, 1920.

TABLE 4
Age Determination According to Brooks's Ten Phases of Pubic Symphysis

I.	17.5–19.5 years	VI.	27.0–33.5 years
II.	19.5–21.5 years	VII.	33.5–38.0 years
III.	21.5–24.0 years	VIII.	38.0–42.0 years
IV.	24.0–26.0 years	IX.	42.0–50.5 years
V.	26.0–27.0 years	X.	50.5+ years

Source: Brooks, 1955.

4. Todd suggested a re-grouping into three main periods: I–III, post-adolescent; IV–VI, building-up of symphyseal outline; VII–X, gradual quiescence and secondary change (Todd, 1920, 1930).

In 1957, McKern and Stewart presented a critical evaluation of age changes in the pubic symphysis based on the overall total of Todd's nine morphological features: ridges and furrows, dorsal margin, ventral beveling, lower extremity, superior ossific nodule, upper extremity, ventral rampart, dorsal plateau, symphyseal rim. They set up a category of three components of the pubic symphysis, with five development stages, as in Table 5. In Table 6, the age limits are set up.

TABLE 5
Age Changes in the Pubic Symphysis

STAGE	COMPONENTS		
	Dorsal Plateau	*Ventral Rampart*	*Symphyseal Rim*
0	Dorsal margin absent	Ventral beveling absent	Symphyseal rim absent
1	Slight margin, mid-⅓ dorsal border	Ventral beveling at superior end ventral border	Partial dorsal rim, superior end dorsal margin
2	Dorsal margin along whole dorsal border	Bevel goes inferiorly along ventral border	Dorsal rim complete, ventral rim begins
3	Grooves fill in, ridges resorb; plateau begins mid-⅓ dorsal demiface	Ventral rampart begins via bony extensions from either or both extremities	Symphyseal rim complete; symphyseal surface fine-grained, irregular
4	Plateau, with vestiges of billowing, is over most of dorsal demiface	Rampart extensive; gaps still in upper ⅔	Rim breaks down; face smooth, flat; some ventral lipping
5	Billowing gone; surface demiface flat, granular	Rampart complete	Rim breaks down more at superior, ventral edge; ventral rim erratic

Source: McKern and Stewart, 1957.

TABLE 6
Age Limits of Component Stages in Pubic Symphysis
(expressed in years)

STAGE	COMPONENT I		COMPONENT II		COMPONENT III	
	Range	*Mode*	*Range*	*Mode*	*Range*	*Mode*
0	17–18	17	17–22	19	17–24	19
1	18–21	18	19–23	20	21–28	23
2	18–21	19	19–24	22	24–32	27
3	18–24	20	21–28	23	24–39	28
4	19–29	23	22–23	26	29+	35
5	23+	31	24+	32	38+	—

Source: McKern and Stewart, 1957.

Taken as a unit, apart from all other skeletal age criteria, the pubic symphysis should register age in lustra of five years, e.g., 25 to 30, 30 to 35, and so on, with a midpoint such as 27.5 or 32. 5 permissible.

Sexing Human Skeletal Remains

The more complete the available skeletal remains, the greater the chances of accuracy. There are basically two methods of sorting for sex: (1) descriptive morphology, and (2) mensurational, which involves either conventional osteometry (measurement and proportion) or statistical evaluation (discriminant functions). The overall chances of correctly determining the sex of skeletal remains are about as follows (numbers reflect percentage):

Entire skeleton = 100
Skull alone = 90
Pelvis alone = 95
Skull + pelvis = 98
Long bones alone = 80
Long bones + skull = 90+
Long bones + pelvis = 95+

"Standards of morphological and morphometric sex differences in in the skeleton may differ with the population samples involved" (Krogman, 1962), especially when dimensions and indices are involved. Standards should be developed with a view to whether or not the remains are those from a population which is predominantly pedomorphic or gerontomorphic, always remembering that within a given population sample the female is the more pedomorphic.

Reconstruction of Stature

Since osteometry is basic to the reconstruction of stature, the student must be thoroughly grounded in osteometric techniques and should critically evaluate all data in terms of measurement methodology. With formulae for adult stature, it is best to use, where possible, more than one long bone, preferably the tibia and femur. Further factors to be noted include the following:

Temporal changes (the most recent data should be used).

Sex differences (Female bones are c. 90 percent of male bones).

Race differences (radio-humeral, tibio-femoral, arm-leg, arm-trunk, leg-trunk ratios).

Age (this should be corrected for possible stature loss in later decades [50 to 60+] of life).

Trotter and Gleser's (1958) adult male/female and white/Negro formulae are the best. Although they are based on American material, I think they are generally applicable, since the probability that the true stature of an individual be within a certain limit must be based on "M ± 2 S.E. (1:22)."

In 1963, Zoraf and Prime measured the tibial length (level medial epicondyle to lower border of medial malleolus) of 177 London schoolchildren: 25 children at 12 years, 149 at 13 years, and 3 children at 14 years. Stature was measured in stocking feet. The regression formulae are

Boy: ht. in cm. = 2.92 (tibial lgth.) + 49.84

Girl: ht. in cm. = 2.53 (tibial lgth.) + 67.22

Zoraf and Prime found that the slopes of the regression lines were not significantly different: "1.37 × S.E." The position of the lines did differ in that, for a given tibial length, the girls' height exceeded that of the boys' by 3.68 cm. (S.E. 0.6 cm.) The S.D. of height for a given tibial length was 3.93 cm. for boys and 3.87 cm. for girls. The 95 percent limits for individual values are ± (1.96 ×3.9) or ± 7.6 cm., below or above the predicted height.

Fragmentary bones may be used for adult statural calculation, provided their morphological details permit an estimate of the percentage present in terms of a total bone. This calculated or restored total length then can be used in adult formulae.

Race Differences in the Human Skeleton

The best data on race differences in the human skull and skeleton are those for American whites and American Negroes. The chances of a correct diagnosis are as follows:

Skull

1. Via morphology and morphometry, about 85 to 90 percent
2. Via discriminant analysis, about 90+ percent

Pelvis — about 70 to 75 percent

Mandible — exclusive of teeth, not diagnostic

Scapula — not diagnostic

Long bones — may be corroborative of skull and pelvis in terms of radio-humeral and tibio-femoral indices.

Residual Data on Individualization

In addition to the preceding data on the registration of age and age changes (epiphyses, sutures, pubic symphysis), sex, and race, there are certain other osteological details which add up to a specificity, a relative uniqueness, and lead to a cumulative build-up of a complex of osteological traits that increasingly narrows the focus of identification to the point of virtual individuality.

1) If the *skull* is completely dried, its dimensions are 1 to 2 percent less, which is not significant. Cranial capacity is of no import, and there are no racial differences in vault-bone thickness.

2) The *vertebral column* loses 2.7 percent of its length by drying. "Lipping" (osteophytosis) occurs on the margins of the vertebral bodies and facilitates aging in lustra of ten years.

3) There are no reliable race or sex differences in the *sternum;* they are useful only in corroborating age.

4) *Rib* epiphyses are united by twenty-three years of age. Rib I is longer in whites than in Negroes, but rib XII shows no race differences. Ribs II–XI show no race differences. Presumably, these ribs are more related to linear or lateral body build.

5) *Bone weight* is variably correlated with total body weight. Baker and Newman (1957) present the following equations:

White

Living wt. = .024 lbs. (dry skel. wt.) + 50.593 ± 20.1
Living wt. = .233 lbs. (dry femur wt.) + 57.385 ± 22.2

Negro

Living wt. = .013 lbs. (dry skel. wt.) + 85.406 ± 13.7
Living wt. = .163 lbs. (dry femur wt.) + 76.962 ± 13.3

Bone weights are most useful in sorting out multiple burials.

6) *Bone density,* even though it lessen with age, is not a reliable age indicator when assessed radiographically, save possibly in terms of a decade or so.

7) The *typing of blood* (ABO system) from bones is not reliable.

8) Where *long bones* are amputated, especially high up in humerus and femur, the corresponding shoulder or hip girdle, respectively, shows atrophic changes, both in dimension and in trabeculation. In fragmentary

skeletal material, the radiography of the bones of a girdle may give leads as to non-amputation vs. amputation.

The Use of Radiography

Finally, because radiography is a very important adjunct to the examination of patterns already discussed in this paper, the graduate student in physical anthropology must be familiar with, and have access to, radiographic techniques. As a rule, use of X-ray film presupposes that postmortem X-ray film of the bones in question will be compared with X-ray films of the deceased taken during life (Krogman, 1965).

I would divide the use of X-ray films into three main categories: (1) general study, (2) study of specific bones, and (3) pre- and post-mortem comparison. Although these categories are not clear-cut, they are useful.

General Study

Into this category falls the problem of epiphyseal union. For the student I have a few recommendations: study a good series of long bones in various stages of union (non-union, beginning union, active union, recent union, long-standing union); analyze the anatomical features of the several stages on the bones themselves; X-ray the bones and analyze the stages on the X-ray films; then compare the time-ratings under the two sets of circumstances.

There are two opposite schools of thought on the determination of of age from epiphyseal union by use of X-ray film. Drennan and Keen (1953) hold that the X-ray film will give an age about three years earlier than the bone itself, "because epiphyseal lines can remain visible on the bone for a considerable time after the radiographs indicate the fusion has taken place." I have stated that, in the X-ray film, "the 'scar' of recent union (the maintenance of radiographic opacity at the site of the piled-up calcification adjacent to the epiphyseo-diaphyseal plane) may persist several years *after* demonstrable complete union in the the bone itself" (Krogman, 1962). The time factor in hand epiphyses has been evaluated by Noback, Moss, and Lesczcynska (1960) as follows: from the first radiographic sign of union (or prefusion) to union (or fusion), it takes 6.5 to 8.5 months (mean prefusion period 6.5 ± 0.69 months; mean fusion period 2.8 ± 0.3 months "fast" to 4.2 ± 0.4 month "slow").

Study of Specific Bones

I shall refer the student to the following studies by various experts of the effects of radiography on specific bones: Todd (1930) on the radiography of the *pubic symphysis*; Graves (1922) on the transillumination of the *scapula*; and Schranz (1959) on the radiography of the proximal end of the *humerus*. All focus on age change categories. Cobb (1952) presents age differences seen radiographically in the *hand* of an "adult" and in "advanced age."

Patterns of the *frontal sinus* (Schüller, 1943) and of the *sphenoid* (Ravina, 1960, after Voluter) involving comparisons of pre- and post-mortem films have been considered unique.

Using roentgenographic cephalometry, or the analysis of the *tracing* of head-films from norma lateralis sinistra, Krogman and Chung (1965) have demonstrated that it is possible to differentiate between white and Negro cranial outlines at the age of one month. This finding is important in adoption cases of white-white or white-Negro crosses.

Pre- and Post-Mortem Comparison

Radiographic data of the presumed deceased taken in life can be compared with X-ray films of the skeletal remains. The classic example is in the case of the "Noronic" disaster, a steamship fire on September 19, 1949, that claimed 119 lives (41 male, 78 female). Of these, 116 were identified by comparison of osteological details seen in pre- and post-mortem X-ray films (Brown, Delaney, and Robinson, 1952; Singleton, 1951). In a more specific study, Greulich (1960) pointed out that osteological details in wrist-hand films are highly individualistic when compared pre- and post-mortem.

In 1953, Thörne and Thyberg suggested that cranial X-ray films in children and adults would be useful in body identification after mass disasters. In 1960, Sassouni employed roentgenographic cephalometry to demonstrate that cranial pattern and detail compared in pre- and post-mortem X-ray films could establish individual identity in young white and Negro males.

COMMENTARY: Gabriel W. Lasker
T. D. Stewart

Gabriel W. Lasker

Dr. Krogman has very clearly detailed how the physical anthropologist can face the task of identification. Constitutional and forensic anthropology, as they have developed, have one thing in common: they deal with the individual. As Dr. Krogman points out, the aim in forensic identification is "a reconstruction of a total individual and a total life pattern. . . . Interpretation must take cognizance of both intrinsic and extrinsic variability: not racial, but individual." Dr. Damon (see Chapter 7, this volume), in speaking of constitutional anthropology, uses the word "person" rather than "individual" to define the subject.

In anthropology, therefore, constitution and identification stress the "whole individual," as does general practice in medicine. Perhaps an examination of general practice in medicine will help in evaluating the role of the parallel fields in anthropology. A patient today often has difficulty finding a physician who will listen sufficiently to his way of stating his problem. Two people may show similar physical signs and have similar laboratory test results, although one may be in pain and the other not. As a rule, only the patient in pain comes to the attention of a physician.

Attention to the individual is one of the chief concerns of medical educators today. The patient's physical condition, psychological state, social relationships, and individual history as seen in repeated visits to the same physician are strongly emphasized. For this reason, some medical schools now provide their students with experience in patient care, and especially in family welfare, early in their studies. Other schools are introducing clinical teachers into basic science courses. This trend reflects an attempt to return to a time when medicine was generally learned by an apprentice accompanying a physician on his rounds.

However, from that era to today, the development of medicine has progressively departed from attention to the whole individual; advances have come through specialization. Many of the major advances have been made by people who would not even be thought of as physicians in any ordinary sense of the word — the experimentalists working as chemists or physicists, often on organisms remote from man or on isolated bits of human tissue. Medical science, like science in general, is analytic. A process is best seen when the material is removed from what the scientist would characterize as "interfering" substances and conditions.

Thus, the current reemphasis on the whole individual is a reaction against the role of science in medicine. In the practice of identification, as in the practice of medicine, one is involved not in the analysis or accumulation of knowledge, but in the practical application of knowledge to the problem at hand.

The question remains of whether anything of the "whole individual" approach can be used to advance basic knowledge in constitutional studies. I think it can, provided it is used only as a broad arena in which individual problems are isolated for analysis. Using an overall anthropometric survey of Harvard students from 1880 to 1920 undertaken by Dudley A. Sargent, twenty-fifth-year reunion reports, and similar later documents, Albert Damon and his co-workers (Damon, Burr, and Gerson, 1965) related measurements of weight and height taken in youth to such subsequent observations as baldness and sex ratio of offspring. In so doing, Dr. Damon dealt with a "constitution" very different from that of the clinical appraisal of an individual patient. This difference has been duly recognized, and a variety of terms have been suggested to distinguish between the bodily form at a particular stage in life and the genetic tendencies of an individual. The "clinical constitution" is the appraisal of the individual as he is observed, preferably repeatedly, under varying conditions, and as he responds. The "analytic constitution" consists of specific measurements and observations, objectively defined, that can be correlated among groups of individuals with other measurable data. Since the technique used is correlation, only very high degrees of correspondence can give rise to a simple inference of causality. As in medicine, the rigorous application of scientific analysis usually yields less reliable prediction than the best practice of the art, but it also provides a basis for further advancement and refinement of factors.

Constitution has come to mean the external form of the human body as it can be rated in a standardized nude photograph. The subtle shadings that suggest softness, roundness, or ruggedness are due to the quantity and disposition of such tissues as bone, muscle, and, particularly, fat. Amount and distribution of body hair and other tissues also can be appraised.

As I tried to show twenty years ago (Lasker, 1947), the overall ratings of somatotype are altered very markedly by sharp curtailment of caloric intake. Subsequently, Garn (1955) demonstrated that, if one examines men before and after a period of weight loss, the remaining subcutaneous fat at the end of the period is distributed in essentially the same pattern as the more abundant fat was at the beginning. There are, therefore, aspects of the external physique which are resistant to this kind of change. These can be approached by separate analysis of different parts of the body.

In a recent report on their reexamination of the somatotypes of East Africans, Bainbridge and Roberts (1966) point out that dysplasia as defined by Sheldon "is simply variation" and therefore subject to appropriate variance analysis. They then show the influence of overall somatotype and tribal background (with differences in diet and occupation as well as genetic endowment) on the distribution pattern of somatotype components in different parts of the body. They find deviations in various parts of the body, which contribute to dysplasia in Sheldon's terms, to be consistently associated with specific constitutions. This pattern is shown to be consistent with that which emerges from a factor analysis of bodily measurements; the consistent and sensible organization Howells (1952) found in measurements of extreme somatotypes. Bainbridge and Roberts (1966) also look to body composition as a way of reducing constitution to analytic terms. They conclude pessimistically that "present techniques are not available for describing the distribution of the body constituents through the regions of the body, except in the case of subcutaneous fat."

To me, this is not really true — it is possible to measure the human cadaver in meaningful terms, structure by structure, and region by region. Such tedious and time-consuming work could be related to X-ray or ultrasonic measurements so that techniques could be developed for percutaneous analytic measurements of the composition pattern of living individuals. I have no doubt that these patterns will follow sensible modes of organization by adaptive natural selection. The skills needed for such studies do not require a medical education; however, as specific influences are evaluated, a new level of basic knowledge will become available for applications to the art of medicine. Some of the same relationships will be useful in forensic applications.

T. D. Stewart

Regarding forensic medicine — the discipline circumjacent to anthropology which Dr. Krogman has dealt with in his paper — the following assumptions can be made: (1) forensic medicine is indeed one of the neighboring disciplines in which anthropologists have had a sustained involvement and to which they have contributed substantially; (2) since the American Anthropological Association (AAA) publication in 1963 on the teaching of anthropology (Mandelbaum, Lasker, and Albert, 1963), the dimensions of anthropological teaching and research relevant to forensic medicine have greatly accelerated and expanded; and (3) there exists a clear and present need for a concerted effort to weigh the philosophical and empirical foundations of the science of man in this neighboring discipline. These assumptions need to be examined.

Forensic medicine may be defined as that body of medical and paramedical scientific knowledge which may be of service in the administration of the law. A very similar definition can be constructed for the recently created parallel discipline of forensic dentistry. The phrase "paramedical scientific knowledge" covers the contribution of physical anthropology to both areas, but does not explain the nature of the contribution: nor does Dr. Krogman's detailed account of skeletal identification procedures make this point clear.

The law requires that corpses be disposed of in a carefully regulated manner. The identification of the body and the cause of death must be reported so that appropriate legal action can be taken if necessary. Medical examiners or coroners handle these matters in the first instance with the Federal Bureau of Investigation often serving as an intermediary agent. Usually the medical officers have little difficulty in making an identification, except when a corpse has remained undiscovered long enough for the soft parts to have deteriorated well beyond the point of recognition, when there has been a disaster (including war) causing loss of individual identification, or when a killer has deliberately made his victim unrecognizable. In these exceptional cases, the administration of the law depends on what can be determined from the recovered skeletal parts. Obviously, for this practical purpose, skeletal identification is just an extension of what some physical anthropologists do routinely when they study skeletons from archaeological and other authorized sources.

Thus, the physical anthropologist who is an expert on skeletal identification makes an important contribution to forensic medicine.

Just how sustained the involvement of physical anthropologists in forensic medicine has been is not clear, simply because the evidence seldom has been reported. The earliest reference to such involvement listed in Dr. Krogman's paper concerns the work of F. Wood Jones in the *Archeological Survey of Nubia* in 1910. I doubt, however, that Wood Jones had the medico-legal applications of his work in mind. A more pertinent reference, although still probably not the earliest, is George A. Dorsey's, "The Skeleton in Medico-Legal Anatomy," published in the *Chicago Medical Recorder* of 1899. Even though the historical record is scanty, anthropological involvement of any sort in the field of forensic medicine is likely to have been relatively infrequent until this century.

Whether one can put a date on acceleration of the relationship is dubious, but certainly the physical anthropologist's contribution to practical forensic medicine received far greater recognition than ever before with the publication of Dr. Krogman's "Guide to the Identification of Human Skeletal Material," by the Federal Bureau of Investigation in 1939. At that time Hrdlička, who handled the skeletal identifications requested of the National Museum by the FBI (which is located just across the street from the Museum), would get, if I recall rightly, not more than half a dozen requests a year. Subsequently, I took over this service and, by 1960, often had two or three cases a month. Dr. Lawrence Angel, my successor, now gets about one a week. As far as I know, this is the maximum for any physical anthropologist in this country.

The American Association of Physical Anthropologists first officially recognized its role in forensic medicine in 1948 when a symposium on various aspects of applied physical anthropology was featured at the annual meeting. Then, in 1955, at the conclusion of the Graves Registration Service program of identifying soldiers killed in the Korean War, the association sponsored a week-long seminar in Washington on the role of physical anthropology in the general field of human identification. One result of these activities was a greater awareness on the part of physical anthropologists of the need for better identification criteria. That considerable progress has been made in supplying this need is evident from Dr. Krogman's enumeration of available procedures. In addition, in the Proceedings of the Second International Conference on Oral Biology held in Bonn, Germany, in 1962, my own statement about "New Developments in Evaluating Evidence from the Skeleton" (Stewart, 1963) gives particular stress to our present, better appreciation of human variability.

I would like to suggest that one of the reasons for this sudden awakening of anthropological interest in forensic medicine was the publication in 1951 of Dr. Sherwood Washburn's well-known article entitled, "The New Physical Anthropology," which he concluded by stating, "We need new ideas, new methods, new workers. There is nothing we do today which will not be done better tomorrow." About the same time, Dr. Washburn produced a series of papers showing that the sex of the pelvis can be determined metrically with a high degree of accuracy. Thus goaded, some physical anthropologists found in forensic medicine an opportunity to follow a fashionable trend. There is scarcely a whisper of all this in the AAA's 1963 publication "Resources for the Teaching of Anthropology" (Mandelbaum, Lasker, and Albert, 1963). Similarly, recent textbooks produced under the influence of the "new physical anthropology" stress evolutionary processes and exclude everything related to anthropometry: nor do any of the current laboratory manuals in physical anthropology, such as those by Anderson (1962), Brothwell (1963), and Kelso and Ewing (1962), mention the applications to forensic medicine. I dare say that even Dr. Krogman's book, *The Human Skeleton in Forensic Medicine* (1962), is not as well known as it should be to many students of physical anthropology.

Despite the newer metrical procedures of discriminant and factor analyses for determining sex and race, skeletal identification is better served by the trained eye than by the computer. The main reason for this is that law enforcement agents are in a hurry for answers and the recovered skeletal remains are often too incomplete for measurement. A quick visual determination by the expert always can be verified at leisure by an objective metrical analysis which will rarely contradict the findings of an experienced eye. Besides, many highly individualistic clues which only the experienced eye can detect and interpret are seldom given much attention in the study of archaeological remains and, therefore, seldom stressed in laboratory manuals.

I will introduce here only a few philosophical considerations. Any physical anthropologist who decides to undertake skeletal identification in forensic medicine should realize that he is making a commitment to society; the skeleton he identifies may be that of the son a father has been searching for or wants to bury, or it may represent the *corpus delecti* that will serve as a basis for a murder trial. Referring to such a trial, Thomas Dwight of Boston wrote in 1878, "It is for the jury, not the expert, to decide on the identity of the skeleton; it is for the expert to show whether the identity is possible or probable. The opinion he will give will depend not only on his professional acquirements but on his honesty and common sense."

In order to assure my own integrity, I have made it a rule not to let the law enforcement agent who brings the bones to me for identification give me any information about the case until I have made my determinations. Otherwise, I might find myself fighting against a tendency to match my determinations to the stated description. One gets much more credit as an expert when one tells the law enforcement agent what has been recovered, rather than *vice versa*. Some years ago in New York, a colleague and I independently examined a severed head recovered in one of the city suburbs and gave identical determinations, much to the amazement of the agents present.

Thomas Dwight (1878) had some other sage advice to which I subscribe:

When the expert receives bones for examination he should at once make a list of them, together with notes of any striking pecularities they may present, and if there is any question of fracture, or if the bones are inclined to crumble, he must lose no time in writing a description that shall be so accurate that he can never be in doubt whether any change of importance occurred before or after they were in his keeping.
Let the expert never forget, both in giving his evidence and in making his investigations, that the result does not concern him. He should not permit himself to be employed either to prove that the remains are those of a certain person, or that they are not. He should be as impartial as a judge.
Let him also remember that absolute certainty can very rarely be reached in the solution of questions of this nature; exceptions and various causes of error are so numerous that strong probability, amounting sometimes to moral certainty, is the most he can generally hope for.

Returning now to the assumptions stated at the beginning of this paper, I would say that anthropology's relationship to forensic medicine has always been limited and sporadic. Only since about 1939 has it intensified noticeably. Even now, relatively few physical anthropologists can be said to be considerably involved in making substantial contributions to forensic medicine.

The involvement of physical anthropologists in forensic medicine has not extended as far as it should in the areas of teaching and research. This is probably due to the fact that good teachers speak from experience and few have had such experience in sufficient degree. Moreover, teachers will not deal with the subject until it is covered more adequately in textbooks. So far as I can see, the AAA 1963 publication (Mandelbaum, Lasker, and Albert, 1963) on the teaching of anthropology has had no effect in this area. There is also a need for greater appreciation of the philosophical implications of the relationship of anthropology to forensic medicine, although it is perhaps understandable that, at the present stage of development, this aspect tends to get lost in procedural details.

REFERENCES

Anderson, J. E. 1962. The Human Skeleton: A Manual for Archaeologists. Department part of Northern Affairs and Natural Resources. Ottawa.

Bainbridge, D. R. and D. F. Roberts. 1966. Dysplasis in Nilotic Physique. Human Biology 38:251–78.

Baker, P. T. and R. W. Newman. 1957. The Use of Bone Weight for Human Identification. American Journal of Physical Anthropology (n.s.) 15 (1):601–18.

Berg, S. 1963. The Determination of Bone Age. Methods of Forensic Science, ed. F. Lundquist, II, pp. 231–52. Wiley: New York.

Brooks, S. T. 1955. Skeletal Age at Death: Reliability of Cranial and Pubic Age Indicators. American Journal of Physical Anthropology (n.s.) 13 (4):567–97.

Brothwell, D. R. 1963. Digging Up Bones: The Excavation, Treatment, and Study of Human Skeletal Remains. British Museum (Natural History). London.

Brown, T. C., R. J. Delaney, and W. L. Robinson. 1952. Medical Identification in the "Noronic" Disaster. Journal of the American Medical Association 148: 621–27.

Cobb, W. M. 1952. Skeleton. Problems of Aging, 3d ed., ed. A. L. Lansing, pp. 791–856. Williams and Wilkins: Baltimore.

Damon, A., W. A. Burr, and D. E. Gerson. 1965. Baldness of Fathers and Number and Sex Ratio of Children. Human Biology 37:366–70.

Dorsey, G. A. 1899. The Skeleton in Medico-Legal Anatomy. Chicago Medical Recorder 16:172–79.

Drennan, M. R. and J. A. Keen. 1953. Identity. Medical Jurisprudence, 3d ed., eds. I. Gordon, R. Turner, and T. W. Price, pp. 336–72. Livingston: Edinburgh.

Dwight, T. 1878. The Identification of the Human Skeleton: A Medico-Legal Study. Clapp and Sons: Boston.

Garn, S. M. 1955. Relative Fat Patterning: An Individual Characteristic. Human Biology 27:75–89.

Graves, W. W. 1922. Observations on Age Changes in the Scapula. American Journal of Physical Anthropology 5(1):21–33.

Greulich, W. W. 1960. Skeletal Features: Visible on the Roentgenogram of Hand and Wrist Which Can Be Used for Establishing Individual Identification. American Journal of Roentgenology 83(4):756–64.

Greulich, W. W. and S. I. Pyle. 1959. Radiographic Atlas of Skeletal Development of Hand and Wrist, 2d ed. Stanford University Press: Stanford.

Howells, W. W. 1952. A Factoral Study of Constitutional Types. American Journal of Physical Anthropology (n.s.) 10:91–118.

Jones, F. Wood. 1910. Anatomical Variations and the Determination of Age and Sex of Skeletons. Archeological Survey Nubia, II, pp. 221–62. "Report on Human Remains." National Printing Department: Cairo.

Kelso, J. and G. Ewing. 1962. Introduction to Physical Anthropology: Laboratory Manual. Pruet: Boulder, Colorado.

Krogman, W. M. 1962. The Human Skeleton in Forensic Medicine. Thomas: Springfield, Illinois.

———. 1965. Radiography in Forensic Medicine: The Skeleton. The Science of Ionizing Radiation, ed. L. E. Etter, pp. 632–51. Thomas: Springfield, Illinois.

Krogman, W. M. and D. Chung. 1965. The Craniofacial Skeleton at the Age of One Month. Angle Orthodontist 35(4):305–10.

Lasker, G. W. 1947. The Effects of Partial Starvation on Somatotype. An Analysis of Material from the Minnesota Experiment. American Journal of Physical Anthropology (n.s.) 5:323–42.

McKern, T. W. and T. D. Stewart. 1957. Skeletal Age Changes in Young American Males, Analyzed from the Standpoint of Identification. U.S. Army, Quartermaster's Research and Development Command. Technical Report EP–45. Natick, Mass.

Mandelbaum, D. G., G. W. Lasker, and E. M. Albert, eds. 1963. Resources for the Teaching of Anthropology, Memoir 94, American Anthropological Association. University of California Press: Berkeley.

Noback, C. R., M. L. Moss, and E. Lesczcynska. 1960. Digital Epiphyseal Fusion of the Hand in Adolescence: A Longitudinal Study. American Journal of Physical Anthropology (n.s.) 18(1):13–18.

Pyle, S. I. and N. L. Hoerr. 1955. Radiographic Atlas of Skeletal Development of the Knee. Thomas: Springfield, Illinois.

Ravina, A. 1960. L'identification des corps par le V-test. Presse Medicale 68:178.

Sassouni, V. 1960. Identification of War Dead by Means of Roentgenographic Cephalometry. U.S. Army, Quartermaster's Research and Engineering Command. Technical Report EP–12 J. Natick, Mass.

Schranz, D. 1959. Age Determination from the Internal Structure of the Humerus. American Journal of Physical Anthropology (n.s.) 17(4):273–78.

Schüller, A. 1943. A Note on the Identification of Skulls by X-ray Pictures of the Frontal Sinuses. Medical Journal of Australia 1:554–56.

Shackleford, J. M. 1966. The Ultrastructure of Mississippian and Archaic Indian Bones from Various Soil and Drainage Conditions. American Journal of Physical Anthropology (n.s.) 24:291–98.

Singleton, A. C. 1951. The Roentgenologic Identification of Victims of the "Noro-nic" Disaster. American Journal of Roentgenology 66:375–84.

Stewart, T. D. 1963. New Developments in Evaluating Evidence from the Skeleton. Proceedings of the Second International Conference on Oral Biology, Bonn (1962). Journal of Dental Research 42:264–73.

Thörne, H. and H. Thyberg. 1953. Identification of Children (or Adults) by Mass Miniature Radiographs of the Cranium. Acta Odontologia Scandinavica 11 (2):129–40.

Todd, T. W. 1920. Age Changes in the Pubic Bones. I. The Male White Pubis. American Journal of Physical Anthropology 3(3):285–334.

————. 1930. Age Changes in the Pubic Bone: Roentgenographic Differentiation. American Journal of Physical Anthropology 14(2):255–71.

Trotter, M. and G. C. Gleser. 1958. Estimation of Stature from Long Bones of Whites and Negroes. American Journal of Physical Anthropology (n.s.) 10 (4):463–514.

Washburn, S. L. 1951. The New Physical Anthropology. New York Academy of Science, Transaction Series II, 13:298–304.

Zoraf, P. A. and F. J. Prime. 1963. Estimation of Height from Tibial Length. Lancet 1(7274):195–96.

Dentistry and Oral Medicine

Dental education is in the throes of rapid evolutionary change. Schools of dentistry are beginning to recognize that they have a mission over and above the production of skilled dental practitioners. This change is due to many factors, but it is probably primarily due to the influence of the academic milieu into which the dental schools only relatively recently have been incorporated. The release of huge federal funds through the National Institutes of Health and increased support for dental research and education by industry and private foundations have been other important stimuli. Although there is no clear agreement on what the dentist of the future is supposed to be, curricular, research, and personnel requirement modifications taking place in most dental schools indicate that the dentist is envisioned as an oral biologist with in-depth knowledge of the anatomy, physiology, microbiology, pathology, biochemistry, genetics, and even anthropology of the head and face: the cranial facial complex as it affects and is affected by the oral cavity.

The dentist of the future will be primarily a diagnostician rather than a technician, a professional as well as a practitioner. He will appreciate and pursue interests in other fields of knowledge and will be conversant and experienced in research. In increasing numbers, he and his colleagues will achieve additional higher degrees, such as the M.S.D. in some special area of dentistry, the M.S., or even the Ph.D. in a physical or biological science.

Will anthropology play a role in the renaissance of dental education? My answer is very definitely in the affirmative, and I should like to point

231

out those areas of education and research in which anthropology will make significant contributions. At the same time, it is obvious that dentistry and dental research have much to offer the anthropologist; it is not merely a one-way street.

First, it is necessary to emphasize the essential differences in the orientation and philosophies of anthropology and dentistry. Each discipline has a deep and long-standing interest in the human dentition, but for quite different reasons. The dentist, as a member of the health profession, is concerned with the well-being of the individual person and, in particular, with maintaining or restoring health to structures of the oral cavity. He focuses upon pathology. People with caries-free dentitions and healthy oral mucosa seldom call upon him. Although he sees many people in the course of his practice career, he sees them as individuals, not as populations.

To learn about early man and the forerunners of man, the anthropologist became familiar with teeth. Since many of the key fossil finds primarily consist of teeth and fragments of jaws, he specialized in the crown morphology of the various teeth. From the study of the evolving human dention, he became interested in odontological differences between the living varieties of man. With the rise of the new science of genetics, he began to study the inheritance of the various morphological structures of the teeth. Those anthropologists who emphasized growth and development also investigated the time and sequence of eruption of the primary and permanent teeth, and the differences in the eruption patterns among living populations, between modern man and his hominoid progenitors, and between man and his primate relatives.

But the anthropologist always is concerned with the dentition of populations, living and dead, with normal or usual forms of teeth rather than teeth affected by disease, attrition, or senescence. The dentists's concern is the health of the living individual. The anthropologist uses dentition as a key to further knowledge about human evolution, about taxonomic positions of man and the animal primates, about dynamics of human genetics and race differentiation, and about the phenomena of growth. The dentist applies his knowledge of the anatomy, physiology, chemistry, and pathology of the oral structures to restore and preserve the individual's dentition as a functioning organ throughout his lifetime.

As we review the interests of anthropology and dentistry, we may wonder what can bring the two disciplines together and whether, indeed, such "togetherness" can be mutually productive. The nature of such a union can best be illustrated by pointing out those instances when anthropologists and dentists have collaborated in education and research. An outstanding example is Dr. Wilton M. Krogman's association with the University of Pennsylvania's School of Dental Medicine and with many other dental schools and organizations throughout the United States. His activities, in concert with dental colleagues, include research in orthodontics, pedodontics, prosthodontics, and periodontics, all important specialties in the dental profession. Dr. Krogman, long interested in human growth and development, has established a growth center in Philadelphia and the records are of inestimable clinical value for obtaining new facts about the phenomena of cranio-facial development.

The research association between Edward E. Hunt, Jr., of the Forsyth Dental Clinic in Boston and Dr. Coenraad Moorrees, head of the Orthodontic Department at the clinic, has produced new and exciting information on the growth and development of the human dentition and has been a great stimulation to graduate and undergraduate dental students at Harvard.

The long-time partnership of Dr. Stanley Garn and Dr. Arthur Lewis of the Fels Institute in Yellow Springs, Ohio, is well known to the dental fraternity, if not to anthropologists. Dr. Garn has, from time to time, brought outstanding dental clinicians to Fels to collaborate with him on research involving the institute's unique serial records, inaugurated some thirty-five years ago. These associations have called attention to many interesting correlations between dentition and other structures of the body and have emphasized the significance of dental growth and eruption in the study of race and evolution.

Among the many other examples of collaboration is Dr. William Laughlin's organized training program at the University of Wisconsin, in which physical anthropologists receive intensive instruction from research-oriented dentists. Dr. Melvin Baer, whose interest in growth and in vivo staining techniques led him to a year of study and research at the National Institute of Dental Research, is now a full-time member of the staff of the Orthodontics Department at the University of Michigan School of Dentistry. Dr. Gabriel Lasker has contributed significant papers on dental genetics. All of these physical anthropologists are well known to their dental colleagues and have had an important effect upon dental education, both graduate and undergraduate, and upon dental research.

The Cleft Palate Research Center, of which I am director, has an interesting relationship with the University of Pittsburgh's School of Dental Medicine. The research staff and the biological scientists of the center are men with clinical degrees — D.D.S. or M.D., or both. The center's program is broad in scope, involving research in some areas which may seem, at first, unrelated to the central research theme — the study of the mechanism and causes of cleft lip and palate in man. All research is undertaken in direct response to a "need to know," established in the course of laboratory experimentation.

Dental research at the center includes topics such as the continued study of the life cycle of each primary tooth in man, the anthropoid apes, and the New World and Old World monkeys, taking into consideration the establishment of a chronological timetable and sequence of events for each tooth that begins with the first proliferation of the dental lamina and ends with the final calcification of the dental crown. Assisting in this study are three full-time dentists, trained in various research techniques and methodologies, and occasional visitors for periods of one to three years. Among the visiting staff have been Dr. Percy Butler of the University of London's zoology faculty, one of the outstanding authorities in the world on the evolution of dentition; and researchers from Canada, the School of Dental Surgery in Liverpool, England, and dental schools in Tokyo and Hiroshima. Sophomore dental students are brought to the center's laboratories each summer to become acquainted with fields of dental research which would otherwise be unfamiliar to them.

Another of the center's interests is the continuing study of the normal range of crown morphology in both its developing and final stages. This exceedingly important work must precede any serious investigation of problems relating to the evolution of the dentition, genetics of the dentition, and dental teratology. The center also studies the occurrences of morphological abnormalities of dental crowns in association with congenital malformations, such as clefts, mongolism, mental retardation, and various genetic syndromes.

Dentition is unique among the organs of the body in that, embryologically, it begins its development when the rest of the body has completed the period of maturation. The human organism is commonly thought to have terminated its embryonic period at the end of the seventh week of prenatal life. Some teeth, however, begin to develop as early as five weeks before birth. The last tooth to develop, the third molar or "wisdom" tooth, undergoes morphogenesis about ten years after birth. Thus, the critical stages of development can extend from the fifth prenatal week to the eighteenth year after birth with the eruption of the third molar. Any insult to the dentition during this period is apt to interfere with the normal development of a tooth that happens to be in a critical stage of differentiation. This should be reflected in the abnormal chemistry or morphology of that particular tooth.

In this way, we have learned that the correlation of our studies of dental morphology and congenital malformations is obviously important. Individual dental units may be used as chronological markers at the onset of disturbances which have widespread effects throughout the body. But, again, this type of discovery is the result of joint collaboration between the anthropologist, who maintains his interest in the delineation of the normal range of dental variation in the population, and the dentist, who has had broad and continuous contact with the dental problems of handicapped individuals.

The role of the center's staff illustrates, in part, the potentialities of anthropological data and perspective in dental education. The subjects taught in individual lectures and in courses by senior staff members of the Cleft Palate Research Center include many that are basically anthropological: evolution of the human dentition, comparative mammalian odontology, embryology and morpho-differentiation of the dentition, tissue culture experiments in odontogenesis, comparative primate odontogenesis, and racial and genetic aspects of the dentition.

Thus far I have referred only to the role of the physical anthropologist. Is there also a future for the cultural anthropologist in the field of dentistry. My own contact with dentistry is perhaps unique in the United States. Over the past nine years, I have been a faculty member at the dental school of the University of Washington and at the dental school of the University of Pittsburgh. During these years, I became conversant with many of the problems besetting dental educators and many of the vexing questions in clinical dentistry that have been submitted time and time again to research without notable success. If I were asked to isolate one area of investigation in dentistry which requires the utmost sophistication in scientific methodology; which area can utilize maximum cooperation between dentistry and other disciplines, particularly anthropology; which area has world-wide urgency in its implications; and which area promises to open new and exciting avenues of research, then I would say, without hesitation, dental epidemiology in its broadest aspects. Further, I would stress the need for a close association of both dental specialists and cultural anthropologists.

If epidemiology is the study of the nature, associations, and frequencies of occurrences of specific traits in selected human populations, it would seem self-evident that the cultural anthropologist, whose major concern is the study of the culture and society of human populations, should be an important participant in the design, prosecution, and analysis of any dental epidemiological project. For example, in the United States, the occurrence of an adolescent or adult with an unoperated cleft of the lip and/or palate is exceedingly rare; most clefts are operated on soon after birth. The same situation prevails in most of Europe. However, in Asia, Africa, and South and Central America, there are vast areas where the adolescent or adult individual with an unoperated cleft is the rule rather than the exception. This situation, of course, is the result of a scarcity of plastic and oral surgeons, difficulties of transportation, insufficient recording of vital statistics, and various local attitudes and traditions regarding medical treatment and surgery.

In Puerto Rico alone, there are approximately one thousand unoperated clefts in a population of over two and one-half million. An epidemiological survey of this population could provide much new and important data on the characteristics of cranio-facial growth in unoperated clefts of various types, and could suggest ways of treating this segment of the population with prosthesis, if not by surgical repair. Clearly, such a survey could provide results for a model of rehabilitation techniques applicable throughout most of the world. In this kind of survey, the cultural anthropologist can make an immense contribution to dentistry and, indeed, to medicine in general. He can do this by understanding how the general population reacts to the presence of a cleft individual; by understanding the attitude of the patient and of his family and friends; by understanding the patient's reaction to medicine and surgery and the effect of changed speech pattern; and by understanding the economic implications of an unoperated cleft.

The mutual exchange of advantages to both anthropologists and dentists is clear. Such a close collaboration can broaden the dentist's understanding of dentition and its importance to such fields as paleontology, zoology, genetics, anthropology, and embryology. Inevitably, he will be stimulated to wider perusal of the manifold aspects of dentition in a broader world context, and will look at his patient from a different perspective. This, in itself, perhaps, will not increase his operative skill, but it will start him on the road toward true professionalism, which is the goal of the modern dental educator.

The anthropologist, on the other hand, can experience excitement and satisfaction as he works in areas directly related to the welfare and health of man, both individually and in groups. Also, he can find added stimulation through close association with his colleagues in medicine, dentistry, and the biological sciences in the fascinating pursuit of answers that will promote better health and well-being for the human species.

COMMENTARY: Edward E. Hunt, Jr.
Coenraad Moorrees

Edward E. Hunt, Jr.

One of the things that excites me most about dental anthropology is its ramifications in the distant past and in the cycle of growth and development of children today.

A study of fossilization and the ancient history of our own vertebrate subphylum helps us to understand what happens to bones when people die. The tissues of a dead vertebrate tend to disappear more or less in proportion to their toughness. Soft tissues usually disintegrate first, followed by cancellous, and then compact bone. The last fragments to disappear are usually the teeth.

As a result, the fossil record for four hundred million years of vertebrate evolution unfolds a richly documented story of dental transformations, more complete than for any other part of the body. This generalization also applies to vertebrates other than man.

An important and recent innovation in the study of fossil and modern teeth is what this study reveals about "behavioral paleontology." Dr. Ronald Every of New Zealand has noted that most tooth-bearing mammals grind their lower teeth against their uppers, in rage or in sleep. This habit strops or grinds the edges of the dental units together and keeps them sharp. An experienced eye can readily see marks of tooth-grinding on both human and animal teeth. Dr. Every and I have seen such marks even on the teeth of mammals of the Mesozoic era, who must have ground their teeth together within earshot of the dinosaurs.

Before Dr. Every's discovery, this auxiliary function of tooth-grinding and sharpening was not very clearly recognized, although it presumably has considerable survival value for the mammals who practice it. Nearly all human beings grind their teeth in sleep, even to extreme or pathological degrees which may damage the jaws. This habit of excessive grinding is called *bruxism*.

Convincing evidence indicates that this habit enhances the survival of animals. In studying the life expectancy and mortality of wild animals, teeth are considered life-limiting organs since many of these animals last only as long as their teeth. Conservatism in evolution is another very important characteristic of teeth, particularly among the higher primates. Dr. Stanley Garn's work on the sequence polymorphisms in dental eruption shows that, in some children, the second molar erupts before the second premolar, whereas, in others, the sequence is reversed. This sequence variation also occurs in the stages of formation or calcification of these two teeth. Dr. Daris Swindler has shown that this polymorphism is not confined to man, but also exists in young rhesus monkeys. Since man and the rhesus monkey have probably not had a common ancestor for at least thirty million or, more likely, forty million years, the persistence of this sequence polymorphism in both the human and monkey lineages is a striking case of the conservatism of the control of morphogenesis in related vertebrates.

Another fascinating phase of dental biology concerns the signs of a hidden malformation. Dr. Kraus, who studies cleft palate, is working with malformations in humans which probably originate in the early or fetal or late embryonic period. Damage in these cases is permanent. For later childhood, the teeth and the brain appear to be the prime indicators of this kind of tissue damage which is associated with toxemia late in pregnancy, difficult labor, anoxia of the birth process, or malnutrition in the newborn. There is good evidence that malnutrition early in life causes permanent damage to the intelligence and mental capacity of the human brain. A similar situation occurs in tooth formation. If conditions are adverse at the end of pregnancy, teeth sometimes will not form. Wisdom teeth and second premolars, which can be studied on an epidemiological basis, are vulnerable in this way. Among the adverse conditions in pregnancy probably related to this condition are twinning, toxemia, or the production of large or tiny babies. As Dr. Kraus points out, the dental lamina is apparently a kymograph of the life cycle. The tooth is a valuable document for analyzing the mechanisms whereby tissue can be damaged or a structure can fail to form.

Thus, the whole realm of dental variation has wide implications for the epidemiologist. As a geneticist, the thing that interests me most about dentitions is the number of enlightening indications of certain chromosomal effects on tooth formation both in man and lower mammals. Garn's work at the Fels Institute indicates, for example, that the large sex chromosome, "X," affects tooth formation. We have evidence, at least circumstantial, that the "Y" chromosome, responsible for masculine characteristics, also increases the size of the teeth, probably by extending the period of their development and creating a slightly different morphology. Perhaps someday we will have a complete understanding of the genetic mechanisms by which some lower primates develop large canines in the male and small ones in the female.

Dentition is a tremendously rich field for genetic and epidemiological research and a very rewarding area for an examination of phenomena of normality and abnormality in the life cycle.

Coenraad Moorrees

Dentists have shown a long-standing interest in anthropology, and in many institutions there is a close, mutually advantageous collaboration between odontologists and anthropologists. Dentistry offers both the physical and cultural anthropologist a fruitful field of endeavor and considerable challenge for research.

Dentists have not only been active in locating research problems, but have participated in interdisciplinary research projects. Yet the nation's dental schools, if judged by inspection of their curricula, have failed to appreciate much of this activity. The early work of Hellman and later contributions of Dahlberg and Pedersen on the tooth morphology of the American Indians and Greenland Eskimos, respectively, have received considerable attention from anthropologists, but only scant attention from the dental profession. The fascinating inferences that can be made from dentition, as determined from population studies, should furnish the clinical dentist with a much needed perspective in his practice.

In addition to defining morphologic differences of the teeth, studies on the Aleut dentition indicate the clear trend toward a master pattern in the dentition of Mongoloid populations; specific modifications of this master pattern permit identification of racial subgroups. The profusion of traits in dentition contributes to population differentiation; in this respect, these studies have only indicated the possibilities that more concentrated future efforts would yield (Moorrees, 1957).

Studies of contemporary man inevitably elicit queries about the past. Dentistry must look to anthropology and paleontology for answers. The evolution of man's dentition as well as the intercuspidation of the teeth brings us to the dynamic or functional aspect of the stomatognathic system and introduces wide vistas for research. Anthropology must join with dentistry to provide answers.

The cultural anthropologist is needed to define the impact of dentition on man's well-being; for example, what effect does a malocclusion of the teeth have on self-concept or self-image, when teeth are viewed as sense organs with an important bearing on mental health. The broader coverage of the population in health care envisioned by the federal government demands a definition of the handicapping effect of malocclusion on the individual. I see it as a fruitful field for future investigation. The Forsyth Dental Center of Boston has already begun preliminary work in this area.

The welcome addition of the physical anthropologist to the research team in a dental research institute has already been described by Dr. Kraus. In addition to clarifying the evolution of the stomatognathic system, the study of the development of face and dentition opens a Pandora's box for research. We are faced with growth as a multivariate problem incorporating somatic growth, constitution as it relates to patterning of growth, assessment of the individual's biologic age scale, and correlation of growth parameters in the body as a whole. Such work must focus on predicting the individual's path or pattern to the attainment of adult potential as the goal for practical application of the findings.

We are also faced with the utter complexity of the genetics of facial growth. The acquisition of the necessary knowledge about the genetics of facial growth also entails an appraisal of the relationship between form and function insofar as it modifies the growth pattern determined by the gene complex. The interaction of muscle and hard tissue conditioned by functional requirements and the adaptability of hard tissue to soft tissue growth combine to present a formidable challenge that will require joint and imaginative efforts if the level of knowledge is ever to extend beyond today's horizon. The yield of such work will be positive and rewarding, the challenge sufficient to whet the appetite of those interested in the welfare of the young — to permit them to grow unhampered by the often serious effects of dental and periodontal ills on individual well-being.

The last ten years have marked a period of unparalleled accomplishments through the work of anthropologists such as Krogman, Meredith, Garn, Hunt, Kraus, and Bear, as well as those from other disciplines, such as Tanner and Moss, and many others who deserve the label of anthropologist for their breadth of vision.

REFERENCE

Moorrees, C. F. A. 1957. The Aleut Dentition. Harvard University Press: Cambridge, Mass.

CHAPTER **10** Donald L. Hochstrasser
Jesse W. Tapp, Jr.

Social Medicine and Public Health

Interaction between the social and medical sciences has developed
rapidly during the fifteen years since Caudill's (1953) exhaustive review
of anthropology in medicine. This recent rapprochement between modern
or Western medicine and the behavioral sciences has been examined at
length in several authoritative works within the last five years. These
studies demonstrate the extensive growth of mutual interest of medicine
and the other sciences dealing with man. However, they also make it
clear that, to date, the greatest amount of cross-disciplinary activity has
been in the direction of medicine or, more generally, toward an expanding infusion of the social sciences into the broad field of health (Freeman,
Levine, and Reeder, 1963; Polgar, 1962.) This direction is evident in
several ways. For example, the main flow of programs and major trends
in interdisciplinary contact and cooperation have involved an increasing
movement of social scientists — especially psychologists, sociologists,
and anthropologists — into medicine and other health fields. At the
same time, researchers, educators, and practitioners from many specialties within the health disciplines are adopting modern social science concepts and methods in their work (Dubos, 1959; McGavran, 1956). Indeed, many health authorities have made some rather strong and somewhat debatable pronouncements to the effect that medicine really is a
social science (Dubos, 1959; McGavran, 1956; Crew, 1956).

Two broad factors underlie the various reasons offered for the burgeoning stream of social science influence in modern medicine over the
past two decades: (1) pressure from technical assistance commitments

of the United States and other Western European nations involving medical programs in the underdeveloped areas, and (2) major changes — sometimes of an almost revolutionary nature — in health and medicine, science and technology, and many other sectors of modern society within the developed areas themselves. With the exception of anthropology, the primary thrust of social science knowledge, projects, and workers into the health field has come about largely through change in developed societies (Polgar, 1962; Scotch, 1963).

During their development from essentially agrarian to highly industrialized and urbanized societies, rich nations have undergone deep and often sweeping alterations in population, basic conditions and levels of living, as well as patterns of disease and environmental hazard, and the organization of health services and medical care. These trends, along with the sociocultural transition accompanying them, have given rise to a host of new economic, social, and political difficulties both within medicine and in its relationship to the rest of society.

In the United States and other Western societies, scholars and other commentators are becoming increasingly aware that technical, human, and ecological conditions underlying many complex problems of medicine in modern society can be resolved or greatly ameliorated only through effective collaboration between the medical and social sciences. Already, this combined approach to health problems has made considerable headway toward general acceptance and support among many fronts throughout the health field. Indeed, in some circles, this collaboration is becoming a more or less established tenet among medical authorities and their social science colleagues. Few today would question the value of such an approach, at least so far as the more pragmatic aspects of the immediate situation are concerned, and many cite the great potential that collaboration holds for advancement and future progress in both modern medicine and the behavioral sciences (Frank, 1948; Gregg, 1956).

The current need for action which this approach presents to the health field, and certainly to the whole community is gaining recognition in many segments of our national society. Consequently, a growing number of private, public, and voluntary health agencies are responding to the challenge with programs and activities which create additional pressures to push and pull social science and medicine toward each other. These activities are opening up new and wider channels for the entry of social scientists into the health field itself: for example, (1) the availability of federal and other funds for research, (2) the many opportunities for study provided by health problems and medical settings, and (3) the call for help and collaboration — sometimes reluctant and full of conflict — which is extended to social scientists by many medical schools, research centers, health departments, and other health-related institutions (Freeman, Levine, and Reeder, 1963).

A complete appraisal of anthropology in public health and social medicine would require a critical assessment of this subject in terms of the above-outlined trends and forces currently bringing medicine and the behavioral sciences closer together in modern society. Such an appraisal is far beyond the scope of this paper. Emphasis here will be given only to a brief and selective examination of (1) the relationship between anthropology and modern medicine in terms of public health and social medicine, and (2) the previous developments and present changes taking place in this relationship. The general frame of reference for these two areas of study is an ongoing program of professional collaboration between anthropology and medicine in the new and developing field of "community medicine" in the United States (Deuschle et al., 1966; Stewart, 1963).

Anthropology, Modern Medicine, and Public Health

Initial ties of anthropology with modern medicine actually go back to the early emergence of anthropology as a scientific discipline in the latter part of the nineteenth century. From this time until World War II, contact between the two fields was largely through connections between physical anthropology and the biological sciences on the one hand, and cultural anthropology and psychiatry on the other hand. The latter interaction between medicine and anthropology started about the 1920's and gave rise to the special interdisciplinary field, or sub-specialty, of culture and personality. This long-established mutual interest and exchange between anthropology and modern medicine has grown considerably since World War II. It now includes not only the biological and psychological areas of medicine but, more recently, public health and, to lesser degrees, nursing, clinical medicine, and other related specialties (Kluckhohn, 1962; Paul, 1956; Wallace, 1961).

As a result of these various developments between anthropology and medicine during the past two decades, an increasing number of anthropologists, as other social scientists, have become involved in interdisciplinary endeavors relating to the health field (Freeman, Levine, and Reeder, 1963; Polgar, 1962; Scotch, 1963). Anthropologists working on health problems in medical settings have succeeded in fashioning the empirical foundations and theoretical outlines of medical anthropology which have laid the basis for a potentially productive professional relationship between anthropology and medicine.

Medical anthropology is concerned with the biocultural understanding of man and his works in relation to health and medicine (Alland, 1966; Roney, 1959, 1963; Scotch, 1963). While this biocultural orientation is basic to the whole field of anthropology, which is the unified study of man as a biological and social organism in time and space (Kluckhohn, 1962; Wallace, 1961), medical anthropology as a subspecialty or as a "synthetic discipline" with multidisciplinary orientations may involve medical scientists, anthropologists, biologists, and sociologists (Roney, 1959, 1963).

Except among some of the more conservative and tradition-bound anthropologists, little doubt exists today that a truly professional relationship between anthropology and medicine will be mutually rewarding for developing and advancing substantive knowledge, theory, and method in each field (Polgar, 1962; Roney, 1963; Scotch, 1963). Caudill (1953) has set forth the long-range goal for a bioculturally oriented and fully integrated collaboration between anthropologists and medical scientists in scientific medicine. In discussing the efforts of psychiatrists and internists to bridge the organic-psychic gap between their two disciplines through a "psychosomatic" approach to clinical health problems, Caudill (1953) states:

Workers in these two groups are interested in the intensive investigation of a small series of individual patients — one might almost say they are learning so much in their study of the trees that they are not aware they are living in a forest. There is little factual or theoretical interchange with workers in public health or social medicine. While this may come in time, it is just at this point that the interest of the anthropologist lies: in attempts to relate the insights gained in intensive study to a better understanding of the larger group phenomena implied in epidemiological statistics.

While it is never explicitly formulated, the need for a biocultural integration of clinical medicine and public health is implied in Caudill's statement. This integration would call for a number of far-reaching changes not only in the internal structure of the medical fields and disciplines, but also in the external organization of its relationship to the rest of society. Indicative of the difficulty of working toward such an integration is Suchman's (1963) restatement of this need for integration a decade later.

In discussing the current trends in public health, Suchman (1963) points out that the "dividing line between preventive and therapeutic medicine" is "becoming increasingly difficult to draw." He also indicates that with the changing health needs of modern society "came the need for developing new relationships between public health and the public, on the one hand, and public health and organized private medicine on the other." However, he does not emphasize that current trends in both public health and clinical medicine call for a merging of personal and social approaches to community health and medical care problems (Gregg, 1956; McGavran, 1956; Stieglitz, 1949).

Services of medical scientists, social scientists, and others working together will be needed to bridge the existing gap between clinical medicine and public health. Since the ultimate goal of this collaboration is to integrate personal and social medicine, a strategy of intervention must be forged for promoting and enhancing health, as well as for preventing and curing disease. We need to view, investigate, and change society, both as the patient and as the doctor (Frank, 1948; McGavran, 1956). Thomas Gladwin (personal communication, 1966) has suggested that, "Anthropology, if it uses its resources creatively, can make a major contribution toward this goal." This will depend largely upon anthropologists working on health problems and in medical settings, and the degree to which they can and will enter into a fully professional and collaborative effort with medical colleagues who are working toward this same goal. For his part, the anthropologist in a medical setting will have to assume the full professional responsibilities of his clinical and basic science work in research, teaching, and service. He must go beyond the much too passive and limited explanatory-educational role he has tended to play in the past in applied work (T. Gladwin, personal communication, 1966).

Assumption of professional status further means that the medical anthropologist's clinical role of "doctor of society" (L. Thompson, 1965) cannot be limited to that of only providing biocultural understanding and "diagnosis" of the health and medical care problems of individuals and groups in the community. He also must assume ethical responsibility for selecting and evaluating alternatives for action and developmental change from his knowledge and findings and for implementing and guiding (in cooperation with the patient) a recommended course of intervention. This approach must achieve results agreed upon by both the patient and the doctor in a bioculturally dynamic and meaningful way. Medical anthropologists must remember that their clinical intervention into human affairs should not only be directed at taking an active professional role in development programs. They also must focus on sociocultural settings and on the behavior of the providers as well as the consumers of health and medical care services (Batalla, 1966; Hochstrasser, Nickerson, and Deuschle, 1966; Peattie, 1957; Quentin, Gladwin, and Bower, 1966).

This kind of professional help and collaboration from anthropologists is what physicians, medical scientists and educators, and other health workers need and want. Only in this way can anthropologists enter the area of clinical medicine and hope to gain and, indeed, deserve the full respect of their medical colleagues. Anthropologists "should have graduated long ago from their practice of telling physicians and other health personnel about the native culture and native medicine and then leaving the rest up to them" (T. Gladwin, personal communication, 1966). This applies equally at home and abroad. Despite all these compelling arguments, anthropologists by and large are still far from having graduated from this explanatory-educational approach in interdisciplinary work with the other sciences and professions. Consequently, they have made only limited progress toward establishing a fully professional collaborative effort with medical colleagues in the health field, even in their more "action-oriented" endeavors (Batalla, 1966; Quentin, Gladwin, and Bower, 1966).

Anthropology and Public Health

In their work with public health and social medicine, anthropologists have been especially slow to recognize the need for developing a professional role for medical anthropology. No doubt, one reason for this situation has been the rather recent entry of anthropologists into these fields. Even now they are still few in number and involved primarily in overseas medical settings or intercultural health programs (Paul, 1963; Polgar, 1962).

The problems of major concern here relate to the way anthropologists have gone about their work in public health as well as to the nature of the public health field.

In the following discussion, we make no basic distinction between public health and social medicine, although we are aware that there has been some conflict between the two fields over their respective differences. As Caudill (1953) points out, "Such quarrels have their historical roots" in the fact that while public health grew out of the practical concerns of epidemiology and preventive medicine, social medicine arose from "a more scholarly European tradition" which tended to view "medicine as a social science." Much more important here, however, is the basic similarity that has always existed between public health and social medicine: the emphasis upon the population or group approach to the study and solution of health problems.

Some of the main difficulties encountered by anthropologists in public health stem from the tendency to define anthropology's role in this field essentially as an academic discipline. Also, public health's role in medicine and society has been viewed as necessarily or exclusively grounded in the population or group approach. This passive acceptance of the more traditional and conservative orientations prevailing in both anthropology and public health has had various consequences. One of the most pervasive assumptions has been that the primary reason for the relationship lies in their reliance on the group approach to man and his works (Paul, 1963). This not only distorts the basic principle of modern American anthropology as a unified study of man, but also omits important areas in physical and cultural anthropology, including culture and personality. Beyond these theoretical considerations, little or no recognition is given to the strategic and increasingly critical need for merging the personal and social aspects in applied or policy matters in each field as well as in professional collaboration between them.

A major consequence of the status quo approach has been the excessive concern with fitting anthropology, especially cultural anthropology, into public health (Paul, 1955; Suchman, 1963). For the same reason, only limited attention has been focused on the equally crucial need for bringing about developmental change in the health field and in the relationship of the health field to society (Freeman, Levine, and Reeder

1963; Paul, 1963). Moreover, the prevalence of very special academic and research interests has led to a rather limited perspective on the scope and potential of anthropology's contribution to public health and community medicine (Foster, 1961; Paul, 1955, 1956).

Foster's (1961) recent discussion of public health and behavioral science reflects several of these general problems and may serve as an example. First, an earnest concern exists to distingush anthropology as an "academic discipline" from public health, seen essentially as a "goal-directed, practicing" profession. A key point is that public health "draws upon the scientific knowledge of a number of fields" and "differs from academic disciplines in that it is a directly applied venture" (Foster, 1961). This definitely seems to be the basic difference separating anthropology as a "discipline" from public health as a "profession.' Both fields suffer from such a comparison, since no consideration is given to a possible professional role for anthropology. Little or no attention is paid to the very important fact that the public health profession includes not only clinical practice, which is a "directly applied venture," but also considerable organization and activity in preclinical and clinical research and training.

The eclectic nature of anthropology in its history, development, and present situation is analogous to that of public health, which also draws upon other sciences and disciplines. On the other hand, many, or even most, anthropologists have little interest in using their knowledge of anthropology in a directly applied and action-oriented fashion. This also may tell us much about the current state of anthropology as a whole. Here again, however, the particular predisposition of many anthropologists to shy away from goal-directed endeavors would not seem to make any particularly telling or inherent distinctions between the two fields. Indeed, in an attempt to establish the academic detachment of anthropology in contrast to that of public health, Foster brings out most decisively that "he is not immediately concerned, as a scientist, with the goodness or badness of his discoveries, nor with their immediate practical utilization" (Foster, 1961).

Foster (1961) raises a number of other issues in discussing his views on how anthropology fits into public health:

Speaking now as an anthropologist, I would say that problems where behavioral scientists can help most are most apt to be found in the fields of sanitation, mental health, tuberculosis, maternal and child health, and perhaps aging and dental health. The subjects that afford least opportunity appear to be air pollution, medical and surgical care for the indigent, radiological health, rehabilitation, urban and suburban expansion, and safety. The common characteristic of the first category is that success is marked by changes in individual and small group behavior . . . legal, political, and economic factors intrude in the second category to a far greater extent than in the first.

Thus, human situations falling into the second category are considered the more difficult social science problems of modern society. These are areas of study where anthropology — apparently due to some inherent limitations in its nature — is expected to make only "minimal" contributions, since the problems fall largely, if not entirely, outside the purview of anthropology as a field of study, be it a discipline or a profession.

However, anthropology is viewed by many not only as a unified study of man, but also as a field that has the potential for becoming a profession which can make major contributions in modern society both at home and abroad. To these people, Foster's view of the relationship of anthropology to public health and medicine is disquieting on several counts. Foster's statement may be true of cross-cultural settings and situations involving individual and small group behavior in underdeveloped areas. But, it is highly doubtful that the many economic, legal, and political factors in modern society that intrude into the first category — tuberculosis control, environmental health and sanitation, population problems including aging, mental health, and the like — are really any less difficult or complex in their own way than those of the second category which includes medical care for the indigent, rehabilitation, and so forth. For example, while rehabilitation is cited in the second category, it is a critical function of tuberculosis control which is given in the first category.

It is equally clear that, from the biocultural standpoint of anthropology, the problems of the second category are no different from those of the first in their essential nature. Both involve man's relationship not only to the natural and man-made elements of his physical environment, but also to the economic, political, and religious aspects of his social environment and to interactions with his fellow man. Since the second category of human situations, like the first, includes some major health and medical care problems faced in current trends of modern society, they, therefore, require collaborative efforts of medical and social scientists to bring about an integration of clinical medicine and public health.

Additional substantive, theoretical, and methodological issues are raised by Foster's (1961) further contention that social scientists, and especially anthropologists, are particularly well equipped to work in settings where there is a "cultural chasm separating the innovating and recipient groups." This has to be considered in conjunction with Foster's admonitions that anthropologists also are not only best suited for study of "individual and small group behavior" but "perform better in situations where social, cultural, and psychological factors hold the key, rather than where legal, political, and economic factors are dominant." All of this adds up to a rather puzzling set of circumstances. Since general ability to handle "social, cultural, and psychological factors" necessarily includes intra- as well as inter-cultural situations, whole communities and societies, as well as small groups and individuals, it becomes extremely difficult to understand exactly why intracultural situations and communities together with legal, political, and economic factors are seen to be no longer a part of "society" and "culture" or a part of the anthropologist's study of sociocultural phenomena.

While Foster's fairly typical general formulation of the behavioral science relationship between anthropology and public health may be accepted as far as it goes, the essence of the issues raised here is that it remains incomplete in our view of anthropology and the neighboring sciences and disciplines. "Cross-cultural" situations and "individual and small group" behavior are certainly important areas of study both at home and abroad and in developed as well as underdeveloped countries. However, these areas do not constitute the entire study of anthropology, even as an academic discipline, nor are they sufficient to define the professional role of anthropology — even cultural anthropology — in medicine and public health. The central problem touched upon is the danger of letting our own special research interests and theoretical inclinations intrude into, and color our, conception of the role of anthropology in its relationship to the other disciplines and professions.

Another and somewhat more immediate problem is pointed out by Robertson (1965) in his review of recent advances in social science and public health. In discussing some of the difficulties involved in "securing the most profitable of relationships between social scientists and public health people," he says: "Another major difficulty, I believe, has lain in the mistaken belief that the social scientist can only be of help in dealing with problems like the organization and distribution of health services, with the acceptance of programs by those of different cultures and so forth." Some social scientists are starting to eliminate this "mistaken belief" in their own work on health problems and in medical settings. Consequently, we can expect this problem to be overcome as medical anthropologists and other behavioral scientists, including those in public health, increasingly turn to the study of health and disease problems in addition to the study of health behavior and medical care problems. Indeed, more research in both of these areas is being carried out by social scientists in conjunction with their medical colleagues (Freeman, Levine, and Reeder, 1963; Polgar, 1962; Scotch, 1963).

Sociomedical research is contributing not only to ecology of human health, including demographic and population studies, but also to epidemiology and etiology of human diseases. With growing interest, this field promises to become one of the most important areas of interdisciplinary research between social and medical scientists. Scotch (1963) suggested that sociomedical research may well represent the major focus for improving the quality of research involving medical and behavioral science. In relating this point to medical anthropology, Scotch states:

We have discussed many of the problems and barriers to improved research. As I see it, the central problem continues to be the failure of medicine and anthropology to come to grips with the role of social factors in disease, and vice versa. . . . The failure to integrate theoretically these two sets of factors (disease and culture) is the biggest stumbling block to real development.

While we agree wholeheartedly with Scotch concerning research on health and disease problems, we suggest that this may not be *the* "central problem" or "biggest stumbling block" to development, either in modern medicine and its relationship to society or in improving collaboration between anthropologists and physicians.

The need to integrate theoretically the two sets of factors, biology and culture, does include health and disease problems. However, it actually goes far beyond this to include other broad problems of health behavior and medical care systems in modern society. There is a growing agreement among authorities from many fields in, as well as outside of, the medical field that disease and health behavior problems of modern society have to be solved together, if they are to be solved at all. These solutions will require major changes in the nature, structure, and function of medicine in society. The most strategic and productive approach for developing and improving collaboration between anthropologists and physicians in all areas of their work would be to focus on the major problems within the structure of modern medicine and within the social organization of medicine's relationship with the rest of society (Baehr, 1965; Deuschle et al., 1966). This approach would include the significance as well as the quality of research.

Overwhelming evidence on current trends in health and medicine indicates that, while many important problems remain in epidemiology and etiology which call for interdisciplinary efforts between the social and medical sciences, technical advances in controlling disease are presently far ahead of their effective application to individual and public health needs. This progress in medical care will result in greater progress in disease control.

Development of new patterns of social organization for providing and delivering health services is fundamental for advancement, both in solving disease problems and in meeting health needs. Mounting recognition and appreciation of the most critical elements for progress in both preventive and curative medicine is necessary for the eventual integration of personal and social medicine within the health field and in its relationship to the community (Badgley, 1963; Baldwin, 1963).

Once again, we return to the basic need for bridging the gap between public health and clinical medicine and to the question of how, and to what extent, research on health behavior and medical care problems by medical anthropologists has contributed toward this goal. The overall behavioral science achievements in this field have been impressive and are documented in many recent reviews. Numerous studies of health beliefs, healing techniques, medical institutions, and health systems in domestic and foreign settings have produced empirical data demonstrating the importance of sociocultural factors in defining the meaning of illness as an individual and group phenomenon. These studies also have defined the organizations and means for counteracting sickness with both therapeutic and preventive measures. Despite these records, this work still suffers from several major deficiencies in helping to integrate personal and social medicine. Such difficulties are especially noticeable among anthropologists and other social scientists in public health (Polgar, 1962; Suchman, 1963).

The first and most obvious shortcoming is that a far greater amount of social science research has been done on the patients or clientele than on modern physicians or practitioners (Paul, 1955; Robertson, 1965). A closely related difficulty is the heavy preoccupation of medical behavioral scientists with the consumers rather than providers of health services, which is often accompanied by what Roth (1962) so aptly called "management bias." These problems have even affected applied research in public health, where the greatest emphasis has been by far upon social science study in learning how to motivate, influence, and change the lay consumers rather than the official providers and professional dispensers of public health services. Interest primarily has been focused on the need for public health workers to account for sociocultural factors affecting community cooperation and on the behavior of "recipient" individuals and "target" groups in planning and implementing health services and programs (Paul, 1956; Suchman, 1963).

A second major difficulty occurs because far too few studies have been done on the organizational aspects of health agencies, and the research to date has concentrated mainly on an essentially static structural-functional approach. Existing medical settings in both the clinical and public health fields have been accepted as more or less necessary institutional conditions. Hence, little attention has been given to a dynamic and developmental view of modern medicine. In the relatively few studies directed toward change in the therapeutic setting, emphasis has usually been fixed on improving the adjustment of health workers and their clients to each other within the structure of the existing medical system, rather than on making organizational and functional changes in the system (Suchman, 1963).

Medical behavioral scientists, then, are just beginning to investigate the many urgent national, state, and local problems involved in coordinating numerous fragmented health programs and in developing new patterns of distribution of health services and new approaches to financing needed health resources. Roemer and Elling (1963) discussed these points in detail in their recent comprehensive review of sociological research on medical care. These authors posed two basic questions: "How can health manpower needs be met?" and "How can more physicians be developed to work in settings where community and preventive aspects are fully incorporated in their work?" Too few medical anthropologists and other social scientists have been concerned with these questions. All these issues and problems in the broad field of health are relevant to professional collaboration between social and medical scientists in bridging the gap between clinical medicine and public health.

Difficulties inherent in the public health field which tend to block its integration with clinical medicine are rooted in the deep dichotomy that has developed in the tradition of Western medicine. Anthropologists and their medical colleagues in public health are facing a historically created differentiation between personal and social medicine that is essentially false but which, nevertheless, is still maintained as an organizationally viable fact in modern society. Nowhere is this basic division among the health sciences and disciplines more rigidly and widely adhered to than in the United States where it now is centered primarily in the fields of clinical medicine and public health (Rosen, 1958; Stewart, 1963).

In response to this general situation, clinical medicine has developed into essentially a private and mostly curative form of personal medicine concentrating on individual patient care research, teaching, and practice. In the process, the two main citadels of the mainstream of American medicine have become organized academic medicine, located in the medical school, and private medicine at work in the community (Baehr, 1965; Deuschle et al., 1966). Conversely, public health has evolved basically into a governmental and largely preventive form of social medicine focused on health promotion. Most of its major centers of research, teaching, and practice are now stationed outside or in a satellite relationship to the mainstream of American medicine (Stewart, 1963; Suchman, 1963). This primary division between the labors and centers of public health and clinical medicine has relegated preventive and social medicine or public health research and teaching to a very small, usually marginal, and often ineffectual activity in most medical schools throughout the coutry (Shepard and Roney, 1964; Deuschle et al., 1966).

Many currents of opinion about both the need and the means for bridging this present gap between public health and clinical medicine are evident in both fields. From all sides comes increasing evidence that new patterns of social organization for provision and delivery of health and medical care services to people must be developed for solving disease problems and meeting health needs. Changes and new directions are just beginning to take shape in American medicine. In public health, Americans seek changes which involve not only structure and organization as a whole, but also public health theory, practice, and its relations, dealings, and confrontations with organized academic and private medicine (Deuschle et al., 1966; Stewart, 1963; Stieglitz, 1949). Within the general context of dealing with current trends in contemporary social and medical science problems, the public health and social medicine services must move their basic research, teaching, and service functions back into the mainstream of American medicine, both in its academic and community settings.

Anthropologists must play a significant part in collaborating with medical researchers, educators, and practitioners for the eventual integration of personal and social medicine within modern society. In doing so, anthropology must be prepared to take on three tasks. First, it must adopt a fully professional role that includes both basic and clinical sciences on an equal basis. Accordingly, anthropologists working in medical settings must accept the scientific and humanistic responsibilities of both "pure" and "applied" research, teaching, and service activities. Second, in its professional role in medicine, anthropology must exert as much effort toward developmental change in the behavior and social organization of the providers as it exerts on behalf of consumers of modern medicine. This professional effort at sociomedical change with medical colleagues also must be carried out both on basic and clinical science levels. Third, anthropology must move its primary base of operation for interdisciplinary work with medical scientists and other health personnel into the mainstream of medicine.

Community Medicine: A New Approach

Opportunities for establishing a professional role for medical anthropology in public health and social medicine are just beginning to open up on several fronts. One important new front is "community medicine." Because no generally accepted definition of community medicine exists, it still represents an undifferentiated field of modern medicine. Nevertheless, training programs in community medicine have begun to function in several university medical settings. These programs have been initiated on the assumption that differences between community medicine and other health disciplines are more than semantic. Several authorities agree that the basic distinction is that community medicine is concerned primarily with bridging the gap between public health and clinical medicine (Deuschle et al., 1966; Gregg, 1956; McGavran, 1956; Stewart, 1963; Stieglitz, 1949).

A completely adequate, general model for establishing community medicine at any given university medical center does not yet exist. New programs in the field will have to be developed according to particular circumstances and special resources available within each unique professional and community setting. Moreover, for the body of knowledge of community medicine to be fully effective, it eventually must span the medical and behavioral sciences; any planned program in this field can be viable only if it is based on continued interdisciplinary activity. Concepts of community medicine apply on all levels of medical research, teaching, and service, and thus cannot be separated from other developmental elements of the health field in the medical school and in the community. These concepts relate to current improvements in relevant academic disciplines and university settings, as well as to present changes in state and local health and welfare programs.

As defined and organized at the University of Kentucky Medical Center, community medicine follows a basic orientation that aims at integrating personal and social medicine within the structure of modern medicine and in its relationship to the community (Deuschle et al., 1966). In this conceptualization, the health and disease process, along with the whole person and total society, become the foci of medical attention. The overall effectiveness and long-term results of the Kentucky experiment are, of course, far from complete. Revisions and further developments undoubtedly will be required in the future. Nevertheless, as an ongoing project, the Kentucky experiment can serve as an example and offer certain guidelines in the kind of medical and community settings and in the type of programs and institutions that presently appear to be particularly conducive to building this new approach to health problems in modern society.

The University of Kentucky's Department of Community Medicine works toward a close alignment with public health and clinical medicine through its preclinical and clinical activities within the medical school. This alignment is further developed in research, teaching, and service activities where collaborative efforts are essential to the practicing fields of public health, private medicine, and the allied health disciplines centered in the community. Anthropology is incorporated into this organization with a full professional role which includes interdisciplinary work in both basic and clinical sciences and collaboration with medical scientists, educators, and practitioners from public health and clinical medicine.

Through a strong extramural orientation to the health and medical care problems of the Kentucky community, community-centered teaching and training activities are facilitated throughout the state; this policy also provides full institutional support for major medical education and curriculum innovation. Unique in the curriculum is a program of extramural clerkships and research projects for medical students.

The teaching and educational programs of community medicine are further augmented by the Department of Behavioral Science which provides medical behavioral science instruction in the basic science courses of the medical college (Strauss, 1965; Willard, 1965). This department brings together the social and statistical sciences on an interdepartmental basis. Medical and social sciences also are allied on an interdepartmental basis in this department's teaching, research, and administrative activities within the medical center (Strauss, 1965). The Department of Community Medicine plays a similar but differently structured and extramurally oriented role that draws strength from, as well as reinforces, the departmental and cross-departmental position of the behavioral sciences in the College of Medicine.

The professional relationship between social sciences and medical sciences and public health disciplines is established and provided by the community-medicine faculty itself. Broad and sustained collaboration is built into the structure and function of the department. Departmental ties with other medical faculties, social science faculties, health units, groups in the medical center and the university, and with various colleges, health agencies, and medical organizations throughout the state further promote and reinforce interdisciplinary considerations and team collaboration.

Since the cultural anthropologist and other faculty members of the department work on both an individual and a team basis, their professional interaction in the teaching and training programs include a one-to-one, faculty-to-student pattern and a faculty-group-to-student-group pattern. Some of these activities take place in classrooms and seminars, in service and administrative programs at the medical center; others take place in the community — in student research projects and clerkships. This pattern also holds for faculty research and service activities. In the basic and preclinical sciences, the department's primary field of operation is centered in the medical school, while its primary field of operation is extramural in the clinical and applied sciences.

The department's basic objective in its medical student teaching and research programs is to develop and impart scientific knowledge and technical skills necessary for identifying and solving community health and medical care problems at local, state, and national levels. For example, together with the his medical colleagues, the anthropologist instructs the the senior medical student during a regular six-week field clerkship of living and working in urban and rural communities throughout Kentucky. In essence, therefore, the anthropologist with other members of the faculty works toward the aim of enlarging the future physicians's understanding and appreciation of the ecology of health and disease and of the biocultural means necessary for maintaining and enhancing health (McGavran, 1956; Tapp and Deuschle, 1964).

Like his student counterpart in anthropology, the medical student participating in this uncoventional field clerkship in a "hospital without wall" (Tapp and Deuschle, 1966) is able to observe, confront, experience, and study the "whole way of life" and its relation to health and health behavior. The medical anthropologist with both a public health and social science background can direct his teaching and research activities to the sociocultural aspects and implications of illness on the individual, family, and small group levels. He also can go far beyond this to the broader dimensions of social institutions, becoming involved in such matters as social organization and occupational structure of health agencies, or provision and delivery of health services. Perhaps most important of all, the medical anthropologist can significantly contribute to the enhancement of the role of the physician and modern medicine as an "agent of social change" (Dixon, 1965) for the improvement of the quality of human life in the community.

From the standpoint of the long-range philosophical and theoretical aims of community medicine, the anthropologist can help develop a better understanding of the human community as it relates to both the scientific method and the humanistic purpose of modern medicine. There are two basic scientific principles of community medicine involved in integrating personal and social medicine into a universal knowledge of the human community:

1)   Health and disease are neither separate states nor distinct processes in man and his environment. They are interrelated, dynamic proc-

esses within the larger and more basic biocultural realities and conditions of human life (Virchow, 1958).

2)   The fundamental biocultural unit and organizing principle in the interrelated life of the human individual and the human group is the human community (Arensberg, 1961).

Conclusion

In conclusion, two general positions concerning the nature and function of anthropology in modern society must be adopted if anthropologists wish to enter into a full and truly professional collaborative effort with medicine. First, the basic value of anthropology to mankind is to serve as a unified study of man with both the scientific and ethical responsibility of developing a complete and legitimate professional role for itself among the other professions in the contemporary world. The primary relationship of anthropology to the neighboring sciences and disciplines is working toward an integrated biocultural understanding of man and his works and in using this knowledge for the humanistic and scientific betterment of human individuals and groups in the global community (Lindsay, 1959).

Second, anthropologists must accept the fact that medicine and anthropology share a fundamental concern over man's capacity and means of survival. Both disciplines are committed ·to the intellectual inquiry into the biocultural "fitness" of the human animal and the individual organism for the comprehensive phenomenon of life. Because life is rooted in adaptational processes and adjustmental efforts under specific environments and conditions, the scientific- humanistic problem of human life involves reciprocal transactions between man and the natural and man-made aspects of his total milieu (Dobzhansky, 1962; Dubos, 1959).

The professional partnership of anthropology and medicine, therefore, must strive together toward a scientific-humanistic understanding of both the biocultural nature of man and his works and the biocultural processes underlying his organic and behavioral well-being. Application of this knowledge to the human needs and conditions of contemporary man must focus on improving and developing mankind's biological and cultural circumstances by giving anthropological as well as medical em-

phasis to optimizing physical, psychological, and social sufficiency in
health and meaningful living for all men.

COMMENTARY: Clifford R. Barnett
             Steven Polgar
             Arthur J. Rubel
             Edward Wellin

Clifford R. Barnett

One of the most common ways in which medical schools have included social sciences in their curricula has been to build a new school.
Another way has been to move the school from one city to another, as
Stanford did. Both are rather drastic methods taken to involve anthropologists and other social scientists in relationships with physicians.

I start with this point in order to emphasize the importance of the
setting in which Drs. Hochstrasser and Tapp work. They have been able
to work collaboratively because the medical power structure has said,
"Yes, we do want to work with anthropologists and other social scientists." I would suggest, on the basis of my own experience in two different
medical schools, that medical schools and physicians must make the
first move toward collaboration with anthropologists in medical settings.
Only after this first step is it the responsibility of the anthropologist to
make his appropriate contribution.

However, once the way to collaboration with medicine is open, there
must be enough trained anthropologists to take over the positions that
become available. The professionals who initially enter into the development of a cross-over area such as this one — an area on the frontier or
borderline of anthropology — do so because they recognize interesting
and challenging problems. They are not, however, trained in the cross-
over discipline, and usually must learn on the job. But it seems to me
that we have reached the time when such on-the-job training is unrealistic. Now, when a new Ph.D. in anthropology begins work in a medical

school, he is being asked to do three jobs all at once: (1) to learn about the medical subculture, including medical concepts, modes of professional interaction, the medical social structure, and the medical vocabulary; and to be familiar with problems he did not know existed before he became involved in the subculture; (2) to work with a patient population or community with which he is unfamiliar; and (3) to do some productive research and perform various services.

The anthropologist in a medical setting has a far better chance of being productive as an anthropologist and as a member of a teaching and research team if he first receives some training for the job. The Stanford Medical School now provides facilities for graduate social science students who wish to learn about the medical subculture early in their careers. This policy also permits medical students to work with anthropologists and sociologists during the early, formative stages of their careers.

The exchange in a cross-disciplinary area must work two ways. Ordinarily, the physician who works with a social scientist for the first time operates under the same handicaps as the social socientists working with a physician for the first time. Thus, the physician must look for the most appropriate social scientists with whom to collaborate, and must learn to communicate with him so that they can attack the problem jointly and productively. The Stanford Medical School has solved the problem of collaboration by providing training on an elective basis so that medical students can pursue an M.A. degree in anthropology, psychology, or sociology while they are working toward an M.D. degree. This training is possible only because the medical school curriculum is arranged so that students have considerable elective time in which to pursue work in the social sciences. Such training also may be incorporated directly into the medical school curriculum, as at the University of Kentucky. Thus, it can be seen that the "neighboring discipline" which controls its own institutional setting must make certain institutional changes before the anthropologist can work collaboratively.

Collaboration with medicine as a neighboring discipline, however, raises certain, as yet unsolved, methodological and theoretical problems. Anthropologists are oriented toward the study of populations and the uniformities exhibited by groups of people, while the physician's central focus is still, and I suspect will remain for a long time, the individual patient. Thus, for certain purposes, a physician may find it helpful to know what Navajos do generally, but usually he must know about the specific individual Navajo whom he has just treated. There is almost a direct conflict between the social and cultural factors in disease and the contribution an anthropologist or other social scientist can make on a specific case. When teaching, it is usually easier to illustrate than to demonstrate the relevance of social variables in approaching the individual patient. The physician himself must always choose from what is known of the occurrence of a disease in a population at risk, that information which may or may not apply to his individual patient. Therefore, in the course of working with physicians, anthropologists have to be aware in many cases of the specific, individual variations present in a given culture, rather than in a cultural pattern as a whole.

Thus, one long-range outcome of medical-anthropological collaboration may be a reemphasis within anthropology upon individual differences and variations within cultures and communities. Medicine will benefit from collaboration through an increased appreciation of the larger cultural and social context within which disease occurs and within which their patients live. The actual demonstration of pertinent relationships will come when the physician, with the anthropologist, begins to view the community and the culture as a unit for study and treatment.

In conclusion, it seems to me that both physicians and anthropologists have a lot of research to do before they can begin to translate whatever they know in social areas and apply it frequently to the individual case, since, even in social medicine, the physician is still treating the individual case.

Steven Polgar

The last ten years of my professional career have been spent in various medical settings and it is relevant to the comments which follow that I am suffering from "battle fatigue" at the moment. The abundance of ex-medical anthropologists and the scarcity of students wishing to enter this field, perhaps, confirm that my condition is not unique.

A major message of the paper by Drs. Hochstrasser and Tapp is that anthropologists should join forces with forward-looking medical colleagues in trying to reunite preventive and curative medicine. Some years ago Milton Roemer made a similar plea to social scientists and my reaction then was the same as now: anthropologists, as outsiders, would not make particularly powerful allies in the struggle within the ranks of organized medicine in the United States. If we were to become engaged in this movement to the extent our friends would like, we could succumb to battle fatigue even more rapidly than otherwise. There is no reason, on the other hand, not to evaluate the relative merits of integrated and separated systems of medical care, or analyze the cultural-historical background of current trends in medical philosophies and institutions. Such investigations could then be used by others in the political arena extending beyond medical organizations.

It is quite common in discussions of the relationships between anthropology and medicine to spend more time on role problems than on substantive issues. Drs. Hochstrasser and Tapp are to be congratulated for not repeating these familiar refrains. However, there are grounds for complaint, the persistence of which might help explain the scarcity of active medical anthropologists.

Drs. Hochstrasser and Tapp alluded to an article by Julius Roth (1962) on "management bias." This article is extremely significant in that it outlines a process whereby the anthropologist, or other social scientist, who joins a medical institution is often quickly and effectively "seduced" into placing medical priorities ahead of those of his own discipline. For an anthropologist to work fruitfully in a medical setting, it is necessary that he concur with the most significant values of his medical colleagues; however, it is also important that he constantly fight to maintain those priorities which made him an anthropologist. To concur with values, in my view, does not mean that one cannot have different priorities and roles. The situation at the University of Kentucky Medical Center could lend itself well to such a combination.

Until we can significantly further our discipline, programs in applied anthropology will have difficulty attracting first-rate students. This is partly because the graduate departments through which we have access to these students are run by traditional anthropologists who look down on applied anthropology. Applied anthropology has yet to prove its worth in traditional anthropological terms but, once it does, the traditionalists will have to stop relegating applied anthropology to second-class status.

We have not published enough studies that have helped to further anthropology as a "biocultural understanding of man and his works," as Drs. Hochstrasser and Tapp call it. I would like to ask Dr. Hochstrasser: "What have you done recently to further the understanding of man and his works as a biocultural unit?" I am not asking this question in a hostile manner, because it is the same question I am asking myself.

In a more positive vein, I would like to give some examples of new ideas that we can bring back to mainstream anthropology from our learning experiences in medical settings, ideas which will not only attract more students and perhaps enhance our reputation in the eyes of traditional anthropologists, but which, in the long run, also will increase our usefulness to the medical professions as scientific collaborators rather than as technicians.

Perhaps the best example is the study of disease ecology. The article by Frank Livingstone (1958) on the sickle cell trait in West Africa best renews my faith in the unity of anthropology. The outcome variable explained in this study was both medical and genetic — the uneven distrubution of sickling — and the independent variables were both ecological and cultural. Yet, the study can also be interpreted as showing interrelations between the independent factors, thereby advancing our understanding of ethnohistory and cultural ecology.

Other examples are studies of sleeping sickness, pastoralism, and agriculture — topics which have been examined recently (Duggan, 1962a, 1962b; Hocppli, 1964; Hoeve, 1967; Langride, Kernaghan, and Glover, 1963; K. D. Thompson, 1967). Further study of the complex relationships, which include human and cattle disease and succession of flora, fauna, and cultural types, would much advance our understanding of ethnology in the "matrilineal belt" of Africa.

Still another interesting question is that raised by Muriel Hammer and Joseph Zubin (1968) concerning schizophrenia: Might there be a balanced polymorphism operating, not only in terms of greater resistance to burns and other injuries, as Julian Huxley and others had suggested, but also in terms of a capacity for idiosyncratic-innovative behavior? Their reflections on schizophrenia lead to considerations of culture in terms of information theory, a novel approach to a basic problem.

I have given some thought to ways of looking at cultural contact and social evolution which benefit from epidemiological concepts. Like some other social anthropologists and archaeologists who no longer concentrate exclusively on the evolution of single cultural entities through time, I have become interested in the notion of "epicultural systems," or "social fields," as Alex Lesser terms them. Although people transmit parasites much faster than they exchange axes or religious ideas, the perspectives one gets on evolution by looking at exchange networks in these terms are akin to one another and also differ greatly from perspectives which start from monadic culture units, with their functional crystallizations and culture brokers vaulting over boundary-maintaining mechanisms.

The very fact that I have trouble explaining this last notion is perhaps symptomatic of the pathology in my present situation. I will have to postpone elaborating this framework to a day when I am free of constant requests to give fast help in endeavors which I value, but which bear on the mainstream of anthropological thought in only the remotest fashion.

Arthur J. Rubel

Several thoughts occur to me when considering Drs. Hochstrasser and Tapp's paper. First, people engaged in so-called medical anthropology seem to be going through a soul-searching period in order to discover how close they are to the mainstream of anthropology. A particular problem we in medical anthropology face is that, by working in clinical medical settings, we are working with individuals. But individuals have not been the traditional primary subject matter of anthropologists. Perhaps Drs. Hochstrasser and Tapp have helped to resolve this conflict by suggesting that anthropologists could work appropriately within the general framework of medical anthropology; that is, in social medicine and public health, where groups rather than individuals are the targets of attention.

Drs. Hochstrasser and Tapp also compared the handling of medical problems in the developing nations and in already developed industrialized nations, of which the best example is the United States. I would make two comments on this comparison. First, the two-factor model for approaching problems of illness uses the factors or variables of biology and culture, or of the individual and culture. This model reflects the fact that, in countries like the United States, chronic illness rather than acute and infectious illness is the major and increasingly important problem. However, we know that chronic illness has little to do with what I would submit as a third necessary variable: the physical environment. Therefore, presentation of a working model with only two interrelated, interdependent variables — biology and culture — probably is also a reflection of the far greater concern and interest demonstrated by anthropologists in so-called psychiatric illness than in physical illness.

The two-factor model is far more appropriate for a country like the United States than it is for developing nations such as Venezuela, Costa Rica, China, or India where it would be impossible to work on problems of illness without using a three-factor model with the interacting variables of biology, culture, and physical environment. In terms of this model, a contrast can be made between developing and developed nations. The difference of approach lies in whether it is essential to include two or three variables.

Second, in reading about the role of social science in the development of health programs and services in Latin America, I am struck by the fact that Latin American nations and, presumably, other underdeveloped nations, are struggling with problems in both social medicine and public health very similar to ours. We all are concerned about the gaps between development of medical knowledge and delivery of medical services to the population. Recently, a project in Vermont in which I was engaged sought to discover how to provide first-class medical services to local townships in rural areas where the number of general practitioners and internists is decreasing. Latin America is struggling with much the same problem — delivering the medical payload to all sectors of the population. There are some very creative schemes for developing sub-professional workers to assume responsibility where there are not enough professionals. There are also entire systems of transportation operated by health departments to deliver health services to rural areas. It seems that our country could learn much from some of the efforts by nations like Venezuela, Mexico, Haiti, and Brazil in providing health services for people who do not have easy access to urban-based physicians, hospitals, and public health facilities.

Edward Wellin

I would like to discuss two matters raised by Drs. Hochstrasser and Tapp. The first concerns the current, predominant trend in medical models which is explicitly given in their paper. The second matter, a disease model, while not discussed by the authors, certainly is implied.

Drs. Hochstrasser and Tapp seem to have the mistaken idea that the nature of the mainstream of medicine in American society is private, curative, and personal: that medical care is conveyed to individual patients by practitioners in the workshops of individual physicians. This outlook confuses the ideological position which still dominates the organized medical profession, primarily through A.M.A. channels, with the hard realities of medical and public health practiced in the United States. In actuality, the mainstream of American medicine has been concerned with the provision of medical care for individuals in the context of highly organized and multi-professional systems and settings, and with the hospital, which is becoming the center of gravity for medical care, as well as for important research. Physicians increasingly are becoming organization men and one can no longer speak of the traditional individual practitioner-patient relationship as a mainstream, although this relationship still is an open channel in American medicine. The very aspect used to distinguish the public health field is becoming the primary context for rendering medical care. Thus, some of the problems which are raised by Drs. Hochstrasser and Tapp tend to have less reality than the authors believe.

We now can turn our attention to the matter of the disease model. Anthropologists, as well as other social scientists, have brought about some important developments which have had significant consequences for medical practice, for practice in public health, and for research.

Scientific theories are useful only to the extent of their explanatory and predictive functions. In that sense, the theory of the specific causation of disease, which held a specific pathogen to be the full cause of a specific disease, was of enormous utility from the 1880's until the development of antibiotics. Now it is clear that the bacterial and viral pathogens were never in any simplistic way the causes of disease. Rather, we know that although pathogens triggered certain conditions, the "triggering" itself was caused by behavioral, physiologic, and genetic factors, both of short and long term. Since the acute and communicable diseases had not yet been brought under control, it was possible to conceive of germs as causes and still obtain very definite accomplishments in curative medicines. However, with increasing dominance of chronic diseases, the underlying cause of disease is more clearly conceived as involving genetic transmissions, in part, and long-term patterns of behavior, diet, and aspective responses. Thus, specific disease causation theory has become less useful.

I think the work of such men as Rene Dubos and Edward Suchman provides the raw material for new theories concerning the nature and causes of disease. These contributions have broad implications in areas of medicine and public health, as well as in social science where disease causation is seen as part of the intersection of cultural and non-cultural systems, and where research by the social and medical scientist, each working along independent and collaborative lines, is of great significance.

REFERENCES

Alland, A., Jr. 1966. Medical Anthropology and the Study of Biological and Cultural Adaptation. American Anthropologist 68(1):40–51.

Arensberg, C. M. 1961. The Community as Object and as Sample. American Anthropologist 63(2):241–64.

Badgley, R. F. 1963. Social Sciences and Public Health. Canadian Journal of Public Health 54(4):147–53.

Baehr, G. 1965. Medical Care — Old Goals and New Horizons. The 1965 Michael M. Davis Lecture. University of Chicago, Graduate School of Business, Center for Health Administration Studies.

Baldwin, R. D. 1963. Impediments to the Acquisition and Use of Medical Knowledge. Science 141:1237–38.

Batalla, G. B. 1966. Conservative Thought in Applied Anthropology: A Critique. Human Organization 25(2):89–92.

Caudill, W. 1953. Applied Anthropology in Medicine. First International Symposium on Anthropology (New York, 1952). Anthropology Today, ed. A. L. Kroeber, pp. 771–806. University of Chicago Press: Chicago.

Crew, F. A. E. 1956. Medicine as a Social Science. Journal of Medical Education 31:399–403.

Deuschle, K. W. et al. 1966. The Kentucky Experiment in Community Medicine. Milbank Memorial Fund Quarterly 44(1), Part 1:9–22.

Dixon, J. F. 1965. Teaching Physicians to be Agents of Social Change. Archives of Environmental Health 10(5):713–18.

Dobzhansky, T. 1962. Mankind Evolving: The Evolution of the Human Species. Yale University Press: New Haven.

Dubos, R. 1959. The Mirage of Health: Utopias, Progress and Biological Change. Harper and Row: New York.

Duggan, A. J. 1962a. The Occurence of Human Trypanosomiasis Among the Rukuba Tribe of Northern Nigeria. Journal of Tropical Medical Hygiene 65: 15–63.

————. 1962b. A Survey of Sleeping Sickness in Northern Nigeria from the Earliest Times to the Present Day. Transactions of the Royal Society of Tropical Medical Hygiene 56:439–86.

Foster, G. M. 1961. Public Health and Behavioral Science: The Problems of Teamwork. American Journal of Public Health 51(9):1286–93.

Frank, L. K. 1948. Society as the Patient: Essays on Culture and Personality. Rutgers University Press: New Brunswick.

Freeman, H. E., S. Levine, and L. G. Reeder, eds. 1963. Handbook of Medical Sociology. Prentice-Hall: Englewood Cliffs.

Gregg, A. 1956. The Future Health Officer's Responsibility: Past, Present and Future. American Journal of Public Health 46:1384–89.

Hammer, M. and J. Zubin. 1968. Evolution, Culture and Psychopathology. Journal of Genetic Psychology 78:151–64.

Hochstrasser, D. L., G. S. Nickerson, and K. W. Deuschle. 1966. Sociomedical Approaches to Community Health Programs. Milbank Memorial Fund Quarterly 44(3):345–59.

Hoeppli, R. 1964. Old Ideas Regarding Cause and Treatment of Sleeping Sickness Held in West Africa. Journal of Tropical Medical Hygiene 67:60–68.

Hoeve, K. von. 1967. The Epidemiology of Trypanosoma Rhodesiense Sleeping Sickness in Alego Location, Central Nyanza, Kenya. II. The Cyclical Transmission of Trypanosoma Rhodesiense Isolated from Cattle to a Man, a Cow and to Sheep. Transactions of the Royal Society of Tropical Medical Hygiene 61:684–87.

Kluckhohn, C. 1962 .Culture and Behavior: Collected Essays. Free Press: New York.

Langride, W. P., R. J. Kernaghan, and P. E. Glover. 1963. A Review of Recent Knowledge of the Ecology of the Main Vectors of Trypanosomiasis. Bulletin WHO 28:671–701.

Lindsay, R. B. 1959. Entropy, Consumption and Values in Physical Science. American Scientist 47(3):376–85.

Livingstone, F. B. 1958. Anthropological Implications of Sickle Cell Gene Distribution in West Africa. American Anthropologist (n.s.) 60:533–62.

McGavran, E. G. 1956. Scientific Diagnosis and Treatment of Community as Patient. Journal of the American Medical Association 162(8):723–27.

Paul, B. D., ed. 1955. Health, Culture and Community: Case Studies of Public Reactions to Health Programs. Russell Sage Foundation: New York.

Paul, B. D. 1956. Anthropology and Public Health. Some Uses of Anthropology: Theoretical and Applied, pp. 49–57. Anthropological Society of Washington: Washington, D.C.

———. 1963. Teaching Cultural Anthropology in Schools and Public Health. The Teaching of Anthropology, eds. D. G. Mandelbaum, G. W. Lasker, and E. M. Albert, pp. 503–12. American Anthropological Association, Memoir 94. Washington, D.C.

Peattie, L. R. 1958. Interventionism and Applied Science in Anthropology. Human Organization 17(1):4–8.

Polgar, S. 1962. Health and Human Behavior: Areas of Interest Common to the Social and Medical Sciences. Current Anthropology 3(2):159–205.

Quentin, A. F., T. Gladwin, and E. M. Bower. 1966. Mental Health, Social Competence and the war on Poverty. American Journal of Orthopsychiatry 36 (4):652–64.

Robertson, A. 1965. Recent Advances in Social Science and Public Health. Canadian Journal of Public Health 56:365–71.

Roemer, M. I. and R. H. Elling. 1963. Sociological Research on Medical Care. Journal of Health and Human Behavior 4:49–68.

Roney, J. G., Jr. 1959. Medical Anthropology: A Synthetic Discipline. New Physician 8(3):32–33.

———. 1963. Medical Anthropology. An Introduction. Journal of the National Medical Association 55(2):95–99.

Rosen, G. 1958. A History of Public Health. M. D. Publications, Inc.: New York.

Roth, J. A. 1962. Management Bias in the Study of Medical Treatment. Human Organization 21(1):47–50.

Scotch, N. A. 1963. Medical Anthropology. Biennial Review of Anthropology, ed. B. J. Siegel, pp. 30–68. Stanford University Press: Stanford.

Shepard, W. P. and J. G. Roney, Jr. 1964. The Teaching of Preventive Medicine in the United States. Milbank Memorial Fund Quarterly 42(4), Part 2:1–311.

Stewart, W. H. 1963. Community Medicine: An American Concept of Comprehensive Care. Public Health Reports 78(2):93–100.

Stieglitz, E. J. 1949. The Integration of Clinical and Social Medicine. Social Medicine, ed. I. Galdston, pp. 76–89. Commonwealth fund: New York.

Strauss, R. 1965. Behavioral Science in Medical Curriculum. Annals of the New York Academy of Sciences 128, Part 2.

Suchman, E. A. 1963. Sociology and the Field of Public Health. Russell Sage Foundation: New York.

Tapp, J. W. and K. W. Deuschle. 1964. Medical Care Teaching in the Community. Medical Care 2:214–17.

———. 1966. Teaching Community Medicine in the Hospital Without Walls. Journal of the Kentucky Medical Association 64(7):569–72, *passim*.

Thompson, K. D. 1967. Rural Health in Northern Nigeria: Some Recent Developments and Problems. Transactions of the Royal Society of Tropical Medical Hygiene 61:277–302.

Thompson, L. 1965. Is Applied Anthropology Helping to Develop a Science of Man? Human Organization 24(4):277–87.

Virchow, R. 1958. Disease, Life and Man: Selected Essays, ed. L. J. Rather. Stanford University Press: Stanford.

Wallace, A. F. C. 1961. Culture and Personality. Random House: New York.

Willard, W. R. 1965. New Objectives in Medical Education. Annals of the New York Academy of Sciences 128, Part 2:480–88.

Medicine and Psychiatry

The formal relationship between anthropology and medicine began one hundred years ago when the pathologist Rudolf Virchow helped found the first anthropological society in Berlin. Although ties between cultural anthropology, psychoanalysis, and psychiatry were developed by Sapir and Dollard in the late twenties and early thirties, a continuous history of the many-sided partnership between physician and anthropologist cannot yet be written. What we are witnessing and experiencing is still prologue.

These beginnings, however, are reason enough to ask what it is that anthropologists share with physicians and psychiatrists, and to bring into focus areas of significant mutual interest to explore assumptions and approaches to the systematic study of man and disease.[1]

The Problem of Disease in Man

When considering the nature of disease in man, the first expectation is that "the observation and classification of diseased patient . . . begins, scientifically, as well as medically, by realizing their individual distinctions as sick persons and not merely diseased tissues" (Feinstein, 1963a). Thus, the proper study of the ill human being assumes that each individual lives with both the symptoms and consequences of disease

1. For a general historical and critical review of social science research in the United States on social-psychological aspects of disease between the mid-fifties and mid-sixties, see G. Gordon, W. Anderson, H. P. Brehm, Sue Marquis, *Disease, the Individual and Society,* College and University Press, New Haven, Conn., 1968.

in its physical and mental, medical and social aspects. While attempting to alleviate disease, the ill become involved in a variety of specific or non-specific internal and external problem-solving processes (von Mering, 1962a). The following questions are appropriate in beginning to explore these processes of life under altered conditions.

1) Is man in disease and health behaving in ways that are relevant to his condition and appropriate to his cultural context?

2) Can "the disease be thwarted by changing or restoring the altered form [of life] or function"? (Ackerknecht, 1953).

3) Can "health be retrieved by 'driving out' the cause of the disease rather than the disease itself"? (Ackerknecht, 1953)

4) Is the health condition separable from other changes in the life of the community?

A half century ago, L. J. Henderson (1913) spoke eloquently on individual fitness, which can be defined as a reciprocal relationship between the organism and the natural materials and cultural realities of the environment. This concept, combined with man's animal origin, gives us the only fixed point of departure from which to describe and analyze the pattern and changes of man's responses to the universal categories of experience of sex and reproduction, hunger, disease, and work (Simpson, 1966; Dubos, 1965; Dobzhansky, 1967; Kluckhohn, 1962). The proper study of man must reconcile the universal study of the diseased organism with the unique study of the sick person in his environment.

Cause and Meaning, Context and Process

The historical perspective shared by anthropologists and physicians is essential in exploring relevant causes of disease and health in the functioning organism. This perspective includes a clear understanding of the slow historical accretion of verifiable knowledge about disease and man (Leake, 1965). The first diagnoses were based on human malevolence, magical powers, or dieties; *post hoc propter hoc* treatment preceded the observational, classificatory, and empirical ways of diagnosis and treatment. Subsequently, medical practice changed to the scientific, experimental, and measurement approaches. At present, societal (Burns, 1967), as well as medical, emphasis on achieving optimum health for every man is being grafted to all the previous developments.

A distinction should be made, however, between the search for causation of illness and the analysis of the meaning of illness in the life of the individual and his culture, although a contingent relationship exists between them. Since the "language" of pathology, like that of culture, has many dialects, the local, social, and institutional context (Spence, 1955) of the disease and its diagnosis and treatment must be examined. Hence, the anthropologist seeks operational distinctions between the so-called patient-care process, or sequence of healing, and the anticipated results of this process.

A systematic study of the significance between the nature of a disease episode to its setting, the care process, and the outcome may well begin with an examination of the various meanings of health *needs* from a cultural or medical viewpoint. This study must then assess the desired health *wants* of the individual as well as consider how to achieve a "cultural balance" between objective needs and possible wants. An absolute yardstick for determining when a health aberration requires therapeutic intervention cannot be obtained in this way. Much, however, can be learned about the actual context and process of patient care and its relation to the course of a particular sickness.

To use these findings, culturally relevant specifications and statements of common treatment objectives are needed, particularly on the meanings of "prevention of death," "reduction of disability," and "impairment of function." Adequate definitions of relief or cure of suffering, discomfort, and dissatisfaction also are required.

For most research purposes, the end result may be defined as change — change from the altered human condition designated as disease, ailment, or malaise. Such a preliminary definition would encompass both organic or tissue change, as well as restoration of individual well-being and reestablishment of expected behaviors. The utility of these definitions depends on whether we can relate a given disease condition to selected aspects of relevant patient-care processes and their outcome.

Organic Disease, Mental Illness, and Treatment

The contemporary Western ways of dealing with physical and mental illness illustrate the complex interplay between meaning, cause, treatment, and outcome of the disease.

In usual medical practice, the patient only has to acknowledge and describe his particular physical problem to his physician. It is a hallowed expectation that the scientific procedures the physician will use can heal bones, limbs, glands, and vital tissue with no more than tacit cooperation from the patient (von Mering, 1962b).

Mental illness, on the other hand, requires a different approach in diagnosis and treatment. Both the patient and society must acknowledge the patient's thinking, feeling and behavior as "sick" before effective treatment can be undertaken. The expectation of therapeutic effect from a clinical relationship of talk, reflection, and listening is also a major departure from traditional scientific medical procedure for diseases of the body (von Mering, 1962b).

The clash between these two orientations to disease and treatment underlies all contemporary experiments in comprehensive medicine. This often is echoed in the patient's belief that drugs, tests, and instruments are "good medicine" and that thorough history-taking and physical examination are old-fashioned or prescientific. In this age of promoting optimum health for Everyman, these views often are paired with the expectation that life can be lived without the presence of pain, anxiety, episodes of illness, or chronic disease (von Mering and Earley, 1969).

Tribal and Folk Practices

In preliterate tribal societies and folk cultures, such value conflicts do not occur except with rapid cultural change or modernization. Characteristically, understanding and treating illness focus on those disequilibrating moments of the diseased person which have cultural or environmental significance. The therapeutic effort rather than the disease-specific conception of cure tends to be institutionalized. This also may explain why most anthropological reports on "primitive theories" of disease have consisted of statements about social structural-functional interpretations of disease. Such statements represent the result of an examination into the meaning of illness to the individual and his tribe in light of certain identifiable functional implications of cultural health practices. Any therapeutic "success" attributed to a folk practitioner does not have to "depend upon real etiological knowledge of causal treatment" (Ackerknecht, 1959). Folk medical practice often has achieved a favorable outcome by "combining" natural restorative powers of the organism with an induced belief in recovery, "the same condition of 'expectant faith' which answers a similar purpose" (Freud, 1959) in the psychological treatment of mental illness today.

Restated, in tribal society, emphasis is placed on the process of therapy which is a standardized procedure, and often complex ritual, directly involving community, family, *and* the individual patient in the "cure." The validity of the treatment — its *presumed* "specificity" to the disease — is measured by how accurately it reflects and reaffirms the traditions, beliefs, and customs of the tribe, and how well it "exorcises" (Evans-Pritchard, 1937) the current imbalance between man and the unknowable. It matters a great deal how certain culturally recognized and consensually validated classes or categories of ill-being are treated. The efficacy of treatment rests in other-wordly hands; it is not establishable through backtracking on the nature of treatment. To calculate probable outcomes in relation to given, independently measurable processes of disease is inconceivable.

The examination of significant normative belief systems underlying folk medical practice would be one-sided if we neglected to take note of the persistence of equivalent assumptions and treatment in contemporary psychiatric practice (von Mering, 1961a, 1965). This phenomenon is readily observable in the institutional care of all those who suffer from seemingly intractable conditions (von Mering, 1958; von Mering and King, 1957). Careful observation of psychiatric facilities reveals that we are in fact dealing with culturally sanctioned and medically condoned "therapies" which are situationally and nosologically predetermined rather than appropriate to the known or putative underlying disease processes. As in the case of tribal or "primitive" medicine, the care-taking effort is legitimated as a perennial ritual of categorical treatments; the "cure" of the individual patient is a secondary concern.

Contemporary Western Medical Practice

In contemporary Western society, the individual and his community seem less concerned with the process of medical treatment than with the result. The therapist generally pays more attention to specific factors in the course of the disease and less attention to the nonspecific factors in its healing. For example, he is inclined to administer fever-reducing drugs to a virus-infected patient rather than to allow that patient to build up antibody titers by "sweating it out." Restated in more clinical terms, the nonspecific factors of temperature, acidity, and inflammatory reaction controlling the primary infection receive proportionately less attention in treatment. A comparable medical quandary arises when a heart condition may be alleviated by surgery or drugs, although the associated or underlying conditions of stress and anxiety cannot be corrected by such means.

Accordingly, the anthropological study of disease and treatment tries to account for elements of belief contained in the outcome. The anthropologist recognizes that, while many theories about causes of disease and ways of healing are possible (von Mering, 1961b), none are compelling apart from their cultural context. He judges the role that "faith" plays in the treatment of a particular illness tempered by the understanding that if man should ascribe a health crisis to the loss of one faith, man also believes that it may be soluble through the use of another.

The Study of Mental Disease

The meaning of sickness as it relates to diagnosis, treatment, and outcome has been a particular problem in the anthropological study of mental diseases. The difficulties stem from several sources. First, many anthropologists doing culture and personality studies have not considered physical and emotional disorders or abnormality essentially as a problem of life under altered conditions (Virchow, 1958; Engel, 1960). They seldom have considered disease in man as an "ailing-healing unit" (von Mering, 1962a) involving both internal and external problem-solving. Although anthropologists would vigorously deny being influenced by the ancient mind-body dichotomy, they, nevertheless, have studied mental illness as if it were a distinct disease entity, best explained in terms of the moral-magical order of tribal existence.

If anthropological literature on mental phenomena in different cultures has been rich in descriptive detail, all too often the relevance of co-existing or underlying physical diseases to psychological processes has been left unexplored. Thus, important research questions do not adequately reflect that emotional aberration and bodily changes are *both* part of man's reactions to his total environment.

A recent statement by Manfred Bleuler (1963) on schizophrenia in Africa may serve to illustrate an appropriate cultural, organic, and psychological formulation of the course of the disease:

Psychoses of schizophrenic symptomatology developing in close temporal and thematic correlation with trauma of all kinds, and from which the patients recover entirely, are much more frequent in Africa than in Europe. The trauma is sometimes a somatic disease, but even more frequently a psychological catastrophe by which the whole family is affected. These psychoses are always connected with magic fears and magic defense reactions against these fears. The course is often favorable, despite the lack of modern therapy. The patients recover without traces of the psychosis. Frequently, however, such a psychosis ends with death. The outcome as a chronic schizophrenic psychosis is seen sometimes, but is not the rule.

Quite apart from their seeming reticence to use this investigative approach, anthropologists also have been unclear in conceptualizing causal and meaningful relationships between personal character, emotional disorder, and cultural milieu. Thus, following the lead of many "early" psychiatric researchers, they have incautiously used psychopathological or psychodynamic labels to delineate significant social processes, or to "describe what are characteristically normal behavior patterns for certain societies" (Kiev, 1965).[2]

The "Shape of Madness" in Man

At this point, we may ask why anthropologists have been studying physical and mental diseases. In striving for the deepest level of understanding of man's many "experiments in living" (MacBeath, 1952), the anthropologist has gone beyond traditional historical reconstruction and structural-functional interpretations of man's works and thoughts to explore the "shape of madness" in man. In so doing, he has moved steadily closer to analyzing this phenomenon as a form of life under altered conditions.

Using the thesis that the "mad" individual openly practices what is concealed in the healthy, the anthropologist has been inquiring into the

2. For a recent controversial statement equating mental illness with social deviance, see the work of the psychoanalyst Thomas S. Szasz, especially *The Myth of Mental Illness,* Hoeber-Harper, New York, 1961.

range of normal and abnormal behaviors, feelings, and thoughts in different cultures. He has been less concerned with strictly medical questions of "what pathogenic force destroys the healthy and creates" the mentally sick person, and more interested in "what changes the limits between two forms of life" (Bleuler, 1963).

In anthropology, as compared to psychiatry, the concept of psychosis as an endogenous process without manifest somatic, psychological, and cultural background has had little currency. With his trained senses, the anthropologist has focused on the study of everyday intimacy and familiarity with madness in the family, kin, clan, neighborhood, and society. This is the milieu which nurtures mental aberrations, gives it shelter and care, and also serves as one of its expressions. Thus, he has been exploring and defining the typical personifications of madness in terms of its unfolding, its spread, its diagnosis, confinement, and treatment in the context of different cultures.

To permit dialogue between cause and meaning, the anthropologist often pursues the study of the unusual or "sick" in man as the usual or ordinary. The use of the principle of disease as an altered human condition has permitted the examination of certain mental disturbances as a legitimate, albeit painful, way of life for a few individuals in some cultures: for example, the Siberian (Bogoras, 1904–1909), Okinawan (Lebra, 1964), or Nubian shaman (Nadel, 1946). Furthermore, certain mental phenomena, such as hallucinations (Wallace, 1959), are not necessarily personally disturbing or denotative of illness. To the contrary, such phenomena may have great social interest for the folk practitioner and the community within the framework of specific, dominant cultural values. Hence, if we scrutinize the value which illness may have in an individual's life task and way of life, we can obtain more exact knowledge about the natural history and particular contextual conditions of a disease.

If the anthropologist only tried to explain disease by specific causes such as physiological change, gene mutation, or trauma, he could not ask why a given culture expends collective effort to suppress or expand individual sensitivity and familiarity with the phenomenon of mental illness. Unlike preliterate or non-Western societies, Western civilization during the past several centuries has tended to "conceal the interrelationship between exterior trauma and schizophrenic psychosis" (Bleuler, 1963). The anthropologist's views about mental aberrations, unlike those of the psychiatrist, have developed primarily from his extensive experience with tribal life where only the combined utterances and behavior of "reason" and of "unreason" can reveal fundamental truths about human adaptation.

In working with primitive peoples, the anthropologist has been more than a patient and careful observer. "Knowing that what we observe is not nature but nature exposed to our method of questioning" (Heisenberg, 1958), the anthropologist has encouraged every informant to use his own interpretation rather than report facts alone. He has practiced listening for the sound of deeds and the silence of thoughts dipped in the mold of private hopes, fears, and sloths; and, in so doing he has acquired a special sense about man's social history and individual development.

Long experience with man's ways of creating direction and signification through words and nonverbal means assists the anthropologist in understanding the relationship between personality and culture. It has opened his mind to study minute departures from regular bodily functioning and personal activity to obtain evidence on the processes generating both extraordinary and everyday behavior (von Mering, in press). Also, it has taught him how to ask questions about the extent to which a given altered condition of life approaches cultural or medical conceptions of "genuine" or "real" disease (von Mering and Earley, 1965, 1966).[3]

In the past, some psychiatrists and analysts have dismissed anthropolgical studies of so-called culture-bound syndromes like "amok," "latah" (Van Loon, 1926; Yap, 1952), "windigo" (Hallowell, 1938), "pibloktoq" (Gussow, 1960), or "susto" (Rubel, 1964) as reports on quaint "variants of basic psychopathological states" (Kiev, 1965). The issue of the clinical significance of culture and values in determining pathoplastic features of mental illness, such as delusions, is, however, a long way from being resolved.

Few contemporary psychiatrists will deny the importance of the relationship between cultural factors and the patterning and "character of psychic stresses (and conflicts) in different human societies quite addi-

---

3. The scientific importance of analyzing small, everyday breaks in normal functioning, as exemplified by epileptiform seizures, was first stressed by Hughlings Jackson, an eminent nineteenth-century English neurologist. Freud subsequently demonstrated the wisdom of this approach in his studies of slips of mind, tongue, and hand.

tional to situational and organic factors" (Hallowell, 1936). Also, no disagreement exists between anthropologist and psychiatrist about the continuing lack of precise answers from the many attempts to specify sociocultural factors which exist as initiating, perpetuating, or causative (i.e., etiological) agents of named disorders (Leighton and Hughes, 1959; Leighton et al., 1963; Murphy and Leighton, 1965).

Further, no one in psychiatry seriously questions the "contribution of culture . . . to the forms and context of primitive therapies" (Kiev, 1965, 1966). Field studies have shown the relative worth of alternative therapeutic goals, such as symptomatic relief or improved functioning in particular contexts. As yet, neither the anthropologist nor the psychiatrist has found the answer to why no single psychiatric treatment model appears to fulfill the needs of every society. This knowledge can be attained only by systematic, comparative studies of clinically specifiable and culturally definable complexes of altered conditions of life. In other words, this approach recognizes the basic medical procedure where the initial impression of the "apparent diseased state" has to be translated into a reasonable approximation of the "true clinical condition" of the patient. This judgment is reached only after a prolonged and often elaborate process of ruling out possible causal and contributing factors which may constitute a health hazard to both the individual and his environment.

The Contextual Study of Illness

The anthropologist neither begins nor ends by describing or explaining mental illness in terms of heredity, symptoms and traumata, or in terms of episodic flareups and chains of reaction, inner conflict and defense, or outer stress and strain. Despite many promising research leads, knowledge about the etiological significance of these and related factors in mental illness is still embrassingly inconclusive (Jackson, 1960; Sanua, 1961; Handel, 1965; Rabkin, 1965).[4] Just as Freud achieved a "return to madness at the level of its language . . . " that is, "restored, in medical

4. For a comprehensive statement of the *nature* of the genotype-environment interaction as the central issue in the understanding of schizophrenia, and also a review of recent findings, see D. Rosenthal and S. S. Kety, eds., *The Transmission of Schizophrenia*, Pergamon, New York, 1968.

thought, the possibility of a dialogue with unreason" (Foucault, 1965),[5] the anthropologist must say something meaningful about man's general condition while studying individual instances of his "fall from reason."

Like the practicing psychiatrist, the anthropologist does not deny reality to the continuous tie between man and madness. He is also not given to reduce all that can be said about man and madness to people who are "mentally diseased" and need care. He cannot allow himself to succumb to the unconscious, but culturally sanctioned, need to repress the irrational, deranged, or impulsive element in all forms of human existence.

A great many of us still underestimate the dangers to research created by the current fashion of transvaluing mental illness into a purely psychological or social problem, and of treating it exclusively in terms of various related nosologies. Neither psychological nor social factors completely explain all forms of mental illness. While one could be persuaded that neurotic patients do not suffer from a disease, this is less possible with schizophrenic patients (Brill, 1966) whose "spontaneous" symptoms approximate those provoked by many known pharmacological substances. Although similar agents have been found in the schizophrenic, we cannot as yet label them the cause of this condition. However, the burden of proof is on those who fail to see any possible relationship.

A brief digression into the history of tarantism, the "dancing mania" of Apulia during the Middle Ages, will demonstrate the problem which values can play in the conduct of research. During the hot Italian summer, the old and young of both sexes manifested "symptoms" of wild dancing, singing, talking to the sound of music in the streets, loss of inhibition, and excessive drinking. Not uncoincidentally, Apulia is located in the same geographic area where the ancient Greeks practiced the Dionysian rites which were vigorously suppressed as sinful with the spread of Christianity. Yet, the rites continued to be performed in secret, "until one day — we do not knew when — the meaning of the dances changed. The old rites appeared as symptoms of a disease. The music, dance, all that wild orgiastic behavior were legitimized. The people who indulged in these

---

5. In the psychoanalytic doctor-patient relationship, reality may be "re-viewed" as if it were a myth, and myth may be "relived" as if it were reality. As such, the relationship is something outside ordinary human awareness and experience, and hence beyond normative social expectations and reciprocities.

exercises were no longer sinners, but the poor victims of the tarantula" (Sigerist, 1962).

This transformation of a particular form of "madness" into a symptom cluster presumably indicative of a physical disease is analogous to contemporary ways of conceptualizing mental illness wholly as a social issue and of reducing the meaning of appropriate treatment to social problem-solving techniques. From the tale of tarantism, we should be cautioned not to build similar assumptions into our investigative work.

A common legal-medical dilemma in contemporary psychiatric treatment (Ross, 1959; Goffman, 1959) is a telling example of the unanticipated consequences of values in action. The psychiatrist, who is expected to be both clinician to the patient and conservator of health for society, must not only make the medical judgment of when to suspend or terminate care and return the hospitalized patient to the community but, by virtue of his dual function, must also "certify" a person's chances to remain sane.[6] Hence, contingencies of age, sex, financial status, previous confinement, and length of stay in treatment settings are critical outcome predictors. In actual practice, they may influence decisions about the discharge of patients as much as the clinical judgment about the degree of improvement in mental function.

Judging by the current proliferation of "Nurturant Society" programs to promote "adequate personalities" (Whithington, 1966), the trend toward progressive conversion of mental illness into a social problem will continue unabated for some time to come. This conversion is likely to further diminish the already limited public understanding of the clinical reality of pathological processes, and also may seriously dislocate existing patterns of everyday familiarity with sickness. Some of the critical issues involved have already been voiced by the noted British social economist R. M. Titmuss (1965):

Is community care being pushed too fast — especially by hospital staffs? Are hospital discharge rates being seen as indices of efficiency and productivity, while the family — like the community care — is being romanticized and sometimes penalized? . . . At present we are drifting into a situation in

6. In this connection, such powers over social life and death of the sick individual historically have not been conferred upon the tribal shaman, medicine man, or folk practitioner, but upon the sorcerer. Consequently, the indigenous healer was no generally placed in an ethical dilemma comparable to that of the contemporary psychiatrist.

which by shifting the emphasis from the institution to the community, we are transferring the care of the mentally ill from trained staff to an untrained or an ill-equipped staff, or no staff at all.

Experts in forensic psychiatry have begun to consider the related problem of justly determining the limits of community, personal, and professional responsibility and liability in a growing number of individual cases of mental illness (Herbert Thomas, personal communication, 1968). The extent of this added burden on the physician who must wisely discharge this dual responsibility to patient and society may well be incalculable.[7]

For the anthropologist who seeks to illuminate the particulars of the problems of abnormality within the context of culture, the significance of these "case studies" of values in action is clear: the more socially useful a concept, the less apt it is to produce scientific data. Clearly, neither historical nor contemporary social efforts to redefine or improve the human condition can replace the etiological treatment of specific health problems (Lewis, 1967).

Meaning and Cause, Disease Pattern and Change

This discussion has stressed the need for a well-articulated frame of reference to study meaning and cause in the *interplay* between (1) the disease condition, which is the clinical problem and the complaint; (2) its context in terms of the relevant circumstances, plights, and crises; (3) the differential diagnosis, or what is known about the etiology, pathogenesis, and symptomatology; (4) the therapy or prophylaxis; and (5) the outcome. Such a conceptual framework has singular importance for observation, analysis, and interpretation, regardless of the particular anthropo-medical research focus in a given field situation or world area.

---

7. Just how adversely health delivery patterns can be affected by inappropriately applying the mental health umbrella or the disease-medical care model to every conceivable form of social and emotional distress is discussed in William Ryan, ed., *Distress in the City, Essays on the Design and Administration of Urban Mental Health Services,* Case Western Reserve University, Cleveland, Ohio, 1969.

For a revealing discussion of contemporary socio-legal realities affecting the hospitalization and discharge of mental patients in the United States and Britain, see R. S. Rock, *Hospitalization and Discharge of the Mentally Ill,* University of Chicago Press, Chicago, 1968. See also F. E. Kenyon, *Psychiatric Emergencies and the Law,* John Wright and Sons, Ltd., Bristol, England, 1968.

Hence, if Tanzania were chosen as the area for studying a given question about disease and man, a formulation of the problems must consider the history of prevailing disease patterns in this "developing," largely pre-industrial or tribal society. In contrast, the analyses of given health problems in a highly developed sociopolitical entity such as England must be formulated in terms of changes in disease patterns characteristic of more technologically advanced countries.

Change in the pattern of disease occurs universally and incessantly. Although it is a fairly slow and not necessarily cumulative process, it is "ultimately related to . . . changes in society — technical, economic, and social. The pattern of disease and the vital statistics — birth rate, death rate, and longevity — are interdependent" (Björck, 1965). This is seen through comparative studies of disease patterns from developing, pre-industrial or tribal societies to more developed and more technologically advanced countries.

What is known about an ailment generally depends on the kind of recognition it receives, since both health and disease are words with many different connotations and behavioral consequences. Hence, the question, What is the pattern of disease? is a constant challenge to the anthropologist investigating man's relation to particular diseases.

Although the history and the geography of disease are time-honored sciences, our concern as anthropologists with this field relates to the general study of man and disease. The anthropologist's traditional lag in interest may be explained, in part, by the fact that "by 1940 the very concept of a geography of diseases had been virtually erased from the memory of the practicing physician. [Moreover], . . . in the last decades the history of diseases was no less neglected than their geography" (Acker-knecht, 1965).

Both the volume and quality of research in medical ecology has increased greatly since World War II, although it is still largely concerned with the descriptive mapping of "who" has "what" and "where" in different parts of the world (Stamp, 1964). Many world atlases as well as continental, national, and regional maps of specific, named diseases, are now available. These charted diseases range from acute and chronic communicable diseases and endemic tropical parasistic diseases to deficiency diseases and food poisoning. Maps also deal with oral disease (Kreshover and McClure, 1966), diseases of the endocrine glands, such as goiter and diabetes, and numerous distributional studies of diseases of uncertain or unknown origin, such as cancer, rheumatic diseases, mental disease, allergy, and multiple sclerosis (Kurtzke, 1966). Many of these cartographic studies of disease have not relied on age-specific measures for the deceased population, and most have employed mortality rather than morbidity statistics. The interpretations of mortality from a particular disease condition have been variously related to such ecological factors as climatic zones, high and low altitudes and temperature, nutrition, water and soil conditions, as well as to population genetics, and, occasionally, to available human and technological medical resources.[8]

All this laboriously collected material constitutes a rich lode of information showing that histories of diseases are intimately connected with their distribution and ecology. It also invites the question of why significant variations in disease exist within certain mapped regions. The answers still await local and detailed anthropological research into actual conditions. Many theoretical and methodological problems must be solved before the readily available biostatistical facts can be related directly to a particular context of human adaptation and reaction to disease.

For instance, the anthropologist must acquire new cross-cultural information on the prevalance (and incidence) of "symptoms" of altered life to see whether these manifestations are culturally recognized threats to health and well-being. Scattered evidence has documented man's differential responses to a variety of common and less common physical malfunctions. For example, among some modern Greek peasants, trachoma is endemic and not regarded as indicative of a serious disorder (Blum and Blum, 1965). Many Spanish Americans do not consider persistent diarrhea, sweating, and coughing unusual enough to cause concern about their health (Clark, 1958). Some South American tribes view pinto (dichromic spirochetosis), a widespread skin condition, as

8. For a more detailed coverage of theoretical issues and special problems in the ecological study of disease, see the following: J. M. May, ed., *Studies in Disease Ecology*, Hafner, New York, 1961. ———. *The Ecology of Malnutrition in Middle Africa*, Hafner, New York, 1965. R. M. Prothero, *Migrants and Malaria*, Longmans Green, London, 1965. E. S. Roger and H. B. Messinger, "Human Ecology: Toward a Holistic Method," *Milbank Memorial Fund Quarterly*, Vol. 45, No. 1, 1967, pp. 25–42. R. F. Gray, "Medical Research," in *The African World*, edited by R. A. Lystad, Praeger, New York, 1965, pp. 352–70. J. Cravioto, E. R. Delicarde, and H. G. Birch, "Nutrition, Growth and Neurointegrative Development: An Experimental and Ecologic Study," *Pediatrics*, 1966, 38:319–72.

normal, and the Thonga of Africa think that intestinal worms are necessary for digestion (Ackerknecht, 1947). Peptic ulcer morbidity has been under-reported for certain African tribal groups (Raper, 1958), and neither pregnancy-associated nausea nor dysmenorrhea are matters of special health concern among the Arapesh in New Guinea (Mead, 1950).

Changes in disease pattern cannot be assessed without more particulate knowledge about man's capacity to live with disease as if it were a natural hazard of living or an outward sign of normality. Such knowledge would be essential when trying to relate change in morbidity and mortality due to selected chronic, prodromal, and endemic disorders to man's basic life-cycle activities, especially to his food production and distribution patterns or to his food preferences and eating habits.

Disease Pattern and Human Response

Surprisingly few anthropologists realize how much their recent research in health and disease has been predetermined by known differences in disease patterns. In developing countries, anthropologists have focused on folk illness, tribal healing ways, epidemiology, and mission-oriented public health practices. In developed areas they have emphasized the study of medicine as an institution, doctor-patient relationships, and institutionalized patterns of care.

The physician-researcher will always study the ecology and etiology of specific or named diseases. The anthropologist, however, will concentrate on specific and nonspecific manifestations of disease in light of local conditions and indigenous human responses. His special perspective from this multi-objective approach must not falter before the potent blandishments of current research fashion. A brief examination of the medical and human conditions prevailing in specific geographical areas will sharpen our understanding.

Athough most human effort in the developing countries is still directed toward securing food and shelter, the ruling elite of most new nations is intent on overhauling the traditional socio-economic order with inordinate haste. This elite, imbued with a simplistic faith in rapid, linear human progress, regard their respective countries as "only temporarily backward" (Lévi-Strauss, 1966) and have little or no concern for whether their countries are unique in their adaptation to health and disease.[9]

The clash between resistance to change and forces for "modernization" is shaping the present and future patterns of disease and medical care.

Despite many variable factors . . . rarely is a single condition present alone. The salient feature is the superimposition of a particular disease on a malnourished, anemic and parasite-burdened individual. The underlying problems will weaken the person, undermine his resistance, create a far more serious medical problem of management, and most likely increase the complications and militate against survival. [Although] . . . under-nutrition and malnutrition constitute perhaps the most serious . . . [problem], the natural balance of selection which at present functions in many countries is gradually being interfered with by developing preventive medicine and curative services (Brown 1966).[10]

This illustration again shows that culture and nature are the soil of disease. While disease can be defined by a particular organic condition and disability by the culture wherein it occurs, the combination of *both* determine the pattern of disease. Altered bodily conditions and emotional aberration, the "multiple disease syndrome" (Hinkle, 1961) involving more than one organ and system, as well as disturbances of mood, thought, and behavior, are not rare, only different in developing countries.

9. For a comprehensive statement of the significance of the interlocking magnification of sickness, poverty, and ignorance in economic development planning, see C. E. Taylor and M. F. Hall, "Health, Population, and Economic Development," *Science*, 1967, 157:651–57.

10. The degenerative diseases associated with the aging process do not constitute a health problem. However, certain common and largely preventable childhood diseases loom large in a population of which nearly 25 percent are under five and close to 50 percent under fifteen years of age.

"Leading the list invariably are malnutrition, diarrhea and respiratory illnesses, often interrelated. The pediatric list continues with malaria, tuberculosis, intestinal parasites (especially hookworm and roundworm infections), and the so-called childhood infectious diseases (particularly measles and whooping cough), followed by accidents such as kerosene poisoning and burns.

Among adults are found various types of anemia and deficiency diseases, tuberculosis and leprosy, such parasitic diseases as malaria, schistosomiasis, filariasis and others caused by locally prevalent parasites, trachoma, venereal diseases, mental illnesses, dysentery and cholera. Also present are all the other medical conditions which are found throughout the rest of the world. There are, of course, a number of unusual diseases peculiar to one region or another, but these usually do not constitute significant problems (Brown, 1966)."

We are immediately struck by the significantly changing pattern of disease when we look at the technologically advanced nations. By medically extending the normal life span by twenty-two years since the early 1900's, "we have, in effect, traded mortality for morbidity" (Gregg, 1952), and disability for medicated survival. The substantial rise in the United States of the average life expectancy from 47.9 years in 1900 to 68.2 years in 1950 has slowed markedly since then. Americans who today can expect to live slightly more than 70.2 years, also can expect to spend two years disabled in bed, and women can expect to outlive the average man by almost nine years (Boggs et. al., 1962; U.S. National Health Survey, 1960, 1962, 1966, 1968; Sanders, 1964). This progressive transformation of a natural to a man-made environment has ushered in an era of unanticipated threats to health and to social well-being.

In essence, we only "sicken and die differently than in the past" (Cooper, 1969). The growing list of essentially unpreventable, long-term diseases with multiple clinical manifestations of unknown etiology has become a primary medical concern (Weinerman, 1965). Most critical are the "diseases of regulation" (Page, 1965), with their extended presymptomatic or "lanthanic" development (Feinstein, 1963b), and the long-life expectancy "degenerative diseases" such as hypertension, atherosclerosis and other cardiac and circulatory disorders, cerebral vascular accidents, neuro-musculo-skeletal problems, and neoplastic diseases.

Of equal importance, a major part of daily health care is expended on middle-aged patients who suffer from "undifferentiated health aberrations" in addition to accumulated diagnosable and treatable illnesses (von Mering and Earley, 1966, 1969). These conditions include sub-acute, diffuse somatic, and psychic dysfunctions. Although these ailments are essentially nonfatal, they may be incapacitating or chronic (Earley and von Mering, 1969). Medicine has yet to arrive at a definitive diagnosis of these forms of disease, or to discover an effective, systematic treatment. Expected improvement, with or without treatment, appears to be negligible (von Mering and Earley, 1965). Instead, "retirement from life into active ill health," or a career as an intermittent patient, may become a fixed pattern of adaptation for some patients (von Mering, in press; von Mering and Schiff, 1968).

In addition to health problems, the perils to social well-bring involve such problems as ways to control biosomatically (Barnes, 1965) the social "pathologies" stemming from the sexual appetite and reproductive capacity of man. No one can calculate the possible side-effects on the fabric of society. Furthermore, despite the medical conquest of certain diseases like syphilis and gonorrhea, advanced countries are again experiencing a marked resurgence of these most human afflictions (Feldman, 1965).

Perhaps it is too early to worry about whether the human race will breed increasingly physically unsound progeny (Dubos, 1959). More immediately useful benefits will accrue to mankind from the discovery of new ways of postponing premature social invalidism, psychological maladaptation, and decay during the lengthening middle years of life. A greater balance between scientific energy expended on medically prolonging life and that directed at retarding degenerative processes is needed. Also, scientific interest in the life-long effects of acute disease and nutrition and sanitation on infants and young children must be matched by a concern with those kinds of human environments which evoke creative behavioral responses from the individual throughout his life cycle (Dubos, 1968).

The constantly changing variety of human response to disease and environment cannot be explained on the basis of simple mechanistic or historical-casual systems alone. Instead, anthropo-medical studies of life under altered conditions are moving toward new formulations of the processes of multivariable interaction between man, disease, and environment (von Bertalanffy, 1968). As yet, we do not have sufficient wisdom to make a sound appraisal of the right amount of concern with the different ages of man and the related ways of responding to the total environment. Such insight, however, is the best possible stimulus for more anthropological studies of the multivariable relationship between the phenomena of disease in man and of the many mansions of culture.[11]

11. A most promising focus for such studies would seem to lie in the relationship between nutrition, infection, cultural environment, and mentation. See H. F. Eichenwald and P. C. Fry, "Nutrition and Learning," Science, 1969, 163: 644–48. A growing focus of anthropological interest is the interrelationship between cultural factors, human fertility, and population control in industrial and nonindustrial societies. See the following: J. B. Birdsell, "Some Predictions for the Pleistocene Based on Equilibrium Systems Among Recent Hunter-gathers," in Man the Hunter, edited by R. B. Lee and I. De Vore, Aldine, Chicago, 1968, pp. 229–40. M. Nag, Factors Affecting Human Fertility in Non-industrial Societies: A Cross-cultural Study, Yale University Publication in Anthropology No. 66, New

Concluding Reflections

The medical spectre of an infinite number of aging people, cerebrally incompetent and socially obsolescent, despite corporeal survival through antibiotics and organ replacements, may seem unreal to many of us today. We also may be reluctant to envisage a relentlessly onrushing technological society which dooms ordinary man to obsolescence before he is born and leaves him a "genuine fossil" at the end of his days (Eiseley, 1965). Yet, such ultimate consequences of man-made environment already have been projected in scientific circles.

Whatever their intrinsic merit, they can only sharpen our perception of the basic continuities and differences in anthropo-medical research in various regions of the world. No matter how much a society may refuse to recognize the biological function of death, or how much an individual may crave "indefinite life, perhaps in the end with somebody else's heart or liver, somebody's arteries, but not with somebody else's brain" (Pickering, 1967), man's goal of freedom from illness is only a utopian dream. As Sir William Osler (1951) noted: "A shrewd old fellow remarked to me the other day, 'Yes, many diseases are less frequent, others have disappeared, but new ones are always cropping up, and I notice that with it all there is not only no decrease, but a very great increase in the number of doctors.' "

Total freedom from illness is a possibility that can only be an invention of man acting against himself. Let us also hope that one's day and hour of death should not become elective, and then only for those who are "sufficiently important, wealthy or influential to command the ultimate in medical resources" (Hofling, 1966).

In this paper, I have discussed man under altered conditions of life and posited the principle of multiple causation in disease. Also, I have raised the issue of contextual definition and the problem of meaning and motive in anthropo-medical research. Anthropological strategies of inquiry and learning must encompass both "knowing about" through the analysis of fact and "knowing" through face-to-face experience and the analysis of pattern. These strategies cause us to ask many significant

Haven, 1962. S. Polgar, and R. A. Hatcher, "Sociocultural Factors in Contraceptive Practice," in *Manual of Contraceptive Practice*, edited by M. S. Calderone, Williams and Wilkins, Baltimore, 1969.

questions at once, rather than a few at a time (Huxley, 1964; Winch, 1958; Wax, 1965; Yates, 1964; Lwoff, 1966), since we should never be content to "solve" only fragmentary questions about the tapestry of action and belief woven by changing man in sickness and in health.

COMMENTARY: L. William Earley
Zachary Gussow
Charles C. Hughes

L. William Earley

This discussion of anthropology in medicine and psychiatry prompts me to consider the reasons for my close collaboration with Dr. von Mering over the past several years, first in research, then in teaching resident psychiatrists, and, finally, in teaching medical students. I will take the position stated in his paper as a point of departure for considering why and how a psychiatrist, psychoanalyst, and schoolteacher on a board of public instruction in the local community became a partner in "mission-oriented" basic research with an anthropologist.

Dr. von Mering, an anthropologist, and I, a physician, have found ourselves sharing assumptions and areas of concern and grappling with problems of relevancy in a very specific manner. This collaboration came, in part, from the breadth of vision which he, as an anthropologist, brought with him from his field, although neither of us has been able to find easy answers or to formulate operational assumptions from the data collected on men and women afflicted with physical and mental disorders.

Certain reasons are obvious why a collaborative effort such as ours is not only possible, but mutually advantageous. We share the principle of multiple determination which is easier to name than to explain. We also share a basic approach that surveys the logic of a proposition and the history of that logic, the results of which are pragmatic. In my opinion, when a social scientist proceeds in this fashion he can always find a collaborator from medicine.

An anthropo-medical approach to the nature of man as a complex unit involving certain simple principles historically offers significant overlapping. For example, the two fields share an interest in the knowledge and understanding of the development of tools, the development of language, and the relevance of the opposition of fingers one and five. Perhaps even more important is the willingness of a behavioral scientist to make searching inquiries into health aberrations and comparative analyses of disease theories in order to relate them to past and present healing practices. These approaches provide excellent ways to develop contructs at the interface of the two disciplines.

A further construct becomes apparent when considering Dr. von Mering's paper. It is relatively natural for me to be concerned with illness because I deal with many patients who have many kinds of illnesses and because of the nature of my background, training, and biases. In working with an anthropologist, however, I have come to see illness more from the perspective of behavioral adaptation, in terms of a progressively complex historical view stretching from magic to scientific experiment, and from matters societal and medical to actual patient care.

As a physician, I have always been interested in the setting of the healing process. Working with an anthropologist has given me an even broader concept of what needs to be defined about both the setting and the process. Indeed, I often think that the progressive sharpening of definition is the most valuable result of collaboration. The value of collaboration between physicians and anthropologists can be realized in many other ways. For instance, a lot more can be said about the meaning of either organic or mental illness in their actual contexts. Thus, the anthropologist who focuses on the "shape of madness" in man can make a most valuable addition to the psychiatrist's training.

Another reason for my acceptance of sound anthropological constructs is my own long-standing interest in the relevance of character to mental illness and to cultural milieu. Inevitably, Dr. von Mering's anthropological pursuits have led him to similar concerns. Cause and meaning for disease have never seemed to be a matter of a simple one-to-one relationship, or necessarily a case of more complex or circular change. Rather, the problems of disease seem to have more to do with a network or web of casuality. Our collaboration has introduced significance into the meshing of this web.

One would hardly expect total compatibility between two disciplines which have been so disparate in the past. For example, if an anthropologist in discussing mental illness should state that his experience with nonliterate societies does not necessarily apply in literate societies, especially in disorders like schizophrenia, I might be tempted to say that this anthropologist's relationship with a member of the medical profession has been incomplete. In reality, however, it is not necessarily a poor relationship, since the problem may be one of disparity between the physician's and anthropologist's definitions of schizophrenia. If this is the case, extended discussions about similar questions have convinced me that we can, with effort, satisfactorily resolve definitional and analytical issues.

As a medical educator, I am sensitive to the importance of cross-cultural studies on treatment of disease. Many significant questions can be raised about their relevance in furthering the understanding of man as as a creature of culture. But, it is also true that cross-cultural studies of man in relation to disease teach us much about the nature of disease because we are backtracking the nature of treatment. In the more complex contemporary medical problem of understanding nonspecific health aberrations, the key role of treatment patterns in disease development can be clarified by using an appropriate anthropological perspective.

Although the general condition of man is proper study for anthropology, Dr. von Mering's stress on what anthropology contributes to the study of life under altered conditions is of particular value. Such study can be done not only on the individual, but on the meaning and cause of disorder, including the development of descriptions of disease patterns and of change. Increasingly, it has become apparent to those in medicine that anthropology has much to offer to the study of changes in disease patterns. I believe that this study could become more important to medicine in the technologically developed countries than in the "primitive" cultures.

Other fascinating questions are posed by the history and geography of disease. I am especially intrigued by their relevance to Ilsa Veith's recent study of the history of hysteria (1965). Perhaps an anthropological mapping of disease — the who, what, and where — coupled with a discussion of the stage of development of a particular period could add much to our knowledge. Some areas of psychiatry are roughly in the position of medicine when lack of insulin was considered to be the "cause" of diabetes. The complex relationships between lack of insulin and diabetes suggest a similar complexity in establishing causes of mental illnesses, which affords a wealth of opportunity for contribution by anthropological thinkers.

The scientific difficulties of making specific questions about disease relevant to local conditions appear to be equally great in the developed and underdeveloped countries. Much fresh thinking about this problem is needed, and Dr. von Mering has been willing to stimulate thinking in this area, rather than to hold simplistic diagrams.

We are not only trading problems of mortality for problems of morbidity, but we are bringing down on our heels a most involved series of new questions, as the accelerated trading of "old" organs for artificial organs suggests. With the introduction of artificial and transplanted organs, we will be given a chance for longer life. Unquestionably, evidence of disease will change as a result. We desperately need the methodology of many disciplines to study these changes so that rational decisions will be possible.

Zachary Gussow

An important conceptual distinction exists between medicine and psychiatry. One would hardly make such a strong distinction between medicine and internal medicine, medicine and neurology, or medicine and pediatrics. But, coupling medicine and psychiatry does not sound odd. Perhaps this is because, at the clinical level, there are two psychiatries: one is a somatic therapy and the other, a variety of psychological therapies. Somatic psychiatry is empirical with the psychiatrist-patient relationship closely following the "activity-passivity" or the "guidance-cooperation" models of the physician-patient relationship described by Szasz and Hollender (1956). The similarity of these relationships is based on commonalities in the nature of clinical intervention. Somatic psychiatrists treat functional disorders with drugs and other medical procedures, as other physicians do. The psychological therapies, on the other hand, operate from theoretical bases and involve therapist and patient in a mutual symbolic participation using social learning, development, education, and problem-solving techniques. In many ways, the psychological therapies are becoming closely allied to the behavioral sciences, while somatic psychiatry remains closer to the basic sciences. The differences between the two psychiatries become obvious whenever a psychoanalyst and a general psychiatrist attempt to discuss the same patient.

The medical models of somatic psychiatry and the social learning, problem-solving models of symbolic therapy compel us to examine the crucial question of whether organic diseases and emotional disorders belong to the same order of reality. Ever since Descartes separated mind from body, efforts have been made to reunite them by conceptualizing functional disorders and physical illness into a unified schema. The field of psychosomatic medicine and such concepts as homeostasis and equilibrium-disequilibrium have provided the bases for these attempts at unification.

Engel (1962) defines disease as disturbance in total organismic equilibrium, and health as the restoration of that equilibrium. Following Engel, organismic functioning involves the growth, development, functions, and adjustments of the whole organism or of any of its systems at all levels of organization: biochemical, cellular, organic, psychological, interpersonal, and social. Pleune (1965) noted that by this definition "practically any event or condition of life may be interpreted as needing diagnosis and/or treatment." Grinker's model (1961), molecular-neurophysiological–symbolic-interpersonal–social-cultural, follows a pattern similar to Engel's.

I think Dr. von Mering is trying to get around this dilemma by framing "physical and emotional disorders or abnormality as a unitary problem of 'life under altered conditions.' " It is unclear whether this is a conceptual schema or a means of facilitating anthropological research into questions of illness and health. Dr. von Mering seems to be aiming strongly at the former; at the same time, he offers the failure to think of *all* diseases as an " 'ailing-healing unit' involving both internal and external problem-solving" as the reason why non-psychological disorders have been neglected by anthropologists. The two elements of Dr. von Mering's definition seem to be related. We confront some of the same questions and difficulties raised by the equilibrium-disequilibrium model when we try to define the meaning of "life under altered conditions."

One difficulty in using the concept of disequilibrium as an indicator of emotional disorder is that in specific situations at significant phases in individual development, emotional disequilibrium becomes a beneficial and necessary prerequisite for continuing psychological growth and development. The infantile "neurosis" of oedipal resolution, the identity crisis of adolescence, the "eighth-month anxiety" of infants in differentiating psychic self from the symbiotic relationship with mother, the "normal" depressions of middle age, and the like, all represent psychic and, often, somatic turmoil. The failure to experience disequilibrium under these situations may later result in some form of "disorder."

An example more familiar to anthropologists is found in grief reactions and behavior during the mourning process. Emotional and physical disequilibrium is the usual, socially expected, accompaniment of grieving. Considerable literature postulates that the failure to experience adequate grief reactions at the appropriate time may indicate some underlying psychopathology (Cobb and Lindemann, 1943); as in the case of Monsieur Meursault in Albert Camus' *The Stranger* (1946), it may even lead society to suspect the individual of possessing criminal tendencies. One reason some people are inclined to think that grief is a disease is that grieving persons are treated somewhat like patients and are expected to act much like patients. However, while disease is considered undesirable, the grieving process and the "working through" of loss are thought to be essential to emotional functioning.

Our society seems to evaluate disease as "evil." Not only do many feel under a moral obligation to conquer it, but many firmly believe in our technological capacity to do so. In this conceptualization, disease is dysfunctional and maladaptive, since our national "theology" preaches adjustment and adaptation.

Medical sociologists define illness and illness behavior as deviant and, in our relentless pursuit of so-called normality, deviance becomes either a profitable research area for behavioral scientists or a symbol of human discreditation. The functional utility of deviant persons and behavior to the stability of society has been documented (Erikson, 1962); perhaps the adaptive value of physical disease, at both the individual and social levels, also merits further consideration. It is conceivable that, under specific ecological and environmental conditions, certain diseases may have important adaptive value and that their premature eradication might lead to serious consequences. One might also hypothesize that certain common childhood diseases actually have adaptive value for continuing growth and maturation. One major difficulty facing a viable relationship of anthropology to the study of disease, as Dr. von Mering indicates, is insufficient knowledge concerning this aspect of how culture and nature interrelate.

There is another aspect of illness that has to do with significant human experience. Without laboring the point and without resorting to dramatic instances of conversion or transformations of human personality under the stress of disease, I do think that perhaps for some people illness or the threat of illness may sometimes provide one of the deepest "human" crisis they may come to experience.

In conclusion, I wish to take minor exception to Dr. von Mering's use of the term "the whole person" in disease. In pedagogy, one speaks of "teaching the whole child" and psychiatrists often say that the patient must come "to admit that he is sick as a whole being." Although we may fully understand the implications of the concept, the patient may be overwhelmed by its connotation. While the patient must realize in psychological therapy that his problems lie within himself, he also must discover his own areas of strength and health, and not think of himself as totally sick. It is his strength and health that facilitate improvement and permit him to take a hard look at his "sickness."

Charles C. Hughes

I shall discuss two points presented in Dr. von Mering's paper which I think are of enduring significance to both a medical-biological viewpoint and an anthropological perspective: the concept of adaptation and its implications, especially its relations to questions of sociocultural change; and the persistent problem of definition of the "pathological" in contrast to the normal.

Dr. von Mering has singled out the starting point for all investigations of human behavior: because of man's psychobiological character, all statements of behavioral science about man must be referable to the dynamics of the adaptational process. Such statements cannot be simplistic expressions of a biological reductionism or narrow applications of ecological concepts relating man only to a "physical" habitat. In the case of man, there is a special environment of his own making, a psychocultural environment enmeshed in particular social contexts. We are a long way from grasping the most significant parameters which the processes of adaptation must follow with reference to this psychocultural aspect of man's surroundings.

The primary reason for this lack of understanding lies in the evolving nature of the psychocultural environment and in the unsuitability of some of the concepts usually employed to study it. We eventually need to cast all concepts, approaches, and techniques into a framework which regards human behavioral phenomena as constantly fluctuating, changing, and striving, and which aims to understand the oscillating and spiralling processes that indicate the main patterns of continuity in change. In this light, terms such as "structure," "form," and "category" are merely halfway houses to concepts molded on a dynamic base; they become a means to understanding *process* in the behavioral sciences as well as in medicine. Ludwig von Bertalanffy (1952) put the matter nicely:

Actually, [the] separation between a pre-established structure and processes occurring in the structure does apply to the living organism. For the organism is the expression of an everlasting, orderly process, though, on the other hand, this process is sustained by underlying structures and organized forms. What is described in morphology as organic forms and structures, is in reality a momentary cross-section through spatio-temporal pattern. What are called structures are slow processes of long duration, functions are quick processes of short duration.

Although concepts relating to dynamic adaptional processes are at least implicitly at the heart of medicine and psychiatry, they sometimes appear to have a curious place in anthropology as well as in other behavioral sciences. Lack of understanding of the concepts or their implications frequently leads to their being relegated to "biology" and, thus, discarded. A recent example, the tone of which is much too common, is the statement made by Zollschan (1964) during a discussion dealing with social change and its psychological involvements: "Concepts such as *adaptation, adjustment,* and *function* have exercised a truly pernicious influence in the study of behavior. They appear to be hanging on in psychology and sociology, although biology is on the verge of abandoning them." I am sure that this latter statement will be news to many biologists!

One reason some behavioral scientists turn away from use of such concepts as function, adaptation, or process, is that they conceive of an organism in simplistic, trait-like terms. They think of adaptation statically rather than dynamically as a noun, not a verb. Little allowance is made for functional alternatives such as direction of activity or modification of adjustive pattern. If a given conception of *the* function of a part or activity fails to produce understanding or conform to prediction, the entire concept is discarded. But, primarily, the study of man must be approached with full recognition of man's multiple capacity (conscious and unconscious) for justifying any course of action to himself. This should be the starting point of any comprehensive theory concerning his behavior.

Dr. von Mering points out that implicit emphasis occurs in both medicine and anthropology on "the whole man." The concept is expressed in contemporary scientific language as an emphasis on the system properties of the individual human organism, on man as a psychobiological system whose principal structural components are derived from a given sociocultural environment through processes of continuous transaction. In medicine, we see concern for training students to view not a disease, nor a patient who has a disease, but rather the disease as an aspect of the person's total behavior. Thus, behavior takes place in a context having widely disparate meanings for different patients, as well as different social and etiological parameters. This holistic approach has long been a hallmark in anthropology.

In his final section, Dr. von Mering discusses the problem of disease and sociocultural change, and man's persistent search for freedom from ailments. Closely implicated in the utopian search is the problem of defining "pathology," when standards of abnormality and normality are relative and vary according to time and circumstance. Neither the question of the search for freedom from disease, nor that of the definition of pathology, can be freed from an adaptational framework.

The pace and scope of directed and inadvertent sociocultural change will increase with burgeoning technological and social developments; such developments will further alter the nature of the environment toward which behavior is directed. But, as Dr. von Mering points out, it is doubtful how much man will actually gain in his effort to eliminate all disease and discomfort. In Europe and North America, medicine has achieved a high level of both therapeutic and preventive control over the traditional killing and debilitating diseases and, in the "developing" nations, it is making inroads. But if the goal of medicine is not to just lower the death rate, but also to eliminate disease, then the goal is illusory, as Dubos (1961) and others have insisted. The elimination of one health hazard frequently creates a niche for another disease or malady, resulting in only a change of the nature of man's ailments, not in the fact, or even the degree, of his affliction. Thus, while modern technology and affluence have helped create a more comfortable micro-environment in many respects, they also have created the smog-bound, corpulent, anxious, self-disparaging, unexercised, alienated, and pesticide-threatened human organism. A colleague of mine has remarked that, through the ages, the physician has searched for ways of preventing death; now the task of medicine, in industrialized societies, at least, is to search for ways to make life not only possible, but worthwhile.

In this quest, medicine must join with the behavioral sciences and psychiatry. In this time of rapid change, developing affluence, widespread communications, and more exposure — but with differential access to the "goods" of life — many people are confronted with an increasingly demanding, if not "punishing," informational environment. This has not been alleviated by those same socioeconomic conditions which appear to be moving toward the solution of many basic medical problems. A central task will be to help the individual create effective defenses against invidious comparison, self-disparagement, lowered self-esteem, "alienation," or the erosive irritations of "relative deprivation."

In his chapter on "Medical Utopias" in *The Dreams of Reason,* Dubos (1961) makes the following points, which are relevant to medicine and psychiatry, as well as to anthropology:

The crucial consequence of this rapidity of change is that future generations will have to meet emergencies without benefit of their forebears' help or experience. The best thing that we can do for them, perhaps the only thing worth doing, is to create an atmosphere in which they will develop such non-specialized adaptive powers that they can respond rapidly and effectively to all kinds of new and unexpected threats for which they cannot be specifically prepared. . . .

The reason that we know so little about how to make people develop their own adaptive powers is that modern civilization has not concerned itself with this problem. Everywhere in the world, and in the United States in particular, the trend has been toward controlling and modifying the external environment for the sake of human comfort, with total elimination of effort as an ideal. We do little, if anything, to train the body and soul to resist strains and stresses. But we devote an enormous amount of skill and foresight to conditioning our houses against heat and cold, avoiding contact with germs, making food available at all hours of the day, multiplying labor-saving devices, minimizing the effort of learning, and dulling even the slightest pain with drugs. Needless to say, I am not advocating a retreat from these practices which have made life so much easier, although not necessarily very much happier. But I would urge that we emphasize more than we do now another approach to dealing with the external world—namely, the cultivation of the resources in human nature which make man potentially adaptable to a wide range of living conditions.

REFERENCES

Ackerknecht, E. H. 1947. The Role of Medical History in Medical Education. Bulletin of the History of Medicine. 21:135–45.

———. 1953. Rudolph Virchow: Doctor, Statesman, Anthropologist. University of Wisconsin Press: Madison, Wisconsin.

———. 1959. A Short History of Psychiatry, p. 84. Hafner: New York.

———. 1965. History and Geography of the Most Important Diseases. Hafner: New York.

Barnes, A. C., ed. 1965. The Social Responsibility of Gynecology and Obstetrics. John Hopkins Press: Baltimore.

Björck, G. 1965. The Next Ten Years in Medicine. British Medical Journal 2: 7–11.

Bleuler, M. 1963. Conception of Schizophrenia Within the Last Fifty Years and Today. Proceedings of the Royal Society of Medicine 56:945–52, 948.

Blum, R. and E. Blum. 1965. Health and Healing in Rural Greece. Stanford University Press: Stanford.

Boggs, S. E. et al. 1962. A Health Study in Kit Carson County, Colorado. United States Public Health Service Publication No. 844. Washington, D.C.

Bogoras, W. 1904–1909. The Chuckchee. The Jesup North Pacific Expedition, ed. Franz Boas, III, Memoirs of the American Museum of Natural History (Volume 11, Parts 2, 3). E. J. Brill: Leyden.

Brill, H. 1966. Contributions of Biological Treatment to Psychiatry. Biological Treatment of Mental Illness ed. Max Rinkel pp. 62–70. Farrar, Straus and Giroux: New York.

Brown, R. E. 1966. Medical Problems of the Developing Countries. Science 153: 271–75.

Burns, E. M. 1967. Social Policy and the Health Services: The Choices Ahead. American Journal of Public Health 57:199–212.

Camus, A. 1946. The Stranger. Knopf: New York.

Clark, M. 1958. Health in the Mexican-American Culture. University of California Press: Berkeley.

Cobb, S. and E. Lindemann. 1943. Symposium on Management of Cocoanut Grove Burns at Massachusetts General Hospital: Neuropsychiatric Observations. Annals of Surgery 117:814–24.

Cooper, J. A. D. 1969. Institutional Responses to Expectations for Health Care. Journal of Medical Education 44:31–35.

Dobzhansky, T. 1967. Changing Man. Science 155(3761):409–15.

Dubos, R. 1959. The Mirage of Health, p. 138. Harper: New York.

———. 1961. Medical Utopias. The Dreams of Reason, pp. 91, 92. Columbia University Press: New York.

———. 1965. Humanistic Biology. American Scholar 34(2):179–98.

————. 1968. Environmental Determinants of Human Life. Environmental Influences: Third of a Series on Biology and Behavior, ed. David C. Glass, pp. 138–54. Rockefeller University Press and Russell Sage Foundation: New York.

Earley, L. W. and O. von Mering. 1969. Growing Old the Out-Patient Way. American Journal of Psychiatry 125(7):963–67.

Eiseley, L. 1965. Freedom of the Juggernaut. Mayo Clinic Proceedings 40:11.

Engel, G. L. 1960. A Unified Concept of Health and Disease. Perspectives in Biology and Medicine 3:459–85.

————. 1962. Psychological Development in Health and Disease. W. B. Saunders Co: Philadelphia.

Erikson, K. 1962. Notes on the Sociology of Deviance. Social Problems 9(4): 307–13.

Evans-Pritchard, E. E. 1937. Witchcraft, Oracles and Magic Among the Azande. Clarendon Press: Oxford.

Feinstein, A. R. 1963a. Conclusions. Journal of Chronic Diseases 16:1132–33.

————. 1963b. Boolean Algebra and Clinical Taxonomy. New England Journal of Medicine 269:929–38.

Feldman, W. H. 1965. Yesterday's Triumphs: Today's Problems. Journal of the American Medical Association 194(1):33–37.

Foucault, M. 1965. Madness and Civilization. Pantheon: New York.

Freud, S. 1959. On Psychotherapy. Collected Papers, I, pp. 249–63. Basic Books: New York.

Goffman, E. 1959. The Moral Career of the Mental Patient. Psychiatry 22:123–42.

Gregg, A. 1952. The Scientists Look At Our World, W. V. Houston et al, pp. 83–108. University of Pennsylvania Press: Philadelphia.

Grinker, R. R. 1961. Psychosomatic Research, rev. ed. Grove Press: New York.

Gussow, Z. 1960. Pibloktoq (Hysteria) among the Polar Eskimo: An Ethno-Psychiatric Study. The Psychoanalytic Study of Society, eds. W. Muensterberger and S. Axelrod, I., pp. 218–36. International Universities Press: New York.

Hallowell, A. I. 1936. Psychic Stresses and Culture Patterns. American Journal of Psychiatry 92:1291–1310.

————. 1938. Fear and Anxiety as Cultural and Individual Variables in a Primitive Society. Journal of Social Psychology 9:25–47.

Handel, G. 1965. Psychological Study of Whole Families. Psychological Bulletin 63:19–41.

Heisenberg, Werner. 1958. Physics and Philosphy: The Revolution in Modern Science, pp. 206, 58. Harper: New York.

Henderson, L. J. 1913. The Fitness of the Environment. Macmillan: New York.

Hinkle, L. E. 1961. Ecological Observations of the Relation of Physical Illness, Mental Illness and the Social Environment. Psychosomatic Medicine 23: 289–96.

Hofling, C. K. 1966. Terminal Decisions. Medical Opinion and Review 2(1):40–49.

Huxley, J. 1964. Essays of a Humanist. Chatto & Windus: London.

Jackson, D. D. 1960. A Critique of the Literature on the Genetics of Schizophrenia. The Etiology of Schizophrenia, ed. D. D. Jackson, pp. 37–87. Basic Books: New York.

Kiev, A. 1965. The Study of Folk Psychiatry. International Journal of Psychiatry 1(4):524–52, 536, 540, 548.

———. 1966. Pre-scientific Psychiatry. American Handbook of Psychiatry, ed. S. Arieti, III, Ch. 12, pp. 165–79. Basic Books: New York.

Kluckhohn, C. M. 1962. Culture and Behavior: Collected Essays. Free Press: New York.

Kreshover, S. J. and F. J. McClure. 1966. Environmental Variables in Oral Disease. AAAS Symposium Volume. Washington, D.C.

Kurtzke, J. F. 1966. An Evaluation of the Geographic Distribution of Multiple Sclerosis. Acta. Neurol. Scand. 42 (supplement):91–117.

Leake, C. D. 1965. Why Search and Research. Journal of the American Medical Association 194(1):54–58.

Lebra, W. P. 1964. The Okinawan Shaman. Ryukyuan Culture and Society, ed. A. H. Smith. University of Hawaii Press: Honolulu.

Leighton, A. and J. Hughes. 1959. Culture as Causative of Mental Disorders. Causes of Mental Disorders: A Review of Epidemiological Knowledge, pp. 341–83. Milbank Memorial Fund: New York.

Leighton, A. et al. 1963. Psychiatric Disorder Among the Yoruba. Cornell University Press: Ithaca, New York.

Lévi-Strauss, C. 1966. Anthropology: Its Achievements and Future. Current Anthropology 7(2):124–27, 125.

Lewis, A. 1967. Health as a Social Concept. The State of Psychiatry: Essays and Addresses, pp. 179–94. Science House, Inc: New York.

Lwoff, A. 1966. Interaction Among Virus, Cell and Organism. Science 152:1216–20.

MacBeath, A. 1952. Experiments in Living. Macmillan: London.

Mead, M. 1950. Sex and Temperament in Three Primitive Societies. Mentor Books: New York.

Murphy, J. M. and A. H. Leighton, eds. 1965. Approaches to Cross-Cultural Psychiatry. Cornell University Press: Ithaca, New York.

Nadel, S. F. 1946. A Study of Shamanism in the Nuba Mountains. Journal of the Royal Anthropological Institute 76:25–37.

Osler, W. 1951. Teaching and Thinking. A Way of Life and Selected Writings of Sir William Osler, pp. 194–204. Dover: New York.

Page, I. H. 1965. Medical Research as I See It. Journal of the American Medical Association 194(3):1355–62.

Pickering, G. W. 1967. Reflections on Research and the Future of Medicine: A Symposium and other Addresses, ed. C. E. Lyght. McGraw Hill: New York.

Pleune, F. G. 1965. All Disease is not Disease: A Consideration of Psycho-Analysis, Psychotherapy, and Psycho-Social Engineering. International Journal of Psycho-Analysis 46:358–66.

Rabkin, L. Y. 1965. The Patient's Family: Research Methods. Family Process 4(1):105–32.

Raper, A. B. 1958. The Incidence of Peptic Ulceration in Some African Tribal Groups. Transactions of the Royal Society of Tropical Medicine and Hygiene 152:535–46.

Ross, H. A. 1959. Commitment of the Mentally Ill: Problems of Law and Policy. Michigan Law Review 57:945–1018.

Rubel, A. J. 1964. The Epidemiology of Folk Illness: Susto in Hispanic America. Ethnology 3(3):268–82.

Sanders, B. S. 1964. Measuring Community Health Levels. American Journal of Public Health 54:1063–70.

Sanua, V. D. 1961. Socio-Cultural Factors in Families of Schizophrenics. Psychiatry 24:246–65.

Sigerist, H. E. 1962. Civilization and Disease, p. 226. University of Chicago Press, Phoenix Books: Chicago.

Simpson, G. G. 1966. The Biological Nature of Man. Science 152:472–78.

Spence, J. 1955. Disease and Its Local Setting. Society and Medicine, ed. Iago Galdston, pp. 3–19. International Universities Press.

Stamp, L. D. 1964. The Geography of Life and Death. Collins: London and Glasgow.

Szasz, T. S. and M. H. Hollender. 1956. Contributions to Philosophy of Medicine, Basic Models of Doctor-Patient Relationship. American Medical Association Archives of Internal Medicine 97(5):585–92.

Titmuss, R. M. 1965. Community Care of the Mentally Ill: Some British Observations. Canada's Mental Health, Supplement No. 49, November-December.

U.S. National Health Survey. 1960. Limitations of Activity and Mobility Due to Chronic Conditions: U.S. 1957–1958. U.S.P.H.S. Publication No. 548. Washington, D.C.

———. 1962. Chronic Conditions Causing Limitations of Activities: U.S. 1959–1961. U.S.P.H.S., Statistical Series B–36. Washington, D.C.

———. 1966. Disability Days: U.S. 1963–1964. U.S.P.H.S. National Center for Health Statistics, Vital and Health Statistics, Series 10, Number 24. Washington, D.C.

———. 1968. Disability Days, U.S. July 1965–June 1966. U.S.P.H.S., National Center for Health Statistics, Vital and Health Statistics, Series 10, Number 47. Washington, D.C.

Van Loon, F. H. G. 1926. Amok and Latah. Journal of Abnormal and Social Psychology 21:434–44.

Veith, I. 1965. Hysteria: The History of a Disease. University of Chicago Press. Chicago.

Virchow, R. (1849). 1958. Disease, Life and Man: Selected Essays, ed. L. J. Rather. Stanford University Press: Stanford.

von Bertalanffy, L. 1952. Problems of Life, p. 134. Watts and Co.: London.

———. 1968. General System Theory, pp. 139–154. Braziller: New York.

von Mering, O. 1958. Beyond the Legend of Chronicity. Nursing Outlook 6:290–93.

———. 1961a. A Grammar of Human Values, 288 pp. University of Pittsburgh Press: Pittsburgh.

———. 1961b. Healing Experience and Disease Causation. Family Centered Social Work in Illness and Disability, Monograph VI, Ch. 4, pp. 51–67. NASW: New York.

———. 1962a. Disease, Healing and Problem-Solving: A Behavioral Science Approach. International Journal of Social Psychiatry 8(2):137–48.

———. 1962b. Value Dilemmas and Reciprocally Evoked Transactions of Patient and Curer. Psychoanalysis and the Psychoanalytic Review 49(2):119–43.

————. 1965. Cross-cultural Study of Medical and Lay Values in Clinic Practice. Year Book 1965, pp. 402–05. American Philosophical Society: Philadelphia.

————. in press. An Anthropo-medical Profile of Aging: Retirement from Life into Active Ill Health. Journal of Geriatric Psychiatry.

von Mering, O. and L. W. Earley. 1965. Major Changes in the Western Medical Environment. Archives of General Psychiatry 13:195–201.

————. 1966. The Diagnosis of Problem Patients. Human Organization 25:20–23.

————. 1969. The Ambulatory Problem Patient: A Unique Teaching Resource. American Journal of Psychiatry 126:146–50.

von Mering, O. and S. King. 1957. Remotivating the Mental Patient, 216 pp. Russell Sage Foundation: New York.

von Mering, O. and S. B. Schiff. 1968. The Intermittent Patient: His Reference Groups and Intergroup Tensions. Archives of General Psychiatry 18:400–404.

Wallace, A. F. C. 1959. Cultural Determinants of Response to Hallucinatory Experience. Archives of General Psychiatry 1:58–69.

Wax, M. 1965. The Tree of Social Knowledge. Psychiatry 28:99–106.

Weinerman, E. R. 1965. Anchorpoints Underlying the Planning for Tomorrow's Health Care. Bulletin of the New York Academy of Medicine 41(12):1213–60.

Whithington, H. G. 1966. Psychiatry in the American Community, p. 68. International Universities Press: New York.

Winch, P. 1968. The Idea of a Social Science and Its Relation to Philosophy. Routledge & Kegan Paul: London.

Yap, P. N. 1952. The Latah Reaction. Journal of Mental Science 98:515–64.

Yates, F. 1964. Sir Ronald Fisher and the Design of Experiments. Biometrics 20:307–21.

Zollschan, G. K. 1964. Explorations in Social Change, eds. George K. Zollschan and Walter Hirsch, p. 187. Houghton Mifflin: Boston.

12 Richard G. Snyder

Aerospace Sciences

In 1911, a young pilot, stylishly attired in a leather helmet, goggles, and flowing scarf, made a 3,220-mile fllight from New York to Pasadena, survived sixty-five crash landings, and became the first man to fly coast to coast (Kane, 1950). That same year Franz Boas published *The Mind of Primitive Man*. Anthropology and the young science of aviation seemed completely unrelated.

During the fifty-odd years since these two events occurred, both anthropology and aerospace science have undergone radical change. The technological developments in manned interstellar space exploration have been achieved only through the concomitant efforts of scientists of many disciplines transcending traditional barriers. As man has probed exotic environments and gained the ability to escape from the environmental limitations of terrestrial ecology, so too the study of man has changed. Serious concern exists among anthropologists about the current and future role of anthropology in the cross-disciplinary interactions of the behavioral sciences. Those of us relating anthropology and aerospace sciences share this concern. Clinically, a healthy patient has the best chance of staying healthy by undergoing periodic examinations even when symptoms of distress are only vaguely defined.[1] Before providing an appraisal and assessment of the relationship between anthropology and the aero-

---

1. It is of interest to note that a previous AAA symposium on Aerospace Anthropology was held in 1964 at San Francisco, and that in April 1966, at Berkeley, an AAPA symposium surveyed activities in physical anthropology related to technology and aerospace. As a result of apathetic reaction among anthropologists, the press reported several controversial discussions (*Product Engineering*, May 23, 1966, p. 87).

space sciences, I should like to define what is meant by aerospace, what activities and disciplines are involved, what the anthropological role is, how currently pertinent issues apply, and finally, how educational curricula might be improved to meet new requirements in this field. I shall approach these questions as a physical anthropologist and a researcher.

The term "aerospace,"[2] now only a decade old (Allen, 1965), pertains to both the earth's atmosphere and to space. The two are generally considered a single realm of activity in the flight of air vehicles and in the lauching, guidance, and control of ballistic missiles, earth satellites, and space vehicles. Man's behavioral and physical activity and tolerances in both aircraft and manned space vehicle environments pose problems which are rarely, if ever, encountered in terrestrial environments. To solve these new problems, indeed even to define them, a number of new specialties have been conceived as the offspring of various scientific disciplines. Thus, there are now astrobiologists, exobiologists, astrophysicists, astrogeologists, astrochemists, and aerospace physicians, and, technically, aerospace anthropologists (Snyder, 1959, 1961, 1964; NASA, 1966). Each specialty has been given strong impetus by technological advances which have provided new tools, techniques, and knowledge.

Due to these exploding technological advances, aerospace activities involve most challenging concepts. What is considered impossible today may be commonplace tomorrow. Since Sputnik I (COSPAR, 1957) was launched in 1957, our aerospace knowledge has increased to the point where we may be ready to explore Mars (Voyager) within another five years. We now have the technical capability to fire passengers in a ballistic rocket to any point on earth in forty minutes. The 36-ton Lockheed 750-passenger transport (C5A) has been tested, the three-decker Boeing 747 Superjet has now entered passenger service, and mockups of 1,000-passenger airliners have been built. The French-British Supersonic Concorde has been tested, and the Mach-2.7 Boeing B-2707-300 (SST) should be operational sometime after 1971. Flying platforms and propulsive belts that enable man to fly through the air have been developed.

2. The term "aerospace" apparently first appeared in print in the *Interim Glossary: Aero-Space Terms* (Woodford Agee Heflin, editor, Air University: Maxwell AFB, Alabama, Feb. 1958). For a more recent publication, see W. H. Allen, editor, *Directory of Technical Terms for Aerospace Use*, NASA SP-7, Washington, D.C., 1965.

Within this decade, the annual anthropology meeting may be attended by participants who dial in the proper computation on their personal rocket, literally shooting themselves there, or they may stay at home and participate in the proceedings through video communication (Futurists, 1966).

These technological changes are occurring with tremendous rapidity as invention and innovation pyramid the process. Technologically, we have progressed further in fifty years than in all of the preceeding history of man; even the wheel soon may be obsolete. But technological advances produce difficulties as well as provide solutions. What effects will they have on man in the future? Is technology progressing faster than man's capability to utilize it? These changes offer great challenges to the anthropologist through their side effects on cultural change, language, community and government structure, economy, and even personality and folklore. The anthropologist must keep abreast or, better, try to project ahead of these developments in determining how such advanced technological changes may affect his particular area of interest. It is more important than ever that anthropologists have a close cross-disciplinary contact with aerospace scientists.

In the past, anthropology has largely been an extrinsically motivated science concerned with man's history, evolution, and physical and cultural development. Anthropologists have borrowed techniques, tools, and even some of their major anthropological concepts from cross-disciplinary contacts in neighboring sciences. The very nature of the anthropologist's approach and perspective often has been historical. The in-depth study of a Witoto village, the phonological structure of an obscure Altaic linguistic family, or the excavation of an archaeological site require a patient, cautious, scholarly approach and, unless some "urgent anthropology" consideration occurs (or grant funds are expended), a concern for the future loses relative significance.

In contrast, aerospace research must be forward-looking. The aerospace anthropologist is not only confronted with offering solutions to advanced problems posed by other disciplines; he also must have a wider perspective of man than that of his colleagues, pointing out or predicting pitfalls in their approaches. He may thus act as a catalyst, or even as an initiator, in finding solutions to these problems. In effect then, the anthropological role in aerospace may have quite a different perspective than it has in traditional pursuits within the discipline. The important contribution which the anthropologist can make to collateral aerospace efforts is his breadth of knowledge of man. The anthropologist will not generally know as much about individual function as the physiologist, as much about personality function as the psychologist, as much about group function as the sociologist, or as much about mechanical function as the engineer; but he is the *only* scientist capable of considering man in an aerospace environment from the viewpoint of total culture and intrarelationships.

The team approach is not uncommon in scientific research; it becomes almost a necessity in aerospace sciences. While the astrobiologist may concentrate his investigations on a speciality interest, he cannot proceed far toward predicting the presence of an exospore in 3C-295, the farthest known galaxy, without consulting the astronomer, the astrogeologist, and other scientists. Similarly, the anthropologist engaged in aerospace activities today will not find himself in an insulated cubbyhole, but may find himself exposed to hard scientific scrutiny from his colleagues in cooperative efforts involving a much wider range of cross-disciplinary efforts than in the past. For example, one of our recent research studies, which concerned the monitoring of the fetal and maternal physiological reaction of a pregnant female baboon (*Papio cynocephalus*) during capsule impact, required the joint efforts of a veterinarian-pathologist, obstetrician, physiologist, electronic engineer, and primatologist. It also involved the concurrent cooperation of two federal government agencies, two state government agencies, a university medical school, and some fifteen physicians scattered throughout the country. Another research study included a chemical engineer, neurosurgeon, mechanical engineer, neurophysiologist, anthropologist, and a Ph.D. candidate in English.

The reason for such variegated teams is that, in dealing with many problems in aerospace, as well as in more traditional disciplines, no one individual has the training or educational background to understand all of the variables involved. Competent scientists with diverse academic backgrounds contribute entirely different viewpoints to the solution of the same problem. Concurrent with this emphasis on specialization, particularly as seen in aerospace research, there seems to be an increased need for the scientist who has an overall view of man. Here the broad training of the anthropologist is important. The requirements of most anthropology departments for work in linguistics, archaeology, ethnology, and ethnography are often completely out of proportion to the extensive zoological training required of the physical anthropology graduate student. Yet, this training can equip him more completely than the physiologist, psychologist, or physician. However, this is due more to the perseverance of the student than to the design of the program. Present graduate curricula are badly in need of revision. If anthropology is to keep up with her sister disciplines in the aerospace age, there will have to be increasing compromise between and modifications in the traditional educational curricula and the newer scientific training requirements. I know of no department of anthropology in the United States today providing a curriculum which prepares a student for work in the aerospace sciences.

In light of this, what educational and training requirements should be considered necessary for the aerospace anthropologist? An important point to any discussion of the anthropological role in aerospace is that most of the anthropologists, and all of those holding doctorates, working in industrial or governmental organizations today do not hold their positions by virtue of being anthropologists. Most have additional academic training and experience at the graduate level in at least one, and often two, adjunct disciplines such as mathematics, psychology, statistics, medicine, or engineering. Besides the additional cross-training backgrounds, most also have had unusual technical experience in electronics, intelligence work, communications, medicine, or aviation. One cultural anthropologist who has worked in physical anthropology and archaeology also holds a degree in marine engineering, was a former airline pilot, advanced aircraft design engineer, and information retrieval specialist. My own credentials for discussing this subject include basic research contributions in human tolerances to ultra-high gravitational force fields, and test and research pilot experience technically qualifying me for both astronaut and astronaut-scientist.

Obviously, such credentials far exceed those required for normal research or teaching. One may ask why it is necessary for the anthropologist to have this ancillary experience. Is the present curriculum for anthropologists not adequate? Perhaps the most important reason for such extensive experience is that anthropologists are in a poor competitive position in the aerospace world. Their image outside the academic grounds is a cross between that of a philosophical tailor who makes odd measurements of people and that of the doddering archaeologist wearing a pith helmet and digging for dinosaur bones. If this seems hard to believe, I challenge anyone to walk into a governmental or industrial research or administrative aerospace organization and ask for a definition of an anthropologist. The results probably will make you wonder if anthropologists talk only to each other. Who is to know that the anthropologist might be an authority in chemical analysis or just the person to evaluate a soft landing on the lunar surface, to predict intrapersonal relationships in long space voyages of whole communities or the community responses to a new ion-powered supersonic transport, to establish new language techniques for extra-solar communications, or the best way to transport an island community being taken over for a satellite tracking station — or to prevent this by scientific prediction of undesirable results?

There appears to be an educational problem on both sides of the fence, with lack of communication a major factor. The aerospace employer, be he the government, industry, or private research, believes he has progressed very well without anthropologists, has no positions for anthropologists as such, and often does not really know what an anthropologist is or what he can do in an aerospace environment. Psychologists do not have this problem. They have infiltrated everywhere and everyone presumably recognizes their usefulness. Anthropologists in academic environments, on the other hand, often appear apathetic, suspicious, and even hostile to their colleagues actively engaged in aerospace research activities. This is reflected in the attitude of the professor shaking his head over his colleague who has fallen to the evils of a non-academic environment, in the innuendos and direct counsel to students from teachers, and in the quantitative courses occasionally offered as applied anthropology, but which ignore huge areas of application. This is hardly the preparation or the background to encourage competent graduate students to enter scientific aerospace research.

A current estimate of the anthropological involvement with other disciplines in aerospace may help demonstrate the poor competitive (and professional) position of the anthropologist. A survey of anthropologists in federal government compiled in 1963 indicated that, at that time, only eleven anthropologists were actively working in aerospace research for either government or industry (Snyder, 1964). Since that time, eight of these have left aerospace activities and only four more have entered, for a net loss of four over a three-year period. This leaves a total of eight anthropologists known to me who still engage in aerospace as anthropologists. They represent the following two industrial corporations and two federal agencies: Hughes Aircraft Company, and North American Rockwell Corporation; the United States Air Force, and the Federal Aviation Administration. McDonnell-Douglas Aircraft Corporation, which has employed as many as three physical anthropologists, lost their last one subsequent to the cancellation of the USAF manned orbiting laboratory in June 1969. Ironically, the Civil Aeromedical Institute of the Federal Aviation Administration probably has the best equipped physical anthropology laboratories and facilities in the world today (Snyder, 1964). There is not one anthropologist employed as such by the National Aeronautics and Space Administration (NASA), the primary governmental aerospace agency. According to NASA, there are over 130,000 scientific and technical personnel representing some 5,000 companies, universities, and other organizations working on Project Apollo, the United States' program to place a crew of three astronauts and astronaut-scientists on the lunar plain in 1969 (NASA, 1965). To my knowledge, only four physical anthropologists have been even indirectly involved.

Since there are approximately 5,000 members of the world-wide American Anthropological Association at present (4,700 in the United States), aerospace anthropology currently plays a very minor role in the total employment picture. By contrast, there are over 1,000 psychologists of a 28,785 total 1969 American Psychological Association (APA) membership, and an estimated 450 physiologists of a 3,528 total 1969 American Physiological Society (APS) membership who are engaged in aerospace activities. It is apparent, at least for this area, that anthropology not only is not the cross-disciplinary leader of the behavioral sciences, but lags so far behind that it is in danger of losing even its present tenuous position. Psychology is already a formidable competitor. For example, for several years now, the number of psychologists professionally employed outside academic pursuits has exceeded those in academic work (R. Emrich, personal communication, 1966).

The brief assessment provided so far certainly does not imply outstanding interest and participation by anthropologists in aerospace sciences. This fact is particularly distressing to those few who are actively contributing to aerospace research and continually observe the need for application of knowledge which they believe the anthropologist can best provide. In my judgment, the major cause of the present, tenuous relationship between anthropology and aerospace sciences is the lack of education or communication noted previously. The aerospace employers, administrators, and researchers have little knowledge of the capabilities of anthropologists because they seldom have contact with them. Conversely, anthropologists in general are not knowledgeable in the fields broadly termed "aerospace sciences" because of lack of interest, participation, or communication.

This background is essential in any attempt to assess anthropological curricula today. How can a student best be counseled to prepare himself for work in areas totally foreign to his advisors? Perhaps even more important academically, why should a promising student be encouraged to enter this field?

Despite the dearth of anthropologists in aerospace positions or ancillary activities, their research contributions have carried considerable weight in the planning, design, and conduct of all manned space flights to date, and their influence has been much greater than their numbers might indicate. Anthropologists have had a decisive hand in such activities as the selection, training, equipment, and study of astronauts and in the design and control of their environments (Clauser, 1964; Pierce, 1964, 1966; Snyder, 1964; Collins, 1964, 1966). They have been active in space communication and intelligence, but their major activities have focused on aviation, rather than on space, populations, and environments (Emrich, 1964; Kennedy and Clauser, 1966; Snyder, 1966).

Anthropological contributions to aerospace sciences may take many forms. The investigations of National Transportation Safety Board's air transport accidents in U.S. chiefly involve lawyers, physicians, and engineers. In a recent jet airliner crash, the addition of an anthropologist to the team resulted in a considerable improvement in interview techniques, a completely new analysis of the problem of post-impact evacuation and crowd disaster reaction, introduction of the first use of voluntary hypnosis of a passenger to provide critical recall information, as well as new information on injury and communications problems (Snow, 1964). Some of the results of this investigation have already affected air travel.

I do not propose to outline an "ideal" curriculum to be thrust upon departments of anthropology. Rather, I should like to make some more general remarks, based on my own experience with universities, government, and industry, which might provoke further meaningful discussion and guidelines.

Regardless of which major field of anthropology an individual chooses, or whether he is a new graduate or an accomplished scientist, there is no substitute for a solid background in experimental design and good research procedure. In addition, ethics must be emphasized. These are acquired fundamentally through good teaching and course work in subject areas which make ample use of application. The statistical concepts received in basic studies should be reinforced through graduate statistics aimed toward the solution of anthropological problems, and should be continued in both laboratory and fieldwork exercises. The student should be allowed, in fact required, to do independent work which continually challenges his ability and utilizes the research techniques, methods, and procedures he has learned. Good teaching includes setting a good example. The teacher who instructs his students in proper scientific technique, but who is observed by his students taking shortcuts or liberties with data, is shortchanging the student.

The student whose interest is in genetics as well as the student whose interest is in cultural change still may be an anthropology major and, while each may utilize different approaches and techniques in his studies, the basic tenets of experimental design will be similar. Each could continue his particular field of interest in aerospace studies, but the criteria of judgment in research design may suddenly take on considerably greater importance than commonly may be found in other research environments. Experiments in aerospace today can require decisions involving millions of dollars, national security, and major scientific breakthroughs. The anthropological researcher can recognize possible sources of error or omission not obvious to scientists trained in other disciplines.

The student must learn to think for himself rather than parrot back the instructor's viewpoint or recite memorized lists. Marked changes are desirable in both the physical and social sciences "toward fundamental analysis and basic principles, away from mere memory work and dependence upon fixed segments of subject matter" (Goheen, 1966). Intelligence should not be judged so much by a student's recall ability as by his knowledge of where to get information and how to use it. In one oral defense of a dissertation, a respected zoology professor startled his anthropology committee colleagues by asking the candidate's opinion on the priorities of research tasks involving a large sum upon which there were many demands. This turned out to be a rather prophetic question since this student, less than two years later, was responsible for assisting in the design of a $7.5 million laboratory and research program.

Student training should include considerably more opportunity for oral examinations: a chance to stand in front of informed people and answer tough questions extemporaneously. The student should learn to admit he does not know an answer but knows where to get the best current information. The educational emphasis upon written examinations unduly penalizes the student when oral, not written, examinations occur most often in our day-to-day activities. Similarly, language preparation today does not prepare the graduate for well-rounded communication. The aerospace scientist may do considerable traveling and usually will have contact with scientists in many countries. All too often, graduate language requirements are aimed at passing written tests for advanced degrees and virtually ignore conversational ability.

The graduate curriculum should be based on the individual student's needs and interests, rather than adhere strictly to course requirements. This requires an honest appraisal of the curriculum. For example, cross-training or specialization in additional disciplines is almost imperative in the case of the physical anthropologist. He must meet the requirements established for the linguistics or archaeology major as well as those established in the biological fields of his interest. This means that the student either devotes an extraordinary effort to completing the requirements or else transfers to the zoology department. This problem has long been recognized, but equitable solutions have been difficult. Instead of discouraging the student by imposing stringent departmental barriers, anthropology departments should allow greater deviations reflecting their traditional interdisciplinary role and should provide the student with the necessary cross-training without weakening his overall anthropological training.

The introduction of materials and concepts from aerospace sciences to anthropology is much more difficult than the introduction of materials from such cross-disciplinary studies as psychology, geology, or zoology. In the latter areas, curricular and scientific exchange have already occurred on most campuses. Many of the aerospace fields of study, however, are so recent that not all universities have the requisite departments. In this case the student may wish to select a college where departments such as astrobiology may be available, or arrange to take selected courses elsewhere. Perhaps more immediate assistance could be provided by the anthropology department library. By subscribing to several space science journals, the library could greatly assist in making current knowledge of activities and developments in these fields available to students. It could include several basic books on current space activities and research which might inform and stimulate both students and faculty (Ordway, Gardner, and Sharpe, 1962). For a budget of six dollars a year, any department can have a weekly subscription to one of several scientific magazines in the field, such as *Aviation Week and Space Technology,* which provides authoritative and comprehensive coverage of developments in both aviation and space research. By simply reading such a journal once a week, one can keep very well informed. The availability of such materials in the library, directly accessible to students and faculty, could go far toward acquainting them with activities in this area. Seminar discussions and independent problem-solving could lead to further interest.

The student also can prepare himself, and at the same time learn more about the field at first hand, through part-time or vacation employment. While they rarely have a full-time position open, most governmental laboratories have student summer employment available and are glad to hire temporary help for research problems in a multitude of areas. Similarly, industry hires students for summer training programs. These are excellent opportunities for the student to learn more about the activities involved and to broaden his outlook. In addition, the presence of anthropology students in industry and government may well arouse interest in utilizing the anthropologist. Such positions most often will not have an anthropological title, again because aerospace scientists are used to getting along well without the anthropologist and vice versa.

It would seem desirable to arrange an informal summer training program with the cooperation of several governmental agencies and industry in which formal academic training would be supplemented by research participation in each of several diverse aerospace activities. At present, no such program exists, although grants for study under several aerospace industrial and governmental programs are available for senior scientists.

Anthropology should "update" courses to present an introduction to some of the questions which are being considered by space scientists, but which intrude upon areas in which the anthropologist has long held scholarly competence, such as extraterrestrial life which is being seriously

investigated by several disciplines. Basic to such a study is solid understanding of life on earth. Ordway (Ordway, Gardner, and Sharpe,
1962) notes that one research path being followed by the astrobiologist
is the study of life processes and experimental studies of life's reactions
to abnormal environmental conditions in the hope of learning more about
evolutionary cause and consequences. Another research area provides
new motivation to determine what the terrestrial environment was like
at various stages in the development of life. Anthropologists can no
longer afford to smile at such "visionary thoughts"; evidence of extraterrestrial life and even communication is beginning to mount. The in-
jections of such developments into already existing evolution courses
could greatly stimulate student interest. Relatively few anthropologists
have even contributed opinions as to what form extraterrestrial life
might take, although Howells (1961) has speculated on extragalactic
body form. The possibility of intelligent extrasolar communities as well
as extraterrestrial communications poses many questions which should
be of interest to the anthropologist; several researchers have already proposed the possibility of cosmic linguistics (Hogben, 1958; Freudenthal,
1960; MacGowan, 1962).

In the past, the anthropologist has too often waited for someone else
to make the discoveries upon which he could discourse and form endless
typologies. The "new look" in anthropology must include a more progressive philosophy. Perhaps this is why the tempo of aerospace sciences
has so far outstripped that of developing anthropology. The aerospace
anthropologist must, through his knowledge of terrestrial man, take the
initiative and assist his colleagues in such fields as astrobiology to investigate the ramifications of the possibility of extraterrestrial life. This will
require a basic change in traditional anthropological perspective.

In summary, there are few anthropologists in the aerospace sciences
now, and there appears to be no evidence which would indicate a significant increase in the near future. Anthropology seems to have lost its traditional cross-disciplinary leadership in the behavioral sciences, at least
insofar as this important new scientific endeavor is concerned. This is
ironical since the few anthropologists actively involved have contributed
to a wide range of aerospace programs and their potential contributions
are felt to be significant, both in terms of application of anthropological
knowledge and of techniques to aerospace problems. The concurrent infusion into anthropology of the aerospace sciences' technology explosion,

which is daily innovating new techniques and tools adaptable to all forms of anthropological study, could offer valuable new life to the discipline. It should be evident that "dynamic anthropology" requires an active contribution to and participation in man's attempt to adapt to the new environments of aerospace. If we fail to do this in the future we will find that all tasks formerly considered to be within the competence of the anthropologist will have been taken over by other behavioral sciences. Our loss will be by default.

COMMENTARY: Lloyd R. Collins
Robert L. Emrich
Robert C. Suggs

Lloyd R. Collins

Dr. Snyder feels there is an urgent need for the study and application of anthropology within the technological framework of aerospace science because the technological pace of an exploding — not disappearing — culture may far outstrip the ability of anthropologists to participate in challenging research for sociotechnological regularities in modern complex technology. Such participation would require the concomitant study and application of anthropological principles in terms of process theory, the most concrete avenue toward the definition of regularities and the acquisition of sociotechnological laws.

The incredible and increasing pace of our technology has no parallel in anthropology. This perhaps demonstrates the inadequacy of the current historically oriented concept of "process" and its shortsighted attempts to define regularities in modern complex societies. Such a concept of process must be refined in terms of predictive recurrences. But history is not recurrent; it is an open-ended, static continuum. Process, on the other hand, is a closed dynamic system. The many definitions of culture do not conceive of it as a closed dynamic system, but as an open-ended static continuum adaptable to the ethnographic method which does not permit the investigator to record and scale the cultural change that is always concurrent with anthropological studies of complex societies.

To implement anthropological studies in complex technologically oriented cultures, students must have had advanced training in such aspects of scientific administration as planned experimental design, testing, and instrumentation, as well as in present methodologies and techniques.

Anthropologists currently acquire data by personally interrogating and observing members of a complex sociotechnological unit in order to accumulate all possible information required to adequately sample the entire idea configuration of the unit. After field experience, the data must be put together, like a jigsaw puzzle, into a total and realistic description of the cultural system. This kind of "study" offers little to aerospace science since it tends to embrace the void between traditional anthropology and modern complex technology. Regardless of present methodological shortcomings, the strength of the ethnographic method lies in its characteristic "systems" approach to cultural analysis. For example, anthropologists who describe whole communities in terms of cultural institutions and elements responsible for the linkage and overlap between and among the institutions are, by definition, working within the framework of cultural systems. If consideration of information feedback with a time dimension is added, we have a systems engineering approach to cultural analysis. Systems engineering is a feedback method for rapid implementation of advanced technological designs with no time lag.

The program of the aerospace anthropologist is basic to science. He is preoccupied with solving complex problems, within strict time constraints, problems which will lead to the formulation of sociotechnological laws applicable to complex technological situations. These problems are solved by anthropologists who are participant innovators and members of a team utilizing the following feedback procedure:

1) Designing research in terms of the problem statement.

2) Examining the technological content of a prototype or a model.

3) Defining independent and dependent variables as test parameters.

4) Instrumentally analyzing the prototype or model to obtain measures on the independent variables.

5) Accepting or rejecting the model according to test results.

6) Testing for applicability within the technological environment where the problem was first originated.

In essence, this adaptation of systems engineering methodology is a dynamic process tool, best handled by a cross-trained team concerned with timely solutions to a problem. This procedure is often called "closing the loop."

The technological emphasis is not to be minimized as a means of classification. Herskovits (1948) has stated that "the study of technology is essential for an understanding of culture . . . technology is the only aspect of culture susceptible to objective evaluation."

I recommend that this call for "urgent anthropology" be met by a workshop designed to discuss and demonstrate the feasibility of applying systems engineering to the study of modern complex societies.

Robert L. Emrich

Dr. Snyder paints a bleak picture of the anthropologist's current participation in aerospace research and adds that the immediate prospects for increasing this participation do not look very hopeful. He indicates that the anthropologist must have some understanding of the advanced technological concepts which typical anthropological training does not provide if he is to function well in a technological setting. I share Dr. Snyder's belief that anthropology can make many important contributions to the development of modern technology. The power of technology to reshape our lives has been dramatically increasing, particularly in the areas of defense and aerospace, and the anthropologist can help to adapt these advances to the human condition.

In view of the great need for anthropologists to participate in technological change, and the opposition of the industrial and academic worlds to the entrance of anthropologists into industrial research, I propose that anthropology departments move toward more active participation in those problem-oriented, multidisciplinary, academic departments which undertake studies such as operations research, systems, public administration, business administration, criminal justice, human factors engineering, and urban planning. These disciplines, relatively empty in content, have been carved from industrial experiences and have resulted from an interaction of contributing social sciences and hard sciences. Through contribution to these multidisciplinary programs, anthropological perspectives will be made available to industrial research efforts and, in time, will establish the basis for a dialogue between anthropology and industry which could lead to a genuine demand for anthropologists in industrial research and a fuller appreciation of the practical value of their talents.

I would like to supplement Dr. Snyder's excellent discussion of the contributions anthropologists can make to industrial and aerospace research by touching on two additional areas which are especially characteristic of cultural anthropology.

The first area is ethnography. The development and introduction of large-scale computer systems into a production organization, such as a military command, an industrial organization, or a governmental department, has extensively disrupted existing social relationships and job functions. Many social relationships are produced by, or within, the computer system and many tasks stem from its operation. The creation of a large-scale computer system requires an understanding of the nature of the initial organization; this is best accomplished by the development of an ethnography of that organization. The design of a new organization based on an existing computer system requires the development of a speculative ethnography to describe the culture of the organization to be created in order to estimate consequences of the new system for operators and users. Finally, an ethnographical study of the new system should be performed to permit the evaluation of its effectiveness. This last step is frequently omitted, probably because system developers are so unsure of themselves.

The second area is the study of values. This study poses an important and difficult challenge to the researcher who is concerned with effecting large technological changes in industry and government. An ability to understand and deal with values is preliminary to coherent decision-making in complex situations. The technological revolution has made decision-making increasingly difficult in several respects. The consequences of decisions are intensified by technology — one decides to launch a rocket to the moon, to target nuclear weapons, to launch nuclear weapons, to redevelop the heart of a city, or to reorganize the Post Office Department. Decisions are more technical — one does not target strategic nuclear weapons without first running many simulated war games, investing heavily in strategic intelligence, and developing elaborate military and political objectives. Decisions are now being made by more objective, explicit, and mathematical processes. Game and decision theory have given rise to strategies and techniques of decision-making. The development of analytic and statistical models permits the testing of the probable consequences of a decision, using a computerized analogy of the "real world." Techniques of economic analysis, such as program planning and budgeting, and the analysis of cost effectiveness, focus the attention of the decision-maker on how the components of his decision relate to his objectives.

All really important decisions promise to bring about major changes in contemporary society. These decisions are judged successful if they realize the aspirations and best interests of the community. The assessment of these aspirations and interests, that is, the relevant values by which major decisions must be judged, is not susceptible to the sophisticated technology of decision-making.

The anthropologist in his study of values, along with the philosopher of ethics, has gone furthest in devising ways to discover and analyze the principal values of a society. Without this sensitive probing into human values, decision-making tends to be based on superficial, incoherent values which are more easily expressed and quantified, but which give frustrating, unsuitable, and inhuman results. Major decisions are being made which hardly fit the interests and desires of society — witness the ugliness of our urban renewal projects or the tragic state of the international situation. Anthropology can help the decision-maker tailor his decisions to the community which is ultimately affected. In addition, the anthropologist can work with applied mathematicians, statisticians, and economists to develop stronger, more coherent techniques of decision-making, which have greater relevance to the needs of society.

Robert C. Suggs

In addition to providing a laboratory for testing specific anthropological theories and evaluating or developing field practices, the aerospace industry has developed a number of techniques and an experimental psychology which may have considerable potential for the field of anthropology.

Anthropology has claimed to deal with total cultural systems but, in fact, it has never done so. Momentary reflection will indicate that the description of a total cultural system is a very large undertaking. Systems engineering could prove helpful to anthropologists since it involves the application of a great number of mathematical techniques in the analysis, design, construction, and evaluation of large, complex, man-machine systems. It provides an effective way of conceiving and portraying relationships, reducing the complexity of systems to manageable proportions without sacrificing significant factors, and isolating malfunctions in various subsystems or system segments. Its application to anthropology could include the analysis of functional relationships in social systems, the study of peasant economics or primitive technology, or, specifically, an investigation of the relationships between Polynesian social stratification and environment as originally considered by Sahlins (1958).

A second group of aerospace techniques of interest to anthropologists are those generally grouped under the heading of "operations research" or what has been known in Washington as the "McNamara Approach." The goal of operations research in industry, the military, and government is to achieve an optimal relationship between the cost of a system, a piece of equipment, or a policy, and its effectiveness. In weaponry, this is called "getting the most bang for the buck."

Operations research techniques also can be used to evaluate the cost and effectiveness of ongoing social systems without any consideration for optimizing the relationship. A wide variety of games (not game theory) are used to test hypotheses, plan and develop concepts, and train personnel. In addition to its current extensive use in the United States by business and the military, gaming has potential for use in anthropology. For example, we might cite studies of primitive warfare or studies of economic systems. The procedure involves developing a model and some rules based on estimates of how the particular system works. The model is then tested against varying environmental conditions to see what kinds of results can be obtained while the system is constantly adjusted for a better approximation to reality.

Mathematical modeling, an important part of gaming, has achieved a high level of development in the operations research field. Anthropologists speak frequently of models, but few attempt to phrase their models in mathematical terms. This procedure can yield considerable benefits to the investigator as well as to his audience. Simulation techniques developed in the operations research field also might be of considerable value in anthropological interpretation. Low level simulation already has been used in testing hypotheses concerning prehistoric voyaging capabilities.

A third technique used by the aerospace industry of considerable value for anthropology is *experimental* psychology. The use of this technique can make a significant contribution in the areas of experimental design, quantification, and statistical analysis. Work in these areas would allow anthropologists to increase their objectivity and precision in field investigation. The methodology of experimental psychology — rigorous yet flexible — has become an invaluable tool for both applied and behavioral science research in the aerospace industry.

The field of industrial psychology offers techniques such as task analysis, link analysis, and time and motion studies. It also has developed data on the relationship of work output to environment. These data would have considerable value in ethnological investigations of technology of technologically underdeveloped countries.

In summary, the exchange between anthropology and the aerospace industry is a two-way street. Aerospace industry can profit from anthropological contributions and anthropology can profit from the stimulation of contact with the many scientific disciplines operating in the aerospace industry.

REFERENCES

Allen, W. H., ed. 1965. Dictionary of Technical Terms for Aerospace Use, 1st ed. National Aeronautics and Space Administration. NASA SP-7. Washington, D.C.

Boas, F. 1911. The Mind of Primitive Man. Macmillan: New York.

Clauser, C. E. 1964. The Role of Comparative Anthropometry in Aerospace Anthropology. Symposium of Aerospace Anthropology, Annual Meeting, American Anthropological Association, San Francisco (1963). (Also in Anthropology, Psychology, Engineering. Occasional Paper No. 1. Phoenix, Arizona. 1964.)

Collins, L. R. 1964. Anthropology and Modern Technology. Symposium on Aerospace Anthropology, Annual Meeting, American Anthropological Association, San Francisco (1963). (Also in Anthropology, Psychology, Engineering. Occasional Paper No. 1. Phoenix, Arizona. 1964.)

Collins, L. R. 1966. The Case for Greater Application of Physical Anthropology in Technological Development. Symposium on Applied Physical Anthropology — A Survey, A Prospectus, and a Call to Increased American Association of Physical Anthropology Activity, Annual Meeting, April 1966. American Association of Physical Anthropology: Berkeley.

Emrich, R. 1964. The Anthropology of Command Control Systems. Symposium on Aerospace Anthropology, Annual Meeting, American Anthropological Association, San Francisco (1963). (Also in Anthropology, Psychology, Engineering. Occasional Paper No. 1. Phoenix, Arizona.

Freudenthal, H. 1960. Lincos, Design of a Language for Cosmic Intercourse. North-Holland Publishing Co.: Amsterdam.

The Futurists: Looking Toward A.D. 2000. 1966. Time. February 25. pp. 28–29.

Goheen, R. F. 1966. The Teacher in the University. American Scientist 54(2):223.

Herskovits, M. 1948. Man and His Works. Knopf: New York.

Hogben, L. 1958. Astroglossa, or First Steps in Celestial Syntax. Journal of the British Interplanetary Society 11(6):258.

Howells, W. W. 1961. The Evolution of "Humans" on Other Planets. Discovery 22(6):237.

Kane, J. N. 1950. Famous First Flights, p. 62. H. W. Wilson Co: New York.

Kennedy, K. W. and C. E. Clauser. 1966. Man in Aerospace Environments: Physical and Geometric Aspects of Air Force Anthropometry. Symposium on Applied Physical Anthropology — A Survey, A Prospectus, and a Call to Increased American Association of Physical Anthropology Activity, Annual Meeting, April 1966. American Association of Physical Anthropology: Berkeley.

MacGowan, R. A. 1962. On the Possibilities of the Existence of Extraterrestrial Intelligence. Advances in Space Science and Technology, IV. Academic Press: New York.

National Aeronautics and Space Administration (NASA). 1965. Apollo Lunar Mission Profile. MSC-65-24S, (3d rev.). Houston, Texas.

———. 1966. Exobiology. Significant Achievements in Space Bioscience 1958–1964. NASA SP-92, pp. 5–23. Washington, D.C.

Ordway, F. I., III, J. P. Gardner, and M. R. Sharpe, Jr. 1962. Astrobiology. Basic Astronautics, pp. 244–308. Prentice-Hall: Englewood Cliffs.

Pierce, B. F. 1964. Anthropology and Biotechnology. Symposium on Aerospace Anthropology, Annual Meeting, American Anthropological Association, San Francisco (1963). (Also in Anthropolgy, Psychology, Engineering. Occasional Paper No. 1. Phoenix, Arizona. 1964).

———. 1966. The Ethnic Factor in Biotechnology. Economic Development and Cultural Change 14(2):217–29.

Sahlins, M. D. 1958. Social Stratification in Polynesia. University of Washington Press: Seattle.

Snow, C. C. 1964. Human Factors in Aircraft Accident Investigation. Civil Aeromedical Research Institute, Federal Aviation Agency. American Association of Physical Anthropologists, Annual Meeting. University of Colorado, Boulder, Colorado.

Snyder, R. G. 1959. Bracing Man for Space Flight. Paper presented to American Anthropological Association and Sociedad Mexicana de Anthropologia. Mexico City.

———. 1961. Manned Space Flight and the Physical Anthropologist. American Journal of Physical Anthropology 19(2):1–12.

————. 1964. Aerospace Anthropology in Federal Research. Symposium on Aerospace Anthropology, Annual Meeting, American Anthropology Association, San Francisco (1963). (Also in Anthropology, Psychology, Engineering. Occasional Paper No. 1 Phoenix, Arizona. 1964.)

————. 1966. Man in Extra Terrestrial Environments: The Role of Physical Anthropology in Advanced Space Technology. Symposium on Applied Physical Anthropology — A Survey, A Prospectus, and a Call to Increased American Association of Physical Anthropology Activity, Annual Meeting, April 1966. American Association of Physical Anthropology: Berkeley.

Index

Throughout this index the abbreviation *bib.* is used for the term *bibliographic entry*.